Pat Harrison: The New Deal Years

PAT THE NEW DEAL YEARS
HARRISON

Martha H. Swain

University Press of Mississippi
Jackson · 1978

All photographs are courtesy of the Department of Archives
and Special Collections, University of Mississippi
Library

Library of Congress Cataloging in Publication Data
Swain, Martha.
    Pat Harrison : the New Deal years.

    Based on the author's thesis.
    Bibliography: p.
    Includes index.
    1. Harrison, Pat, 1881–1941. 2. Legislators—
United States—Biography. 3. United States. Congress.
Senate—Biography. 4. Mississippi—Politics and
government—1865–1950. 5. United States—Politics
and government—1933–1945.
E748.H385S9   328.73'092'4 [B]   78-7919
ISBN 0-87805-076-0

To
the Memory of
Jim Henry and Verna Welborn Swain

Acknowledgments

MY WORK in researching and writing this book has been
made pleasurable by the assistance of many people. Dr. Glover Moore at
Mississippi State University first encouraged me to make a study of Senator
Harrison. More recently, Dr. John K. Bettersworth, another of my professors at Mississippi State, read the manuscript near its final stage and
made many helpful suggestions as to style and emphasis. I am grateful to
these two men for their teaching of southern history and for the professional encouragement and models of scholarship that they have provided me for many years.   It is to Dr. Dewey W. Grantham of Vanderbilt
University that I owe the most. His high standards of scholarship, his wisdom, his gracious manner, and his demanding but always kindly insistence
upon quality work will always, I hope, be reflected in my endeavors.
Another gentleman-scholar at Vanderbilt who assisted me is Dr. V. Jacque
Voegeli, whose critical judgment and meticulous reading of my dissertation
were of inestimable value. Drs. Herbert Weaver and Henry L. Swint
likewise made many suggestions as to how a massive dissertation should be
rewritten as a book. Also, I want to thank Dr. William F. Holmes of the
University of Georgia, who critiqued the dissertation and suggested ways to
sharpen my focus on Senator Harrison.

I should like to thank Pat Harrison, Jr., of Gulfport, Mississippi, and
Mrs. James (Marianne) Cummings of Bethesda, Maryland, for their
cooperation and willingness to answer all questions about their father.
While the bibliography cites a number of Harrison's associates who granted
interviews, I am especially indebted to Turner Catledge and to the late
James A. Farley and Felton M. Johnston. One of the great pleasures of
researching the career of a man as respected and likable as Pat Harrison
is that his friends, remembering him fondly, have been warm and responsive
to my inquiries.   The staff of the libraries and archives that I visited were
cooperative and hospitable. My special appreciation is extended to the
staff of the Franklin D. Roosevelt Library, Hyde Park; to Joyce Taylor,

former director of the Mississippi Collection at the University of Mississippi Library; and to Elizabeth Mason of the Columbia University Oral History Collection. Perry Sansing assisted in selecting the cartoons and photographs from the Pat Harrison Collection at the University of Mississippi. Barney McKee of the University Press of Mississippi has guided me throughout the process of publication, and I am thankful to him for his early interest in my subject. Marilyn Paul as copyeditor saved me many embarrassments and I am very grateful for her careful work.

New friends at Texas Woman's University have rewarded me with the friendship that makes the after-hours work less tedious. Dr. A. Elizabeth Taylor and Dorothy DeMoss have given me daily encouragement and have at all times been interested in my work. Frances Mary Shipley has been the same kind of good friend and has assisted me in proofreading.

Finally, I want to thank my twin, Margaret, for her love, her continued enthusiasm for this project, and the tender care she has always given me.

Table of Contents

Pat Harrison: The New Deal Years

CHAPTER I

The Rise of a Quintessential Conservative

IN 1936 TIME MAGAZINE suggested that "better than any living man, Senator Byron Patton Harrison of Mississippi represents in his own spindle-legged, round-shouldered, freckle-faced person the modern history of the Democratic party."[1] There were other national political figures of whom the same might be said, but the magazine, in selecting Senator Harrison, chose well. Here was a man whose political career had begun in 1906, when his party was in the doldrums, and now, when the Democracy was at the crest of its power, was one of the patriarchs of the United States Senate. Entering the House of Representatives only two years before the Democrats returned to presidential power in 1913, he was prepared to give his unreserved support to President Woodrow Wilson. Elected to the Senate in 1918, just when his party lost congressional control for fourteen years, he played the role of a minority senator with superb skill and zest. Clever in debate, adroit as a Senate tactician, and popular among his colleagues, Harrison rose rapidly to prominence in party circles. After the Democrats won both the Congress and the presidency in 1932, Harrison, as chairman of the powerful Committee on Finance, became one of the key senators to whom Franklin D. Roosevelt would turn.

Byron Patton Harrison was born on August 29, 1881, at Crystal Springs, a small southwest Mississippi town in Copiah County, a diversified farming center. He never knew much about his ancestors other than that they had come from the Carolinas and had settled in two adjacent Mississippi counties, Copiah and Claiborne. His father, Robert A. Harrison, was a small merchant, a Civil War veteran who had been wounded in that conflict. He died when the boy was only six years old, leaving a widow, Anna Patton Harrison, and four children. [2] When old enough to help support the family, Byron Patton, the third of the children, sold newspapers brought in from New Orleans and Memphis, and in the summer he supplemented the income from paper sales by driving a two-mule carriage from the train station to the local chautauqua grounds. [3]

Young Patton attended the public schools of Crystal Springs, graduating from high school in 1899 as valedictorian of his class. Little is known of his school days other than the fact that he played baseball extremely well and excelled in oratory. (Harrison liked to practice his speeches before the boarders at his mother's rooming-house.) In 1899 he attended the summer term at the University of Mississippi, but in the fall he transferred to the University of Louisiana on a baseball scholarship. He also waited tables in the college dining hall. As a consequence of his work and baseball, his grades suffered and he remained in college for only two years. Harrison's ability on the mound brought him an offer to pitch for the Pickens, Mississippi, semiprofessional team in the Old Tomato League, an opportunity which he accepted with alacrity. He then moved to Leakesville, in southeast Mississippi, where he taught school and became the principal of the local high school. By studying law in the evenings he was able to gain admission to the bar in 1902 and began his legal practice in Leakesville. Evidently, he also studied a local girl, Mary Edwinna McInnis, for the two were married in January, 1905. To them were born in the course of their married life five children, the first two dying in infancy from diptheria, and the latter three, two girls and a boy, surviving to adulthood. [4]

Harrison was a gregarious individual, and it was only natural that as a smalltown lawyer he would join the Elks, the Odd Fellows, the Masons, and the Woodmen of the World. Fraternally fortified, he ran for district attorney in the newly created Second Judicial District of Mississippi. Elected in 1906 after a vigorous campaign against three opponents, Harrison served the term and was reelected. Meanwhile he moved to Gulfport, the largest town in the judicial district, and became active in the Democratic party, attending the national convention in 1908 as a delegate. [5]

No ambitious Mississippi officeholder could escape the factionalism that divided the state in the rough and tumble days of James Kimble Vardaman and Theodore G. Bilbo. Harrison soon came to the attention of the colorful and aggressive leaders; for a time each would attempt to claim him but the rising young politician from Gulfport was able to maintain his independence, eventually becoming the most formidable rival both Vardaman and Bilbo would face in the course of their own Senate careers.

In a notorious secret caucus in 1910, the state legislature selected LeRoy Percy, a prosperous Delta planter, rather than ex-governor Vardaman for the Senate vacancy caused by the death of Anselm J. McLaurin. The caucus had many reverberations, one of which was a challenge to a series of debates issued by District Attorney Harrison to a state senator who defended the caucus. Harrison, who sympathized with the defeated Vardaman, debated with the state senator for several days at picnics and other gatherings. Subsequently, friends of Vardaman backed the young prosecuting attorney for Congress, placing him in the running for the seat of Eaton J. Bowers, who was not seeking reelection. It was during the campaign that "Byron Patton" was shortened to plain "Pat," and he seldom again used the full name.[6]

The 1910 congressional campaign first introduced Mississippians to the Harrison brand of oratory, and they found it compelling and delightful. His longtime friend Clayton Rand, a Gulf Coast editor, described the style as spellbinding, "an eloquence that flowed like a babbling brook through a field of flowers."[7] Harrison led in the first primary and defeated his opponent in the runoff. Having won election to the House of Representatives, he resigned his post as district attorney and prepared himself to enter the Sixty-second Congress.

On March 4, 1911, when Pat Harrison began his thirty-year congressional career, he was only twenty-nine years old and the second youngest member of the House. At first he "looked and listened, and somewhat in the manner of a brainy ball player studied his colleagues, making ready for the day when he would be summoned to the bat."[8] That day came on June 10 when Harrison made his maiden speech. His topic was the Payne-Aldrich Tariff Act of 1909, the primary target of his congressional campaign speeches. A low-tariff Democrat who never forsook his belief that tariffs should be applied for revenue only, Harrison gave his full support to the Underwood-Simmons tariff reduction bill of 1913.

The young Democrat became one of the most devoted followers of

Woodrow Wilson, whom he named nearly thirty years later as "the greatest President of all I've known in my congressional career."[9] Despite his adulation of Wilson, Harrison did not always support the administration. He was a leading proponent of the Glass-Owen federal reserve banking bill and worked closely with North Carolina's Claude Kitchin in obtaining favorable loans for farmers. On the other hand, although Harrison voted for the Clayton antitrust bill in spite of his objections to its stringent provisions on hydroelectric monopolies, he abstained in the vote on the conference report. Likewise, in the creation of an interstate trade commission, he preferred a commission with limited authority rather than the somewhat stronger agency that was eventually created. Harrison also voted for a railroad securities control bill, but not until after he had warned the House that the bill infringed upon the powers of the railroad and public service commissions of the various states.[10] Never a radical, Harrison's reservations about significant aspects of the New Freedom suggest that he was hardly a truly committed progressive.

The Mississippian's record on the social legislation of the period reveals that he was too bound by his belief in states' rights to accept the program which Arthur S. Link has called "advanced progressivism." Harrison strongly opposed successive child labor bills. "My State legislature knows more about conditions there and is better enabled to pass appropriate legislation . . . than is the Federal Congress," he insisted. When a proposal was made to alleviate illiteracy among adults through an adult education program, Harrison remonstrated that a national literacy program smacked of "Federal encroachment" upon the right of local communities to conduct their own educational affairs and tore at the "roots of the rights of the States." "I think it is wrong for the federal government to appropriate money for education in the States," he declared. He abstained in the vote on a bill to provide compensation to injured federal employees; but, in view of an impending crippling railroad strike, he favored the Adamson eight-hour day for railroad workers. He endorsed the prohibition amendment and voted against the woman suffrage resolution, although he said little on the latter issue.[11]

The new congressman dipped into the pork barrel to obtain for his local district a naval training station, a coastal dredge, and river navigation aid. He also worked incessantly, but in vain, in the interests of

the Mississippi Choctaw and Chickasaw Indians to have the tribal
rolls reopened (they were closed in 1907) in order that the Indians
could share in the financial advantages of tribal membership and land
allotments in Oklahoma. The opposition of Oklahoma representatives, as well as that of the War Department, prevented the passage
of any of Harrison's four bills, but as a result of his work the federal
government undertook social betterment programs which materially
assisted the Mississippi Indians. [12]

Since the freshman congressman rarely addressed himself to
domestic issues, it is difficult to determine just what philosophic convictions motivated him. (But then the same difficulty reappears in
assessing his service under another Democratic reform president in a
later decade.) Harrison certainly cannot be categorized as one of the
"Southern Agrarians," who are the subject of a debate between the
historians Arthur Link and Richard M. Abrams, although each has
offered phrases which are useful in understanding Harrison's actions
not only during the Wilson years but also in the New Deal. Link's
conclusion that the administration supporters were "for the most part
conservatives" who had "no fundamental political principles [but
were] loyal party men" seems to be an apt description of Harrison, as
does Abrams' judgment that southern congressmen were motivated to
extend the power and credit of the federal government only in response to the "exigencies of an impending national election and a
world war." [13] During the three distinct eras in which Harrison sat
in Congress—the Progressive Era, the New Era, and the New
Deal—he is best understood in terms of his personal devotion to his
party and to its two presidents and his emulation of his congressional
idols, Senators John Sharp Williams and Oscar W. Underwood during the early years and Senators Joseph T. Robinson of Arkansas and
James F. Byrnes of South Carolina during the later years. The latter
two men were in the House with Harrison and he first developed his
close friendship with them there.

Both because Harrison was a protégé of Senator Williams and an
ardent supporter of Wilson's preparedness program, he was destined
to break with Senator Vardaman. When the state Democratic convention met in Jackson in 1916, it was apparent that Harrison could
not remain a political friend of both Vardaman and Williams. When
Vardaman blocked Harrison's appointment as the temporary chair-

man of the convention, the young congressman determined that he
would one day claim Vardaman's Senate post. Elected against Vardaman's opposition as the permanent chairman of the 1916 state convention, Harrison obtained a ringing endorsement of the president
and then left the state to enter Wilson's campaign for reelection,
speaking primarily in the Midwest. [14]

While Harrison balked at supporting some aspects of Wilson's
domestic legislation, he failed to back the president's foreign policy in
only two instances. Convinced that there was "no more ardent
Member for the restriction of undesirable immigration in the House"
than himself, Harrison twice voted to override Wilson's vetoes of a
literacy test for immigrants. [15] When Wilson asked for repeal of the
exemption of American shippers engaged in coastwide trade from paying tolls for the use of the Panama Canal, Harrison dissented. Having
voted for exemption in 1912, he spoke against repeal in 1914, denying
that the exemption was a form of subsidy for the shipping interests.

On other occasions Harrison gave the president his unqualified
support. He defended Wilson's Mexican policy—the refusal to recognize the government of Victoriano Huerta, the subsequent intervention of American troops, and the expedition of John J. Pershing
against Mexican bandits. When the European war began, Harrison,
as a member of both the Rules and Foreign Affairs committees, substantially aided the administration in tabling the McLemore resolution warning Americans against travel on armed belligerent ships and
he spoke on behalf of the war resolution in April, 1917. [16] His support
of Wilson was much like that which he would give to another Democratic president some twenty years later. His "stand by the President"
reflected the habit of most Southerners of supporting Democratic foreign policy. It was Harrison's mentor in the Senate, John Sharp
Williams, who has been categorized "the most vociferous Wilsonian
and probably the ablest." [17]

At one time Harrison considered resigning from his seat in the
House to enter military service, but Wilson asked that he remain at
his congressional post. "I do not feel that we have the right to weaken
one branch of the government to strengthen another," the President
wrote him. The statement proved invaluable in the congressman's
candidacy for the Senate. In August, 1917, at the Neshoba County
Fair, long the political sounding board in Mississippi, Harrison an-

nounced against Vardaman and ex-governor Edmund F. Noel. It was soon apparent that the campaign would be a two-way tilt between the veteran senator and the young representative.[18]

The campaign that followed was reported to have "scorched the leaves on the trees and caused the rivers of Mississippi to smoke and steam."[19] In 1915 Vardaman had been the political leader of the state, but his opposition to the armed merchant bill, the declaration of war, the draft legislation, and the espionage bill in addition to Wilson's inclusion of the senator as one of the obstructionist members of the "little group of wilful men" lost for Vardaman much of the popularity that he had once enjoyed. Pitching his campaign on the one issue of support for Wilson and the war, Harrison reproached Vardaman for his pacifist views.

The campaign was waged in the summer of 1918. Vardaman declined to meet his opponent in joint debate and remained in Washington, leaving the conduct of his campaign to what remained of his loyal press. In the spring during a tour of the state to promote the sale of liberty bonds, Harrison began his campaign. On Independence Day he spoke at Meridian on the administration at Washington and its correct conduct of the war. Elaborate arrangements were made for the July 4 celebration. One of the spectacular features was a forty-yoke team of oxen, some of them the identical animals used by Vardaman six years earlier when, in his Senate campaign, he had been carried about the state in a wagon pulled by eighty white oxen. For the Meridian rally the Harrison forces captioned a sign borne by the animals, "We helped pull him in and now we are helping pull him out again."[20]

The Jackson *Daily News,* edited by Frederick Sullens, wholeheartedly backed Harrison as did the metropolitan dailies from Memphis, Mobile, and New Orleans, all widely read in the state. Sullens asserted that there was but one issue in the campaign. "It is loyalty— loyalty to the Democratic administration, and to the ideals for which thousands of United States soldiers are fighting." The *News* gloated over the unenthusiastic reception which Vardaman received at his speaking engagements. Yellow paint streaked the speaker's platform at Amory and the same hue splotched the grandstands at Ackerman when Vardaman spoke there. The senator's attacks upon Harrison gained little credibility. While the incumbent called his opponent "an insignificant creature incubating an ambition to serve his country, or rather himself, in the halls of state," few people were impressed. [21]

One of the most decisive factors in the election outcome was a letter written by Wilson to a Hazlehurst attorney, Myron McNeil, who had asked the president for his view on the election. Wilson replied that, should Mississippians reelect Vardaman, he would regard their action as a "condemnation of my administration, and it is only right that they should know this before they act." [22] The reply was splendid grist for the Harrison press. Still, Harrison feared that Vardaman's strength in the rural areas would give him a margin of victory. A Harrison supporter warned John Sharp Williams that there was "no telling what those red-necks will do." [23]

The returns gave Harrison a first-primary victory. He won with 56,715 votes to Vardaman's 44,154 and Noel's 6,730, carrying fifty-seven of the state's eighty-two counties and showing weaknesses only in the northeast Mississippi hill counties. According to rumor the anti-Vardaman camp had put out orders not only to "beat Vardaman but to drown all the pups." Thus other defeated candidates attributed their losses to earlier associations with the discredited senator. One of the losers was Bilbo, who had run for Harrison's congressional post and been soundly beaten by a rising young attorney from Hattiesburg, Paul B. Johnson. [24]

Thus, at the end of 1918, the team of Vardaman and Bilbo which had dominated Mississippi politics for ten years was eclipsed by a new leader who always would strive to avoid identification with factions within the state. Vardaman was conquered for good, but Bilbo would rise and torment Harrison as no one else was ever able to do. [25]

When Harrison entered the Senate in March of 1919, he won immediate acceptance by the Democratic leaders. The "grand old man" of the Democrats, Senator Williams, was nearing the end of his career and he shifted much of his work to the junior senator. Harrison may have consciously patterned himself after Williams, to whom he was deeply devoted, or perhaps he simply acted from a natural bent. For whatever reason, the new senator developed a witty yet effective style of debate aptly suited for the role of a minority senator. There were many comments years later that during the 1920s Pat Harrison was at his best. Certainly, they were his happiest years. Before the end of his first term, he was easily one of the most popular men in the Senate, a happy circumstance that he would enjoy for the remainder of his life. Moreover, his personality, the rapier of his wit, and his jaunty courage would boost the Democratic party throughout twelve years of successive losses in presidential elections. [26]

In the 1920s the Mississippi senator struggled to vindicate the internationalism of Woodrow Wilson. Unfailing to the last in his devotion to the Democratic president, Harrison spoke time and again before public audiences and his Senate colleagues on behalf of the League of Nations. Although he compared the treaty obstructionists with the "never-ceasing hell hounds Milton stationed at the infernal gates," in the end he joined other Wilson devotees in voting with the irreconcilables against ratification of any treaty to which the Senate had attached reservations opposed by Wilson. Pursuant to his fight for the treaty, the Mississippi senator voted against the joint resolution for a separate peace with Germany. Of the World Court, he affirmed in 1926, "I am for the World Court. I have been for it from the beginning." [27]

Harrison became a staunch restrictionist of immigration, as were most of his southern colleagues. He proposed to prohibit immigration for a period of five years, but his bill was never reported out of the Committee on Immigration of which he was a member. During a summer on the chautauqua circuit in 1923 he advocated immigration restriction, and the topic was the subject of his first experience with radio broadcasting in December, 1923. While Harrison's general position pleased Samuel Gompers, who responded favorably to the radio talk, the labor leader was "astonished" to hear Harrison call for the registration of all aliens within the country. The Mississippian's hard line on immigration did not issue from a sympathy with organized labor; apparently his phobia manifested the provincialism of the South. "It matters not how much you spend on the youth of this land educating them in the ideals of this Government if . . . you are going to admit those from other countries illiterate in character to come here and pollute the stream," he told an immigration conference in 1928. [28]

Harrison's distrust of Europe, moreover, was revealed in his attitude toward cancellation of the allied war debts. He accepted a scaling down of both the principal and interest on the British and Belgian debts, but he drew the line at concessions to France and Italy, primarily because he saw no effort on the part of the two nations to reduce their production of armaments. Furthermore, he believed that the terms offered to France and Italy would aggravate demands for greater concessions from other European countries in future settlements.[29] It was not until a period of international depression that Harrison temporarily altered his views. In the summer of 1931, when President Herbert Hoover proposed a moratorium on the foreign payments due in the new fiscal year, Harrison hailed the proposal as a "proper and constructive move" which would restore worldwide confidence and economic stability. But after the Democratic victory of 1932, when talk was rife that debt cancellations would jeopardize the economic program of the new administration, Harrison reverted to his former opposition. He now expressed a fear that leniency to foreign nations would shift the burden of payment to American taxpayers.[30]

It is hard to reconcile the internationalism of Harrison's stand for the League of Nations with the economic nationalism of his opposition to liberalized debt and reparation programs. The fact of the matter is that, while Harrison was a member of the Foreign Relations and Finance Committees throughout most of his Senate career, he devoted most of his time and thought to domestic issues. He looked at every American commitment to Europeans, whether it be for debt concessions or immigrant education, from the standpoint of the American taxpayer and the maintenance of a balanced budget.

Serving as a minority member of the Senate Finance Committee, the Mississippian spent a decade on the congressional battle line over the tax policies of Republican Secretary of the Treasury Andrew W. Mellon. The much maligned Mellon was a perfect target for the minority party and he received the brunt of the partisan-inspired oratory of Senator Harrison, who once charged that Mellon believed that "prosperity should come from the crumbs that fall from the tables of the rich."[31] Nonetheless, the senator was a stronger foe of the Treasury secretary as a convention keynoter and campaigner for his party during midterm congressional races than he was on Senate roll calls.

The record shows that in the early twenties Harrison supported his party leaders in their fight to retain the excess profits tax, to reduce excise taxes upon consumer goods, and to grant relief to taxpayers of moderate incomes. He opposed what he called the "inexcusable and

disproportionate reduction of the surtaxes of the enormously rich"
carried in the revenue bill of 1923. He supported successive proposals
of minority leaders, particularly those of John Nance Garner in the
House, to provide greater relief to small taxpayers, but at the same
time he was not willing to support the demands of certain of his party
leaders to go the limit in wealth taxation. Harrison did not favor
either a federal estate tax or an inheritance tax, and he defended the
issuance of tax-exempt securities. When the Senate debated the revenue bill of 1926, Harrison called for a slight reduction in the levy on
corporate incomes and offered amendments to repeal the war-imposed
stamp tax on capital stock issues. By then he was convinced that tax
relief to corporations would mean increased savings to the consumer,
who, he argued, ultimately bore the brunt of the taxes. "I am not the
champion of the corporations of this country; but . . . I believe in dealing fairly and equitably and justly with every interest," he told the
Senate in 1927. Thus Harrison had evolved over the decade from a
supporter of fairly heavy corporate taxation to something of a wealth
protector himself. [32]

Harrison's vacillation on tax policies during the Republican years
indicated that he had no well-articulated tax philosophy and presaged
the ambivalence which would characterize his leadership as chairman of the Finance Committee during the New Deal, when the
Democrats would be forced to grapple with incessant demands for
more and more taxes. On one tax issue, however, he was firm. He
opposed a federal sales tax, and in 1932, during the last battle over a
tax bill before he became the New Deal taxmaster, he was one of the
Senate leaders of the rebellion against a sales tax proposed by members of his own party in the House. [33]

While Harrison had few fixed views on how to levy federal taxes,
he did not waver in thirty years on the tariff, a subject which he
injected into almost every issue he debated. He led his party's opposition to the Republican tariff bills from the time of the emergency
tariff of 1921 through the passage of the Hawley-Smoot bill of 1930.
He opposed protective tariffs because he felt that they were devastating to all consumers, including farmers. Moreover, high tariffs restricted international trade, which he considered to be the only solution to the European debt question and the pall of a worldwide depression. "I have never voted for protection in my life, and I shall

never do so. I believe in a tariff for revenue only," he told the Senate
in 1922 during the debate on the Fordney-McCumber bill.[34] Harrison was not, however, a free trader. He supported what he called a
competitive tariff, and in 1930 he voted for a duty on long-staple
cotton while resisting the appeals of some Mississippi constituents for
protection on a number of other items including lumber. Still, he
remained one of the most ardent southern supporters of tariff reduction. A future Democratic administration would provide an opportunity for Senator Harrison to serve as a master strategist for tariff revision.

When Harrison first went to Congress, he intended to devote himself primarily to the relief of the agricultural distress from which
most of his Mississippi constituents continually suffered, and he
sought membership on the House Agriculture Committee. For a time
he served on the Senate committee also, but his interests shifted and
he was always on the periphery of the various shifting agricultural
blocs of the 1920s. The Mississippian never considered himself as a
member of the farm bloc, but he defended the alliance of southern
and western farm senators without which "little or nothing would
have been done for the great agricultural interests of the country." At
other times he lectured the farm senators on their misguided efforts,
notably in respect to tariffs on farm products and farm relief finance
measures that were dependent upon the retention of tariffs. He also
was unsympathetic to agrarian relief measures limited to the Midwest. Thus, he opposed the first two of a series of bills offered by
Charles L. McNary of Oregon and Gilbert N. Haugen of Iowa which
reached the Senate in 1926 and 1927; but he later offered reluctant
support when the terms of a subsequent bill in 1928 were satisfactory
to cotton farmers, and he even voted to override the veto of President
Calvin Coolidge of the final McNary-Haugen bill.[35]

Unwilling to accept any scheme by which the government would
"go into the mercantile business to purchase agricultural products,"
Harrison never supported solutions directed to the problem of farm
surpluses beyond the mild measures that extended rural credits and
created voluntary marketing cooperatives. Constricted by his basic
opposition to federal activism, Harrison promoted the government's
acceptance of the private enterprise proposal of automobile magnate
Henry Ford, who promised to develop the government's holdings at

Muscle Shoals into a great fertilizer factory. When the Ford proposal was rejected, Harrison turned to the plan of Alabama's Senator Oscar W. Underwood to lease the holdings to private power interests. Only reluctantly did Harrison finally accept the proposal of George W. Norris of Nebraska that the federal government develop a giant multipurpose flood control and power production facility. When the Norris bill cleared the last of many Senate hurdles, Harrison was one of two southern senators who voted against public control of Muscle Shoals. It was not until the vote was taken on the conference report that Harrison cast a "yea" vote for the Norris plan. He had finally resigned himself to the fact that government ownership was the only system under which the Shoals could ever be developed for the production of nitrates for fertilizer and power for cheap electricity.[36] He was, however, never able to feel any warmth for the great federal enterprise eventually founded at Muscle Shoals.

Harrison's record from the onset of depression in 1929 until the end of the Hoover administration in 1933 indicates that he had changed his views little since the early 1920s when one of his popular chautauqua topics had been "Less Government in Business and More Business in Government."[37] As the depression deepened, he acquiesced to more extensive government aid for distressed groups. He supported an unemployment bill offered by Robert Wagner of New York as well as the use of federal funds to relieve drought-stricken farm areas. "Let the arm of the government be extended to give employment, if possible, to the millions of men and women who are out of employment, and to relieve the distress that is rampant," he said in late 1930. Nevertheless, he drew the line at the idea of a dole for direct relief, and he voted against the La Follette-Costigan bill of 1932 to provide federal grants to states for direct relief. "I have opposed this dole legislation," he wrote a constituent. "It is not my idea of how the situation is to be met," he explained, although he never addressed the Senate on the subject. On the matter of public works, he was more explicit. He spoke in favor of the Rainey-Wagner bill to provide the Reconstruction Finance Corporation with funds for public works. After Hoover promptly vetoed that measure, Harrison voted for the Emergency Relief and Construction bill, a version more palatable to the president. Later action of the senator from 1933 through 1939 indicated that he continued to believe that public works programs were far preferable to a direct dole to the unemployed and distressed. [38]

As an opposition senator during the administrations of Warren G. Harding, Calvin Coolidge, and Herbert Hoover, Senator Harrison's congressional behavior must be judged almost exclusively in terms of his keen partisanship. [39] His remarks in the Senate seldom transcended party politics, and the inconsistencies in his voting record on such issues as the Mellon tax proposals reflected little more than his party's efforts to embarrass Republican presidents as well as his own uncertainty as to the right course to take. These were what the journalists called his "gadfly" years, when his "chief joy in life [was] to jerk up Republican Senators by their Achilles heels and skin them alive." [40] Remarking on Harrison's role as a minority assistant, Mark Sullivan quipped that the senator played "Stonewall Jackson to Senator Underwood's Robert E. Lee" (Underwood was the Democratic Senate floor leader from 1921 to 1923.) Near the end of his life Harrison reminisced about the 1920s: "I was somewhat free and easy without the weight of heavy responsibilities and the openings were so many and large that I could not restrain frequently from enjoying the art of throwing the political javelin." [41]

Based on his public record prior to 1933, Pat Harrison was nearly the quintessential conservative in his approach to economic questions. He believed essentially in a limited government, a balanced budget, a tariff for revenue only, and a federal tax program which produced needed revenue without penalizing the producers of wealth. But, above all, Harrison was the most loyal of Democrats, devoted to the party's presidents and voraciously hungry for Democratic victories at the polls. At some point prior to 1933, he sensed that an economic revolution was under way and that he must make philosophical capitulations and practical adaptations if prosperity for the nation and victory for his party were to return. Just how far he was willing to follow a new Democratic leader and to support his party regardless of his own personal predilections was a question to be answered in the future.

CHAPTER II

The Terrible Twenties: "I Want to See our Party Win"

THE PRESIDENTIAL ELECTIONS of the 1920s were exercises in frustration for Pat Harrison. In each of the three contests he threw himself wholeheartedly into the Democratic struggle to win the presidency, and then, after successive Democratic defeats, he worked at high levels in Democratic councils to rebuild the party for its next quadrennial combat. He was vastly disappointed by the defeat in 1920 of James M. Cox, and four years later the Mississippian, whose political talents won him the position of convention keynoter, was stunned by still another decisive defeat of his party. In 1928 Harrison worked incessantly for Alfred E. Smith despite the risks for himself in Mississippi. Recognized as a master strategist in Democratic circles, Harrison was invited to counsel the party's leaders in their search for a winner in 1932. His associations with Franklin D. Roosevelt from 1928 to 1932 convinced him that the New Yorker was "the most available man" to head the ticket in 1932, and at the Democratic convention in Chicago that year the senator from Mississippi played a vital role in the nomination of the New York governor and in his subsequent election.

The senator's first significant role at a nominating convention came in 1920 at San Francisco where, because of the illness of John Sharp Williams, he led the Mississippi delegation and seconded the nomination of Governor James M. Cox with a rousing statement castigating the Hearst papers for attempts to dictate the party's nomination.[1] In fact, the behind-the-scenes maneuvers of Harrison in behalf of Cox led some journals to credit Harrison with doing more than any other delegate to bring about the nomination. Cox himself later referred to Harrison as "a distinct factor" in his nomination. Harrison was not as confident in the wisdom of the party's choice for a vice-president. According to Arthur F. Mullen, a party wheelhorse from Nebraska, Harrison was not averse to paying deference to the political influence of William Randolph Hearst for, when the senator learned that Franklin D. Roosevelt was to be nominated, he had hotly said to Mullen, "If you'd said Bainbridge Colby, we'd have had the Hearst newspapers."[2] Colby was never warm to the idea of being nominated, and when Cox approved Roosevelt as his running mate, Harrison joined with others in winning Tammany boss Charles F. Murphy's approval of Roosevelt's nomination.[3]

The convention over, Harrison moved to New York City to serve as chairman of the Speakers' Bureau and sporadically as temporary head of the campaign headquarters. His numerous statements to the press indicated that, to him, the League of Nations was the pivotal issue of the campaign.[4] For his ceaseless activity at the headquarters, Harrison won the praise of Joseph P. Tumulty, an old Wilsonian, who singled him out as a party faithful of "great assistance" upon whom a major burden of the campaign's direction fell. Cox, who went down in a November defeat humiliating to the party, remained on close personal terms with Senator Harrison and liked to boast of Harrison's often repeated statement, "He is still my candidate."[5]

Personally endowed with the resilience that his party needed, Harrison quickly rebounded from the 1920 defeat and called upon the Democrats "to bury all past differences and forget about the recent campaign." He wrote the Mississippi Democratic committeewoman, "What we need now is complete cooperation with a militant and united front."[6] Unity was his keyword. But unity was never as elusive for the Democrats as it was at the 1924 convention where Harrison was one of the most visible of the party leaders. By the early spring of 1924 he was being mentioned for the post of convention temporary chairman and keynoter. Chosen unanimously by the Committee on Arrangements, Harrison was a happy choice among the backers of Oscar W. Underwood, William Gibbs McAdoo, and Alfred E. Smith, the leading presidential hopefuls. One of the New York leaders, Franklin Roosevelt, remarked that he was very well pleased with the committee's decision, for he had reached the conclusion "some time ago" that Harrison's qualifications marked him as the best man for the post.[7] Some dissatisfaction was expressed in Harrison's home state by former United States senator LeRoy Percy, who asserted that Harrison would stand before the convention as a spokesman for a Ku Klux Klan delegation (although he admitted that the senator was not a member of the Klan), since the Mississippi delegation was Klan-controlled. Harrison, who had not attended the state Democratic convention, made it a point to avoid public contact with the Mississippi delegates and the chance that he might be forced to take issue with them in New York City. He was skittish because he would make his own bid for a second term in the Mississippi August primary. [8]

Some distinction lay in the fact that Pat Harrison, at the age of forty-two, was the second youngest keynoter in history. Apprehensive about the speech that he had prepared to deliver before a divided party, he revised it so often that it became stale to him. Party chairman Cordell Hull advised him to consult Claude G. Bowers who read the manuscript and assured Harrison that it was "a very fine speech—nothing wrong with it." [9] As it turned out, the address delighted both the audience and the party leaders during the hour and a half that Harrison lampooned the Republican party for its political sins with "revelations" that Will Rogers declared "would have made anybody but Republicans ashamed of themselves." [10] In time little would be remembered about Harrison's keynote address other than that the combination of his drawl and the usual muffled convention hall acoustics caused some of the gallery visitors to mistake his clarion call for Paul Revere to bring duty and high resolve to America as a call for "real beer." The statement drew prolonged cheering. The New York *Times* described it as an excellent keynote for a "fighting campaign," a speech of "good ole bonded pre-war stuff." [11]

Harrison never publicly revealed his choice for the Democratic presidential nomination in 1924, although he had confided to John Sharp Williams in late 1923 that McAdoo appeared to be the strongest contender. "I lean very strongly towards [him] because I want us to win." [12] Years later he would say that of all his congressional colleagues he thought "Oscar Underwood would have been the greatest president," but in 1924 Underwood's stand against the Klan made him anathema to the South. When the convention assembled, Harrison carried his own state's vote until the sixteenth ballot when the Mississippians turned to Senator Joseph Robinson and then swayed alternately between McAdoo and Samuel M. Ralston of Indiana, never casting any ballots for either Underwood or Smith. [13] When John W. Davis of West Virginia was finally nominated on the

Washington *Evening Star,* 1924
Courtesy: Archives and Special Collections, University of Mississippi

103rd ballot after nine exhausting days, Harrison declared it a "master stroke" which would bring victory in November. As he had done four years earlier, Harrison joined the national headquarters staff and spent much of the summer on the campaign circuit, concluding his efforts in late October with a radio speech, a campaign medium used by only a few of the party leaders. After the defeat of Davis in November, Harrison, keenly aware of the party schism revealed by the nomination marathon, called upon leaders to "cease wrangling among themselves, compose their differences, and cease the promotion of selfish ambitions."[14]

In 1928 Senator Harrison was freer to participate in national preconvention affairs in Mississippi for, having carried every county in the state in his 1924 race against former governor Earl Brewer, his

own political position was secure. (In fact, he would not even have an
opponent in 1930.) With the Mississippi Democratic convention in
the hands of moderates, Harrison chose to attend.[15] The political
climate of Mississippi had cooled to the point that Al Smith was now a
plausible contender for Mississippi support even though the Klan and
temperance societies in the state opposed him. In 1927 Harrison had
stated that Smith would carry Mississippi and he had written to the
Klan that he favored sending an uninstructed delegation to the national convention; he knew that an instructed group would go anti-
Smith.[16] When the Mississippi convention met in June, Harrison's
speech loaded the scales in favor of an unmandated delegation.[17]

Three weeks later Harrison's appearance on the podium as acting
permanent chairman on the final day of the Houston convention
hinted that Arkansas Senator Joseph T. Robinson, the permanent
chairman, was to receive the vice-presidential nomination, a reward
with which the twenty Mississippi delegates were in perfect accord.
It was while Harrison was presiding that the famous telegram from
Smith was received calling for the repeal of prohibition. Roosevelt,
who had placed the "Happy Warrior" in nomination, was on the platform with Harrison and shared his fear that the message would
prompt a floor fight that would irreparably damage party unity. As
Harrison put it, "My God, this will cause a riot!" Bowers, Roosevelt,
and Harrison all agreed that the "wet" wire would have to be read but
that Harrison should read it as rapidly as possible and then immediately recognize a delegate who would move for adjournment. He
speedily read the telegram, got his adjournment motion, and gaveled
the session to an end. Thus the convention ended and, as one wag put
it, "The Democratic donkey with a wet head and dragging a dry tail
left Houston."[18]

Senators Harrison and Robinson, who had already formed a lasting
political and personal friendship, were acutely aware even before the
nomination that Smith was unpopular in the South as much for his
Catholic religion as for his wetness. Former senator Williams had
predicted both a Smith nomination "by default" and a subsequent
overwhelming defeat that would break the Solid South. The senators
knew, too, that Smith's selection of John J. Raskob, a Catholic and a
wet, as party chairman had further agitated already troubled
waters.[19] Harrison moved to New York City for the duration of the

campaign to serve as a member of the Democratic Executive Committee which remained in almost constant session. [20] Assigned to handle the southern states, his correspondence with party faithfuls there reveals his frustration over the reluctance of elected leaders in some quarters to risk their political necks by a forthright endorsement of Smith. He at least enjoyed the confidences and cooperation of Senator Carter Glass of Virginia. "I am just praying that the reaction will not be as bad as we anticipate," Harrison wrote Glass in mid-August. The Mississippi senator was also disturbed by the lingering bitterness of preconvention discord which the press continued to nurture. [21]

In Mississippi, Harrison's problems were not insurmountable because the leading politicians—his Senate colleague Hubert D. Stephens, Governor Bilbo, and the influential Congressman Ross A. Collins, as well as the revered John Sharp Williams—all supported Smith. Before joining the advisory committee in New York, Harrison had spoken in Mississippi to the Patrons' Union at Lake and to a larger crowd at the annual Neshoba County Fair. Assailing religious intolerance and insisting that there were questions of greater importance to the South than prohibition, he argued the essentiality of Democratic unity for the success of the party's progressive programs in agriculture and tariff reform, and he pointed to Smith's record in New York as indicative of "his keen mind, his undaunted courage and candor, his grasp of public questions." The endorsement without a dissenting vote of the Democratic ticket by both houses of the Mississippi legislature was a welcome note at party headquarters in view of the reports coming in from other states in the South, particularly Alabama where J. Thomas Heflin was girding the state for a papal invasion in the event of Smith's election. [22]

By late October, Harrison's concern at party headquarters had grown beyond his anxieties over the blatant exploitation in the South of Smith's religion and his wetness to worries over charges that Smith was an advocate of racial equality. Acutely aware of scurrilous statements that Smith had a long record in New York of promoting social relationships between whites and blacks, Harrison directed his attention to dispelling the charges. In a mimeographed circular sent to prominent southern leaders Harrison denied that Smith had appointed Negroes to New York state offices, that he believed in interracial marriage, or that he had placed Negro teachers over white chil-

Byron Patton Harrison, age 22, as a young teacher (1903)

Senators Hubert D. Stephens and Harrison (1920)

Harrison umpiring a ballgame of congressional pages (1921)

Harrison and William Jennings Bryan (1923)

Senators William E. Borah and Harrison (1923)

Harrison delivering Democratic National Convention keynote address (1924)

Harrison at radio microphone during 1928 campaign

Sen. Dennis Chavez (N. Mex.), White House legislative liaison Charles West, Harrison, Sen. Joseph T. Robinson (Ark.), Postmaster-General James A. Farley, and Sen. Joseph O'Mahoney (Wyo.), after Senate sustained bonus vote on May 23, 1935

George E. Allen, Vice-President John Nance Garner, and Harrison (1936)

Rep. Robert Doughton and Harrison on Dec. 17, 1936, consulting on revenue bill nuisance taxes

dren in New York schools. On the other hand, Harrison himself engaged in some political profit-taking on the race issue when he described to Mississippians in his Patrons' Union speech the efforts of Hoover to desegregate the Republican campaign headquarters. [23]

While the nucleus of opposition to Smith in Mississippi may have been anti-Catholicism, [24] most Mississippians maintained a racial commitment to the Democratic party. John Sharp Williams' unequivocal statement "I will support the Democratic ticket nominees because I am a white man and a Democrat" explains more than anything else Mississippi's appearance in Smith's column in November. [25] When Harrison later praised his home state for having "answered the poisoned hisses of intolerance" in casting for a Catholic candidate the largest vote accorded a presidential nominee in Mississippi's history to that point, he overlooked the racial intolerance that was possibly the strongest undercurrent in the victory. [26] Even in defeat, Harrison remained loyal to Smith, and when the vanquished "warrior" chose to go to Biloxi for post-election relaxation, Harrison accompanied him. [27] His close Mississippi friend and confidant Eugene Fly later said that the senator had risked political oblivion by his support of Smith. [28]

Harrison's post-election loyalty to Smith did not mean that he intended to follow the "brown derby" into another election ring. When he wrote to a Democrat in Texas that "factional differences must be wiped out and past mistakes forgotten," [29] he may have deeply sensed that Smith's candidacy was one of those mistakes. Harrison soon became the most prominent Mississippian who had come to look upon Franklin D. Roosevelt, the new governor of New York, as the promising contender for the 1932 nomination. The Harrison-Roosevelt relationship now blossomed beyond the casual acquaintanceship of earlier years. Even while Roosevelt was governor-elect in 1928, he turned to Harrison for advice on problems concerning New York. Harrison responded in a number of "Dear Frank" letters. A short time later Harrison congratulated the governor on his "deportment" and the "manner in which [he was] handling the affairs of the State of New York." Pleasantries between Roosevelt and Harrison were exchanged through the New York lieutenant-governor, Herbert Lehman, and extended to such trivialities as Roosevelt's intercession with President Nicholas Murray Butler of Columbia University in arranging a

football game between that university and the University of Mississippi (it never came off). [30] The personal pleasure that Harrison enjoyed through his relationship with FDR is revealed by a statement
made to a Mississippian who had asked the senator just how well he
knew the New Yorker. "I call him Frank," Harrison replied with
obvious satisfaction. [31]

When Democratic party chairman John J. Raskob attempted to
force through a wet plank at an important conference of the Democratic National Committee in March, 1931, Harrison revealed his
fears about the disaster inherent in such a move to one of Roosevelt's
associates, who in turn wrote the governor of an important "confidential" conference with the Mississippian in which the latter insisted
that the issue should "lie dormant" until the convention. The confidant wrote that "the Senator will gladly back your candidacy," and
that he would be useful for preliminary work in southern states.
Harrison was not yet willing to espouse Roosevelt's nomination publicly, he continued, but would be happy to confer with him at Hyde
Park or New York City, where the newspapers would be less likely to
"make a noise" about it than at Albany. Nonetheless, a conference
was arranged at the governor's mansion on March 12. [32] During the
talks Harrison suggested people capable of doing some preconvention
publicity for the Roosevelt cause. Writing to Roosevelt on March 19
he concluded, "I have given some thought to the advisability of my
coming out in a strong statement at this time for you but I believe it
might be better to wait a little while." He was willing to act "whenever we agree that the psychological time is at hand." [33]

As for the Raskob attempt to commit the party to prohibition repeal, James A. Farley, by now a leading manager of the Roosevelt
campaign, succeeded in marshaling enough opposition, particularly
among southern senators, to bypass the ploy. Senator Robinson put it
bluntly: "You cannot write on the banner of the Democratic party . . .
the skull and crossbones emblematic of an outlawed trade." [34] Harrison's own problems with the "outlawed trade" were just beginning,
for his involvements with prohibition repeal would haunt him politically in his 1936 campaign for reelection to the Senate. As matters
stood in late March, 1932, Harrison, who had gone to Mississippi for
a month and planned to confer with FDR at Warm Springs on his
way back to Washington, wrote a Roosevelt agent, "I believe Gover-

nor Roosevelt can be elected. And quite naturally I want to see our Party win." By July, Harrison still had not made a public commitment but was certain that the governor was "far in front . . . and if he should be elected . . . he will make a great President."[35]

The Roosevelt managers were convinced that Harrison's open support would be necessary in carrying the Mississippi delegation at the national convention. Colonel Edward M. House, another of the Roosevelt "general staff," was also taking the political pulses of various state leaders and learned from one influential Mississippian that a Roosevelt nomination "will not be hard if his cause is espoused by Senator Harrison at the outset."[36] In September the senator in a Labor Day speech at Tampa publicly stated that Roosevelt was "far in the lead" and that he would be the standard-bearer "if the convention would be held today."[37]

By January, 1932, organizational work for Roosevelt was under way in Mississippi, but it apparently had fallen into the hands of an incompetent lot. Ellen S. Woodward, a former Mississippi legislator and a woman of remarkable political astuteness, warned Harrison that the only men who had appeared on the scene as Roosevelt organizers "were such types that would drive people away," and she described a pathetically ill-planned dinner put on in Jackson as "the poorest arranged affair I ever attended." Harrison relayed her confidential report to Louis Howe along with his own embarrassment over the fact that the free-lance promoters served only "to bawl things up." Roosevelt, too, was alarmed by a group of fund collectors who had appeared not only in Mississippi but elsewhere in the South, and he wrote Harrison to spread the word in Mississippi against the group "out to make a money racket out of my candidacy."[38] Banishing these irregular interlopers fell not to Harrison but to Farley, who refused to open the party purse for reimbursement of expenses.

By early summer Roosevelt had won instructed delegations in a number of southern and border states that he considered crucial for the first ballot victory that he sought. He was most desirous that the Mississippi Democratic convention instruct its delegation and hoped to achieve the coup through Senators Harrison and Stephens as well as Congressman John E. Rankin, all of whom had already been designated by Howe as "those whom we have relied on to conduct the fight for delegates." While Harrison had appeared evasive about coming out for an instructed delegation (it had long been the custom for Mississippi's contingent to go to national conventions uninstructed), there was no question within the coterie of Roosevelt's advisers regarding his stature as "our loyal friend," and they sought Harrison's advice about the conduct of the Roosevelt boom in states outside the South, particularly Massachusetts and Rhode Island.[39] Harrison, in turn, was calling for outside help to do missionary work among Roosevelt's opponents in Mississippi, of whom Governor Martin Sennett (Mike) Conner was the most formidable.

Governor Conner, who declined an invitation to visit Roosevelt at Warm Springs in May with the excuse that the legislature was in session, was closely identified with the forces within the state advocating the candidacy of Newton D. Baker, Wilson's secretary of war and now a favorite among the internationalists and older progressives. Even without a formal organization the Baker name had become increasingly popular at county conventions held throughout the state in May prior to the June 7 state convention, and his popularity probably contributed to attempts made by Rankin to win instructions for Roosevelt in the county meetings. Despite the fact that only nine of the state's eighty-two counties had been pledged for Roosevelt, Rankin wrote him of the "marvelous showing."[40]

Roosevelt, aware of the probability that the Mississippi state convention would endorse him through a resolution as the South Carolina convention had, was concerned that any state resorting to a stratagem short of instruction "is made the immediate target of a drive by blockaders and furnishes a faint ray of hope that something may yet be done by them." When the state convention did follow just such a course, thus adhering to its tradition, Roosevelt was disappointed. His wire to Harrison—"Good for old Mississippi. I am delighted."—was not the truth for he found more believable the Mississippi picture described by another admirer who wrote that direct instructions "would have been a knock out for you."[41] Pat Harrison had not attended the Mississippi convention, for he had remained in Washington for day and night sessions of the conference committee, threshing out the revenue bill of 1932. He was, however, selected as one of the delegates to the Chicago convention scheduled to open on June 27. When the Mississippi delegates left for the convention two days before, it was common knowledge that they carried a fragile one-vote margin for Roosevelt with which Harrison was expected to hold the twenty votes for the governor under Mississippi's time-honored unit rule.

On the opening day of the convention the Mississippi delegation elected Governor Conner as chairman, and Harrison spent the day calling on Mississippi delegates grouped in the Sherman Hotel. Roosevelt's strength within the delegation surfaced when it voted on the second day to seat the Louisiana delegation headed by Huey P. Long, as well as a pro-Roosevelt group from Minnesota, and then voted for Thomas P. Walsh as permanent chairman rather than Jouett Shouse, who was known to be the choice of the stop-FDR delegates. At the exhausting Wednesday night session when the platform was brought out, the Mississippians kept their banner out of the parade that followed the adoption of the prohibition repeal plank and Harrison voted for the minority report calling for resubmission of the Eighteenth Amendment to the states. The Mississippians also voted down the plan of William K. ("Alfalfa Bill") Murray advocating cash payment of the veterans' bonus although Congressman Rankin gave it vociferous support.[42]

On June 29, at the sixth caucus of the Mississippians to settle upon a first ballot vote, Senators Harrison and Stephens finally got the expected 10 1/2 to 9 1/2 vote for Roosevelt. When the convention balloting began, Roosevelt failed to win the first tally; nor did he win the second. By that time the convention had been in session so long (the sun had risen) that Harrison, relying upon a statement of the Roosevelt leaders that there would be an adjournment, returned to his hotel three miles away and undressed for bed. Turning on the radio, he heard "Mississippi passes" and realized that the convention had not adjourned temporarily after all; rather, a third ballot had begun. Knowing that some of the Mississippians were wavering due to talk among other state delegations that Roosevelt would be weak in northern and western states and to numerous telegrams coming in to Conner from Mississippi urging Baker's nomination, Harrison was certain that his absence would be disastrous. Only partially dressed, he dashed from the hotel into a taxi and completed dressing during a fast ride back to the Chicago Stadium. He arrived just in time for the roll call of the Mississippians and cast the crucial vote for Roosevelt that kept the governor ahead by one vote in the Mississippi balloting.[43]

There is some dispute whether it was really Harrison who held the

Mississippians in line that dawn of July 1. Senator Burton K.
Wheeler who was implacably for Roosevelt was certain that Harrison,
as well as other Southerners such as Josiah William Bailey of North
Carolina and John H. Bankhead of Alabama, had supported Roosevelt
all along only because they thought they had to. Edward J. Flynn, the
political boss of the Bronx who personally thought Harrison to be too
conservative to be a genuine Roosevelt man, was convinced that the
senator would welcome an opportunity to break the unit rule and turn
Mississippi to other candidates. According to Flynn's postmortem,
Huey Long was put in charge of holding in line both the tottering
Mississippi and Arkansas delegations. Long charged into the Mississippians and shook his fist in Harrison's face with the threat "If you
break the unit rule, you sonofabitch, I'll go into Mississippi and break
you." Flynn recorded, "There is no question in my mind but that
without Long's work Roosevelt might not have been nominated."[44]
Nonetheless, the doubts cast upon Harrison's constancy for Roosevelt
do not seem to be supported by the senator's action in holding the
crucial Mississippi votes. His efforts to control the delegation were
honest and they were of consequence. Arthur Krock, a veteran reporter and columnist, reminisced in 1950: "Had that delegation broken,
Roosevelt could never have been nominated, because he would have
gone down so far that Ritchie or Baker would have come up."[45]

As the bedraggled delegates streamed out of convention hall to rest
until the convention reassembled that night for a fourth ballot, there
was no rest for the Roosevelt field marshals who feared that the convention had been deadlocked. Mississippi and several other states
were still a source of worry. Meanwhile, Harrison was asked by Farley to find Representative Sam Rayburn of Texas, who had come to
Chicago determined to nominate John Nance Garner, and arrange a
meeting of the Roosevelt and Garner leaders in a place safe from
reporters. A short time later Harrison summoned Farley to the room
at the Congress Hotel that he shared with his close Mississippi friend
George E. Allen, a popular Washingtonian who had headed an organization of hotel men boosting Roosevelt's candidacy. There Farley
met with Rayburn who had brought along Silliman Evans, a powerful
Texas publisher. While in Harrison's room, Rayburn told Farley that
he would telephone Garner, who had remained in Washington, to
negotiate the release of the Texas delegates to Roosevelt. After a hec-

tic day of pressure politics to win Garner's withdrawal and the support of the Texas and California delegations for Roosevelt, Garner gave in and agreed to accept the vice-presidential slot. During the day Harrison caught up on his sleep and, according to Lewis W. Douglas, an avowed Baker man, took the telephone receiver off the hook in order not to be subjected to pressure to assist in realigning delegations about to switch to Baker. That night, just before the balloting began, Evans ran into Harrison near the speaker's platform and told him, "John Garner is out and Texas is going for Roosevelt." Harrison, who had begun to race to his delegation, reeled and ran back to grab Evans by both shoulders. "Are you sure?" he asked. "You can't mean it! We have just voted to leave Roosevelt." Reassured, he double-timed it back to the Mississippi delegates who returned to Roosevelt in a hurried caucus.[46] When the fourth ballot was completed, Roosevelt had won the nomination.

Pat Harrison never claimed for himself a decisive role in the swing to Roosevelt although others made that claim for him. "Senator Harrison is entitled to all the credit for keeping the Mississippi delegation from switching to Baker," Thomas Grayson, a Baker supporter, wrote Roosevelt on July 5. Although a number of Mississippians wrote to the new nominee to assure him that an overwhelming number of the state's citizens had supported him from the start, Roosevelt must have had a lingering suspicion that he had had a close call with the entire Mississippi delegation including Harrison. Arthur Krock mused in his New York *Times* column on July 1, "It is still a mystery why Mississippi has been so lightly infused with the pro-Roosevelt sentiment of all its Southern neighbors." Indeed, there had been open support for candidates other than Roosevelt within the Mississippi delegation for many of the group considered the New Yorker to be too liberal. One delegate had seconded the nomination of Ritchie, and Governor Conner's support of Baker was well publicized.[47] A week after the convention ended, Conner, who was in New York scanning the bond market for the sale of Mississippi issues, admitted that if Roosevelt had not been named on the fourth ballot, Mississippi would have swung to Baker. He wrote the same to Ralph Hayes, who had been Baker's "Howe."[48]

All things considered, it would appear that any claim that Harrison led the southern Democrats in opposition to Roosevelt in 1932 cannot

be substantiated. Nearest the truth is a statement made to Baker in
late 1932, "Pat Harrison . . . will end up being for you." Harrison
probably considered Baker as the first alternative should Roosevelt's
nomination fail, but that does not lessen the fact that Harrison's first
loyalty was to the New Yorker. [49]

The nomination over, preparations began for the conduct of the
campaign. Key Pittman, the Nevada senator who served as a speech
writer on the campaign train, suggested to Roosevelt in mid-July that
Senator Harrison be appointed to an advisory committee. On July 26,
when Farley presented campaign plans to Democratic congressional
leaders meeting in Harrison's Senate office, it was agreed that the
Mississippian would open the speakers' campaign on July 29 with a
radio address. Harrison then went to Mississippi to spend the first
week in August conferring with leaders on the conduct of the national campaign in his home state. Unlike in 1928, Mississippi gave
Harrison no worries at all and he did not feel it necessary to carry on
an extensive campaign there. Thinking it imperative, however, to set
his own record straight with the home folks, he used the Neshoba
County Fair as an occasion to defend his vote against the soldier
bonus plank as a vote against a wrecked budget. As for the prohibition
plank, while protesting that he was personally dry, Harrison avowed
that as a representative of the Democratic party he would abide by the
platform. After spending six weeks in Mississippi, he allotted the
remainder of the congressional recess to the national headquarters
and in mid-September he joined the Hotel Biltmore headquarters battalion of writers and speakers in New York. [50]

Harrison's services in 1932 were much as they had been in the
1928 campaign, but he had a far easier time than in the earlier contest. When he wrote the southern state leaders on this round, his
letters were rosy in their optimistic reports of progress. "I do not see
how they can beat us this time," he wrote to Florida, and he predicted
to a Tennessean who was concerned about a factional rift in that state
that "I cannot believe that there is the slightest chance to defeat
Roosevelt." An inveterate movie-goer, Harrison could be counted on
to know what the newsreels were showing of the campaign, and he
wrote Howe that Hoover was getting larger coverage than Roosevelt.
"They are not giving us a fair play," he complained, and he recommended that the Smith-Roosevelt reconciliation scene at the New

York state Democratic convention be given wide circulation in the movie houses. He also circularized the Roosevelt story through influential newspapers. "There is no better medium for reaching Mississippi than the *Commercial Appeal,"* Harrison wrote to editor Thomas Fautleroy. [51]

In late September, Harrison returned to Washington to make preparations to go on the stump for Roosevelt. The Democratic headquarters, which had worked out an October itinerary for Harrison covering ten states, counted upon the Mississippian to advance the campaign against the Republican tariff and spending programs. Of Republican warnings of business uncertainty in the event of a Democratic victory the senator scoffed: "It takes a lot of nerve for this bunch to give that bunk to the people in view of their own broken promises and indefensible record." Fortified by ammunition from the party general staff, Harrison attacked the grants made by the Hoover administration to big business through the Reconstruction Finance Corporation and concessions given Henry Ford. The senator covered some of the Midwest which Roosevelt crossed on his western trip, but he never made it to California even though McAdoo had issued a Macedonian call for aid in the state races there. [52] In speeches outlined by the party "ghosts," Harrison espoused the same brand of fiscal conservatism that Roosevelt epitomized in his Pittsburgh speech on October 19. That speech, with its pledge of a 25 percent cut in federal spending, and Roosevelt's endorsement of the National Economy League reassured his Mississippi campaign agent that the party's standard-bearer was indeed a man admirably suited to the nation's needs. If the Pittsburgh call for fiscal responsibility did represent Franklin Roosevelt's basic beliefs well into the New Deal, as Frank Freidel has said, then the Roosevelt-Harrison New Deal honeymoon of some three years duration becomes much more understandable. [53]

The November 8 returns proved Mississippi to be the bulwark of Democracy that Harrison predicted; the Republicans won a paltry 2.8 percent of the vote in the state. Roosevelt apparently appealed to Mississippians from all walks of life. "It's funny, but I don't believe I could write Mr. President Hoover this letter even tho he were a Democrat, but it's different with you—probably we feel it's your humanness and ability to understand," one Mississippian wrote

Roosevelt.[54] The Roosevelt image of confidence and action that exerted such a tremendous appeal to the rank-and-file voter in Mississippi was certainly as valuable to the new president as the factor of political availability that had endeared him to Harrison. Mississippians looked forward to the inauguration and the role that their senior senator would play in the new administration.

CHAPTER III

"I am a Good Democrat & I go Through"

1933

THE YEAR 1933 was probably the busiest of Pat Harrison's Senate career. Even before Franklin D. Roosevelt assumed office in March, the senator was involved in committee work on economic policy-making. From inauguration to the end of the session in June, Harrison presided over a committee responsible for the passage of key segments of the new president's program. A close look at the senator's work during this time as well as a brief survey of his late summer and autumn recess activities should answer some interesting questions about the Mississippian's outlook on the responsibilities of the federal government in a time of total depression. Was he an innovative thinker or did he rely upon the judgments of others? Was he so inflexible in his stand for a balanced budget that he would be unable to accept record-high federal expenditures on domestic programs?

When Congress reconvened in December, 1932, for a short, lame duck session, Senator Harrison, as the rising chairman of the Committee on Finance, was something of a man of the hour. Hundreds of letters and telegrams were coming in from all over the country and his telephone jangled constantly. "It's a bombardment," he said on December 2. Republicans and Democrats intended to make a last drive for the balanced budget promised by both candidates in the recent campaign, and talk of new taxes filled the air. When President Hoover was rumored to have turned to the sales tax idea once again, Harrison conferred with him and helped scotch the idea. At the same time President-elect Roosevelt threw his influence against House leaders who wanted to put forward a revenue plan. He had already announced his opposition to the sales tax as oppressive to the "forgotten man," but he wanted to inherit a balanced budget. Writing to

Harrison, he said, "I have not bothered you in any way about the appropriation bills because I have the utmost confidence that you will do the right thing."[1]

Budget-balancing admonition came to Harrison from another source, his close friend Bernard M. Baruch, the Democratic party patriarch whose economic advice was gospel to many of the senators who still served in the shadow of Woodrow Wilson. In January, Baruch wrote Harrison a long letter which called for "a complete and honest balance of the budget." He knocked Hoover's budget as "too thin to fool anybody and it is we who must answer for its errors." He closed by suggesting to Harrison that very soon some senator "of about your size and contour should rise in his seat and deliver one of those speeches that continue to live in Senate annals," a speech that would leave a clean slate for the New Deal. By the middle of January, however, the congressional Democrats had abandoned hope for the enactment of budget-balancing legislation by the Seventy-second Congress. They preferred drift and discord to the acceptance of any of the tax and economy measures offered by Hoover. As a perennial recorder of successive Congresses wrote, the congressional players were "holding poor hands and [were] distracted by thoughts of the new deal that was to come."[2]

In that bleak winter Franklin Roosevelt was drawing upon an intellectual bank whose board of directors came to be known as the "Brain Trust." Senator Harrison proposed to draw upon the wisdom of another set of men, those who worked not in the classrooms of prestigious universities but in the practical everyday business world. These were the sort of men whose views he had always respected. In December he announced that after the holidays he would introduce a resolution authorizing the Finance Committee to undertake a broad investigation into the causes of the depression. "We have now groped in economic despair for more than three years. . . . The methods which have been adopted are merely palliative," he complained. His own remedies were suggested in a press release in late December: a radical curtailment in government activities, economy in government, a balanced budget, increased commodity prices, and tariff reductions. An essentially conservative program, it drew favorable comments from a number of journals, including the Chicago *Tribune*, whose editors seemed pleased that a senator of such convictions would direct

a clinic to diagnose the nation's economic ills. "Just how you have
won the Tribune no one knows, but you certainly have that terrible
'Republican sheet' endorsing every d—n thing you do or propose,"
wrote an Illinois friend of the senator. William Hard of Hoover's
"medicine-ball cabinet" went so far as to call Harrison "capitalism's
savior." The press generally agreed that the purpose of the investigation was to stave off the inflationary schemes threatening in Congress
from the supporters of Senator Elmer Thomas of Oklahoma, although
there was an undercurrent of fear that the inquiry would open the
floodgates to every radical idea that had gained any currency whatsoever. When Harrison offered his resolution during the first week in
January, he admitted that the currency question would be among the
subjects to be examined. It gained approval on January 26. [3]

Meanwhile, the senators who were expected to become the floor
leaders in the new administration were in close communion with the
president-elect. Harrison, along with Robinson, Pittman, Hull, and
Byrnes, met with Governor Roosevelt in New York on January 5 to
unify a party program that would touch on farm relief, prohibition
repeal, and fiscal legislation. From the meeting came the gloomy
news that an increase in normal taxes would be required to balance
the budget since Hoover had estimated a deficit of $492 million. Har-
rison told reporters, "An extra session will come along pretty soon, I
imagine." He already had plans to call the Democratic members of the
Finance Committee together to work jointly with the Ways and
Means Democrats in framing a new tax law. To an automobile show
group in New York City a few days later, Harrison revealed much of
the program—repeal of prohibition (not merely a modification of the
Volstead Act), lowered income tax exemptions, and a 25 percent cut
in federal expenditures. In addition Congress would clothe the president with broad powers. Of Roosevelt, he confided, "The more I have
come into contact with [him], the more I am impressed with his
ability, his vision, his courage, his heart, and his grasp of these great
questions."[4]

Harrison's Finance Committee forum ran for two weeks in February. He was not oblivious to what was likely to come from the fund
of over 250 "best minds" that had been invited to appear or send
statements. "We expect to give every school of thought its day in
court," he said, and he anticipated soundings from gold standardists,

bimetallists, free silverites, deflationists, inflationists, drys, wets, technocrats, wealth distributors, high protectionists, and free traders. The first witness to appear before the committee was Baruch, fresh from a visit with Roosevelt at Warm Springs that coincided with Senator Wheeler's fight in the Senate for free coinage of silver at 16 to 1. Among all Democrats, Baruch was the most aggressively insistent upon a sound currency, and he "held school" for the committee, lecturing it upon the necessity of maintaining a sound money system, a balanced budget, and an intensified fight for reciprocal trade agreements. Warning against certain popularly advanced inflationary and spending remedies, he declared, "The most dangerous are the projects to inflate the currency." He added that "delay in balancing the Budget is trifling with disaster." *Business Week* aptly described the effect of Baruch's testimony. He had "kicked the whole currency inflation plan . . . right out of Senator Harrison's committee room at the first meeting."[5]

From those who actually appeared before the committee or who sent briefs came a variety of schemes. Some were impertinent and facetious, some contained "sure-fire remedies," and some were unorthodox to say the least. Other than putting down the threat of inflation and a currently popular but costly soldier bonus plan, the hearings did little else than support the international economic conference that the Democrats already had on the planning board. Harrison thought that his committee had fulfilled the mandate of the Senate and deemed the hearings a "success in every way" in offering to Roosevelt "material assistance." By the time the hearings officially ended in late March, the New Deal was well under way.[6]

On the misty and windy March 4 of Roosevelt's inauguration, a three-day "Carnival of Confidence" ended in sunny Jackson, Mississippi. On the grounds of the Old Capitol stood a specially built scaffold awaiting the first public execution in Jackson in more than fifty years. The despised victim? "Old Man Old Deal." After the hanging and burning, "The New Deal" was crowned before thousands. Acting Governor Dennis Murphree intoned that "the darkest hour is just before the dawn" and hosannaed: "Thank God today for Franklin D. Roosevelt." In Washington, Senator Harrison had nothing but praise for the inaugural address. Vague as it was concerning details for a recovery program, the senator was certain that the new president

Washington *Evening Star,* February 15, 1933
Courtesy: Archives and Special Collections, Univeruity of Mississippi

would "particularize" when Congress met in the special session
called for March 9. [7]

Particularize Roosevelt did in one message after another until fifteen major measures had been enacted by the time of the congressional adjournment on June 15. Senator Harrison's committee was a
busy group, implementing many of the presidential mandates, and
the senator was seldom on the floor during those first hundred days.
Tied up as he was in committee sessions, his "gadfly days" were over.
Now he had become the chairman of one of the most powerful committees in Congress. He necessarily became something of a legislative
drudge; as a *Time* pundit put it, it was "as if W. C. Fields were to
begin playing Othello." [8]

On his second day in office Roosevelt, in a swift move to stymie the deepening banking morass, proclaimed a national bank holiday. Harrison was not directly involved in the banking crisis, but he had discussed the matter with Roosevelt in late 1932 at the behest of Francis Gloyd Aswalt, the acting comptroller of the currency. Harrison knew how the depression had affected Mississippi, where 59 banks had failed in 1930, 56 in 1931, and 12 in 1932. On March 1, 1933, the state superintendent of banking, J. S. Love, had ordered restricted bank withdrawals. Harrison had no more reason to oppose the emergency banking bill, which zipped through to enactment from its introduction in the House to presidential signature in eight hours on March 9, than did any of the other fifty-six Senate Democrats who voted for its passage. After the holiday the majority of Mississippi's banks were never in serious difficulty, and eventually only six national banks in the state failed to be licensed for reopening. On the first anniversary of the banking holiday, Mississippi banks were described as being in the best condition in their history. [9]

Only an hour after signing the banking act, Roosevelt awed congressional leaders by his plans to fulfill his campaign pledge to reduce federal expenditures by 25 percent, particularly slashing veterans' compensations and federal salaries. Harrison thought that the president's message was "one of the finest in [his] long experience in Congress." Immediately following the message majority leader Joseph T. Robinson introduced the economy measure and Harrison called his committee into session to expedite a bill carrying out the president's wishes. The chairman insisted that he would stand for no delay; he intended to hear "only briefly" on the following day from groups representing veterans and federal employees and to report out the bill on the same day. [10]

Within minutes of House passage of the bill, "to maintain the credit of the United States" Harrison reported out of committee a bill exactly as it had come from Roosevelt's draftsmen via the House. The expected Senate testing of the bill came early on March 13 when Harrison moved for its consideration. His plea that "we handle this matter with chins up and chests thrown out [to] take the consequences" was not convincing to some senators who were ready to do battle against delegating authority to the executive department to handle budget cutting. Nor did the objectors like the idea of saving

$500 million at the expense of disabled servicemen and federal employees whose purchasing power would be decreased. [11]

Inundated by amendments, the bill did not pass the Senate on the first day as Harrison had predicted. The Senate fell into such a snarl over the extension of the cuts to Spanish-American War veterans that Harrison sought and got a limitation of debate. His acceptance of amendments protecting those veterans and leaving undisturbed the pensions of service-connected disabled veterans smoothed the way for passage. On March 15 the Senate passed the bill by a vote of 62 to 13 (with only four Democrats voting "nay"), thus imposing a 15 percent cut on all federal employees and reducing veterans' benefits virtually all along the line. The House willingly went along with the Senate's forty amendments by an amazing vote of 374 to 19. The president signed the legislation on March 20. [12] Speaking on the Washington *Evening Star* forum over the National Broadcasting Company network that night, Senator Harrison proclaimed that the economy program had eliminated the feared billion-dollar deficit and the threat of a general tax increase. The $500 million savings in veterans' compensations and general expenditures together with the anticipated $150 million from a beer tax and $137 million from a continued levy on gasoline would keep the budget in balance. Taking his cue from a Roosevelt axiom, Harrison compared federal budget balancing with family budget strictures. "We balance our domestic budget. It is no less important that governments balance their budgets," he insisted. [13]

Harrison's support of prohibition repeal and the beer bill was something of an anomaly for a Mississippi politician of his astuteness. The Mississippi legislature had passed a statewide prohibition law in 1908 and had been the first to ratify the Eighteenth Amendment; the state was said to have the most rigid "bone-dry" laws in the nation. In earlier days Harrison had seen the wisdom of skirting the prohibition issue. When he had spoken in Tampa in 1931, he had faced an awkward moment when the local chairman of the occasion had asked him how he stood on prohibition. The smiling senator turned to the audience and remarked, "I'm just wondering if your distinguished officer is making an inquiry or extending an invitation." While the crowd roared, Harrison left the stage. [14] He had been equally equivocal shortly after Roosevelt's nomination in defending his hurried shift from his support of the convention minority plank to submit repeal to the states to his acceptance of the majority plank of outright repeal. By the fall of 1932 he had moved further toward an unqualified stand for repeal both by Congress and the states, his own included. The anticipation of added revenue from beer and wine sales was stronger than the home state resistance to legalized alcohol. His public speeches now gloried in the great heady hope for new taxes.[15]

The initial test of repeal as a recovery palliative came early in 1933. Ironically it was left to two Mississippians to promote repeal—James Collier, chairman of the House Committee on Ways and Means, and Harrison, who threatened to wrench the bill from the hands of the Finance chairman, Reed Smoot, the Utah Mormon who was anything but happy about quenching the great American thirst. Harrison voted for repeal, but his Mississippi Senate colleague Hubert Stephens did not. After Senate passage on February 16 of the proposal to submit the Twenty-first Amendment to the states for ratification, the House fell in line four days later. Of the nine Mississippians in Congress, only three voted for repeal—Harrison, Collier, and William Whittington, a former chairman of the Mississippi Baptist Convention! Collier then introduced the House bill to legalize beer, but the drys killed it and its passage had to await the new Congress and a new president.[16]

Two days after the economy measure passed its first Senate test, President Roosevelt sent a surprise message of only seventy-two words to Congress requesting the amendment of the Volstead Act and the legalization of beer with a presumably non-intoxicating alcoholic content of 3.2 percent. The House burst into applause upon hearing the message and voted the next day (March 14) for beer by a vote of 316 to 97. The Finance Committee received the bill on the same day, and the chairman promised the quick action that was now his habit with all administration measures.[17]

The Senate Finance Committee reported out the beer proposal, now called the Cullen-Harrison bill, on March 15 without a record vote after only one hour of discussion. The committee added a provision for 3.2 percent wine, which it recognized as neither very palatable or salable. The chairman was correct in his prediction that the beer and wine bill would pass the Senate at its next sitting. The six hours of debate were consumed mainly by discussion on the sale of beer to minors and a ban on radio advertising of beer as well as Harrison's surprising amendment to reduce the alcoholic content to 3.05 percent, the British beer standard. The Harrison amendment passed. Harrison and Stephens cast opposite votes on the final bill; the somewhat drier senator from north Mississippi was dead set against repeal. In passing the bill (43 to 30), the Senate went for beer in one day just as Harrison had predicted and fulfilled the House slogan of "Light Beer Before Dark."[18]

The House conference members did not find Harrison's 3.05 percent "near beer" to be inspiring at all; in fact, they questioned whether enough of such blandness could be sold to produce any appreciable revenue. So anxious was the Senate to act upon a conference report that it stood by in temporary recess while the conference was going on. When Harrison brought the report in, it revealed that the Senate had quaffed the House's 3.2 percent beer and the House had downed the Senate's wine. The Mississippi senator's move for adoption shortly carried by a vote of 53 to 36. The House approved the report on the same day (March 21), and Roosevelt signed the bill within five minutes of its arrival at the White House a day later, presenting one of the four signature pens to Harrison. On April 17, 1933, when twenty-one states plus the District of Columbia rolled out the barrels, an estimated $7.5 million fell into the treasury till from the one day's take. The beer bill efforts of the tax-minded Finance Committee had paid off.[19]

Roosevelt originally had called Congress into session only for the enactment of emergency banking legislation. After he had kept it in session for the deliverance of an economy program and a beer bill, some congressmen thought that the special session would adjourn. Senator Harrison on March 15 had said that the beer bill would be the last measure of the emergency session.[20] He was wrong. The next day FDR sent to Congress his message for an agricultural relief program to deal with the major economic problem of depressed prices and the still-declining farm income. No measure of the new session had done anything but tighten and deflate the economy.

Perhaps because he had grown up as a "town boy" (albeit a small town), Pat Harrison had never become an authority on agriculture or farm relief nor had he developed a reputation as a cotton senator as had his ebullient colleagues, J. Thomas Heflin of Alabama and E. D.

Smith of South Carolina ("His name is Ellison Durant, and he sure do."). Harrison's involvements with agriculture during his Senate career were always episodic. His remedies for the agricultural difficulties of the 1920s had been limited to appropriations for such programs as experimentation and reforestation coupled with farm credit extension; he assuredly had not looked upon the higher tariffs as an effective approach to the seemingly insurmountable problem of increasing surpluses. His initial opposition to the McNary-Haugen bills suggested that he basically opposed any programs to relieve agricultural distress that called for federal activism. But, lacking any real understanding of the remedies advanced by farm experts, Harrison tended to rely upon the judgments of his friends, which accounts for his eventual vote for a McNary-Haugen bill. He was a close friend of George N. Peek, who had been one of the proponents of the measure.[21]

Riding on the "Capitol Limited" to the Chicago convention with Milburn L. Wilson, an agricultural economist from Montana who had done more than anyone else to advance the idea of a "domestic allotment" for production control, Harrison had confessed to the professor that he knew little about the control program, but it surely had a "sixty-four dollar name." Senator Peter Norbeck, an agrarian Republican from South Dakota, had told him the plan "was just the thing for cotton."[22]

Thus, in nine years Harrison had evolved from his 1924 opposition to any governmental control of agricultural production to a position in 1933 of qualified acceptance of federal intervention. When the agricultural adjustment bill reached the Senate in late March and bogged down before a conservative onslaught, Harrison held his fire. His trust in Peek was so implicit that he had told Secretary of Agriculture Henry A. Wallace that he would support anything acceptable to Peek. He assumed that Peek, as head of the production control program, would have the "sensible" advice of men such as Baruch, Frank O. Lowden of Illinois, and Alfred H. Stone, a Mississippi tax expert. Harrison particularly singled out Rexford G. Tugwell and Mordecai Ezekiel as professorial types that "people were scared to death over." Hubert Stephens had been especially alarmed over the rumored excesses in acreage curtailment, but, when he learned that his own views coincided with those of Peek, he too withdrew his opposition to the farm bill and joined Harrison in its support.[23] Harrison never spoke in the Senate on the farm relief provisions of the bill and voted with the administration senators to defeat those amendments which were anathema to the president—a veterans' bonus scheme, an embargo on imported goods to be sold below the United States cost of production, and the coinage of silver.

Senate discussion of declining farm prices opened a wide avenue for a growing number of inflationists who attempted by one means or another to commit the Congress, if not the chief executive, to drastic measures to hike commodity prices. On April 17 Senator Wheeler fell short by only ten votes in getting his amendment to coin silver at the ratio of 16 to 1 appended to the farm bill. Harrison was far from being radical enough to take his cue from Wheeler; instead, he adhered to the soft-spoken word from the White House, translated not so softly by Joe Robinson, against the inflation amendment. Two days later, President Roosevelt, thoroughly frightened by violence in the corn belt and the congressional rebellion against deflation, took the country off the gold standard. If a stand for maintenance of the gold standard was a litmus test of conservatism, then Pat Harrison appeared to be no conservative. A year earlier, he had confessed his admiration of the British statesmen who had had "the courage and forethought to do something," including going off the gold standard. "I think we have deflated too greatly, too precipitously, and now we have to inflate back a little bit," he had told the Senate in defending both the lending propensities of the Reconstruction Finance Corporation and the Glass-Steagell Act of 1932, which had liberalized federal reserve rediscounting. He said that "the proof of the pudding is in the eating thereof." And so it seemed to be when on the day following Roosevelt's gold move the price of cotton moved upward on the commodity exchanges.[24]

During the week following the defeat of Wheeler's silver amendment, congressional Democrats coalesced behind an amendment offered to the farm bill by senator Elmer Thomas of Oklahoma whose greatest passion was currency inflation. Thomas proposed that FDR be given power to inflate the dollar through alteration of its gold content. Harrison defended the amendment in a Falstaffian thrust at Republican opposition reminiscent of his gadfly days. Inspired by the retorts of an old adversary, Pennsylvania's Old Guard Republican

David A. Reed, Harrison made one of his few speeches of the
Hundred Days. Convinced that the RFC and the Glass-Steagall Act
had been "little sugar-coated" failures, he was now ready for "controlled inflation." By that he meant the presidential discretion to devalue the dollar that the administration Democrats succeeded in writing into the Thomas amendment over the protests of those who preferred a mandatory provision that would have forced the president's
hand in the devaluation of gold or in issuing greenbacks. Roosevelt's
fear of an uncontrollable Congress was justified after the three days
of running debate that began on April 25, described by one reporter as
a "jolly day which had called up every inflationary experiment since
the fat and indolent times of Greece and Rome." The end product of
the running fray of roll calls was the passage of the Thomas amendment by a vote of 64 to 20, with the southern opposition coming from
only Bailey of North Carolina and Glass of Virginia. On the same day,
April 28, the completed agricultural adjustment bill passed the Senate. [25]

In late March, Roosevelt sent a message to Congress calling for the
relief of the nearly fifteen million unemployed. The first of his proposals, that of a civilian army to work in reforestation, passed both
houses of Congress without a roll call vote. The Civilian Conservation Corps, which enjoyed immense popularity throughout the country, was particularly helpful to Mississippi where forests had been de-
nuded and water erosion was a continuing crime of nature. On the
day that Roosevelt signed the conservation bill, Senator Harrison held
conferences with several Mississippi officials, among them state
forester Fred Merrill, to review the results of a land use survey for
reforestation of the Tennessee River watershed. That northeastern
section of the state was one of the earliest selected for camp locations
and Harrison dogged the president during the early summer of 1933
to designate a larger number of southern sites for a winter relocation
of CCC camps. In mid-July FDR, concurring with his secretary of
agriculture, who had also heard from Harrison, set aside $20 million
to purchase land in more than twenty states across the southern section of the nation. [26]

Only two Democrats—Bailey and Thomas P. Gore of
Oklahoma—voted against Roosevelt's request for unemployment re-

lief via the creation of a federal relief administration and an allocation of $500 million to states whose own funds to handle the unemployed were near depletion. Although Harrison had given only halfhearted support to the relief measures of 1932, he had come to see what federal money could mean to Mississippi. His home state had been highly dependent upon the funds disbursed under the Emergency Relief and Construction Act of 1932 which had allotted $300 million for low-interest RFC loans to states for relief and public works projects. The largest bid-letting in the history of the Mississippi Highway Department came in early 1933, and by June the state's welfare board had distributed nearly $4 million for work relief and direct relief. Thus Harrison had no reservations in supporting the new FERA program with its horn of plenty. When Harry Hopkins, the new relief czar, set about spending $5 million during his first two hours in office, Mississippi came in fifth from the top of his list of state grants.[27]

To numerous owners of Mississippi homes and farms burdened by high taxes and five-cent cotton, the depression had brought the heartbreak of property loss. On a single day in April, 1932, more than one-fourth of the property of the state had gone under the auctioneer's hammer and had been sold for taxes from the courthouse steps. It was estimated that in another eighteen months the state would acquire through tax forfeits more than three million acres of farm land. In the face of such tremendous property losses, Senator Harrison had introduced a measure in December, 1932, authorizing the RFC to lend owners of mortgaged property sufficient money to pay their taxes for two years, but the proposal was never reported out of the Banking and Currency Committee. In the face of this rebuff the Mississippi solon was as amenable to the Home Owners' Loan Act and the Farm Credit Act, both passed in June of 1933, as was the overwhelming majority of Congress. Two months before the passage of the former act, Harrison had made an open appeal to all lending agencies in Mississippi to defer foreclosures pending the assured passage of a home owners' relief measure. The response of Mississippians to the new opportunity to refinance mortgages was immediate; within eighteen months the Home Owners' Loan Corporation had received over 18,000 applications in Mississippi covering

$30,209,805 in property; also one-third of the loans made had been closed out at a saving to the owners of over $12,000,000 in property values.[28]

As chairman of the Finance Committee, Pat Harrison's most important duties during the New Deal would be those of a taxmaster. During the Hundred Days the administration, because of the pressures to pass emergency measures and the president's campaign pledge to reduce taxes, deferred the heavy taxation which vast public expenditures obviously would eventually necessitate. There was, however, the need to continue certain excises which the congressional finance committees routinely extended through a measure that was never seriously threatened. As the new administration's first tax bill, it did provide an opportunity for Huey Long to proffer his notion of confiscating incomes over $1 million through taxation. His amendment was decisively defeated.[29]

One of the final measures of the Hundred Days was the National Industrial Recovery Act, which was designed to meet Roosevelt's double request for unemployment relief and a system of industrial self-regulation of wages, hours, and employer practices. The multipurpose bill contained tax provisions worked out primarily by Lewis Douglas which, in addition to increases in normal income and corporation dividend levies, included a small manufacturer's sales tax and a "breakfast table" tax on certain foodstuffs.[30] Because of its tax features the NIRA bill was to be coursed through the finance committees of Congress. Robert L. Doughton, chairman of the House Ways and Means Committee, whose own state of North Carolina had recently rejected a sales tax, dourly remarked at the end of a long White House parley held on May 15, "I didn't know they [the executive draftsmen] had been called upon to write the financial end of the bill." His remark revealed the resentment that Congress increasingly would harbor over White House deference to its own inner circles rather than to congressional leadership. Harrison, who also had attended the conference, came away doubting that the sales tax would ever get past Congress. The next day he began informal discussions with his revenue-makers to determine what levies the Senate would accept. Using a procedure he would often turn to throughout his tenure as chairman, he began hearings concurrent with House debate of the measure so that he could take the bill to the floor immediately after House passage.[31]

As predicted, the Ways and Means Committee rejected even a modified sales tax. Rather than taxing the "little man" and his breakfast table, the House was tempted (as was the Senate a week later) to turn to a general revision of the revenue laws. Only the necessity of getting out the recovery bill restrained the House. It passed the bill on May 26 by a vote of 323 to 76 essentially as it came from the committee, carrying an increase in normal income tax rates and corporate dividends.

Caustic remarks directed during public hearings to Senator Robert Wagner of New York by conservatives on the Finance Committee, William King of Utah and Bennett Clark of Missouri in particular, were mere warm-ups to the heated proceedings that followed in the committee's executive sessions and on the Senate floor. Disclosures of financier J. P. Morgan's tax lapses in 1932 led chairman Harrison to lay before his committee a plan to increase the NIRA taxes upon private bankers and partnerships through a tax on corporate dividends collected at the source, the reenactment of a tax on declared capital stock values (it had been repealed in 1924), and the removal of certain exemptions private bankers had enjoyed under the 1932 Revenue Act. Held to be a shrewd proposal, Harrison's tax schedules eliminated the unpopular House increases in normal income tax rates. Estimated to raise considerably more revenue than the House plan would, Harrison's scheme, which he insisted was his own and not of the White House, won the approval of most of his committee.[32]

When, with the tax provisions out of the way, the committee turned to the industrial control segment of the bill, an open revolt broke out against the extension of executive power. The committee insurgents—Democrats Bailey, Byrd, Clark, Connally, Gore, King, and McAdoo and Republicans Henry W. Keyes and Jesse H. Metcalf—mustered enough support to eliminate the licensing provision and to reject the administration plan to control the oil industry. Harrison, who termed the licensing provision a "birchrod in the cupboard" against cut-throat competition, was appalled at his committee's action and announced his intention to save the administration features when the measure reached the floor. Clark, the principal

Washington *Evening Star,* June 9, 1933
Courtesy: Archives and Special Collections, University of Mississippi

opponent of the whole bill, almost won a vote to strike out all but the
public works title (the vote was 10 to 8).[33] The revolt subsided when
five of the prodigal Democrats returned home politically and voted in
a second test on the licensing provision to restore it to the bill. Only
Harry Flood Byrd still held out. Thomas Connally's "hot oil" amendment, granting the president authority to ban interstate shipments of
illegally produced oil, also went back into the bill. Only minutes after
committee approval of the final form of the bill, Harrison carried it to
the Senate floor and asked for an early consideration.[34]

When debate began on June 7, Harrison, in deference to Robert
Wagner's deep commitment to the bill, yielded to the New Yorker to
open the floor discussion. The latter provoked cogent arguments from
Idaho's William E. Borah, who protested the recovery bill's "ultra

concentration of wealth," and a scornful attack from Huey Long who thought it to be the "most tyrannical law" he had ever seen. Senate votes scuttled the amendments offered by Finance Committee conservatives to eliminate the enforcement provisions of the industrial recovery title. As floor manager of the bill, Harrison accepted Borah's amendment to prohibit code authorities from engaging in price-fixing or other "monopolistic practices," but he was reluctant to accept other revisions that he feared would obstruct passage of the measure. By the end of the two long bristling sessions of June 8 and 9, the president's lieutenants were in control of the NRA bill and had kept it virtually clear of all amendments certain to rankle Roosevelt.[35]

Senate revisions left the industrial recovery title essentially as it came from the House. The principal differences in the bill, as passed by the Senate on June 9 by a 58 to 24 vote, were the Harrison tax features. With a show of speed unusual for a conference committee, the House and Senate managers brought out a report at the end of a nine-hour, shirt-sleeve Saturday session. The House accepted the report that same evening, but Harrison's plan to obtain an immediate adoption was abandoned when the Senate became jammed with unfinished business.[36] A unanimous consent agreement maneuvered by Harrison and Robinson set the vote for June 13, when the report won Senate approval by a close 46 to 39 vote (fifteen Democrats rejected the report, including Finance committeemen Clark, Connally, Costigan, and Gore). Only the "yea" votes of five Republicans released the bill from Senate clutches to send it on its way for a presidential signature on June 16. Senator Harrison made one parting statement: "This is a great piece of legislation." He predicted that the NRA would be a "noble experiment."[37]

The passage of the omnibus recovery bill marked the end of the first session of the New Deal Congress, a session that had overturned the long established personal and political postures of many an administration leader. Early in the session, veteran newsman William Hard had predicted that the New Deal would throw to the winds the time-honored terms "conservative" and "progressive" and he had pointed out the essential conservatism of the budget-balancing economy bill and the irony of the so-called "progressive" support it had enjoyed. For the two finance committee chairmen the session had launched a new era in governmental activity, the end of which they had no way of knowing just then. Doughton confessed to a constituent, "I'm going along with the Administration in its program, and while there is some of it I do not fully understand and think it may be of doubtful merit, if anything is tried and does not work, it can very readily be repealed or amended." Senator Harrison had spoken rather cryptically at one point during the debate on the Thomas amendment to the AAA. "I am naturally a conservative," he said. "I prefer to follow precedents, and in this country no one suspects me of being a radical."[38] That the Mississippian could champion and pilot to passage the economic program of his president was a testament to one of two things. Either Pat Harrison was more progressive than he thought he was, or Franklin D. Roosevelt had ushered in an essentially conservative program. Whatever the case, the senator had nothing but praise for the historic spring session of 1933. "I haven't the slightest doubt that we are now out of the throes of despair," he told his fellow Mississippians in the summer of 1933.[39]

During the hectic days of the congressional session, FDR had given little attention to appointments, postponing all that were not necessary until a later date. As one observer said regarding the patronage "carrot" that the president held before Congress, "his relations with Congress were to the very end of the session tinged with a shade of expectancy which is the best part of young love." If hewing the line to administration goals was the supreme criterion for patronage handouts, as indeed it was, then Senator Harrison was due his share. He had anticipated such, for he had written Thomas E. Campbell, the civil service commission head, in early January, 1933, to find out how many openings would be available for Democrats. A multitude of job-seekers thought that Harrison was the man to see. His office was flooded by job requests, but it was not until the end of the session that he was able to draw upon his account with the president. "Right now I am trying my best," he wrote to a Mississippi supporter, "to find out what it is all about with reference to opportunities for some of our friends down in the State."[40]

During most of the latter months of the session an average of five hundred letters a day arrived at the Senate office building requesting the intercession of Mississippi's newly heralded "administration leader." The letters came not only from Mississippians but also from

neighboring states, particularly Louisiana, where Senator Long had
been stripped of his patronage by Postmaster General Farley and
President Roosevelt, both of whom were furious over attacks from
"the Kingfish." When Mayor John J. Kennedy, a Biloxi friend of
Harrison, was appointed customs collector for the port of New Orleans, the Mississippi senator's stock went up as much with
Louisianans as it went down with Long. The Mississippi press reported that the Kennedy appointment was a reward to Harrison for
his work on the economy and industrial recovery bills.[41]

When Harrison told his colleagues at the next session of Congress,
"I have gone around with my basket for a long time, and nothing has
yet fallen in," his smiling colleagues knew better. He and Stephens
were instrumental in the March, 1933, appointment to the Tariff
Commission of James W. Collier who had lost his congressional post
in a politically inspired reapportionment move in the Mississippi
legislature.[42] For two of his closest personal friends Harrison secured
highly coveted positions when Roosevelt named Eugene Fly as internal revenue collector in Mississippi and George E. Allen as one of the
three commissioners of the District of Columbia. Fly had served as
Harrison's personal secretary for seventeen years and more recently
had been Collier's clerk for the Ways and Means Committee. Allen, a
lawyer and a nephew of the popular turn-of-the-century representative "Private John" Allen, had made a host of friends in Washington
when he had managed the Wardman Hotel properties. His appointment in November, 1933, came as a surprise and was attributed more
to his friendship with Harrison than to his widely recognized administrative abilities and broad knowledge of business affairs.[43]

With the launching of the New Deal in Mississippi, Harrison and
Stephens obtained the appointment of home-state supporter Hugh L.
White, who had been defeated by Mike Conner in the 1931 gubernatorial race, as state administrator of the public works program. It
was an appointment particularly lauded by those Mississippians who
looked upon the industrial development of the town of Columbia as a
testament to the former mayor's executive talents.[44] The appointment of Wiley Blair, a Tupelo lawyer and state senator who had been
a coauthor of the redistricting bill that had cost Collier his congressional seat, to be manager of the state home loan organization was not

as highly regarded within some political circles. "Pat and Hubert have torn a big hole in their political pants," surmised Harrison's editor friend Fred Sullens.[45]

The adjournment of Congress did not mean the adjournment of politics. Senator Harrison remained in Washington for several weeks hoping to gain some rest, but he found that "the task has been more strenuous than when Congress was in session." In order to "run away from some of these job hunters" and rest in preparation for what lay ahead in a Mississippi summer of mending his own political fences and shoring up the New Deal, he took a golf and fishing vacation at White Sulphur Springs, West Virginia, and Eagle River, Wisconsin. In late July he returned to Mississippi after an absence of nearly six months and spent the balance of the summer in Gulfport and Jackson. During those days when he was not speaking on a "cold tongue and potato salad" circuit, he made three return trips to Washington for White House conferences and greeted New Deal officials who came to Mississippi on goodwill missions.[46]

When Harrison arrived in Jackson in July, 1933, he fired the first shot in a campaign to spur Governor Conner into calling a special session of the legislature to repeal prohibition. On the day that the president signed the beer bill, Conner, bone dry in conviction and practice, had predicted that Mississippi would reject the Twenty-first Amendment, and he did not intend to call a special session. There were already rumors that he intended to measure lances with Harrison in the Senate race in 1936, making prohibition one of the key issues. Basing his stand upon a belief that liquor revenues were needed to reduce other taxes, that beer was being sold openly in Mississippi anyway, and that 3.2 beer was not intoxicating, Harrison argued for a popular referendum. He had voted for repeal because the Chicago platform had called for repeal. "I am a good Democrat and I go through," he reaffirmed. Once known as one of the pillars of the dry cause in the Senate, Harrison had "gone over lock, stock, and barrel to the wet side," the Washington *Post* noted, adding that "no one . . . has his ear closer to the ground than Pat." Already moist on the Alabama, Tennessee, and Arkansas edges, Mississippi was about to be drowned by repeal in Louisiana; and it is possible that nothing could have irritated Harrison more than knowing that Senator Long stood to swell the Louisiana state coffers at the expense of thirsty Mississippians. [47]

While Conner toyed with the idea of a "mail order" poll of the legislature on a special session, Harrison modified his forthright stand for repeal by making statements that the Democratic party would have to find a way to prevent the return of the open saloon. He naïvely suggested that each federal revenue stamp bear the imprint "This liquor shall not be sold in an open saloon," without attempting to define an "open saloon." By the fall of 1933 Conner's poll had revealed that the Mississippi lawmakers were not anxious to convene for beer, wine, or any other spirits, and the issue was deferred to the regular session of 1934. Harrison was not free to drop the issue, for he would face the liquor tax measure of 1934 that would come on the heels of national repeal, not to mention a drubbing from Mississippi drys for his role in the whole matter of beer, repeal, and liquor taxation. [48]

Anxious that the National Recovery Administration be endorsed by Mississippi businessmen, Harrison was amenable to the requests of NRA administrators that he "make a few speeches before important groups." In an opening volley against "industrial bootleggers" who chiseled against the newly drawn codes, Harrison pled for cooperation with the recovery program. On August 11 he keynoted a giant NRA rally in Jackson attended by two thousand citizens from all sections of the state. Emphasizing the NRA public works features that affected Mississippi, he extended his remarks to other New Deal measures. "The New Deal does not seek to promote the interests of any one class of people to the detriment of any other class," he proclaimed. In a later speech to the Mississippi Bar Association meeting in Vicksburg, he lashed out at the "selfishness, subterfuge, and cowardice" of slackers. [49]

Before a crowd of fifteen hundred attending a rally at McComb, Harrison named as a New Deal malcontent Huey Long, who had attacked FDR in a Louisiana state fair speech, and labor "agitators" who were blocking the recovery program. "As one who helped write the National Recovery Act," Harrison boasted, "I subscribe to the labor provisions." Labor's counsel must be considered in the drafting and administration of the codes, he continued. Invited by a Hatties-

burg civic leader to inspire the masses "to dedicate their lives to a
New Deal," Harrison responded with still another lesson on New
Deal magic for a record-breaking crowd that had come into the city by
train, automobile, truck, wagon, and on horseback.[50] The senator's
speeches may have helped inspire home state acceptance of the NRA
program, but the retailers and manufacturers of the state were more
noticeably impressed by cash register performances that picked up by
the end of October. In that month the collection of the state sales tax
broke all records for the eighteen months of its existence and business
activity increased by some $10 million during the month. Mississippi
editors credited the NRA with a major share of the increase, and one
renamed the Blue Eagle program "Noticeable Relief Accom-
plished."[51]

Likewise Harrison's praise of the Triple-A cotton acreage reduction program fell upon already receptive ears. By June 20, 1933, all of
the state's counties were organized for a Cotton Contract Week drive
expected to bring from $10 million to $12 million in benefit payments
to the more than 300,000 cooperating farmers. When Secretary Wallace paid a two-day visit in August to confer with Farm Bureau and
extension leaders, Harrison accompanied him on an inspection tour
of the Delta cotton plow-up program. Because Oscar Johnston, a
prominent Delta planter and a close friend of Harrison, had been
named administrator of the Agricultural Adjustment Corporation,
the financial arm of the cotton program, Harrison retained a close tie
with Wallace's department. By October, 1933, when cotton had
reached 9 1/2 cents per pound from its low of 5 cents in 1932, Harrison defended the Roosevelt agricultural program before an audience
in the north Mississippi hill town of Fulton and called for further
reduction in 1934.[52]

Advocacy of cotton production control did not mean that Senator
Harrison had abandoned the extension of farm credits as a panacea
for southern farmers. In his Vicksburg speech to the Mississippi bar
he openly criticized Robert B. Clark for administering the farm loan
law too restrictively. Clark, a Tupelo banker who had become manager of the federal land bank at New Orleans, was reputed to be out
of harmony with the Farm Credit Administration, for he had consistently turned down loans approved by the FCA. "I will have him
beheaded by [the] Democratic Administration," Harrison declared,

because the "loan laws must be administered sympathetically." Paul
Mallon, a Washington columnist, reported that Harrison was "the
man leading the inner uproar" on behalf of Henry Morgenthau, Jr.,
the head of the FCA. Clark, whose resignation was in the hands of
the directors by mid-October, defended his record of releasing fewer
loans than any of the other eleven federal land banks by pointing out
that farmers had consistently forfeited their loans, thereby placing
ownership of land in the hands of the federal government. Harrison's
open war against Clark, a Conner supporter, was said to be politically
inspired and was another of the 1933 stands taken by the senator that
would reappear in the heated battles of another day. [53]

Harrison was in Washington the last week in August and missed
the visit to Jackson of Harry Hopkins and his assistant Aubrey
Williams. In town primarily to confer with George B. Power, director
of the State Board of Public Welfare, Hopkins's brief mission became
a notable success when he stated that Mississippi would not be asked
to match federal funds dollar for dollar during the coming winter.
Except for disapproval of Harry Hopkins's expletives, Mississippi relief officials would find little else to criticize in the man for the entire
period of his tenure as director of the FERA and its successor agencies. When Hopkins announced the appointment of Ellen Woodward
as his assistant administrator of federal relief, he endeared himself to
Senator Harrison and the Mississippi officialdom, which had been
associated with her in her earlier work as a state legislator, a member
of the executive committee of the state welfare board, and as executive secretary of the state development board. [54]

The great affinity of politics and relief in Mississippi would give
Hopkins plenty of headaches later on, but more immediately problems
issued from Interior Secretary Harold L. Ickes's stewardship of the
industrial recovery program's public works funds. The $60 million
allotted to Mississippi included $10 million for highway construction
to be allocated by a state commissioner who was a political opponent
of Governor Conner. The governor's refusal to call the legislature
into special session to appropriate requisite matching funds irritated
Ickes, who refused to grant Mississippi any more road money. Harrison was not involved but watched the hassle from the sidelines, adding material to the dossier he maintained on Conner. When a state
newspaper supporting Conner later claimed that the idea of the Civil

Works Administration had originated in a conference between Hopkins and the governor, Harrison checked on the story and learned that it was not true. "I am bringing to your attention some editorials which show that my prophecies in our little tête-à-tête with Mrs. Woodward were not far wrong," the senator wrote Hopkins. "While I am sure you have tried to keep politics out in every way, it is impossible for others to keep out," he added. [55]

Meanwhile the senator had his own complaints about the interior secretary's parsimony with the public pocketbook. When the Arkansas, Tennessee, and Mississippi congressmen agreed in early August that the amount released for Mississippi flood control programs was highly inadequate, especially in view of the fact that some 2,000 to 2,500 men had been dismissed from employment due to exhausted funds, Harrison determined to have a showdown with Washington officials "until the matter is ironed out." How could he continue to appeal to industry, labor, and the farmer for cooperation with the recovery program, he asked Marvin McIntyre, "with thousands of men being laid off and agencies of [the] administration fiddling about where funds are to come from?" Aware that work would have to be done in the low-water stage and unhappy with the sum allotted on August 15 by the federal public works board, Harrison returned to Washington to confer with Ickes, Lewis Douglas, and War Department engineers. Within a week he announced that nearly $7.5 million would flow into the Vicksburg area to strengthen flood control facilities. [56]

While finding jobs for others during the summer break, Harrison had to give some attention to keeping his own job, and his friends alerted him to personal appearances that would be to his political advantage. State Democratic chairman Edgar Williams had recommended a McComb NRA rally appearance because of "the occasional digs made by Rey Bonney," an anti-Harrison editor. Reminded that it had been sixteen years since some of the north Mississippi towns had been visited by their senior senator, Harrison fulfilled several speaking engagements there. In mid-October he launched "Recovery Week" at Tupelo, dedicated a stadium built with RFC funds at Columbus, and made a farm talk at Fulton. [57] Altogether, it was a trying summer and fall for most of the congressional Democrats, who found that rest was as elusive at home as in Washington.

By the late summer of 1933, Mississippi's first cards in the national "New Deal" showed that nearly $100 million would be loosed upon the state in federal expenditures for direct relief, public works, cotton subsidies, reforestation, subsistence homesteads, and flood control. There was no way to estimate what it would all mean in growing prestige, popularity, and job security for Pat Harrison. It is not surprising that, after the senator had told his home folks to remain loyal to Franklin D. Roosevelt, the salty editor of the Jackson *Daily News* added, "We must stick to him . . . until hell freezes over, and then skate around with him on the ice."[58]

At the end of 1933 Harrison was as devoted to the aims of the president as were most of his Mississippi constituents. Early in the congressional session it had been clear that Roosevelt and Harrison were in harmony on the necessity to economize in government spending and to compensate by adequate taxation whatever expenditures were made. Harrison was not so adamant about the spending proclivities of the Hundred Days Congress that he would be the "naysayer" that some of his more conservative colleagues were. He was too acutely aware of the needs of his home state, whose economy had responded to the remedies applied. Furthermore, it was evident in 1933 that Harrison was not likely to be an innovator of legislation himself. He was content to serve as a legislative broker for the ideas of others.

CHAPTER IV

"It is My Duty to Work In Harness"

1934

DURING THE SECOND YEAR of the New Deal there were
no signs that Pat Harrison held any reservations about the recovery
program other than his few complaints that some of the president's
advisers were not very practical men. With Roosevelt himself, Harrison remained in perfect accord. While the senator for a time flirted
with inflationists who were more radical than FDR, Harrison was
satisfied with the action eventually taken by Roosevelt toward what
the Mississippian called "controlled inflation." The senator continued to seek tax avenues that would maintain a balanced budget,
and he opposed a costly soldier bonus plan. It became quite clear in
1934 that he opposed revenue measures that would unduly tax corporate income and impede recovery through private channels. It was
equally clear when Harrison returned to Mississippi during the
summer recess that the president's program had done a vast amount
of good for the state. The senator's greatest concern that summer was
the election of Theodore G. Bilbo as his Senate colleague, a man
whom he had found to be quite irksome.

When Harrison arrived in Mississippi in the midsummer of 1933,
the economic outlook for his constituents, nearly 90 percent of whom
were farmers, had seemed promising. By late summer, when the
small boom in prices had turned downward, southern congressmen
began to bombard the president with demands for inflation. Cotton,
which had been at 10.6 cents a pound in July, brought 8.8 cents in
September. It was no surprise when John E. Rankin, an unabashed
inflationist, telegraphed the White House from Mississippi for some
sort of currency expansion, but it was an unusual turn of events
when Senator Harrison, considered to be a fiscal conservative,
boarded a train for Washington intent upon pressing the president

with "whatever influence [he] might have" to move toward inflation. Fearful that a six to eight week delay would put the cotton crop in the hands of the processors, the senator wanted something done before the entire 1933 crop had moved to the market and beyond the cotton growers' bins. In a September 13 conference the senator urged "controlled inflation" with Roosevelt and, leaving the White House, stated that "commodity prices have got to go up. I favor some form of rational inflation. We have got to do more than we are doing."[1]

Roosevelt, ever apprehensive about inflation, was noncommittal to Harrison. When those reporters who took the senator's new stand to be a near apostasy pressed the president for his reaction, FDR merely shrugged, "And so we get off on the same old subject again." The president had more recently been influenced by James Warburg, a New York financier with orthodox views who took a dim view of the Mississippi senator's recent conversion. Thus the White House kept quiet while the senator continued to talk. Although he believed that increased RFC assistance to banks (if they did not "dam up credit as they have been doing") and the formation of RFC mortgage companies would ease the farmers' dilemma, Harrison thought that speedier means of help were in Roosevelt's hands. The Mississippian prescribed an increase in the price of gold beyond the world price, the issue of silver certificates through government purchase of "considerable" amounts of silver bullion, and more immediately, presidential use of the authorization given him by the Thomas amendment to issue treasury notes and alter the gold content of the dollar. Moving beyond mere prescription into threat, Harrison warned that the next session of Congress would make the terms of the amendment mandatory rather than permissive. As for Roosevelt's reliance upon his recovery program to restore prosperity, Harrison became somewhat Byranesque. If prosperity were not restored to the American farmer, he declared, "you can kiss the baby goodbye."[2]

Harrison was only one of several senators who were urging Roosevelt along the path to inflation. "Cotton Ed" Smith, chairman of the Senate Committee on Agriculture, Duncan U. Fletcher of Florida, chairman of the Banking and Currency Committee, and Nevada's "silver senator" Key Pittman were also members of the contingent marshaled by Elmer Thomas, who had assumed command of the drive for higher prices through an inflated currency. Mississippi

Representatives Will Whittington and Wall Doxey were among a southern delegation that made no more headway than others in getting a presidential commitment to "do something" along the lines of inflation for cotton farmers. Counteracting their influence were warnings to Roosevelt from Secretary Wallace that price inflation would endanger his plow-up campaign and from Hugh Johnson that the orthodox business community would have less enthusiasm for signing his NRA codes.[3]

There was more to southern agrarian unrest than plunging farm prices. Based on prewar averages, the purchasing power of the farmer had dropped by 10 percent and appeared to be headed lower, and some farmers pinned that problem on the NRA's boost of industrial prices. "The NRA I think is absurdly radical . . . they are trying to force prosperity upon the industrial world regardless of the status of agriculture—it can't be done," vowed one of Harrison's constituents. The senator declined to criticize the recovery administration, but he continued to associate with the inflationists as forecasts of agrarian ruin increased. As one Washington correspondent explained, "That is why such sound money fellows as Pat Harrison and Duncan Fletcher . . . plead for currency debauchery."[4] The Mississippian was indeed playing a new role and ample publicity followed his various moves.

By November a national debate was on between the defenders of the president's policy and the bankers and financiers who were shocked by a gold-buying spree Roosevelt had begun in October. Senator Harrison had already entered the fray when he told a business luncheon group at the Waldorf-Astoria Hotel that the "crowd in Washington is not for any wild inflation," and a more receptive, if less sophisticated, audience at a Laurel, Mississippi fair that the credit of the government would not be impaired by a treasury note issuance of $3 billion and a cut in the gold content of the dollar. Somewhat mollified by the government's cotton curtailment and lending program, which had moved cotton to ten cents a pound by November, Harrison was not as abrasive in a second conference with Roosevelt on November 13, leaving a parting statement with reporters that "the President is trying to do his duty. If the gold program does not work out, I believe the President will take some other course." In fact he volunteered to presidential press secretary Steve

Early to "take the war path" in a counterattack against administration critics. "Pat says he will go on the air in a national hook-up and fortify himself with facts to blow critics to four letter word region," Early wrote to Marvin McIntyre. Early replied that the time was not yet "ripe" for the counterattack. "Let them go ahead and do some more shooting," he added. [5]

Although he had simmered down in his attempt to thrust the president toward inflation, Harrison still maintained his ties with Thomas's corps of radicals. The Mississippian joined Senators Thomas and Smith and members of the Committee for the Nation to Rebuild Prices and Purchasing Power in signing a resolution in November urging Roosevelt to continue his gold and monetary policy until the level of commodities, salaries, and employment reached their 1926 positions. The resolution also was signed by Robert M. Harriss, a New York cotton broker who had served for some time as a link between Harrison and Thomas. It is a matter of conjecture whether or not Harrison was restrained from later going completely over to the silverites by his friend Bernard Baruch, whose article on "The Dangers of Inflation" appeared just at that time in the *Saturday Evening Post*. "I believe that inflation is an enemy of mankind," Baruch wrote. [6]

Although neither the credit expansion, which Harrison so avidly supported, nor Roosevelt's gold buying did much to raise commodity prices, the inflation battle had resulted in a political alignment of the South and West not seen so clearly since 1896. It would not result, however, in Harrison's going so far as formally to join the silver bloc that had formed around a nucleus of western senators led by Pittman, Borah, and Wheeler. Except for Rankin, Mississippi's congressional delegation began to speak less about inflation and veered away from criticism of their White House chieftain whose other programs appeared to be eminently productive in reviving the southern agricultural economy. Economic indices showed the impact of $40 million in cotton checks and a weekly input into the South of nearly $1 million in CWA money and from the development of Muscle Shoals and Mississippi flood control projects. [7]

In mid-January of 1934, Roosevelt sent a message to Congress requesting that the government be permitted to take possession of all monetary gold and devalue the dollar at a point between 50 and 60

percent. Of the request Harrison remarked, "The President's monetary policy appeals to me." Two nights later he made the national
radio address he had earlier volunteered to make. Praising the anticipated gold program as a means of reducing the national debt, increasing trade balances abroad, and accumulating a large profit to the government (the last becoming the basis for a two billion dollar exchange
stabilization fund), he forecast a more just equilibrium between the
purchasing value of commodities and the value of the dollar. With the
exception of Carter Glass, who termed the gold program "stealing,"
all of the Senate Democrats voted for the gold reserve bill that passed
on January 27 by a vote of 66 to 23. When Burton K. Wheeler attempted to add a silver purchase plan to the gold program, Harrison
voted against it since Roosevelt had said, "This is not the time to
order the purchase of silver." Harrison's opposition was indicative of
an allegiance greater to Roosevelt than to his silver senator friends.[8]

The silverites were not to be put down. With the apparent sympathy for silver purchases that the Wheeler amendment vote had revealed, the administration within six weeks faced another hard-
pressed move from the West. When the House passed a bill put forth
by Martin Dies of Texas, Roosevelt knew that he had no alternative
but to compromise or else see the balance of his program for 1934
subject to reprisal. On April 21, a high-level confrontation took place
at the White House attended by treasury officials and silverites. Harrison was there as a representative of the Senate administration
group. It was a wearisome hassle, and when it was over the Mississippian complained, "We discussed silver from the time of the finding
of the first nugget." He did not think new legislation was now necessary. "The President has all the power he needs to expand the currency through the silver channel under the Thomas amendment,"
Harrison told reporters. The inevitable compromise placed a mandate
upon the secretary of the treasury to purchase silver through the issuance of certificates until the white metal reached one-fourth of the
government's monetary holdings, but at the same time it was permissive about how and when the treasury should act. The measure
passed the Senate on June 11; Harrison voted "yea."[9]

If Roosevelt had capitulated to the silver bloc, he stood firm against
the veterans' lobby which camped out before every congressional session. Still riled over the cuts made in the Economy Act of 1933 and as

persistent as ever for a comprehensive soldier bonus, the veterans
found their champion in Representative Wright Patman of Texas,
who introduced a bill in early 1934 to pay the soldiers a bonus
through the issuance of $2.4 billion in greenbacks. Roosevelt was hor-
rified at the prospect, not only because of its inflationary aspects but
also because of its obvious damage to his hope of eventually balancing
the budget. [10]

The House discharged the Patman bill on petition in February,
1934. Mississippi's veterans, long displeased with Harrison's opposition to bonus plans, gave notice in a statewide meeting in early March
that they would oppose congressional candidates in the August primary who crossed them on bonus propositions. With Mississippi's
ex-soldiers in line for almost $21 million from the bonus plan before
Congress, only Whittington of the House delegation voted against it
at the disorderly session which thumped it through on March 12.
Harrison told Morgenthau that he had first considered bringing up a
bill to pay the bonus with the seignoirage on silver and "kill it by a
good size vote," but finding that there was considerable sentiment in
the Senate for the bonus, he prevailed upon Vice-President Garner to
have the bill lie on the table for so long that its delayed referral to the
Finance Committee would kill it. It languished in Senator Harrison's
committee until June 6, when he reported it adversely, too late for it
to make a run through the Senate. [11]

Meanwhile, when the annual independent appropriations bill
came up in late February, the Senate retreated from its earlier stand
for economy and passed amendments to pay the Spanish-American
War veterans 90 percent of the pre-Economy Act compensation and
restore the federal payroll cuts. Harrison's wire home "It grieves me
that I cannot at all times comply with the wishes of my friends"
foretold his opposition vote on the appropriations bill which restored 5
percent of the pay cuts and carried the increased veteran benefits.
The bill completely riddled the earlier Economy Act with its dis-
pensation of an additional $354 million in benefits to the two groups.
It faced a certain veto. [12]

The House and Senate both swiftly overrode the veto. Whittington
was again Roosevelt's lone supporter from Mississippi in the House,
and both Harrison and Stephens, the latter facing the voters in August, stood behind the chief executive. Robinson and Harrison de-

bated the proponents of the measure to the point of hoarseness, but they were unable to hold all of the Democratic votes that they needed. In one of his few public statements on the Roosevelt program, Harrison confessed, "We may have enacted some legislation that does not agree with my philosophy of government. But we are not out of our economic trouble, and we will get nowhere if we divide and fight among ourselves."[13] Although Roosevelt and his legislative lieutenants deprecated talk that the veto defeat was a sign of growing congressional independence, the news media increasingly commented to that effect. Arthur Krock called the defeat the president's "First Manassas," but Harrison remonstrated that the American people were with Roosevelt. Administration leaders, believing that the worst of the congressional recalcitrance was past, anticipated adjournment as soon as the revenue and tariff bills, the only remaining obligatory matters, were disposed of.[14]

In his January budget message to Congress, Roosevelt requested levies on alcoholic beverages partially to offset recovery and relief expenditures. He knew that the congressional finance committees already had a measure in the mill ready for immediate floor action. More than revenue was involved; there was the problem of setting a tax rate which would satisfy the liquor industry as well as undercut the bootleggers who had stocked nearly fifty million gallons of liquor. Not only domestic excises were involved but also the tariff on imported liquors and wines. Then, too, there were suggestions of a revenue-sharing plan by which the federal government would collect the taxes on liquor production and return a portion to the states.[15]

On December 5, 1933, the fourteen-year-long drought ended when Utah became the thirty-sixth state to ratify the Twenty-first Amendment. Trucks rolled out of the warehouses in twenty-four states on the same day. At a White House conference on December 11 the two congressional chairmen disputed liquor tax increases recommended by an interdepartmental committee. Harrison suggested a levy of $2.20 a gallon, which he estimated would bring in a "sweet morsel" of $400 million in revenue on liquor alone, but James M. Doran, director of the distilling industry's NRA code authority, insisted that the tax be lower in order to thwart the bootleggers, while Herbert Feis, a State Department economic adviser, advocated presidential reciprocal power in fixing import duties. In its executive ses-

sion the Ways and Means Committee settled on a tax of $2.00 a
gallon with revenue-sharing based upon a state's combined production and consumption. [16]

The full House eliminated the revenue-sharing plan and then
passed the remainder of the Ways and Means proposal by a vote of
388 to 5. Harrison was forced to abandon any effort to revive the
revenue-sharing plan in the Senate since half of his colleagues were
from dry states. After the Finance Committee quickly consented to
the House bill the chairman dashed from his Senate office to the
chamber to report it for immediate consideration. It passed unanimously. When the president signed the bill a few minutes before
midnight on January 11, the government picked up $1 million in rev-
enue on the following day, for the act was effective immediately.
Liquor taxes in 1934 would total $375 million. [17]

When in April of 1933 Harrison became the first senator to serve
as chairman of the Joint Committee on Internal Revenue Taxation, a
congressional study committee that had been created in 1926, he increasingly gained stature as a spokesman for the administration's tax
policy. His late summer prediction that the budget would be balanced
by anticipated liquor and beer revenues contributed to a taxpayers'
euphoria which he heightened in a radio broadcast on January 17,
1934. He stated that the revenue bill of 1934 would deal largely with
administrative features intended to prevent tax evasion by persons of
substantial wealth. Such a program could expect immense popularity
since it would follow shocking revelations made in 1933 before the
Senate Banking Committee that J. P. Morgan had paid no income
taxes for either 1931 or 1932. [18]

The revenue bill that came from the Committee on Ways and
Means in January was essentially a tax-avoidance measure, but by the
time the Finance Committee went into executive session, the president's budget had been riddled by the increased expenditures disbursed by the independent appropriations bill. Hence Senator Harrison felt compelled to revamp the House bill, passed in February, to
raise a larger sum of revenue. Also, he was of the opinion that certain
"nuisance" taxes on consumer items should be eliminated, an idea he
had consistently advocated over the years. The revenue thus lost
could be compensated by the reenactment of a defunct tax on the
declared value of capital stock as well as a 5 percent excess profits

tax. The Finance Committee's bill, reported on March 28 and containing $72 million in tax increases beyond the House bill, was expected to face a prolonged Senate debate. Harrison offered assurances that the new taxes would produce a balanced budget by 1936 and that no more tax increases would be necessary. But rumors had it that President Roosevelt would seek taxes beyond those contained in the committee bill, for both houses had just overriden his veto of the appropriations bill. [19]

Although Roosevelt, who was vacationing away from Washington, preferred that Harrison delay Senate debate until his return, the senator conferred with treasury officials and Lewis Douglas and decided that the bill should be pushed through at once. He feared the momentum which Robert La Follette and minority committee member James Couzens might gain for their plan to levy higher surtaxes, which the Mississippian thought would have an adverse effect upon business recovery. When Morgenthau advised Roosevelt that Harrison "had the situation in hand," the president agreed that the best policy was to get the tax bill out of the way. [20]

Harrison's advocacy in the chamber of his committee's bill was followed by the expected barrage of amendments intended to raise income and estate tax rates substantially. After he advanced his fear of thwarting recovery through unnecessary tax burdens, the Senate rejected La Follette's amendment to increase the surtax on incomes above $1 million to 71 percent from the 59 percent figure carried in the bill. In spite of Harrison's attack upon the theory of redistributing wealth through higher income taxes, ten Democrats supported the La Follette amendment, including Hugo Black, Bennett Clark, Thomas Connally, and Huey Long, the latter clashing with Harrison in a six-hour quarrel in the Senate chamber. So bitter was the dialogue that senators of long tenure declared that they had not heard such a personal exchange in years. [21]

The La Follette forces, defeated in their attempt to redistribute wealth via higher taxation of personal incomes, now turned to efforts to increase estate taxes 10 percent above the committee's figure, a move to which Harrison consented. La Follette succeeded in leaving another of his marks upon the revenue bill of 1934 when he persuaded the Senate that income tax returns should be open to inspection. This controversial feature had been a part of the 1924 revenue act, but it had been dropped from later acts because of protests that free-lance operators had sold tax information that subjected taxpayers to "sucker" lists and even to kidnapping threats. A number of Democrats, including the liberal Robert Wagner, joined Harrison in voting against tax publicity even though the provision was watered down to leave tax return figures open only to state officials. With the last of the amendments out of the way, the bill passed the Senate on April 13 by a vote of 53 to 7.[22]

Because Harrison never liked to have tariff items inserted into revenue bills, he strongly opposed the 5 cents a pound levy on coconut oil and copra that the revenue bill of 1934 carried as it came from the House. Describing the coconut tax as "one of the hardest nuts for the committee to crack," he succeeded in reducing it to 3 cents a pound. The item bothered him for several reasons. He knew that southern cotton growers wanted the tax to protect their cottonseed oil by-products from the competition of foreign oils, and he rightly suspected that he would have to answer to them for his own objections to the tariff. He also shared with Millard Tydings of Maryland, a champion of the Philippine independence movement, the belief that the tax was inordinately unfair to the islands because the oils constituted the second largest Philippine import to the United States. "I have never thought that we ought to pass an Independence act one day," Harrison argued, "and the next day undo everything we guaranteed to the people in the act." As an administration spokesman, moreover, he was obligated to protect presidential prerogatives in dealing with the islands. Nonetheless, the Senate, bowing to the farm lobby, retained the tax by a sizable vote.[23]

As soon as Roosevelt returned from his vacation, he made it clear in a conference with his Senate leaders that he wanted the tax on coconut and related oils stricken from the bill. Because the president threatened to veto the bill on that account, Harrison was determined to have the Senate vote again on the measure, a ploy which veteran legislators could not recall on legislation as important as a major tax bill. After long consultation with the president and State and War Department officials, however, he released the bill to return to the House, hopeful that a gentleman's agreement in conference would eliminate the tax.[24]

During conference meetings "Muley" Doughton conveyed the

usual touchiness he felt whenever the Senate virtually rewrote House bills. "I guess it is just another effort of the Senate to show its superiority," he complained. "It has to justify its existence." Allen T. Treadway, the ranking Republican on the House committee, added, "It is evident that the so-called Senate Progressives ran away with the Finance Committee." He was substantially correct, for Harrison had been prodded by La Follette into going beyond the committee's intentions, even though he had never lost control of the bill. In the conference meeting on April 25 the House conferees accepted practically all of the Senate amendments. The completed bill, expected to produce $417 million in revenue, gained Senate approval without a record vote on May 4, and Roosevelt signed it on May 10, flanked by Harrison and Doughton. [25]

While Harrison was herding the administration tax program through the Senate, he was also involved with legislation that had fallen to him not because it was within the purview of the Finance Committee but because of his own expertise in managing difficult legislation. The matter was a sugar control bill designed to bring order out of the chaotic sugar industry. Marvin Jones, chairman of the House Committee on Agriculture, and Edward P. Costigan, a Colorado senator who had long been a student of the problems faced by his sugar beet constituency, wished to bring growers of sugar cane and beets under the stabilization and subsidy features of the Agricultural Adjustment Act. Harrison was sympathetic to their arguments that forty years of sugar tariffs had failed to aid the sugar producers, for he had often lectured Senator Reed Smoot on that subject. He was aware of the multifaceted conflicts involving Roosevelt's and Hull's concern for the rehabilitation of the Cuban economy, the Interior Department's responsibility for Puerto Rico and Hawaii, and the War Department's interests in the Philippines, as well as the complexities of reconciling differences between domestic growers and sugar refiners. [26]

By early February, 1934, the Jones-Costigan bill was ready for congressional action. For a reduced tariff of half a cent per pound, it substituted a processing tax of the same amount, the proceeds of which would defray the costs of granting a bounty to domestic sugar beet and cane farmers to limit production; island producers were also to limit their output in return for guaranteed export quotas. Despite the fact that all parties concerned lamented either the restrictions upon domestic production or upon island exports, the bill made its way through the House Agricultural Committee and went on to the Finance Committee where Harrison was expected to moderate the differences. "We are going to try to work it out," he told the president in mid-March, and in early April he told Morgenthau that he had arranged for passage of the sugar measure as soon as the revenue bill was out of the way. [27]

The sugar bill passed the House by acclamation in early April. Because the bill faced a deadlock in the Finance Committee, Harrison dispensed with hearings while he met individually with the sugar senators and negotiated a bill that they, the Finance Committee, and the administration could all accept. Costigan reported the bill to the Senate and Harrison urged immediate consideration in view of the fact that it was late in the season and sugar beet farmers were anxious to draw up their contracts with processors. Harrison's protest that he had "no interest in the world" in the sugar bill was confirmed by Arthur H. Vandenberg, a Republican from the sugar beet state of Michigan, who described the Mississippi senator as "continuously fair to all of us," and Costigan, who praised the Mississippian for his ability, disinterestedness, and integrity. [28]

Along with the roses came brickbats. Although Rexford G. Tugwell, who as assistant secretary of agriculture had worked hard to obtain a favorable production allocation for Puerto Rico, admitted that the reconciliation of all interests involved was a "wholly impossible" task, he charged that the measure had been turned into a refiner's bill shutting out "any possibility" for developing the industry in Puerto Rico. A year later columnist Drew Pearson wrote that Harrison at the last minute had "tucked away" in the Jones-Costigan bill a prohibition on new sugar refineries that significantly held up economic reconstruction of the territory. In a furious denial, the senator retorted that the charge was a "mendacious [and] damnable lie." [29] The bill, which Roosevelt signed on May 9, was to be effective for three years. Not until 1937 would Harrison face another fight over sugar legislation.

Behind the revenue and sugar bills lay the trade agreements program of Secretary of State Cordell Hull. Roosevelt had declined to push for tariff revision in 1933 when he had elected his own brand of economic nationalism over the internationalism of Hull, who patiently prodded his chief executive to support tariff revision. Finally, on February 28, 1934, at a White House conference attended by cabinet members and congressional leaders including Harrison, Roosevelt decided to tackle the tariff. His message of March 2 requested executive authority of three years' duration to negotiate and promulgate reciprocal trade agreements and to modify tariffs within a range of 50 percent. Neither reciprocity nor flexible schedules was an invention of the Democrats. Both had Republican antecedents in the McKinley Tariff of 1890 and the tariff acts of 1922 and 1930. What *was* new about the Hull-Roosevelt approach was the implication that the bilateral actions of a Democratic administration would result in widespread tariff reduction. Congressional observers predicted that the tariff bill would provide the bitterest fight of the session and supply the Republicans with an issue by which they could reconstruct their faltering party hopes. [30]

On the day of the message Representative Doughton introduced the administration program in the House. By the end of March the bill had completed its round of hearings, committee executive sessions, and debate. House passage came on March 29 by a vote of 274 to 111 after forty amendments offered by the militant minority party were shunted aside. It was the shortest span of time in which the House had ever dispatched a tariff bill. Involved at the time with the revenue and sugar bills, the Finance Committee had to wait until late April before committee hearings could begin. [31]

Harrison planned to hold the hearings to a minimum and confine the bill to presidential designs; he assuredly did not intend to permit logrollers to turn reciprocal tariff legislation into an omnibus revision measure. Robinson had already caucused the Senate Democrats to muster support for the tariff bill while Republicans rallied around Pennsylvania's David Reed, who predicted that presidential trade agreements would "sink long-established American industries without a trace." Secretary of State Hull, the initial witness, insisted that "extraordinary conditions call for extraordinary methods of treatment" and defended the trade program from the bitter denunciation of the Republican committee members. By the end of the second day of hearings Harrison had been won over to Reed's insistence that the bill include a stipulation that a public notice of executive intention to negotiate an agreement be given so that interested parties could be heard. Before the hearings ended on May 1, Henry L. Stimson, recently Hoover's secretary of state, in a nationally broadcast speech urged Congress to grant authority over tariffs to the president. Stimson, who had once endorsed the Hawley-Smoot tariff, was looked upon as something of a turncoat by his Republican colleagues. Some days later Harrison dressed down his fellow senators across the aisle who snickered at his reference to the Stimson speech. [32]

When Harrison reported out the bill, it was essentially as it had come from the House. When the Republicans learned that forty-five Democrats had met on the night of April 30 and almost unanimously endorsed the measure, they were well aware of the outcome of the protracted argument which would ensue once Harrison brought the bill up for debate. This he did on May 17 in an impassioned speech that deprecated the old tariff policy of "heaping up" trade barriers. When minority leader Charles McNary reminded the Mississippian of his 1930 opposition to granting authority to the president, Harrison retorted, "I have been here too long to believe that I can be consistent all the time in all things." Besides, he argued, there was a decided difference in giving Hoover the power to increase rates and giving Roosevelt the authority to make trade agreements that would sell surplus goods, build up international trade, and improve the economic conditions of the country. [33]

After his initial speech Harrison fell back upon a tactic he often used, described by his good friend James F. Byrnes, "If you've got the votes, keep quiet; if you haven't talk." For nearly three weeks the trade bill's pilot permitted the Republicans to talk almost uninterrupted while he organized his own forces through cafeteria and cloakroom activity. Idaho's lion, William Borah, spoke against the tariff in a style reminiscent of his League of Nations speeches, McNary threatened an amendment to exempt farm products (Harrison countered that it would never pass), and protectionist Republicans by the score attacked the bill. The incorrigible Huey Long offered as a substitute the Harrison tariff bill of 1932 which Hoover had vetoed because it would have subjected presidential tariff agreements to congressional approval. Because the Louisianan's speech-making had verged upon a one-man filibuster, Harrison drew his Democratic friends together and forced through an agreement to limit debate. [34]

By June 1 administration leaders realized that the Republicans had launched a filibuster through dilatory tactics aimed at preventing action not only on the tariff but also on other New Deal measures offensive to the minority party. Through McNary's cooperation with Robinson and Harrison, the Democrats got the measure back on the track and, once again in control, they were able to beat down the barrage of crippling amendments laid down by the Republicans. The 54 to 33 rejection of Hiram Johnson's amendment to exempt farm products from trade agreements (only three Republicans voted against it and only three Democrats for it) presaged the outcome of the final vote on the bill itself. On June 4 the trade agreements measure passed by an almost completely partisan vote of 57 to 33. Only five Democrats, among them the Southerners Glass, Long, and Overton, voted against the bill; five Republicans voted for it. [35]

The administration's victory was compounded two days later when the House, in an unusual procedure, approved the Senate's work without even the formality of a conference. On June 8 the Mississippi senator went on the air to give one of the chats which radio listeners had come to expect whenever the Finance Committee had produced a major administration measure. To Republican charges, represented by Vandenberg's statement that the new tariff system was "an extraordinary, tyrannical, dictatorial power over the life and death of the American economy," Harrison countered that the Hawley-Smoot tariff of 1930 had been "the epitome of selfishness and greed, the perfection of political philandering, [and] the sacrificial altar upon which the unprotected many were offered up for the appeasement of the false god of the fanatical few." The senator predicted that, in contrast, the Democratic program would usher in a new and bountiful life for American trade. Roosevelt signed the bill into law on June 12; it would be three years before the tariff would come up again. [36]

Cordell Hull characterized his close Mississippi friend as a "notable chairman . . . whose cooperation was indispensable." [37] Harrison had not, of course, written the tariff bill or any significant portion of it. He had displayed those legislative talents of compromise, cajolery, and congeniality with which he consistently supported the New Deal. While he would never be recognized as an intellectual or an ideologue, he was increasingly gaining stature among his colleagues who respected political skill apart from ideology.

Without fail Harrison supported the administration in other actions of the second session of the Seventy-third Congress. He voted in March for the St. Lawrence Seaway treaty when twenty-two Democrats, among them Stephens, deserted the administration in the Senate's rejection of the treaty. Harrison's supportive votes were neither noticeable nor needed when the securities and exchange bill, the railroad retirement bill, and the national housing bill all passed the Senate by overwhelming majorities. [38]

Because the 1933 cotton yield had been greater than that of 1932 in spite of the plow-up, Alabama's John Bankhead introduced a bill aimed at stabilizing cotton prices by limiting the 1934 crop to ten million bales and levying a high penalty tax on cotton ginned in excess of quotas. In this crucial test of government control over the most important segment of Mississippi's economy, both of the state's senators voted in the affirmative when the bill passed the Senate on March 29 by a seven-vote margin. Although Josiah W. Bailey of North Carolina cast the only "nay" vote in the cotton state column, Stephens, in an unusual move, rose to voice his grave reservations about the bill after the vote was taken. Concerned over the question of constitutionality and the probable effects of a stringent program of control, he wanted to make it clear that he had cast his vote only because of the "strong desire of the people of the South with reference to the legislation." Harrison said nothing, biding his time until the late summer when he could see the results of the cotton cutback. [39]

If Pat Harrison had any qualms about the direction in which his chief executive had led the country up to the time of congressional adjournment on June 18, 1934, he left no record of such reservations. He had told the Senate in April, "I am one of those peculiar individuals who believe that when my party is in power it is my duty to work in harness, and that when the country and my party have chosen a leader, it is my duty to follow him." Ironically, at that very time Rexford Tugwell, who considered Robinson and Harrison as Old Guard southern conservatives, confided in his diary that "F.D.R. has done marvelously in working through the old crowd to get our legislation." Sensitive to the bitter opposition of some of the Old Guard to the young liberals who advised the president. Tugwell, who was up for Senate confirmation as assistant secretary of agriculture, resigned himself to "take it on the chin." Yet he was convinced that the Arkansas and Mississippi administrative adjutants were "discovering more and more that we can be attacked with impunity." Ernest K. Lindley, who wrote candidly of the Washington scene, agreed. Already he had observed congressional clashes with the so-called Brain Trust and its drive for policies to institute social change. Much of the New Deal ran counter to the "ingrained" views of such "party wheelhorses" as Fletcher, Smith, Harrison, and Robinson, Lindley observed at the end of the Seventy-third Congress. [40]

While the social and economic philosophy of Department of Agriculture advisers such as Tugwell and Mordecai Ezekiel disturbed Senator Harrison, it is no exaggeration to say that in 1933 and 1934 he was infinitely more harrassed by the political aspirations of an obscure official in the public relations division of the department—Theodore G. Bilbo. In January, 1932, when Bilbo's stormy second term as governor of Mississippi ended, he was at the nadir of his long and checkered career. Always in need of money, he wrote to Harrison in January, 1933, asking for a federal job. He had in mind either the post as collector of internal revenue for Mississippi or the Washington directorship of the extension work of the Department of Agriculture. Although he knew that Stephens would block an appointment, Bilbo counted upon the senior senator to "maneuver the situation." Confidentially the ex-governor advised Harrison that "either one of these positions would place me in a position where I could be of real help to you when the time comes." Shortly afterward he concentrated on getting the agricultural post and pressed Harrison further, reminding the senator that he could be of great help in lining up "the old Vardaman crowd" in 1936 when Harrison would face reelection. "I will repay you a thousand times," he promised. By March, 1933, however, Harrison's office was deluged with telegrams from Mississippi county agricultural agents protesting the rumored appointment. [41]

Not satisfied with writing letters from Jackson, Bilbo went to Washington to plead with Harrison there. Apparently the senator provided the down-and-out politico with money to tide him over ("coffee-and-cake hand-outs," George Allen called them), and then set about to find a job for Bilbo, who was all but camping out in Harrison's office, in George Peek's division of the Department of Agriculture. Harrison's friends all knew that he was anxious to keep his

politically dangerous constituent off the Mississippi streets, so when
the senator went to see Peek, the AAA administrator agreed to take it
up with Secretary Wallace.[42]

The accounts of Harrison's interview with Peek are legion. Explaining that Bilbo was "at loose ends," he warned of the "disaster" if
the veteran politician were to enter the Senate race against Stephens
in 1934. "The man is a vote getter," Harrison declared. Learning that
one of Bilbo's talents was public speaking, Peek suggested a public
relations position entailing a nationwide presentation of AAA
policies. Harrison interjected, "George, you weren't thinking of having him make speeches in Mississippi, were you?" Pressing the
senator for other caveats, Peek was told that Bilbo should not handle
government money or be placed in an office "where there was a girl
around." Otherwise, Harrison assured Peek, "he's absolutely all
right." (Peek's assistant Chester Davis, who was present, later recalled, "Wasn't that a hell of a recommendation?") After hearing
Harrison's description of Bilbo's frailties, Peek laughed, "In other
words, Senator, this good Democrat Bilbo will be fine for us if we
muzzle him, tie his hands, and lock up the petty cash." That was
about it, Harrison concurred. The outcome was the appointment of
Bilbo as an assembler of current information for the AAA. His work
began in June, 1933, at a salary of $6,000 a year and with a secretary
who looked, according to the reporters Joseph and Stewart Alsop, "as
though she had entered government service in the administration of
Millard Fillmore."[43]

Chester Davis termed the job as "bona fide" because it did involve a
selective analysis of press commentaries and the distribution of critical items to the affected divisions. Almost immediately, however,
numerous newspapers dubbed Bilbo "the pastemaster general" and
described the job as mere scrapbook work. Bilbo refused to pose for
news photographers with a paste pot and scissors and testily insisted,
"I don't clip." He was rankled by a demeaning image created by his
opposition press in Mississippi and comments similar to that of a
Washington *Post* columnist who commended Harrison's "mastery of
the art of patronage distribution" in satisfying a former governor with
a job as "chief scissors-wielder." Bilbo was soon completely disgrun-
tled and intimated that he was biding his time only until a propitious
moment to announce his candidacy for the Senate.[44]

In early 1934, when Harrison knew that Bilbo was about to resign,

the senator went to Chester Davis to find a more dignified job for
"The Man." Davis suggested a position in Puerto Rico with the sugar
and tobacco programs, but Harrison could not convince Bilbo of the
merits of the job in spite of the fact that, as Davis put it, "he really
laid it on" as a position "just a little short of an ambassadorship." In
an encounter between the two Mississippians which Davis witnessed,
Bilbo flatly told Harrison that he intended to run for the Senate,
and the senator as plainly told his rival that he would support
Stephens. Bilbo then warned Harrison that if the senator announced
his support for "Huey Stephens," then he would inform the voters
that "Pat Harrison is for Stephens because with Stephens in the Senate, Pat Harrison casts two votes. If I'm in the Senate, I assure you
he'll cast one." With that, Bilbo wheeled out of Harrison's office.
Shaking his head, Harrison asked Davis, "What can you do with a
fellow like that?"[45]

In February Bilbo resigned. In an ingratiating letter to Harrison
expressing an appreciation for a "meal ticket in the depression" he
spelled out the humiliation the job had brought to him and explained
his inability to take the Puerto Rico position because of its temporary
nature and inadequate compensation (even though Roosevelt had
tried to persuade him to take the job). He warned Harrison not to
oppose him in the race because Mississippians would remember Harrison's neutrality in the 1928 race between Stephens and Congressman T. Webber Wilson. "I might say in passing," Bilbo closed,
"that few Mississippians would endorse the efforts of one Senator
trying to dictate the naming of his colleague."[46]

The new Senate contender had hit dead center, for Harrison was
well aware of the fact that in Mississippi politics a smart man ran for
his own office and let other races alone. It was a rule that he seldom
dared to violate, and he certainly had no intention of doing so in the
Senate race of 1934 which by June had drawn three aspirants, the
incumbent Stephens, Bilbo, and Congressman Ross A. Collins. In a
letter made public through the Jackson *Daily News*, a staunch anti-
Bilbo paper, Harrison made clear his intention to vote for Stephens,
but he explained that he had made it equally transparent to the junior
senator that "under the existing circumstances" he thought the voters would resent his interference with "their right to choose my colleague in the Senate." Three weeks after Congress adjourned, the

senior senator left Washington in the company of close friend
Matthew S. Sloan, president of the Missouri, Kansas, and Texas
Railroad, for a six-week vacation trip through the Midwest and on to
Mexico City where the two were guests of Ambassador Josephus
Daniels. Thus Harrison missed (or avoided) the summer fireworks of
a Bilbo campaign at home. [47]

The campaign was an episode in the long, ongoing struggle among
the traditional factions in Mississippi politics. Geographically, north
Mississippi battled south Mississippi. Stephens was from New Albany, in the northeastern hill country, Bilbo from Poplarville in the
south central piney woods. Moreover, it was an extension of the
socioeconomic conflicts that had colored Mississippi elections since
the days of John Sharp Williams and James K. Vardaman. It was
common knowledge that Bilbo had trained with the forces of the
"Great White Chief." He constantly complained that wealth and af-
fluence were arrayed against him (he would have to subsist through
the campaign on crackers, sardines, and cheese, he glowed), and he
adopted a platform appealing to laborers and farmers. Redistribution
of wealth, unemployment insurance, cash payment of a soldier
bonus, and federal control of federal reserve banks were among the
twenty-seven planks which the populist-minded candidate advocated.
Furthermore, Bilbo styled himself in speech and dress to keep the
faith of the Vardaman flock. Drew Pearson contrasted the private
tastes of Bilbo for flashy dress with his public appearance on the
speaker's platform at Byhalia, for which he donned a "gray sack suit
torn at the sleeve." (At the local boardinghouse prior to the speaking
"you could have mistaken Bilbo for a dry goods salesman out of Memphis.") His speeches, punctuated by folksy stories, homilies, scrip-
tural admonitions, and an overworked reference to the nether world,
delighted audiences. Many Mississippians were indeed excited over
the prospect that Theodore G. Bilbo really would deliver on his campaign promise "If you elect me to the Senate, I will raise more hell
than Huey Long." [48]

Hubert Stephens and Pat Harrison were representatives of a
senatorial line that could be traced through Williams and LeRoy
Percy to the earlier conservatives of the era of L. Q. C. Lamar. A
prototype of the southern Democratic gentleman, temperate in his
manner of speaking and immaculately groomed, Stephens had unob-

trusively served two terms in the Senate by 1934, rising to the chairmanship of the Committee on Commerce, where his interest in flood control and harbor legislation appealed to the Mississippi Delta and coastal areas. Never a campaigner, he had made only twelve speeches in his 1928 race. Plagued by diabetes and a crippled foot, he had not planned to seek reelection until he learned that Bilbo intended to succeed him. In contrast to the multiple planks of his opponent, Stephens offered only one, "Stand by the President and his program." He had the support not only of Harrison but also of John Sharp Williams, Jr., who pointed out that his father, who had died in 1932, had twice voted for Stephens. And, of course, he had the support of President Roosevelt. Shortly before the first primary, the chief executive summoned Stephens to Washington to discuss "matters of national importance," reputedly at Harrison's suggestion. [49]

Collins was eliminated in the first primary and threw his support to Stephens on the grounds that "there must be no hindrance thrown in the way of our peerless leader, Franklin D. Roosevelt." In the runoff primary, Bilbo and Stephens each carried forty-one counties but the incumbent lost by a little more than 7,500 votes. Stephens laid his defeat to "political cross-currents and political deals" as well as to dissatisfaction with the Bankhead cotton act quotas. More likely Stephens lost because his voting record had antagonized veterans, organized labor, and administration supporters who thought that he was anti-Roosevelt at heart. In fact, his fellow senators were reputedly shocked by his claim that he had stood by the New Deal. Also, Stephens had been misled as to his strength in Mississippi and had simply failed to campaign vigorously and match Bilbo's forensics. [50] His loss was a great blow, though no surprise, to Pat Harrison who learned a lesson from the Bilbo-Stephens race which he would recite in his own bid for reelection in 1936.

Harrison returned to Mississippi in late August, 1934, just in time to cast his vote for Stephens in the first primary. He then left for Washington, where he held conferences on budget-balancing with Morgenthau and Daniel W. Bell, who had become acting director of the budget upon the resignation of Lewis Douglas. Going on to Hyde Park, Harrison conferred with the president on several matters, including the Mississippi senatorial race. He returned home to vote in the second primary and then directed his energies toward mending his own political fences, heeding an editorial warning from the friendly Fred Sullens to "get out on the stump." A not-so-amicable member of the Mississippi press corps, who bitterly assailed Harrison's failure to "open his mouth" on behalf of Stephens, claimed that "literally thousands" blamed the defeat upon the senior senator. Already there was talk that north Mississippi would field a candidate in 1936 to claim Harrison's job since south Mississippi now had the governorship and both Senate seats. In October the senator made the rounds of the autumn county fairs and shared the limelight with Bilbo in a mammoth Jackson parade that opened the state fair. Reminiscent of the New Deal inaugural carnival, Mississippians turned out on October 8 for a two-mile parade of bands and floats repledging the state's faith in the recovery program. Two weeks later, at Hattiesburg, the senior senator reaffirmed his own loyalty to the New Deal and railed at "the big financiers in New York" whose opposition to Roosevelt impeded recovery. He appeared already to have taken a page from Bilbo's book. [51]

In November, Harrison returned to Washington where he was joined by Bilbo who wanted to meet (and be met by) the president. "Both Franklin and Theodore survived the shock," Sullens cracked. Harrison went on to do a stint of campaigning in the congressional races against selected New England anti-New Deal Republicans. One of his targets, who lost his race, was Frederic C. Walcott of Connecticut, a member of the Finance Committee. The smashing Democratic victory, unprecedented for an off-year election performance, gave the Senate sixty-nine Democrats. Flushed by the victory, Harrison declared that the Roosevelt administration could move forward "with steady strides and assurance." [52]

After the election Harrison returned to Mississippi to continue his speaking engagements in advocacy of further New Deal attainments. He told a south Mississippi audience at Quitman that he had given assurances to the chief executive that, when the desired course of the new Congress had been determined, he stood ready as chairman of the Finance Committee to support the president "to the limit." Then the senator went to north Mississippi to greet the most distinguished New Dealer who ever visited the state. "The most powerful and best-beloved man in the world slept quietly on Mississippi soil last night," purred the Jackson *Daily News* on November 18. Roosevelt's

inspection of Tennessee Valley Authority facilities ended with a
two-day trip to Mississippi climaxed by a visit to Tupelo, the first
municipality to contract for TVA power. A crowd of 75,000 persons
heard the president praise the city as a "community of rugged individualism." He was impressed also by a subsistence homestead project just north of the town. As the president moved in and out of the
state his special train stopped at various depots where enthusiastic
crowds greeted him. After Roosevelt left the area, Harrison remained
to make more speeches. [53]

In late November Harrison joined the president for still another
conference, this time at Warm Springs, where a parade of governors,
White House advisers, and senatorial chieftains came and went over
a two-week period. Of the Senate visitors, Robinson, Barkley, and
the Mississippian appeared to be apprehensive of the increased government expenditures likely to be requested of the new Congress and
of concomitant tax demands. For Tugwell, who was also present, the
visit provided a "quite chummy" luncheon session, the first time that
the "old Democratic wheelhorses" talked with him intimately about
party matters. He could recall that earlier in the year he and Wallace
both had run afoul of Harrison when they had proposed to nationalize
the liquor industry. Harrison had absolutely blocked the move. [54] In
Harrison, Tugwell had "no faith at all" and "little enough" in Robinson, but in the latter he at least could see loyalty and a "glimmer of
understanding about the New Deal." Tugwell marveled at the way
the president handled the two senators. "They do what he says un-
aware of what he is driving at . . . and on the whole they behave." M.
L. Wilson later described the effect that Tugwell had upon Harrison.
"I think he kind of left Pat saying, 'Here's this smart good-looking boy
from Columbia University, but what the hell does he know . . . about
Mississippi? What the hell.' "[55]

By the end of 1934 Tugwell was not the only "smart boy" from an
eastern university who had gained access to the inner councils of the
Roosevelt administration. The young men, mostly Harvard-trained,
who entered government service under the aegis of their teacher,
Felix Frankfurter, would urge Roosevelt toward new directions in
1935. To FDR, who had joyously written in early 1934 that "We're
on our way," the fall election victories were a blanket approval of the
programs of the first two years. Just what the "way" would be in 1935

was open to speculation; not even Roosevelt knew. While there were those like Tugwell who questioned what lay upon Pat Harrison's heart concerning the whole New Deal, thus far his voting record, his public expressions, and extant private statements did not indicate that he was anti-New Deal. Whether or not there would be fresh directions and new directives to prick the senator's ideological conscience in the years ahead remained to be seen. As the senator himself might have put it, the next two years could well be a "whole new ball game."

CHAPTER V

Emerging Doubts

1935

LEGISLATION CAME SLOWLY from the first session of
the new Congress which convened in January, 1935, until Roosevelt
spurred his leaders into action and demanded passage of the program
that he had outlined in his January message as the condition upon
which Congress could adjourn. Thus it was not until the long hot
summer of 1935 that a "Second Hundred Days" produced the most
extensive reform measures that any Congress had ever enacted. For
Pat Harrison it meant a rigorous spring and summer of hearings and
cloakroom work. He became deeply involved in implementing the
president's request for social security legislation, a new tax bill, and
the extension of the National Recovery Administration; he was
equally busy in thwarting the passage of a soldier bonus measure.
And there were, of course, other issues that engaged his attention
peripherally, primarily the new relief program and a shift of emphasis
within the Agricultural Adjustment Administration.

By 1935 there was a simmering conflict between traditional Democratic party leaders, particularly the southern branch of the party,
and the new "Roosevelt coalition" of independent Democrats, progressive Republicans, urban workers, Negroes, and intellectuals. Related to this clash between what Arthur M. Schlesinger, Jr., calls the
"politics of organization" and the "politics of ideology" was a growing
awareness that the executive wing of government represented the
ideologists while the congressional branch housed the professional
politicians. In time a full-fledged donnybrook would be staged between the two branches of government, but for the enactment of the
president's new program it seemed to Rexford Tugwell that Roosevelt
would have to rely on that congressional group which was the nemesis
of the agricultural official. As much as Tugwell disliked to admit it,

82

the southern Democrats appeared to be the "only dependable body of men who can be counted on to stick by their bargains and pass legislation."[1] As for Harrison, bargaining and sticking were the marks of his trade.

On January 17, 1935, Roosevelt submitted to Congress his endorsement of the report of the Committee on Economic Security calling for old age annuities, unemployment insurance, and grants for maternity and children's services. He called for immediate legislative action. Given the honor of sponsoring the bill were Representative David J. Lewis of Maryland and Senator Robert Wagner of New York, who had been the authors of an unemployment insurance bill that had died from lack of presidential nourishment in the previous Congress. While there was some thought that the social security bill, as it came to be called, should be referred to a special committee or to the House Labor Committee, congressional leaders insisted that the measure should go to the Ways and Means Committee; in the Senate there was no opposition to its reference to Harrison and his committee.[2]

Harrison's work in securing the passage of the social security bill demonstrated once again the managerial ability of a senator who spent a decade in promoting legislation that was always the work of others. Apparently he was not impressed by conservative criticism that the bill infringed upon traditional concepts of self-help and rugged individualism; nor was he susceptible to homegrown fears, later articulated by his friend Fred Sullens, that "able-bodied Negroes [would] sit around in idleness on front galleries, supporting all their kinfolks on pensions, while cotton and corn crops are crying for workers to get them out of the grass."[3]

Harrison intended that economic security legislation "be expedited as the President has asked," and he held an extended conference with Edward F. McGrady, the assistant secretary of labor, to set up the machinery for Finance Committee hearings scheduled to begin simultaneously with the Ways and Means Committee hearings on January 22, a rare procedure followed at the request of the administration in order to hasten passage of the bill. While Edwin Witte, executive director of the Committee on Economic Security, schooled the representatives on the proposals, Senator Wagner appeared before the senators. He was followed by Secretary of Labor Frances Perkins and a battalion of social workers, actuarial experts, labor economists, and civitarians who had worked on an advisory study of economic security. The dialogue in the hearings revealed that certain senators were reluctant for the federal government to make intrusions into the social arenas which the bill encompassed. Clearly, Senator Harrison had his work cut out if he were to bring an unfettered social security program out of committee. [4]

Probably the best known witness to appear before the Finance Committee was the widely publicized Dr. Francis E. Townsend, whose own plan to end the poverty of the over-sixty age group consisted of monthly payments of $200 to be spent within thirty days at a monumental cost of $20 billion. On February 16 he faced a semicircle of hostile senators. Harrison refused to shake hands with Townsend for the benefit of photographers, angrily stating, "I don't want to advertise the Townsend plan." A week later the Mississippi senator, who knew of the widespread support enjoyed by the doctor, telephoned Morgenthau and asked that a Treasury Department expert appear before the Finance Committee on the " 'Old Man' Townsend stuff" and "just tear it to pieces." Morgenthau, who told Miss Perkins that his department was "not crazy about going up there on it," concluded that he would have to comply with Harrison's request: "He's a very difficult man to refuse because he's always been so friendly." Morgenthau realized that for use among constituency fans of the popular physician Harrison and his committee wanted the weight of the Treasury Department thrown against the Townsend scheme. "You can send somebody who can demolish it in ten minutes," Miss Perkins told Morgenthau. Consequently the secretary sent a treasury spokesman to the committee hearings. [5]

Few employer representatives appeared before the committee, partly because business did not yet understand the bill. One of the most influential of the businessmen who did appear was Marion B. Folsom, assistant treasurer of the Eastman Kodak Company and a member of the Advisory Committee on Economic Security. His favorable testimony was highly persuasive since he was able to make himself understood, which few of the government witnesses had been able to do. After Folsom's testimony Harrison invited him into his private office and explained that the committee members were busy on several other bills and that he himself had little time to study the social security program. "We've had these actuaries; we've had Miss Perkins; we've had Senator Wagner—this, that and the other," the chairman explained, and "either we're dumb or they can't express themselves. We don't know what the hell they're talking about." Because Folsom was the first person who could "talk a language" the committee could understand, Harrison asked for his recommendations on amendments and scribbled them down on his personal copy of the bill. The senator later wanted Folsom to attend the executive sessions in an advisory capacity but decided that it was best not to bring in outsiders. Frequent reference to his opinions, however, reflected Folsom's great influence on the legislative revision of the social security bill.[6]

On April 19, in a striking administration victory, the House passed the social security bill by a vote of 372 to 33. Edwin Witte, characterized by one of the drafters of the bill as "a walking encyclopedia on welfare and social insurance matters,"[7] worked closely with Harrison in the two weeks of the executive sessions of the Finance Committee. It was here that serious obstacles to the administration plan were anticipated, for several of the committeemen were known to be among the most conservative members of the Senate. To Harrison's "exceptionally able" management of the committee Witte attributed the eventual discharge of a favorable report. To counteract the May 6 Supreme Court invalidation of the Railroad Securities Act, Harrison had Justice Department representatives appear before his group to distinguish between the pension program of the doomed act and the fledgling bill. The chairman delayed the vote on the compulsory old age insurance title until after a speech by Witte; then when Harrison called for a vote, every senator considered doubtful voted in the affirmative. When the Mississippian was not certain how the vote would go on some motions, he postponed taking a count until later meetings, and on the most controversial items he put off a vote until he was confident of passage. On the crucial last day, when a number of key votes were taken, Harrison held James Couzens's proxy in his pocket and managed to win over the support of three senators who had been in the doubtful column. In short, according to Witte, "with a less adroit chairman, the social security bill would probably have emerged from the Senate committee in a very unsatisfactory form, if indeed a favorable report could have been secured."[8]

The Finance Committee made important changes in its overhaul of the House bill. It eliminated the requirement that state old age pensions provide a "reasonable subsistence compatible with decency and health," a stipulation which was obnoxious to those senators who saw within it the possibility of federal dictation of payment to racial minorities. In particular deference to Senator Harry F. Byrd the phrase was stricken. The committee, in order to reduce ultimate costs, also insisted that recipients of old age insurance be required to cease work, and it authorized the sale of voluntary annuity insurance to those persons not covered by compulsory old age provisions, a plan which had been eliminated by the House and was later rejected on the Senate floor. The senators also lodged the Social Security Board in the Department of Labor, although it had been designated an independent department by the Ways and Means Committee. The senators were no more kindly disposed toward turning the administration of social security over to Miss Perkins than was the House, but the president urged its placement in the Department of Labor. As Witte put it, Harrison "felt rather edgewise" toward the woman secretary. In addition the Finance Committee added a new title which called for annual allotments to states for aid to the permanently blind. [9]

Federal grants for maternal and child health services had created a furor within the American Medical Association, which adopted resolutions opposing the services and condemning government health insurance, a social service that was dismissed by the Committee on Economic Security as unfeasible. Persuaded during committee hearings by the arguments of Dr. Felix Underwood, chief health officer of Mississippi, for a federal health program, Harrison attempted to include a catastrophic illness provision within the social security bill. He gained no support, however, because the committee feared that such expanded services would be too expensive. [10]

Finally, on May 17, the committee reported out the social security bill without a record vote, but other legislation preceded it on the Senate calendar. As was the case when major administration bills were under his wing, Harrison made national radio broadcasts, speaking first on "Old Age Pensions" and a second night on "Unemployment Insurance." For the latter subject he spent a week fortifying himself with evidence that social security was not unconstitutional.

His theme in both broadcasts was that the programs were not emergency measures but rather enduring reforms that looked far into the future.[11]

It took five days for Harrison to get the social security bill through the Senate—a considerable length of time compared with that taken by most of the bills he handled. Anticipating criticisms before they could be offered, he asserted that the bill sought to alleviate hazards of economic insecurity by encouraging state action, that the Justice Department had deemed the program constitutional, and that no private pension plan was as favorable as the pension program of the Wagner-Lewis bill.[12] La Follette, Wagner, Barkley, and Costigan formed the "back-up team" for Harrison, but the persuasive comments of none of the five senators silenced Huey P. Long, who gave notice that he intended to lower the pension age from sixty-five to sixty and enlarge the benefits through his share-the-wealth plan. After a Democratic crackdown began, Harrison won an agreement to limit debate which thwarted a filibuster and Long's wealth-sharing plan was defeated without a roll call on June 17.

Bennett Clark, Missouri's maverick senator, protested Harrison's objections to an amendment exempting private pension plans from participating in the old age insurance program. Clark claimed that Harrison relied solely upon the advice of Murray Latimer, a native Mississippian who had become a prominent actuary and chairman of the Railroad Retirement Board. The Missourian was annoyed, too, that Harrison had arranged for Leonard Calhoun, another Mississippian who had become the majority expert of the Finance Committee on social security, for Thomas Eliot, who had drafted the original bill, and for Edwin Witte to sit near him on the floor to offer information when technical questions arose. Again Wagner and La Follette gave support to Harrison, but the Senate adopted the Clark amendment by a vote of 51 to 35 shortly before the entire bill passed by a vote of 76 to 6 on June 19.[13]

The designation of William H. King and Walter F. George as conference committee colleagues of Harrison alarmed advocates of the bill, for the two were opposed to the old age insurance title. Frances Perkins was especially concerned, because the Senate conferees were known to be wavering toward concessions to the House in its adamant stand that the Social Security Board be made an independent agency.[14] Her fears were justified, for the conference report removed the board from the Labor Department. The old age insurance title remained intact, while the Clark amendment was removed. In the final days before adjournment the House and Senate adopted the conference report, neither house resorting to a roll call. On August 14 President Roosevelt signed the bill into law before a group of more than thirty people who had worked to secure its passage. When Harrison returned to the Senate floor after the rites, he told his colleagues: "This will prove one of the most beneficial pieces of legislation enacted by this administration. I am happy to have had a part."[15]

Participants in the 1930s lawmaking process and some recent historians agree that, while the Social Security Act was one of the "most revolutionary pieces of social legislation ever enacted by Congress" (the words of participant-historian Wilbur J. Cohen), the measure had major shortcomings. The first title, providing for matching funds up to $15 a month for grants-in-aid to needy persons over sixty-five years of age, basically permitted the dollar amount of the monthly payments to be determined by the states. Stripped of stipulations for "reasonable health and decency," widely divergent and inadequate support resulted. By September, 1938, the old age assistance recipient in Mississippi received a monthly sum of $6.37; in California the amount was $32.39. The controversial and almost defeated Title II provided that those employees who were to be covered by the old age "retirement" insurance (and nearly one-half of the workers of the 1930s were not) must make compulsory contributions from their wages; on a matching basis employers were to be taxed on their payrolls. Both provisions were by nature deflationary. The recession of 1937–1938, which came right at the time that the first deductions were made, would partially be laid to social security taxation. Furthermore, in the third significant program instituted by the act, the basic responsibility for unemployment insurance was relegated to the states, resulting in unequal and inadequate payments made in the absence of national standards.[16]

Yet, when viewed from the perspective of the Senate Finance Committee chairman and the Senate chamber, the social security program, with its inherent weaknesses of limited coverage, stingy benefits, state standard-setting, and regressive taxation, was as much as could be gotten in 1935. Neither the legislative nor the executive

leadership was as naïve or purposely negligent as present-day critics
may imply. Morgenthau and his aides knew that the taxes would
divert income from consumption to savings, but the Treasury Department was committed to keeping a firm hand on the budget.
Morgenthau's devotion to economy was excelled only by conservative
senators who would have killed a more expensive program. Roosevelt
viewed the payroll contributions as a matter of political necessity.
"With those taxes in there, no damn politician can ever scrap my
social security program," he told Miss Perkins.[17]

A few contemporaries of Harrison, who were bitterly disappointed
by the limitations of the Social Security Act and preferred a vastly
enlarged federally financed social security program, tended to scoff at
his efforts. One of them, Abraham Epstein, a specialist in the social
insurance field, characterized both Harrison and Doughton as conservatives who "found the entire subject unfamiliar, irksome, and its
aims altogether contrary to their previous convictions." Such critics
were unfair to Harrison. Thomas Eliot, who more than anyone else
wrote the bill, agreed that the Mississippi senator was not warmly
committed to social welfare but he sensed that Harrison, as a loyal
administration senator, was determined to produce the most feasible
and respectable bill possible. Reminiscing two decades later about the
passage of social security, Eliot remembered the Mississippian as a
"keen, industrious, and determined" chairman with whom he and
Leonard Calhoun spent several summer evenings on Harrison's front
porch instructing the conscientious senator on "every detail of every
section" of the complicated and difficult bill.[18]

Pat Harrison, along with other southern congressmen, knew that
some states could contribute little toward assistance for the needy and
temporarily unemployed, but he told the Senate that his committee
had concluded that "in its present financial condition the Federal
Government is going as far as it can go." When he returned to Mississippi in the summer of 1935, he found that Governor Conner blamed
him for the fact that social security legislation called for state fund-
ing, compelling the governor to call the legislature into special session
to consider relief appropriations. Conner had urged the Mississippi
congressional delegation in January to recognize relief to the needy
aged as a national problem to be met entirely through federal taxation. To his constituents the senator again declared that Congress

would have never approved a plan by which the federal government assumed the full financial burden. [19]

Convinced by his budget director that he should present a works program to eliminate direct relief, Roosevelt told Congress in January, 1935, "The Federal Government must and shall quit this business of relief." To end the dole Congress was asked to appropriate the hefty sum of $4.8 billion for a substitute works relief program. [20] As a matter of fact, the federal government was in the relief business on a vast scale in Mississippi. While Washington in 1934 had allotted 72.3 percent of the relief funds dispensed nationwide, in Mississippi 98.1 percent had come from federal sources. The state legislature had refused in March, 1934, to comply with Conner's request for $1.5 million to supplement Federal Emergency Relief Administration funds for the more than 60,000 relief cases within the state. When Hopkins demanded in January of the new year that Mississippi put up the $1.5 million for direct relief of the unemployed by March 1 or lose federal funds, the state's relief recipients faced incalculable distress. Not only had some 14,000 Mississippi "unemployables" reached the point of destitution, but also many schools faced a late winter closing because of lack of funds. [21]

When Malcolm J. Miller, a field representative of the FERA, visited Mississippi in the fall of 1934, he reported that, while Harrison was in "full sympathy" with the relief program, the senator saw little reason why the rural relief load should remain so high. The crop year was good and cotton prices were 100 percent higher than in March, 1933. In late 1934 Harrison told the president, who was preparing his budget for 1935, that rehabilitation work would be less expensive and more desirable than direct relief. As for the South, and particularly Mississippi, the senator said, "I would much prefer to give a fellow a mule and a piece of land and loan him money for implements . . . than to give him direct relief." He was aware, too, of unfavorable public reaction to the latter approach. To his argument that work relief should replace direct relief, he added that an enlarged works program could endow the state with funds for better roads. Thus, the senator would agree with the 1935 decision of Hopkins and Roosevelt that an effort should be made to replace direct relief with some form of work relief. [22]

Harrison took no part in the debate that ran from January through

March, 1935, over an emergency relief appropriation bill reorienting relief towards a works program. Much of the time was consumed by a great deal of flak over Senator Pat McCarran's amendment to require that wages paid by government programs equal those prevailing in private construction programs. Supported by the American Federation of Labor as a protection against a breakdown in union wage scales, the prevailing wage stipulation was opposed by administration leaders, including Harrison, who argued that it would require half again as much as the $4.8 billion figure and also deter workers from entering private employment. Harrison voted against the "prevailing wage" in the two votes that killed the McCarran motion before the Senate passed the bill. His refusal to support organized labor's stand on the works relief wage scale would "come home to roost" at a later date. [23]

Harry Hopkins, who sincerely hoped to keep politics out of the new Works Progress Administration, which Roosevelt created by executive order in May, 1935, inherited a sticky political situation in Mississippi where Senators Harrison and Bilbo vied for patronage control with each other and with Governor Conner, whose political star was still thought to be ascending. Throughout the turbulent life of the WPA, Harrison tangled with Bilbo for the political affections of Hopkins, who attempted to remain neutral. When Hopkins carried Ellen Woodward, his FERA assistant, over into the new agency as director of women's work, her close personal friend and political ally, the senior senator, gained a strong vantage point, for she was in a position to know of Bilbo's political machinations with the WPA. The issue of WPA politics in Mississippi, however, was just beginning. More immediately, conferences with Hopkins over WPA funds for Mississippi and attention to the details of new project applications and job requests crowded the already busy days of the Finance Committee chairman during the closing weeks of the congressional session. For Mississippi the good relationship between Harrison and Hopkins had its rewards. Under the relief program from the beginning of 1933 until the end of 1935, the state allotment totaled $31,028,139, a figure that accounted for 96.2 percent of all funds spent for emergency relief in the state. [24]

In February, 1935, Interior Secretary Harold Ickes recorded in his diary that Roosevelt was consulting with only three senators—

Harrison, Robinson, and Byrnes—to the consternation of Key Pittman, the president *pro tempore* of the Senate. Certainly there was much for FDR to see Harrison about, including the contemplated extension of the National Recovery Administration, which was due to expire in June, 1935, unless given a new lease on life. That controversial agency was already under heavy fire. Disaffected businessmen, particularly representing medium and small-sized units, were by early 1935 outspoken in their hostility toward the NRA, and the U.S. Chamber of Commerce was adamantly opposed to the two-year extension. Numerous senators were already on record in opposition to the codes. When Long and Gerald Nye, as early as February of 1934, had called for an investigation of the NRA, Harrison had dismissed their efforts as "trifling away the time of the Senate." A year later, however, the "Blue Eagle" had to be told of its life expectancy.[25]

NRA opponents failed in an attempt to have the Senate refer an investigation of the NRA to the Commerce Committee rather than to the Finance Committee. Harrison indicated that he would do nothing about the study until the administration plan had taken a more concrete form. The fact that Senator Harrison was now lukewarm to the NRA and likely to be unenthusiastic over the proposed two-year renewal surfaced when he stated that the present law should be strengthened by "more definite standards" of legislative purpose and clearer directives for code administration.[26]

Sensitive to charges that Congress was merely a docile "rubber stamp," Roosevelt was reluctant to produce the extension bill which had been drafted by Donald Richberg, general counsel for the NRA, and his associates. Columnist Paul Mallon predicted that in due time "you will see Pat Harrison shake from his sleeve" a draft of the administration bill. While the Senate waited for that trick, it again battled over Nye's move to short-circuit the Finance Committee in his determination to have an "impartial" investigation of the NRA. Once again the Senate committed the study to the Finance Committee after Harrison had moved about the floor arguing points best suited to win reference of the NRA probe to his own committee. Krock of the New York *Times* observed that Harrison's achievements were "constructive and skillful" and indicative of the fact that FDR "might have less trouble in Congress if he left more to his party leaders and less to his administration associates."[27]

With no bill yet on hand, the Finance Committee began its public hearings. For six weeks a stream of witnesses appeared and gave depositions that made clear only the fact that small businessmen were divided over charges that the code authorities had stacked the NRA deck in favor of large corporations. When Richberg offered to bring in "whole battalions" of businessmen to speak for the agency, chairman Harrison sardonically replied, "I certainly have no wish to hear from any battalion." Rumor had it that the bill finally produced by him on March 29 had been carried about in his pocket for several days after Roosevelt's departure for a short vacation and was flushed out by Richberg's testimony before a closed committee session that Senate dilatoriness was hampering code enforcements. [28]

Senate hearings ended on April 18 with conflicting statements symbolic of the whole six weeks of testimonials. General Hugh Johnson's loyal arguments defending the NRA were practically extinguished when a damaging report of a Brookings Institution study was handed around at the close of the hearings. The result of the first independent report made on the NRA since its beginnings, the study purported to show that the recovery administration had substantially retarded recovery. Richberg was furious that Harrison had requested advance proofs of the report and inserted some of it into the record of the hearings. On the other hand, Senator King was delighted. According to Mallon the Utah senator hated the NRA "even in his sleep." Moreover, Clarence Darrow's critique, biased and limited as it was, denounced the evils wrought upon the "small fellow." His testimony stirred the old Wilsonians on the committee. One of them, Bailey, vouched that "the country is after all supported by the small producers and the small merchants. I could not conceive of a civilization in which they were not properly looked after." [29]

Harrison had concluded that the only feasible move was to extend the NRA for a period of ten months. Robinson concurred, but Roosevelt made clear his displeasure with a short-term extension at a White House conference on April 30. His remarks were so pointed to Harrison and Robinson that one witness reported that they "turned blood red from neck to ears." The meeting, attended as well by McCarran, Clark, Borah, and Richberg among others, ended in confusion and deadlock. When Roosevelt appeared to be converted to a temporary extension, Richberg and Miss Perkins intervened. At the session's end Harrison told reporters, "You can put this down, NRA is going to be extended," to which Borah added, "never in its present form." McCarran provided the press with the only uncontested summary of the meeting: "We agreed to disagree."[30]

Unwilling to approve a two-year extension, the Finance Committee in two polls (16 to 3 and 13 to 4) voted to stretch the life span of the NRA by only eleven months—until April, 1936. At the same time it clipped the Blue Eagle of its price-fixing and intrastate commerce claws. Richberg, afraid that the move would be interpreted as one approved by the president, was dismayed at the committee's action. The break between Senate administration leaders and FDR over the NRA became public when Harrison reported the extension resolution to the full Senate "as the best way out of a difficult situation." He continued, "For my part I believe in the NRA," but he warned that a fight for the full two years would be protracted and such a measure would be unobtainable by the June 16 expiration date of the NRA. Should the House and NRA partisans press for the two years, "they may be in the position of killing the goose that laid the golden egg, and the blame may be on those who are the best friends of the NRA for killing it in the end." Harrison recommended that the Senate "ride along" with the temporary extension until the Supreme Court ruled on the original act.[31]

After only two hours of discussion and with only thirty senators present, the Senate adopted without a roll call the short-term extension. The president "knows what we are doing," Harrison assured his colleagues. The Supreme Court's 5 to 4 invalidation of the NRA on May 27 left the House with nothing to do but hold a requiem service on its own two-year extension plan. While opponents of the NRA were jubilant over the Court's decision, Robinson and Harrison insisted that the damage was not irreparable to the interstate character of the NRA. The latter admitted that "the NRA is limping, but I don't think the action of the Court can forestall us in taking remedial action." From King came a "Thank God for the Supreme Court." He hoped that the codes were knocked out "for all time." Michigan's Republican Congressman Roy Woodruff chuckled, "The Government didn't have a chicken leg to stand on."[32]

The press reported much visitation at the White House during the week following the decision, as Hugh Johnson and Felix Frankfurter entered at the back door while Harrison and congressional leaders came in at the front. The latter group adopted a wait-and-see position in the hope that public opinion on the Court's ruling might clear the air. Harrison ruled out the possibility of a constitutional amendment to sanction the authority of the NRA; and, following an extended session on June 4 with congressional leaders, Roosevelt surprised the press by announcing that he would accede to the Senate resolution. He hoped that piecemeal legislation would restore certain protective features of the NRA and thus the Congress would circumvent the Supreme Court. Harrison agreed that such a tact was feasible and endorsed particularly the president's plan to grant government contracts only to firms maintaining NRA standards. [33]

With FDR's position finally settled, the House produced a bill to extend to the following April an NRA that could comply with the Supreme Court decision. Meanwhile, opposition in the Senate marshaled by Borah, King, Clark, and Nye pressured Harrison's committee to place limitations upon presidential powers to suspend antitrust laws for voluntary adherents to NRA principles. The Mississippi senator thought that the limitations were meaningless, but, as the ace "horse trader" of the Senate, he knew that concessions must be made to any group led by the formidable Borah. The Mississippi and Idaho senators conferred to smooth out an acceptable path for the Senate's own stopgap resolution. As it stood, the voluntary compliance system remained the heart of the extended NRA in the hope that the old features—collective bargaining, minimum wages and maximum hours, and prohibitions on child labor, unfair trade practices, and price-fixing—could live on. Finally at sunrise on June 12 the Senate extended the NRA by a vote of 41 to 13. The next day the House accepted the Senate's skeletonized NRA after only forty minutes of listless debate, and the president added his signature that afternoon. [34]

If Pat Harrison could be taken at his own public word on the NRA, the record would stand that he favored its continuation in an amended form. He was genuinely alarmed about NRA strictures upon intrastate commerce and he undoubtedly had absorbed some of the animosity toward the agency of the small businessmen, who conducted most of the commercial enterprises in Mississippi, as well as the hostility of certain of his close friends and golfing companions who ran some of the nation's largest firms. In the final analysis, however, his position against the Richberg-Roosevelt plan for a two-year extension was dictated by his "horse trading sense," as *Fortune* magazine phrased it. The journal reported in 1935 that Harrison "strides about the Chamber, looks, grins, listens, trades, and returns to the cloakroom with a better idea of what is about to happen than any man on the floor."[35] On the basis of that second sense Harrison claimed that half a loaf was all Roosevelt could have gotten on the NRA.

Contemporaries, who criticized Harrison for habitually compromising the New Deal, believed that he had all but chloroformed the NRA. Hugh Johnson claimed that the Finance Committee hearings were stacked against the National Recovery Administration and that the defenders were not permitted to puncture the "contradictory nonsense" poured into the record. In addition he mourned that nobody on the committee knew enough about the NRA to defend it, much less prepare the bill. The director of NRA litigation, Alexander G. McKnight, declared that neither Harrison nor Robinson "internally" supported the NRA, and Felix Frankfurter was as convinced as Richberg that Harrison had dallied on the extension. Max Freedman, who edited the Frankfurter-Roosevelt correspondence, concluded that the Finance Committee chairman "had played a shuffling and equivocal role in the passage of the rump NIRA." But, if Harrison was not wildly enthusiastic about the way the NRA had worked out in the two years of its operation, neither was Roosevelt, who confided to Frances Perkins, "It has been an awful headache. . . .I think perhaps NRA has done all it can do."[36] All along Harrison had suspected the president's lukewarmness toward the NRA and sensed that he was capable of driving his congressional leaders into legislative battles that he himself preferred to shun.

With the NRA virtually dead, Roosevelt insisted that certain of its desirable features be salvaged through a series of lesser laws, often referred to as the "little NIRAs." The records do not reveal any opinions of Senator Harrison concerning the legislation to fill the NRA vacuum that Congress sent to the White House during 1935 and 1936. He made no statement on the Senate floor on the Guffey-Snyder bill (August, 1935), which sanctioned the bituminous coal code, although he voted for the bill. He did not speak on the Connally Act (January, 1935) to ban interstate shipments of "hot oil," the Walsh-Healy Bill (June, 1936) to grant workers on government con tracted projects the protections of NRA labor standards, or the Robinson-Patman bill (June, 1936) to prohibit preferential discounts for chain store buyers in order to protect small, individually owned firms. Because the latter three measures passed without a roll call, no record is available on Harrison's position.

In the post-NRA period the most significant efforts to stabilize industrial relations were Wagner's bill to solidify labor's right of collective bargaining. In 1934, when Wagner had first introduced his bill, Miss Perkins was ambivalent, Roosevelt gave little support, and his administration adjutants, Robinson and Harrison, were cool to the measure. After withdrawing the 1934 bill, Wagner introduced a stronger measure soon after the start of the 1935 session. Again administration backing was weak. Robinson and Harrison hoped to delay consideration until adjournment could kill the measure. The two Senate leaders, seeking to obtain Roosevelt's approval that the bill should lie over, argued that if it were brought to a vote, it might not pass, thus embarrassing the Democratic party.[37]

Wagner was not to be hoodwinked by such an argument, and he persuaded the president not to stand in the way of letting him have his vote. Wagner's assessment of what the Senate would do in the face of the labor vote was borne out on May 16 by the 63 to 12 passage of the measure. Both Harrison and Robinson joined the large number of Democrats who voted for the Wagner labor relations bill, although they remained silent opponents. Probably a majority of the Southerners in Congress who attended a Southern States Industrial Council dinner on April 29 agreed with regional industrial leaders who maintained that the Wagner bill threatened the South with industrial strife and that the Guffey coal bill would paralyze the southern coal industry. That the public record carries nothing of Harrison's opposition is probably due to a great reluctance to oppose labor publicly. Labor lawyers who worked with the National Labor Relations Board could later recall no statements made by Harrison, and one of them, Charles E. Wyzanski, Jr., has suggested that the Mississippi senator would likely not have trusted the "discretion" of labor officials enough to have talked with them.[38] Certainly, Harrison's vote did not mean that he had undergone a philosophical conversion. He was simply as politically tuned to 1936 as were FDR and a majority of Congress.

If Harrison and Robinson were ineffective in derailing the Wagner bill, they met with greater success in the small role they played in the "housecleaning" that swept a group of liberals from the Agricultural Adjustment Administration in early February, 1935. For some time the legal division directed by the idealistic Jerome Frank had been at loggerheads with AAA head George Peek, Harrison's old friend, and Cully A. Cobb, a pioneer in Mississippi agricultural education and extension work who had become director of the AAA's Cotton Division. In the first round of controversies Frank got the best of Peek, and the latter was eased out of office, a move which angered Harrison in view of his low estimation of Frank's chief backer, Rexford Tugwell. In early 1935, Frank's dictation to Cobb's division that the interpretation of cotton contracts was a question to be handled by the legal division precipitated dissension within the AAA over the retention of tenants under new agreements. On the weekend of February 2, 1935, when word went out to extension directors in three southern states that the controversial paragraph had been interpreted to mean that landowners must retain the same tenants rather than the same number of tenants, a group of powerful southern congressmen moved into action.

Of the AAA officials, Tugwell, Cobb, and Chester Davis, who had replaced Peek, were all out of town. Acting in Cobb's absence, his assistant, Wofford B. Camp, invited a congressional group—among them Senators Harrison, Smith, and Robinson and Congressmen William J. Driver of Arkansas and Hampton P. Fulmer of South Carolina—to meet in Cobb's office. The congressional contingent heard the arguments of the Cotton Division that the new contract interpretation would spell the end of the cotton program. The group was already aware of the difficulties which Robinson's Arkansas Delta planter constituents were having with the Southern Tenant Farmers' Union. (The union had made little headway in Mississippi.) Knowing that the tenants were supported by the AAA liberals and fearing that the agency's legal division had plans to alter southern agricultural patterns radically, the Southerners who met with Camp agreed that the Frank "crowd" should be given the axe. They intended to see Roosevelt on the next day and inform him that, if the group under Frank remained in office, no significant piece of legislation would ever get through Congress again. Within days the "purge" had come about and Frank's lawyers were out of office. [39]

Pat Harrison's role in the matter is not certain, but it can be conjectured that he was as hotly defensive of Cobb's position in 1935 as he was in his action to protect one of his own appointees dismissed from the Bituminous Coal Commission in 1938. At that time he telephoned the proper authority and demanded that the man be returned to his job by midafternoon or he would go on the Senate floor and "offer a bill abolishing your damned commission and firing everybody connected therewith." He punctuated his order with a "I don't mean maybe either." By 2 p.m. the jobholder from Mississippi was back at work.[40] Ordinarily slow to anger, Harrison was known on a few occasions to go into a fury when he detected high-handed tactics on the part of the resident intellectual community which served as movers and shakers in some of the New Deal agencies.

In June, 1935, the Wheeler-Rayburn bill to reduce the power of public utility holding companies ran the Senate gauntlet. The linchpin of the bill, the so-called "death sentence," empowered the Securities and Exchange Commission to dissolve recalcitrant utility companies that refused compliance. When Illinois Senator William H. Dieterich offered an amendment which would have blunted the main thrust of the bill, a number of previously loyal Democrats, including Byrnes, left the administration fold to support the Illinoisan. James T. Patterson has determined that the vote on the Dieterich amendment was "one of the most significant of the New Deal years" as a test of party and presidential loyalty. Thus it is all the more worthy of note that Harrison was not one of the twenty-nine Democrats who supported the amendment that lost by a 44 to 45 count. At final passage he voted for the bill.[41]

In 1935 that hardy perennial, the soldier bonus, came to full bloom; to the administration it was a tare nurtured by the congressional inflationists and a powerful special interests lobby. In January the Texas Democrat Wright Patman introduced his bill to pay the veterans through a $2 billion cash outlay the payments due them in 1945 under the terms of the Adjusted Compensation Act of 1924. Harrison immediately conferred with Roosevelt, who knew that both houses were anxious to get some kind of bonus bill out of the way before the issue could become a political snare in 1936. Following successive White House meetings, the senator continued to reiterate the point that FDR would veto any immediate cash payment plan.

Nonetheless, in late March the House discarded alternatives to the Patman plan and passed the Texan's proposal by a weighty 318 to 90 vote, handing the issue over to Harrison who now had to face the Senate inflationist bloc. It was generally expected that some compromise would be forthcoming now that the chief Senate trader and his committee held the reins. "I have half a dozen compromise bills in my pocket," he told reporters on March 22.[42]

Convinced that Roosevelt would accept whatever compromise plan the Senate proposed, Harrison on April 11 introduced a proposal drafted by Frank T. Hines of the Veterans' Bureau that would set the maturity date for the adjusted certificates at 1938 rather than 1945 and issue negotiable federal bonds to veterans who desired immediate cash. The estimated ultimate cost was put at $1.3 billion with an immediate cash outlay of about $88 million. Actually, the Senate was hard pressed to find time to consider any bonus plan, since an array of other legislation was still in the mill, all of it threatened by a filibuster over an antilynching bill. In a sense Harrison held the key to the legislative situation. With the NRA and social security bills blocked by bonus legislation in his committee, he was anxious to move the veterans issue on and out of the way.[43]

There was still no word from the White House on the Harrison compromise; in fact, rumors existed that the president had not even read it. Anxious to shelve the antilynching bill, a subject far less popular among Southerners than the bonus, Harrison rushed his bill with its 12 to 8 committee sanction to the floor. When debate began, Senator Elmer Thomas charged that Harrison would repudiate a billion dollar debt that Congress "had acknowledged is due to the soldiers of the Nation." The pragmatic Harrison pointed out that other pension plans would "get nowhere for practical purposes" and his own was the only one that could ever win a presidential signature. Although administration senators supported him, Harrison knew from futile telephone calls that his plan would go down in defeat, as it did on May 7 when the Senate opted for the Patman plan. The inveterate vote-counter from Mississippi predicted a veto and boasted of thirty-five certain sustaining votes.[44]

The deluge of telegrams that rained upon the senators and the White House, 250 descending upon the latter by the hour, over the weekend following the Senate vote attested to the political potency of the bonus. Huey Long aptly phrased the dilemma of FDR and the thirty senators who faced reelection in 1936: "If he commits suicide [by veto] he'll be an ex-President. Even an ex-President is something, but an ex-Senator ain't nothing." Harrison's candidacy for an ex-senatorship was in the making according to the Mississippi press. The state's veterans (there were 37,218 on the rolls) joined the White House telegraphic bombardment; Raymond Clapper, a Washington columnist, estimated that $33.5 million was at stake for Mississippi veterans alone. Louis Jiggitts, one of Harrison's political pulse-takers, had written Roosevelt in late 1934 that Mississippi's ex-warriors wanted the bonus paid and that it would be politically expedient for Harrison to support payment. According to Jiggitts, Bilbo had been elected by taking the soldier vote from Stephens, who had consistently opposed bonus legislation. [45]

The expected outcome on the bonus bill materialized on May 22 when Roosevelt broke all precedents in personally delivering a veto message to a combined House and Senate in an atmosphere so tense that Mrs. Roosevelt, who was seated in the gallery, never even took her knitting out of the bag. Staking his veto primarily on the inflationary aspects of the bonus, the president called for congressional support. He had not gotten back to the White House before the House overrode the veto by a resounding vote of 322 to 98. Meanwhile Harrison assisted presidential adviser Charles West and Postmaster General Farley in some hectic cloakroom work among the senators whose economic theories, social consciences, and political savvy were all in the crucible. The American Legion had already classified twelve senators, including Harrison, Robinson, Connally, and Wagner, as "hopeless;" others, including Bilbo, were expected to rebuke FDR. When Harrison took his turn during the five-hour Senate debate over the veto message, he made it clear that his vote to sustain FDR would not mean that he would concede to anyone "the right to argue that [he was] less interested in the welfare of the ex-serviceman than any other American citizen." Whatever effect his remarks may have had could have been lessened considerably by the incorrigible Long, who strolled in late and stood in the center aisle chewing caramels, which he so generously handed about that a number of senators were conspicuously smacking the candies as Harrison concluded his speech. [46]

The Senate sustained the veto by a margin of nine votes. Bilbo and

Harrison were on opposite sides of the count, and Harrison had his qualms about what the veterans would do to him in 1936. His compromise position all along had been dictated, he said, by the practical aspects of going down the way for the only kind of bonus that the Senate would accept. A Senate poll in early June, 1935, showed that nothing could have been passed over a veto except a bill on the order of Harrison's. The political breezes from Mississippi in October carried the news that the state's house of representatives had memorialized Congress to pass a cash bonus bill at the next session. By December, when Harrison returned from Christmas at home, he was beginning to adopt the old argument of the previous session: "I hope we will be able to work out something on the bonus that will put this question behind us . . . and the sooner the better."[47]

On the first day of the new session, House bonus advocates united on a full cash bonus plan and within a week sent it over to the Senate by a 356 to 59 vote. There full cash advocates presented a bill to pay the veterans approximately 98 percent of their demands. Harrison, carefully stating that the president should not be quoted as either favoring or rejecting the plan, introduced it into the Senate on January 13, 1936, and the Finance Committee reported it for floor debate by a vote of 18 to 0, after substituting a Harrison-Clark scheme to pay the certificates in "baby bonds" issued in denominations of $50 and $100. Finance Committee members Harrison, Gore, Costigan, and Couzens all faced their electorates that year. Majority leader Joe Robinson, also up before the same bar of judgment, had fallen in behind the new bonus plan, which Harrison insisted would call for no new taxes.[48] His colleagues were not surprised when Harrison explained his sudden conversion to a bonus payment. The Patman bill had been inflationary, he said, while the new proposal would not be for the simple reason that the bonds would not all be cashed immediately. "The good wife will use her good offices to hold back for a rainy day" many of the $50 bonds, he predicted in the homey style that marked most of his discourses. Contrary to his warnings in 1935 of a veto, he now assured the Senate that the measure would become law whether or not FDR signed it. Three days later the Senate sent the Harrison-Clark bonus bill to a certain White House veto by a vote of 75 to 16. The runaway vote showed that the senators were as anxious to get right with the soldier vote in paying off the bonus in

1936 as they had been in passing it in election year 1924 and liberalizing it in election year 1932.[49]

Bonus history repeated itself on several counts during that January of 1936. Roosevelt sent a laconic 206-word veto message, and, for the first time since the days of Roosevelt I, the message went in a president's own handwriting. Again, it took the House only forty-five minutes to turn the veto aside. On January 27 every senator answered the roll call (Garner could not remember such before in his tenure as vice-president) for the veto countdown, which went 76 to 19 against Roosevelt. Of the nineteen presidential sustainers, fifteen were not facing reelection that year. It was notable that the pair from Mississippi and Arkansas for the first time had voted against their chieftain. In a postmortem on the session one writer concluded that "the President dropped the reins and every man scrambled to political shelter as he thought best."[50] There can be no doubt that political expediency led Pat Harrison to line the pockets of the Mississippi veterans before he asked for their votes.

Contemporary commentators who attempted to assess the New Deal sympathies of the senators serving in the Seventy-fourth Congress disagreed on just where Harrison stood. In May, 1935, Paul Mallon wrote that the reservations Harrison held during the first two years on the New Deal had largely disappeared and that Roosevelt had come to the conclusion that the Mississippian had done an excellent job. The Cassandra of the New York *Herald Tribune*, Mark Sullivan, disagreed, for he was certain that three out of five congressional Democrats inwardly were strong dissenters to the New Deal and only by taking a "count of personal prudence" to election year 1936 did the Harrisons and Robinsons swallow their distaste for the support they were offering the president. And Raymond Clapper concurred. To him both Harrison and Robinson were "cool at heart" to many administration measures, and by the end of 1935 both appeared to be "as unhappy as a man wearing flannel underwear in August."[51]

The difficulty in determining what Harrison really thought is that the public record is not helpful and private communications are inextant. If his voting record is an index to his position, then that record reveals only the one dissenting vote, on the bonus, which was not a true test. Assessing his support of the chief executive would be an easier thing to do if it were entirely clear just where Roosevelt stood on such key legislation as the Wagner Act or the extension of the NRA. Harrison's support pretty well reflected the twists and turns of White House leadership. Critics then and now who characterize Harrison as an administration dissenter would have a better case should they examine some of his equivocal statements while certain legislation was in an initiatory stage and should they raise questions about what really transpired in his relations with other senators, particularly his committeemen, who were parties in his efforts to water down or redirect administration measures. The trouble, however, is that the answers are not likely to be found.

The crux of the matter is whether Harrison worked at successive compromises because he genuinely believed that "half a loaf" was better than no loaf or whether he capitalized upon his great personal popularity and talents at trading as a means of weakening legislation with which he may not have agreed. The solution to the puzzle may become somewhat clearer when his role in the passage of the taxation measures of 1935 and 1936 is examined.

CHAPTER VI

"I Don't Want to be Caught Coming And Going"

1935–36

THE SCRIBES WHO BEGAN to hint in 1935 that Pat Harrison was becoming dissatisfied with the New Deal found some basis for their opinions as they followed the debate on the taxation of wealth. More and more there was talk that federal taxation could be used for social as well as revenue purposes. Congressional discussion in the late winter over the repeal of the publicity feature of the 1934 revenue act provided an opportunity for senators to air their views on the subject of wealth taxation, a topic that would be rekindled during the warmer days of June. The conflict between President Roosevelt and Senator Harrison over the general revenue measure of 1935 was the first clear case of a basic difference over a New Deal program. Never really solved to the satisfaction of either man, the dissonance continued into 1936, when once again the president asked that taxation be used to curb the economic power of the wealthy.

In the early summer of 1935 Harrison thought that the Finance Committee had discharged the principal duties assigned to it for the first session of the Seventy-fourth Congress. Doubtless he must have felt some measure of satisfaction over the passage or anticipated completion of the legislation that had come and gone in a steady stream from his committee room. He could have little reason to suspect that very soon and very abruptly an issue would emerge which would test his loyalty as an administration leader, his faith in Franklin D. Roosevelt's innate fairness, and his basic belief that the New Deal was headed in the right direction. The unexpected dispute would arise over a subject zealously guarded by the senator as his own field of expertise—tax bills and their intended purpose. Just as he had always essentially been a tariff-for-revenue-only man, recognizing only a modicum of the principle of protection, Harrison consistently maintained that revenue bills should raise revenue. That taxation should be used as an instrument for economic and social reform was an idea alien to the senator. As already noted, he had been cool to the attempts of both Huey Long and Robert La Follette to redistribute wealth through taxation in 1934. Although the act that was finally approved in 1934 did attempt to equalize tax burdens by compelling the wealthy to pay a larger portion of income in taxes and to establish a more ethical system of taxation, it did not "soak the rich" or redistribute wealth. Nor, for that matter, did it raise adequate revenue to match soaring government costs. [1]

In February, 1935, Long Island's "blue-blooded" representative, Robert Low Bacon, initiated a move to rescue the nation's taxpayers from the embarrassment of the so-called "pink slips," which were to be attached to the March 15 returns. Under the terms of the publicity feature affixed to the 1934 act at the behest of La Follette's progressive flock, each full return was to be accompanied by a short summary of the taxpayer's income, deductions, tax credits, and the payable tax. Although the information was to be open only to public officials at the national and state levels, there was little guarantee against its becoming public knowledge. As a thrust against tax evasion, the "pink slip" law had had the support of the progressives and "country Democrats" but it had aroused protests from many taxpayers who resented an invasion of privacy and congressmen who shared New York Senator Royal Copeland's conviction that the law "makes Uncle Sam 'finger man' for bandits, kidnappers, and crooks." The anti-pink slip campaigners sent more mail to Washington than had the Townsendites. Dismissed at first as a display of Republican bad grace, the movement soon gained the support of a majority of the House of Representatives who repealed the law by a vote of 302 to 98 after a three-hour shouting match. Except for Whittington, the Mississippi congressmen voted for repeal. [2]

Harrison personally opposed repeal because the experiment had not even had a year's testing, but he sought from Morgenthau the Treasury Department's stand. He told the secretary in late February, 1935, that the Finance Committee had received a lot of "propaganda . . . to repeal this publicity stuff," but Morgenthau gave no help. "The Treasury [is] down here to carry out orders of Congress, see. . . .We're going to stay strictly neutral," the cabinet officer responded. When the chairman brought the subject before his committee, he found the division that he expected. On the one hand, Bailey favored repeal, but La Follette wanted an even stiffer disclosure of returns. The odds were with Bailey, for polls indicated that a majority of the senators opposed the pink slips.[3] A favorable report on repeal came out of the committee in early March after only fifteen minutes of deliberation and without a record vote. The Senate spent little more than three hours debating the report and then lifted the pink slips by a vote of 53 to 16. Only ten Democrats stood by the publicity feature, Bilbo included. Harrison, in the end, went along with the majority position. True to expectations, La Follette attempted to amend the repeal with his standing proposals to raise the normal income tax, lower the standard exemptions, and increase the surtax, but the Senate sustained Harrison's point of order that revenue measures must originate in the House and that the Senate could not initiate tax revision.[4]

Harrison knew of the undercurrent of talk regarding general tax revision, but he did not anticipate that Roosevelt would jeopardize his other legislative requests by submitting a tax program to the already agitated and restive Congress. The senator could recall that in late 1934 Roosevelt had said that he would ask for no new taxes. He knew, too, that Morgenthau had determined that the primary interest of the treasury should be revenue. The treasury secretary, however, had become concerned about the growing problems of depression and the mushrooming costs of relief.[5] In December, 1934, Morgenthau carried to his chief a tax plan that contained a graduated inheritance tax and an increase in gift taxes, an intercorporate dividend tax aimed at breaking up holding companies, and a tax on corporate earnings not distributed as profits to stockholders.[6] The plan reflected the thinking of Felix Frankfurter and Herman O. Oliphant, the general counsel in the Treasury Department. The two were apostles of Louis D. Brandeis and true believers that taxation could and should be used to break up concentrations of wealth and industrial power. Roosevelt rejected the plan, and in his January, 1935, budget message declared that there was no need for new tax legislation. He told the press, "I have not yet got to the point where I am going to say anything on taxes."[7]

In May, Morgenthau renewed his efforts to have the president

consider the treasury proposals, but Roosevelt was buffeted by advice
from Raymond Moley, former "chairman" of the Brain Trust, against
any new tax scheme embodying "dubious social reform." A concate-
nation of events between February and June changed the president's
mind. Intemperate attacks from the right continued, a series of Supreme Court decisions against the New Deal culminated in the invalidation of the NRA, and, perhaps the most galling of all, the
"Share-the-Wealth" movement of Huey Long stung Roosevelt. In
mid-June the chief executive turned to Oliphant's detailed draft of a
"soak-the-rich" plan and told Moley that he intended to send a message to Congress, "blithely" adding, "Pat Harrison's going to be so
surprised he'll have kittens on the spot." Moley was shocked, for to
him the message "signalized the adoption of a policy of reform *through*
taxation" and a departure from "the principles of taxation for revenue
and reform in taxation."[8] Moley's distaste for reform taxation was
shared by majority leader Robinson and Harrison, his legislative
lieutenant and alter ego on most matters.

When Harrison attempted to see Morgenthau to discuss taxation,
the secretary turned him away with the suggestion that it was
Roosevelt whom he should see about taxes because any new program
was "entirely in the hands of the President." Then, on June 19,
Roosevelt telephoned Morgenthau that he had seen both Harrison
and Doughton and promised the former that he would delay the tax
message until he could get the social security bill through the Senate.[9] While there is no evidence that either Harrison or Doughton
knew the contents of the tax message that afternoon of June 19, there
were many signs that Congress was not prepared for the message
when it came.[10] Senatorial eyebrows lifted as the clerk intoned that
"our revenue laws have operated in many ways to the unfair advantage of the few, and they have done little to prevent an unjust concentration of wealth and economic power." Silence prevailed except for
Long, who swaggered and waltzed along the aisles and provided the
only floor comment, "I just want to say 'amen.'"[11] Over in the
House, however, cheers followed the mention of a redistribution of
wealth. Harrison's immediate position was that there was "a great
deal of merit" to the graduated corporation taxes which the president
proposed, but he warned that taxes "should not be so heavy as to
destroy estates or wipe out incomes." Senate leaders were inclined to

wait for House action, mindful that revenue measures must originate there. Harrison, ever consistent in his deference to this special function of the House, told reporters that "no doubt the Ways and Means Committee will decide whether to begin now or to undertake a study looking to consideration at the next session."[12]

Philosophically many congressmen were not prepared to accept Roosevelt's tax requests; nor were they physically amenable to sitting through a long, hot Washington summer haggling over taxes—in addition to the added embroilments of a social security conference report, the utilities holding company bill, and the Guffey coal bill. All hope of adjournment by mid-July seemed to have been dashed unless the tax proposals could be hastily tacked onto the routine extension of the so-called "nuisance taxes" that were to expire on June 30.[13] Did the president intend that his Senate leaders attach his new tax program to the nuisance tax resolution? Was the tax message "more or less a campaign document laying down the principles as to where he stands," as Morgenthau thought, or did FDR intend only to suggest a proposal for a tax study over the summer recess, as Harrison believed?[14] Differences over the matters became a cause célèbre in the Roosevelt-Harrison relationship.

On the day after the tax message was read, the Finance Committee extended the nuisance taxes by one year after the chairman convinced the committee that the president did not want his new tax program tied to the extension resolution, thereby jeopardizing its passage. La Follette, who had charged in an April radio address that the administration had failed to meet the issue of taxation, now announced his intention of attaching the presidential tax program to the resolution when it reached the floor along with his own tax plan for raising additional revenue by reducing tax exemptions on lower and middle income brackets. Rallied by La Follette, twenty-one other senators signed a round robin by which they pledged to stay in session until the president's program was passed.[15] Prodded by this progressive ploy and by noisy demands from Long that he fish or cut bait, Roosevelt was forced to take a stand.

Congressional leaders were divided. Senator Robinson and Joseph W. Byrns, speaker of the House, favored action during the current session. Charles McNary, Republican minority leader, agreed with Harrison that action should await a broad study. Nonetheless, upon leaving a White House conference on June 24, Robinson and Harrison told reporters that Congress would press for immediate action and that Harrison would ask the Finance Committee to add the program to the excise tax resolution pending in the Senate. Newspapermen noted that Harrison remained silent at Robinson's statement that "we should get the matter behind us as soon as possible." Members of the press corps surmised that the Mississippian was particularly unhappy about the whole matter; he was reputed to be embarrassed over an obligation to support a proposal with which he did not agree in order to bolster a president with whom he could not afford to break the year before they both faced reelection. Furthermore, Harrison was fearful that a tax bill would reopen the bonus question, embarrass individual senators, and complicate the passage of other legislation.[16]

The announcement that a new tax program was to be adopted by the Senate as a rider to a measure already passed by the House and enacted in only six days precipitated a journalistic storm. Walter Lippmann, Roosevelt's favorite columnist, described the president's "utterly undemocratic and disorderly methods" as "nothing less than a flagrant abuse of power." To Lippmann the tax program was a reversal of the underlying philosophy of the NRA, and the "indecent haste" of a six-day measure was a capitulation to Long and La Follette. Meanwhile, Harrison, indicating that there would be no time for hearings other than "very brief" statements on the inheritance levies, had gone to work with treasury experts to provide tax schedules embodying the Roosevelt plan. Immediately after the White House conference, Harrison had gone to the Finance Committee room, summoned tax experts, and worked through the night; the next night they worked again until 4 A.M. Explaining to the Senate that "there have been some developments" after his committee had voted not to consider any new taxes, the Mississippian insisted that the extension be granted by June 30 or the treasury would lose $1.5 million a day. When McNary argued against haste, Harrison admitted that he concurred but "others" had vetoed a delay.[17]

The next day Harrison was forced into an about-face. At the president's weekly press conference with about one hundred newspapermen, many of them representing journals critical of FDR's haste and nearly half of them having reported Robinson's Monday night post-conference statement, Roosevelt inquired, "What made you think they were going to pass the new tax measure by Saturday?"

Reminded that Pat Harrison had said it would be passed by then, Roosevelt denied that he had ever said anything to that effect, nor had "anyone ever intimated in any shape, manner or form from the White House, nor was it suggested during the meeting the other night at the White House." Protesting, "Heavens above, I am not Congress. I am just an innocent, peaceful little fellow down here that makes recommendation," the president sloughed off the whole decision on his Senate leaders.[18] Meanwhile, Harrison was at work on the six-day wonder, dashing about the House and Senate wings, the committee room, and the Senate floor when a reporter questioned him about the presidential statement. In disbelief he asked to see a transcript of the press conference. Convinced that Roosevelt had retreated from his previous stand, Harrison went onto the Senate floor and canceled the rush order, asking merely for the simple extension of the excises.[19]

It was just as well. With the Finance Committee in rebellion and the treasury staff unable to provide adequate schedules, it was obvious to the Senate leadership that a six-day bill was impossible. Harrison, Doughton, and Byrns met with Charles West, the presidential representative in congressional matters, and decided upon procedures for a comprehensive tax bill. Senate and House hearings were ordered. The matter was settled. Congress would drag on through the summer, threshing out a revolutionary tax proposal. To the president came congratulations from Frankfurter for "very skillful manoeuvering. . . .you so guided matters that Doughton and Pat Harrison could not escape being committed to the promise of legislation now."[20]

Tempers cooled in many quarters, even within the critical press. The outspoken Baltimore *Sun* called the decision a wise one which now might permit attention to go to a substantive tax proposal instead of "excited speculation as to whether the President let down Senator Harrison." It remained for the senator to explain how the "misunderstanding" had come about. To the Senate he now vowed that he would oppose adjournment until a bill embodying the president's view was considered. Harrison assumed full responsibility for what had happened, "confirming" the White House statement that Roosevelt had never pointedly requested action by Saturday night. He explained that the president had merely asked that the new taxes be attached to the excise resolution, and that it had been his own decision that the measure must then be passed by June 30 to salvage the revenue. Outwardly Harrison showed no pique at what his colleagues knew to be a rebuff from the president. Senator Robinson now laughed at the whole string of events, and Garner, presiding over the Senate, appeared to enjoy it all as if it were just another good show.[21]

Neither the newspapermen, from whom Harrison retreated after the press conference revelations, nor the Senate Republicans absolved Roosevelt as had his loyal lieutenant. Arthur Krock wondered why, if FDR had not desired such haste, he had remained silent after his Senate chieftains had made their Monday night front portico statements, waiting two days to speak, after an avalanche of criticism had been precipitated. Krock declared, "Mr. Harrison has once more taken the rap." Harrison chose to end the discussion: "Let us close this chapter, and let us not talk about the matter any more." Still, in

"I'll Take It!"

Newark *Evening News*, June 28, 1935
Courtesy: Media General, Richmond (Va.)

spite of their contrived appearance of tacit assent, he and Robinson
were disturbed by Roosevelt's abandonment of them. According to
Morgenthau, Harrison was particularly irritated because the president had recently rejected a candidate he had endorsed for the Board
of Tax Appeals.[22]

Why should the reluctant Democratic congressional leaders go
along with the president on his tax program and dedicate themselves
to two more months of legislative fury? Journalist Mark Sullivan conjectured that the desire for party solidarity in 1936 and the personal
support that Democratic candidates would need from Roosevelt in the
primaries were two factors. (Harrison warned his committee that
their political fortunes were "entirely in the hands of the President.
If you vote to discredit any part of his program you are voting against
yourselves.") A conviction that Roosevelt was still the spokesman for
the majority of the people, the power of patronage, and the dazzling
$4 billion voted for presidential discretionary spending were other
considerations Sullivan did not mention. It can be added that both
Robinson and Harrison may simply have enjoyed paying deference to
the president of the United States.[23] Furthermore, Pat Harrison was
deeply loyal to Roosevelt and appreciative of what the New Deal had
done for Mississippi.

At the end of that madcap June week in 1935, Harrison and
Doughton settled into the routine of White House conferences, con-
sultations with treasury experts, and preparations for committee
hearings, hoping now for adjournment by August 1. Harrison promised that every effort would be made to confine the measure to presidential desires. Both he and the president suspected that La Follette
would attempt to turn the bill into a general revision of the whole tax
system in order to raise revenue for increased government relief
spending.[24] Aware that not only social reform but also revenue was a
factor, Harrison proposed a scale of levies on personal incomes, inher-
itances, and corporations projected to yield some $340 million in new
revenue. Although his rates were scorned by House proponents of a
wider distribution of wealth, Harrison explained that he had always
thought that there was a degree beyond which taxes could not go
without reaching a point of diminishing returns. Ernest K. Lindley,
the Washington correspondent for the New York *Herald Tribune*, reported at the time that the Treasury Department disclaimed all re-

sponsibility for the schedules, and he chided Harrison for hastily bringing out a schedule of increases "so trifling as to make the whole program look ridiculous." Senator Long, disappointed that the translation of the sentiments of the June 19 message into actual tax levies had fallen far short of his demands, had washed his hands of the whole thing. He complained that the Harrison schedules would produce "a dime for the Treasury every time we went in the hole one dollar," while La Follette lamented to Morgenthau that "it puts the Administration in a hell of a spot to have a swell message like that come up here and then these futile things proposed to implement it."[25]

With the revenue bill back on the course that tax measures constitutionally followed, Senator Harrison relinquished his role as revenue-originator to the House where hearings began on July 8. The chairman of the Ways and Means taxation subcommittee, Samuel B. Hill of Washington, complained that it had begun to "look like the mountain labored and brought forth a mouse." Hill, Doughton, and Jere Cooper of Tennessee, all from the Ways and Means Committee, told President Roosevelt on July 4 that Harrison's rates would bring in only $134 million and not the $340 million estimated by the Mississippi senator. They insisted that there had to be more than social reform in the new tax program; revenue had to be raised, and the most logical source was from the middle class brackets. Roosevelt was cool to that idea. In fact, according to the Washington *Evening Star*, the whole new tax program seemed to be slipping from his hands, "what with Huey Long tugging in one direction, Senator La Follette in another, and the conservative Democrats sitting on their haunches, whittling, and cussing themselves." While administration leaders crushed an adjournment movement in the House, Harrison called in reporters in mid-July and told them to "tell the country" that Congress would remain in session until the tax bill was passed. He did not know that the president had confided to Morgenthau on July 1 that "he would not fight it" if Congress postponed the tax bill until fall.[26]

By late July the House committee had brought out a bill that carried a tax on excess profits Roosevelt had not asked for. Concurrent with House floor debate the Finance Committee from July 30 through August 8 held its hearings on the House bill so that the Senate could

begin debate without delay upon House passage. When Secretary
Morgenthau steadfastly refused to comment on the merits of the bill,
Harrison complained, "I do not know of any Secretary of the Treasury that hasn't given to the Finance Committee and the Committee
on Ways and Means his views with reference to certain policies."
Morgenthau insisted that his position as secretary had always been
that it was not proper for him to "attempt to tell Congress what the
rates or schedules of any revenue bill should be." Knowing that the
House bill's inclusion of the excess profits tax and its scale of corporate income levies did not completely reflect the presidential program,
Harrison tried to learn from Morgenthau whether there had been any
change in administration attitudes that would make the House version acceptable. His complaint, "I don't want to get caught coming
and going on this proposition," was understandable to those who remembered the last week of June. [27]

After listening to a seven-day parade of hostile witnesses, ranging
from tax lawyers and businessmen to a representative of the End
Poverty in California movement, the Finance Committee reported
out a bill vastly different from the House measure. The committee
repudiated the inheritance tax, Roosevelt's chief recommendation,
but voted to increase the gift and estate taxes to compensate for lost
revenue. Harrison was not convinced by Oliphant and other treasury
aides that abandonment of the inheritance tax was inconsistent with
the president's message. He admitted that his committee had not delivered all that FDR had wanted, but after both the House and Senate
committees had determined to stray from the tax message, he had
concluded that "we had better go in and get some revenue." [28]

Harrison wrote the majority report, which he made public only
minutes before Senate debate began on August 14. Major critics of
the bill were Senators Hastings, Vandenberg, and Long. To Daniel
Hastings it was "a cross between a spendthrift and a social revo-
lutionist . . . its principal object the Presidential election of 1936."
Long sneered that the bill had gotten "into the hands of a very bad set
of friends," and Vandenberg complained that the proposal was a
"tin-foil" measure that had been written "in the slap-dash judgments
of the final days of a Congress consumed by an insistent purpose to
adjourn." Harrison defended his committee's proposals as more in
conformity with the president's message than the House bill had been

and pointed out that his committee had included a tax on intercompany dividends in response to FDR's attack on holding companies, a levy which the House had failed to approve. The Senate also placed slightly higher graduated taxes upon larger corporations and raised the tax on capital stock, but it softened the House surtax on individual net incomes so that the maximum rate of 75 percent would not affect incomes below $10 million.[29]

Harrison and Barkley wielded the cudgels against La Follette's proposals to increase personal taxes upon lower income groups and to reduce the standard individual exemptions, and Harrison also succeeded in warding off attempts to add tariff features to the bill. When debate ended, the revenue bill of 1935 passed the Senate by a vote of 57 to 22 with only ten Democrats in opposition. The Senate had adopted the House maximum levy of 75 percent on incomes of $5 million (the 1934 surtax rate had been graduated to only 59 percent on incomes of over $1 million). Conference agreement came on August 20 and Senate acceptance of the report on August 24. The House had conceded to the Senate's elimination of the inheritance tax and to its increase in the estate tax. The president signed the bill without ceremony on August 31.[30]

The question remains whether Pat Harrison's support of the share-the-wealth tax bill of 1935 was merely nominal. Raymond Moley thought so. Writing in 1937, he interpreted the tax message of June 19 as the "day the split in the Democratic Party began," and recalled that Harrison had "bled inwardly." He wrote that Democratic leaders had said bitingly that "they'd go 'down the line' this time, but that they'd be damned if they ever would again under like circumstances." Moley has added that Harrison's close friend, Senator Byrnes of South Carolina, had told him that Harrison's friends all knew his true feelings, but respected his loyalty to the president and understood his "calculated double talk" in support of the share-the-wealth plan. Contemporary columnists wrote assuredly of the opposition of key Democrats to the tax plan as well as to other administration proposals that came to Congress in early 1935. And, at the same time, FDR's confidants warned him of Harrison's lackluster support. At a White House conference on May 14, when Roosevelt conferred with a group that included Norris, La Follette, Wallace, Ickes, and Frankfurter, Senator Wheeler advised the president "to

get all that he could out of Senators Robinson and Harrison," since
neither senator had any sympathy for the administration's program.
Two months later, while the tax bill was under congressional
scrutiny, Roosevelt told Frankfurter that he knew that Robinson and
Harrison had serious reservations about "the whole New Deal. They
just wonder where the man in the White House is taking the old
Democratic Party."[31]

In retrospect the Revenue Act of 1935 may have been, as Paul K.
Conkin has written, the "most decisive turn by Roosevelt from con-
sensus politics to a clear appeal to the disinherited," but tax policy
was not, in the end, to be a significant feature of New Deal economics beyond the arena of talk. The act of 1935 added only $250 million
to the annual revenue yield, about one-sixth the amount that Congress had shelled out while hassling over the bill. As a share-the-
wealth vehicle, it was not a success; its effect on 98 percent of the
income recipients was negligible, the disappointed *Nation* later
pointed out. The percentage of wealth captured by the top 10 percent
of income recipients actually increased slightly after passage of the
bill. Furthermore, as Sidney Ratner has underscored, the progressive
taxation features of the act were vitiated by the social security payroll
taxes passed only six days before the revenue bill became law. Actually, there would be no real change in the distribution of income until
World War II.[32]

If the wealth tax of 1935 did not raise revenue substantially, it did
raise one thing—a mighty howl from big business. The business press
was apprehensive about what another year's revenue act might bring.
The liberal press was more optimistic. Although disheartened that
the 1935 act added only about two dollars to the wealth of each
American, *Nation* at least hoped that it cast "the shadow of coming
events."[33] That shadow became substance in the Revenue Act of
1936, the product of a set of circumstances similar to those that had
preceded the tax act of 1935. Once again President Roosevelt's
January message called for no new taxes and his balanced budget
expectations were shattered by the Supreme Court (this time the
hatchet went to the Agricultural Adjustment Act and its processing
taxes). Too, there was the thumping passage of the soldier bonus over
a presidential veto. When Harrison and Doughton became aware of
treasury needs and of an impending tax message, they left the White

House under the impression that Congress would write a tax bill from the fund of its own wisdom. The senator promised, "We will try to devise a wise and efficient program in a way that won't interfere with the business upturn."[34]

The president's message of March 3 was jolting enough in its request for $786 million annually in additional taxes for the next three years; it was even more shocking in its call for one of the most sweeping revenue proposals yet submitted by the chief executive. He asked for the repeal of practically all existing corporation taxes (on capital stock, excess profits, and income) and for the substitution of a heavy tax on undistributed profits. As a tax device the new tax appealed to a variety of New Deal policy-makers—the economic planners, the antitrusters, Keynesians, and democrats who sought to restore decision-making to small stockholders.[35] To those who did not care for the advanced thought of Rexford Tugwell, Herman Oliphant, or Marriner Eccles, governor of the Federal Reserve System (and here can be put Doughton, Harrison, and the ambivalent Morgenthau), the tax was attractive as a revenue producer and a loophole-plugger. Hence, Harrison was able to applaud Roosevelt's message as the "complete answer to those who have been continuously shouting about unbalanced budgets."[36]

Committee consideration and floor handling of the undistributed profits tax of 1936 were in many ways similar to the passage of the wealth tax of 1935. Executive sessions of the Finance Committee held concurrently with the open hearings of the Ways and Means Committee prompted jealous suspicions in the House that the Senate would write its own bill anyway. There is little wonder that the measure, embodying the president's views almost completely, sailed through the House on April 29 by a vote of 267 to 93 after less than three hours of debate. Before the measure even passed the House a Washington columnist predicted that "after the Senate Democrats get through compromising La Follette, they will then compromise with the House and that will be the final form of the bill."[37] The prognosis was correct in every respect.

The Senate Finance Committee severely tortured the House bill, giving full rein to a stellar cast of business spokesmen who looked upon the profits tax as prohibitive of the efforts of business to rid itself of debts or to make further investments. The most compelling of all testimony argued that the profits tax would result in a substantial loss of revenue to the government and that a number of "blue-chip" firms would pay no taxes under the proposed plan (they had paid dividends in excess of net income by drawing upon a strong surplus accumulated over the years). [38] Committee conservatives, led by Byrd, Bailey, King, and George, who were galled at the deliberate use of a tax measure to institute reform, led a majority of the committee away from the House plan. Chairman Harrison admitted to Morgenthau in a conference in the senator's office attended by both Lovell Parker of the Finance Committee staff and Herman Oliphant that the House bill would not get past the Finance Committee and that his own idea was to retain the graduated corporate income tax

Washington *Evening Star,* May 25, 1936
Courtesy: Archives and Special Collections, University of Mississippi

and place upon it a small flat tax on undistributed profits. He reasoned that, by offering a compromise acceptable to the opposition, the administration could retain control; not to compromise would sink the president's plan altogether.[39]

When the committee went into executive session, Harrison faced a truculent majority. Advised by his aides that "the President had better talk to Pat Harrison and 'with material,'" Morgenthau took Harrison and Doughton to confer with Roosevelt, who agreed to a compromise provided that it would meet treasury income needs and retain the philosophy of the profits tax. Morgenthau confessed to his staff that he no longer believed in the House bill because he could not easily give up the revenue it lost. Convinced that "the President is not iron clad on what he wants," Harrison urged his committee to accept a compromise which would retain the prevailing corporate income rates but superimpose upon them a flat undistributed profits tax of 7 percent. Based on Harrison's compromise, the committee's product, adopted by an 18 to 1 vote, ended up placing a new flat 18 percent rate on corporate income, superimposing a 7 percent tax on undistributed profits, and retaining the capital stock tax of the 1935 act—reflections of major concessions to the Byrd forces.[40]

Severe sinusitis sent Harrison to bed for ten days in mid-May, and, without what Max Lerner called his "consummate bit of chairmaning," the committee fell into a carnivorous mood. The group was now led by King, one of the leaders of the conservative revolt, and it was anxious to rush a bill to the floor and to passage so that Congress might adjourn for the Democratic national convention. Finally in late May the committee brought out a bill which was a virtual facelift of the House measure.[41] It included not only an increase in corporate income levies but also a slight increase in individual surtaxes that La Follette succeeded in adding to the bill in Harrison's absence.

After three days of debate, in which the Republicans sat out a bit of Democratic infighting over La Follette's perennial amendments to broaden the income tax base, the bill passed by a vote of 38 to 24, La Follette's amendment having been removed. In conference sessions, as had been predicted, the Senate compromised the House in an exchange by which the House won on the undistributed profits issue with sliding rates of from 7 to 27 percent (a far cry from the average 33 percent that the Roosevelt recommendation had carried) and the

Senate scored with the retention of a normal graduated tax of from 8 to 15 percent on corporate income. In short, the House protected the principle of the profits tax and the Senate shielded the revenue yield, the two contending factors of the long debate. Debilitated by the June heat and other divisive legislation, a spiritless Congress took up the conference report. The House passed it without seeing a copy, and, after only a perfunctory debate, the Senate adopted it on the last night of the session.[42] Roosevelt again signed a tax bill without comment or ceremony.

The act satisfied neither the friends nor the foes of wealth taxation. Rather, it represented a temporary truce between those who wanted to adhere to conventional and revenue-dependable corporate income taxation and those who were willing to experiment with a new principle of undistributed profits taxation which carried an element of social reform. Secretary Morgenthau may have been one of the few participants who could say that he had gotten "a real excitement and pleasure out of this thing, out of laying a cornerstone for a new America." To Marriner Eccles, the final act was "better than nothing, but not very much better." In practice the tax confirmed both the hopes and fears of its adversaries. On the credit side, the act did release about $1.1 billion in cash and other assets and increased consumer purchasing power by about $500 million annually during the two years of its existence. On the other hand, it placed smaller corporations at a disadvantage in the maintenance of capital requirements and the retirement of debts, while larger companies, able to tap the open investment market for needed capital at a minimum cost, held the advantage over their smaller brethren.[43]

As Otis L. Graham has pointed out, few New Deal contemporaries realized how the federal revenue measures negated one another or that the "slight progressivity" that Senator Harrison and his committee wrote into the revenue acts of 1935 and 1936 was canceled by regressive taxation at the state and local levels, particularly in Harrison's own state which had pioneered in the enactment of a sales tax.[44]

Even if greater distribution of income during the New Deal through taxation had not been thwarted by a negligible understanding of the possibilities of doing so, there were manifest limitations in both congressional and executive leaders which arrested the passage of

FDR's initial tax recommendations in 1935 and 1936. Roosevelt himself was partly responsible. Suspicious of Harrison and Doughton, he never fully confided in them and often attempted to circumvent their treasured legislative prerogatives. Had Roosevelt not delighted so much in late session "surprises" and had he remained more "ironclad" (as Harrison had found him not to be), his financial handymen in Congress would have been more resolute in their defense of presidential reforms. Harrison, too, was ambivalent in taxation matters. While he flirted with the idea of taxation for social purposes in 1935 and 1936, he was never able to shake loose his fundamental belief that the primary purpose of taxation was revenue, and, as he stated in a later testament of his fiscal creed, "The only way for the federal budget to approach a balanced condition is through an increase in the national income which is *always based upon business activity.*"[45] Although he was temporarily converted by treasury liberals to the taxation of wealth in 1935 and 1936, he was more permanently influenced by the economic "realism" of business minds, represented by Bernard Baruch and such congressional staff personnel as Lovell Parker.[46] Harrison's support of the emasculation of the undistributed profits tax in the Revenue Act of 1938 and its elimination in the Revenue Act of 1939 would be manifestations of the fact that he had completed a full circle return to his basic beliefs.

CHAPTER VII

Time Out for Politics—Mississippi Style

1935–36

"WITHOUT THE GOOD old-fashioned politician the Senate would collapse. And in Pat Harrison the good old-fashioned politician blessedly survives," a writer for *Fortune* remarked in 1935.[1] It boded well for the senator's political health that he did possess striking talents for electoral brokerage or he might not have survived the political strife that engulfed Mississippi in 1935 and 1936. First of all, there were the quadrennial fireworks of a Mississippi gubernatorial election, an interesting enough phenomenon when conducted by Mississippians alone, which sparkled more than usual in 1935 after a little willful meddling from Huey Long. Then, in the following year, after assassination had removed Long as an omnipresence in Mississippi politics, "The Man" Bilbo tried to advance himself to senior senator status at the expense of Harrison. That decision on Bilbo's part came in large measure from his touchiness over Harrison's domination of judicial and relief patronage. Added to home state problems for Harrison in 1935 was the disposition of a political feud in the Virgin Islands involving one of the senator's Mississippi friends. The only political event of the two years that gave Harrison no worries was the presidential contest in 1936.

During the first six months of 1935, Harrison became involved in an argument with Interior Department Secretary Harold L. Ickes, a dispute which eventually had to be settled by Roosevelt. With his remarkable facility in finding suitable and generally satisfying jobs for Mississippi politicos turned out of office by their constituents, Harrison had obtained the appointment of T. Webber Wilson, a former congressman, as United States district judge in the Virgin Islands. This American possession early in the New Deal became what a recent chronicler of the islands' history has called a "laboratory for New

Deal planners." The island governor, Paul Pearson, a Republican appointee of Hoover, was a moral crusader and idealist whose administration had the enthusiastic support of Ickes, whose own moral persuasions dated back to his days as a Bull Mooser. Ickes, already miffed over a cabinet shuffle that had transferred the administration of the insular court system from the Interior to the Justice Department, was nettled when Attorney General Homer Cummings named Wilson to the judgeship at the behest of Senator Harrison and Postmaster General Farley, the party sachem of patronage. The Pearson-Wilson affair became simply another facet of the ongoing conflict between the politically minded Senate and the New Dealers who refused to ascribe any political motives to themselves, and the Virgin Islands became another arena for the sort of controversy that generally accompanied Ickes's administration of the Public Works Administration, an agency that supplied the bulk of the New Deal's input into the local economy. [2]

Whether or not Judge Wilson intended to replace Pearson as governor, as rumor had it, he did succeed in gaining popularity with the local native opposition to Pearson which saw the judge as "a fine Southern gentleman" with no trace of prejudice. To the contrary, the liberal press described him as an out-and-out racist. "Negro-wise," *Time* reported, Wilson appeared to be in a formidable position, enjoying the support of the vocal islanders, the senators, and Cummings. His affirmation "I am answerable only to Attorney General Cummings and to God Almighty" made it clear that neither Pearson nor Ickes held any sway with Wilson. [3]

At the behest of Judge Wilson a federal attorney began an investigation of the local PWA, administered in the islands by Governor Pearson acting as Ickes's agent. Out of the probe only one case came to Wilson's court; it involved an island quadroon who was found guilty of pilfering less than $40 worth of PWA building materials and fined $200. The verdict aroused the ire of Secretary Ickes who thought that Wilson was a "thoroughly bad actor" who "ought to be removed at an early date." By 1935 Roosevelt knew that he had a problem on his hands. "Call up Pat Harrison and say that the President does not want anything done about the Virgin Islands until the President has had a chance to talk with him," Marguerite LeHand told Marvin McIntyre in January. The *Nation* publicized the whole

Virgin Islands controversy in a series of articles written by Raymond Gram Swing, who was indignant that Harrison, Cummings, and Farley had placed Wilson on the bench in the first place. [4]

During the week in which the article appeared Harrison had his conference with Roosevelt. By that time the senator was furious, for the public relations division of the Interior Department had circulated among the press mimeographed copies of the *Nation* piece. The grapevine reported that the senator's friends were ready to retaliate against Ickes when the work relief bill came to the floor. Actually, Ickes had not authorized the public distribution of the article, and it was while both he and his press representative were away that an overzealous official had given copies to newspapermen. Ickes made his apologies to Cummings, Farley, and Harrison, but nonetheless, the feisty secretary had managed to trample the toes of two fellow cabinet members and an administration senator. He remained indifferent to the rancor directed his way by the friends of the offended trio. "I have known for sometime that I wasn't loved by everybody with the fervor with which I should be loved," Ickes rejoined. [5]

Ickes in turn was annoyed because Harrison had written the president a letter which contained what the secretary considered "bitter expressions" about himself. Convinced that "someone" had "poisoned" Harrison's mind against him and determined to "have it out face to face" with the Mississippian, Ickes went to see him. It was not an amicable session, according to Ickes, who left with "a very low opinion of Harrison," whom he found to be "like an old, complaining woman . . . running around in circles." The senator aired his grievances not only about Ickes's outspoken criticism of Wilson but also about the secretary's failure to recognize his interests in Interior Department appointments. Not so, Ickes countered, pointing out to "whiny Pat" that he had more than sixty appointees in the department. They quarreled for over an hour, Ickes recorded in his diary after the set-to ended. [6]

Harrison's pique was heightened by the entry into the wrangle of columnist Drew Pearson, the son of the islands' governor. The senator aired his side of the story to the Senate and candidly reported that he had told both the president and Ickes that the governor of the Virgin Islands should be a Democrat, "sentiments . . . not appreciated by the Secretary of the Interior, Governor Pearson, or his son Drew."

According to his close friend "Jimmy" Byrnes, Harrison was "thereafter the target of the Merry-Go-Round." [7]

The controversy ran on for better than six months. The Senate entered the fracas when it ordered an investigation of the islands. Chaired by Millard Tydings, the select panel of five senators, three of whom were Finance Committee associates of Harrison, was hardly expected to support Ickes or the civil libertarians who backed Governor Pearson. Roosevelt plied Harrison with correspondence and reports from admirers of Pearson, while the senator in turn supplied the president with letters from detractors of the Pearson regime. In July, while the Senate probe was underway, Ickes wrote a public letter to Tydings demanding the removal of Wilson. Roosevelt confided to Felix Frankfurter that he had a "nasty little problem" on his hands because Harrison had enlisted the support of Joseph Robinson and the two administration leaders were asking for Ickes's scalp. The president was apt to alienate either his cabinet officer or his senators however he resolved the matter. [8]

In mid-July FDR talked first with Ickes, then with Tydings, Robinson, and Harrison, and finally with Webber Wilson. Without explanation the Senate investigation recessed. When the press hinted that a resignation or two would result from the rumpus, Ickes made it clear that his own would not be one. "I kind of like my job. It keeps me interested," he remarked. A week later Harrison telephoned the White House that "some of us on The Hill" thought it wise to take immediate action on the Virgin Islands imbroglio, presumably to forestall a resumption of the hearings. Within a week Roosevelt abruptly settled the matter by transferring Pearson to the Public Works Administration as an assistant director and Wilson to membership on the Federal Parole Board. The *Nation* promptly carried another article by Swing, this time lamenting Wilson's new appointment as a move "to save Pat Harrison's face" the cost of which was "very, very dear." The syndicated columnist Rodney Dutcher surmised that the appointment was a payoff to the Mississippi senator for his "steady performances" in supporting New Deal programs which he privately disliked. [9]

The controversy ended with the reassignments of the two antagonists. In time, Harrison and Ickes "made up." The senator never referred publicly to the argument, and Ickes recorded in his diary two years later that Harrison's good friend Edwin A. Halsey, the secretary of the Senate, had told him that "Pat Harrison thinks you are all right now." Ickes concluded that the senator had had a change of heart toward him because he had actually "said something complimentary" about his administration of the PWA.[10]

While Harrison was settling T. Webber Wilson into fitting employment, he was concerned about the political future of his good friend Hugh Lawson White, who was making his second race for governor in 1935. Both White and his opponent Paul B. Johnson, a Hattiesburg attorney and veteran politician, had been defeated by Mike Conner in their earlier gubernatorial bid in 1931.[11] Preferring to watch the 1935 rematch of White and Johnson from the sidelines, Harrison declined to participate because of his "heavy responsibilities" as chairman of the Finance Committee. In delineating his neutrality he denounced the use of the "federal set-up" to advance the cause of either candidate and announced that he had informed the head of all federal agencies in the state that he would not "countenance" the political activity of any officeholder who had been appointed through his own endorsement. He did, however, prevail upon Robert Fechner, the national director of the Civilian Conservation Corps, to give leave to the CCC enrollees in Mississippi to vote in the August primaries. Fechner reported to Roosevelt his willingness to do so on the basis that the customary general election day leave in Mississippi "doesn't mean anything." Neither Fechner nor FDR spoke of Harrison's request as a move to gain the vote of the 5,000 affected young men for White, but that had been the senator's ulterior motive.[12]

Long's intrusion into the Mississippi race in 1935 on Johnson's behalf added a new dimension to the Harrison-Bilbo alliance against their Louisiana nemesis. Wailing "I don't want the poor people penalized with a rapacious millionaire type like Hugh White," Long expected the enrollees in the 612 Share-the-Wealth clubs he claimed to have in Mississippi to vote for Johnson. White, aware that political analysts considered the race as a prime test of Long's strength outside Louisiana, waged his campaign on the issue of whether or not Mississippians would permit Long to dictate their choice of a governor. Before the race ended, however, Long appeared to have renounced any intervention because "We are sure to be repudiated no matter who wins." He was correct, for when White bested Johnson by a close vote a boisterous crowd of two hundred happy partisans of White hanged and burned Long in effigy at Osyka on the Mississippi-Louisiana line. [13]

Mississippi's refusal to become, as Bilbo put it, a "vassal" to Huey Long was immensely gratifying to both of her senators who had feared Long's power for years. Long's whirlwind campaign for Senator Hattie Caraway in Arkansas in 1932 had shaken Harrison, who bore the brunt of constant threats from Long to "get him" in 1936. The two senators had measured lances at the Democratic convention in 1932 and the enmity had continued throughout 1933 and 1934 over patronage, share-the-wealth taxation, and Long's charges that Harrison was a front man for Bernard Baruch and Wall Street. In one of their many clashes on the Senate floor, when Long depicted Harrison's tax leadership as a continuation of Hooverism, Harrison retorted that Long's opinions were "less respected by the Membership of this body as a whole and by the country than that of any other Senator here." On that occasion Long broke away from reporters at the Senate door to stop Harrison and warn him that his wealth clubs in Mississippi "ain't going to vote to re-elect Pat Harrison to the Senate." Harrison did not answer but later remarked to the press, "I pity the candidate who secures his support." [14]

Despite disclaimers of any fear of Long's threat to defeat him in 1936, Harrison was secretly worried. He maintained a correspondence with W. D. Robinson, a native Mississippian and a roving *Times-Picayune* correspondent who aspired to write a grand exposé of Long. Robinson busied himself in collecting a vast amount of anti-Long material that he began to share with Harrison as early as July, 1932. From the Democratic headquarters that year Harrison had written to Robinson that Long was an embarrassment in the campaign. After Bilbo entered the Senate, he too had engaged the services of Robinson and instructed him to "send everything you [have] on Huey Long." To Bilbo's thinking, Long was "smart as hell and crazy as he can be." Bilbo calculated that by 1936 someone would have to "tend to him on the stump" and it was his ambition "to make a damn good job of it." Despite the rumors that Bilbo was "laying in the gap" for Long, the two never bothered to take one another on, and Bilbo liked to boast that he was the only senator to whom Long refused to speak.[15]

According to Raymond Moley, by April of 1935 the Democratic high command feared that Long would thwart the reelection of both Harrison and Joe Robinson, the two senators who Burton K. Wheeler declared "hated Huey like no one was hated in the Senate in [Wheeler's] time." Louis Jiggitts wrote to Roosevelt that April that Long had not made "any appreciable gain" in Mississippi, but he counseled that "groundwork should be laid now for a future attack upon him if it is necessary." The assassination of Long in September removed the threat. Harrison made no statement on Long's death other than a platitudinous comment on the Louisianan's "dynamic and colorful character and his daring and exceptional qualities of leadership."[16] Both Mississippi senators were vastly relieved to be rid of the Long menace.

After a post-session vacation trip in the late summer of 1935 to Arizona and San Francisco, where he had not been since the 1920 convention, Harrison returned to Mississippi. In Jackson he opened headquarters at the Edward Hotel to receive the several hundred visitors who came to "ding dong" him for jobs or to talk politics. Because his Gulfport mail was running so heavy, he opened a second office there and returned to his hometown to avoid politics while the legislature was in session.[17] In reality, Harrison was at the game of politics as he may never have been before. If Long was out of the picture, Bilbo was still very much there. Hence, in the fall of 1935, Harrison set out to canvass the state on behalf of the New Deal and to shore up his county organizations. This time he was particularly sensitive to criticism from the Bilbo faction that he had gone "high hat" and was too much of a national figure to represent the humble folk of Mississippi. In what Turner Catledge, a Mississippi native who had become the Washington correspondent for the New York *Times*, called "Pat's barefoot tour," Harrison went into sixty counties. The perambulating senator presented himself at cotton gins, molasses mills, and crossroads general stores and even made a point to get out to the small farms at milking time.[18]

Harrison found that most Mississippians were still warm to the New Deal. The major factor in the state's rising economy, which was in better shape than at any other time since the World War, was the Agricultural Adjustment Administration. Catledge quoted one Delta banker who told of debt payments on loans cancelled out years ago. "People come in here and ask to pay back interest on notes that we literally have to fish out of the wastebasket," the banker told the reporter. If Delta planters found the AAA a boost to their largescale operations, the farmers in the long blighted northeastern section of the state were even more thankful for the program. The only consistent criticism was that the Bankhead Cotton Control Act of 1934 hampered the operations of low-bale producers. With 100,000 bales in excess of the allotted quotas coming from the 1935 bumper crop and south Mississippi farmers holding cotton from the market in expectation of invalidation of the Bankhead Act, Senator Harrison would return to Washington convinced that changes should be made in cotton allotment policies.[19]

When Congress reconvened in January, 1936, the simmering Harrison-Bilbo feud grew red hot over patronage, long a contentious matter between the two. John Sharp Williams had once warned Harrison, "When you get a man appointed to office, you make twenty enemies and one ingrate,"[20] and in Bilbo Harrison had both the enemy and the ingrate, for the former had done a slow burn ever since his stint as "paste-master general." Eager to rebuild his own faction in Mississippi, Bilbo avidly sought federal patronage, and Harrison was constantly compelled to defend himself both against charges of the junior senator that he had taken the lion's share of appointment opportunities for himself and from critics who faulted him for having permitted the Bilbo "crowd" to assume control of relief activities in the state. To the latter critics Harrison replied that he had made an agreement with Bilbo that the officeholders named by Senator Stephens and himself were not to be disturbed, but that subsequent vacancies were to be filled by the junior senator until he had obtained an equitable share of patronage. As Bilbo saw it, such an equity never materialized.[21]

The first major clash between the two senators came over the naming of Judge Eugene O. Sykes of Aberdeen as chairman of the Federal Communications Commission. Bilbo was incensed because Sykes had campaigned for Stephens in 1934 while serving as a member of the FCC. "Utterly false," Sykes declared before the members of the Interstate Commerce Committee who approved his nomination as chairman in February, 1935. Although Bilbo took his case to the president, Sykes won confirmation by the Senate but served as chairman for only a few months, stepping down to his former commissioner status. Reports circulated that Bilbo's testimony at the hearings on the chairmanship appointment had undermined Sykes's influence as the FCC head. When Harrison later sought to have Judge Sykes named to a federal judgeship on the Court of Appeals for the District of Columbia, Marvin McIntyre protested that he was too valuable a member of the FCC to withdraw him from that agency. More likely the president did not care to provoke a messy fight between the Mississippi senators.[22]

When a vacancy occurred on the Fifth U.S. Circuit Court of Appeals at the death of Florida's Nathan P. Bryan, Harrison immediately endorsed Edwin R. Holmes, a son-in-law of ex-senator Williams and a federal district judge in Mississippi under an appointment from Woodrow Wilson. Harrison headed a group of Mississippi attorneys who called upon Attorney General Cummings to press for Holmes's appointment, and numerous bar associations forwarded endorsements to Roosevelt.[23] When Harrison told the president that the entire Mississippi congressional delegation supported Holmes, there was one vigorous dissent. Writing from Mississippi, where he was "at home fighting Huey Long in the interest of Pat Harrison, President Roosevelt, and the Democratic Party," Bilbo notified Cummings and FDR that he wanted no decision made on Holmes until he could be heard. "This man put me in jail for political reasons," Bilbo complained to the president. About his objection to Holmes, Bilbo was never shy. In 1923 the judge had held Bilbo in contempt of court and sentenced him to ten days in jail for his refusal to testify in a celebrated personal suit involving his protégé, Governor Lee M. Russell. Bilbo had already gotten a good deal of political mileage out of the sentence, for he had announced his candidacy for governor in 1923 from the steps of the Oxford jail. (He lost the heated race to Henry L. Whitfield and then staged a victorious comeback in 1927.) Bilbo now intended to exploit Holmes's nomination to the hilt and vowed that he would fight it "all the way from Maine to Mexico, from Dan to Beersheba, from hell to breakfast."[24]

In January, 1936, with Congress back in session and the appointment pending Senate confirmation, Harrison became disturbed over Bilbo's pleas to FDR and recommended to Marvin McIntyre that the president be advised to leave the matter to Harrison. McIntyre told Roosevelt privately that the senior senator had complained that if Holmes's name should be withdrawn, "it meant his finish in Mississippi." Meanwhile, Bilbo continued to defend his own reputation, charging that Holmes had "prostituted" his judicial office to "brand [him] as a jailbird." When the offended senator sent Roosevelt a letter enclosing the plea that he intended to make before the Judiciary Committee, FDR scribbled on the message "Will you take care of this rather delicate matter!" and turned it over to McIntyre.[25]

Bilbo's testimony before the judiciary subcommittee gave every indication that he was more anxious to unseat Harrison than he was to unbench Judge Holmes. Given an audience of the three subcommittee senators and an avid corps of newspapermen, the junior senator aired Harrison's financial problems which dated back to heavy losses in Gulf Coast real estate investments at the time of the crash. Bilbo argued that Holmes had presided over the liquidation of two Mississippi banks which resulted in the loss of more than $100,000 to depositors and that the proceedings which closed the operations of the First National Bank of Gulfport had protected Harrison as a "favored" depositor. Harrison, who was both embarrassed and irritated over having his financial reverses broadcast so widely, told the committee that he had done "everything humanly possible to take care of the situation down there." He explained that he had suffered most of the reverses when he had had to take back properties which he had sold and pay the taxes on them. Harrison lamented that he was still paying off obligations, that he was insolvent, and that "as always [he was] poor as the devil." Banging his fist on the desk and looking Bilbo straight in the eye, he countered that his colleague had dragged his financial status into the hearings solely to hurt him politically and personally. Nonetheless, the matter was one that he could "take care of before the people of Mississippi."[26]

After hearing statements in behalf of Holmes from twenty-three witnesses compared with only four who supported Bilbo, the judiciary subcommittee reported the nomination unanimously. When the report came up for floor discussion on March 19, Bilbo delivered a five-hour diatribe, but his protests were virtually ignored. The Senate confirmed Holmes by a 59 to 4 vote that reflected Harrison's stature among his colleagues. If the senators had failed to heed his wishes, Bilbo thought that a more significant set of listeners would. After the vote he told reporters, "I am going to notify Hannah," meaning his homestate supporters. [27]

Friction over a federal judgeship in Mississippi did not end with the confirmation of Holmes, for his former bench was now vacant. Bilbo immediately submitted for Harrison's approval the name of Bidwell Adam, a Gulfport opponent of Harrison, but Harrison was not willing to have the vacancy filled on the threshold of his summer campaign for reelection. After Cummings notified Roosevelt that Harrison wanted him to delay the appointment until after the August primary, the post remained unfilled over the summer. Bilbo was furious over what he deemed to be executive connivance with Harrison, and he claimed that his colleague only wanted to transport all the lawyers of the state to "the mountain top and show them the cattle of the thousand hills." Bilbo's criticism that Harrison's delay inflicted a considerable inconvenience upon the attorneys of the state who needed a working judge was valid, as borne out by an offer from an Alabama federal judge, Harrison's friend John McDuffie, to assist in the litigation of cases before the fall term of court. In a September move to outflank his colleague in naming Holmes's successor, Bilbo withdrew Adam's name and sent the president a list of twenty possible candidates. When Cummings tentatively selected from the list the name of Sidney E. Mize, a Gulf Coast lawyer acceptable to Harrison, Roosevelt asked McIntyre to find out "whether he is a liberal or a reactionary." Informed that Mize was a man "of liberal views and sound legal learning" who carried the endorsements of both the AFL's William Green and Senator Wheeler, chairman of the Judiciary Committee, FDR submitted the nomination to the Senate in January, 1937. Unanimous approval within two days finally ended the year-long discord between the two Mississippi senators over federal judgeships. [28]

The Holmes affair led to such enmity between Harrison and Bilbo that neither spoke to the other for more than four years. Thoroughly angry that Harrison had routed him so completely and envious of the apparent influence that Harrison had in the Roosevelt administration, Bilbo was determined to seek his revenge. The senior senator's candidacy for reelection offered an excellent first opportunity. In fact, when reporters asked "The Man" at the end of the first day of the hearings on Holmes if he would support Harrison during the coming summer, the redoubtable little senator snapped, "Hell no. I'm in the market for a colleague who will have some respect for me."[29]

It was a foregone conclusion that Bilbo would support Harrison's opponent whoever he might be. As it turned out, that man was none other than Bilbo's former enemy, Mike Conner. Conner and Bilbo had opposed each other for governor in 1927; after Bilbo won, it was said that he kept a skeleton in his office with Conner's name written on the forehead. When Conner defeated Bilbo's candidate for governor in 1931, the enmity deepened and Bilbo carped that Conner showed not the least "symptom of willingness" to cooperate with the administration in Washington. Conner had never minced words about Bilbo either, for he had once called him "an extraordinary piney-woods liar" who had served four years as governor and ten days in jail when it should have been four days as governor and ten years in jail. Some political savants advanced the notion that Bilbo was out to make the state of Mississippi safe for himself by "trying to drown Mike while the creek is up." There was no doubt that Bilbo intended to show Mississippi in the summer of 1936 who was the boss of the state.[30]

Mike Conner had impeccable credentials to be a senator. Educated at the University of Mississippi and Yale University, where he received his law degree, he had been elected speaker of the Mississippi House of Representatives at the age of twenty-four and had served eight years in the post. Active in state party politics since the age of twenty-one, he had been a delegate to every state and national Democratic convention since 1916. His victory in a field of five in the 1931 governor's race had been something of a political miracle. When Conner announced for senator in March, 1936, armchair forecasters gave him fair odds to win or at least make a good showing in the August primary. Gerald L. K. Smith, heir to Long's share-the-wealth mantle, announced immediately that his clubs would work against Harrison, and Conner was expected to have the support of the Bilbo county leaders, Townsendites, veterans, and those Mississippians who considered him to be the most capable governor the state had had in many years. Even those Harrison partisans who anticipated that their candidate would win expected the race to be chillingly close. After all, Harrison would face two opponents—Conner on the ballot and Bilbo on the stump. "He will have a fight but will win I am glad to say," Judge McDuffie wrote to Sam Rayburn after spending a week on the bench in Jackson.[31]

Harrison had garnered the support of a group of political luminaries and influential familial heirs who had incurred the wrath of either Bilbo or Conner over years of Mississippi political infighting. J. B. (Billy) Snider, a north Mississippi editor who was serving as lieutenant governor under White, and Dennis Murphree, who had been Conner's lieutenant governor, both came out for Harrison. James K. Vardaman's brother Will and his son, James K., Jr., announced their support of Harrison, and, of course, the senator had the backing of the prominent Williams family. T. Webber Wilson reappeared in Mississippi, ostensibly on vacation, to campaign for Harrison, and former governor Earl Brewer joined the senator's team. The force of Gerald L. K. Smith's opposition was canceled by other partisans of Huey Long who could never forgive Bilbo for his intemperate remarks at Long's death. Hence the leader of the wealth clubs in Mississippi, Dr. M. W. Gantt of Meridian, called upon Long's friends in the state to repudiate Bilbo by electing Harrison whose efforts in the passing of the social security bill had been impressive. But, with the exception of Governor Hugh White, who accompanied Harrison on a number of speaking occasions, most of the politicians of the state in office and out observed the political amenity of refraining from participation in the campaign. Paul Johnson, who was said to harbor senatorial ambitions of his own, was conspicuously silent, and Harrison sent word to his orators to "lay off" Johnson.[32] If Harrison called upon any of his Senate colleagues to come to his aid, none of them did.[33] Anyway it was not likely that any outsider still in full possession of his mind would care to dabble in Mississippi politics.

Conner's opening speech on June 9 set the pitch of his campaign when he called Harrison a presidential "rubber stamp" who had become "too big for Mississippi." Claiming that he himself had never vacillated on the veterans' bonus, Conner charged that Harrison had only "made a grab at the caboose" when the bonus train passed

through. To the farmers, he argued that Harrison had fought a reduction in the farm bank loan interest rates and opposed the coconut
oil taxes carried in the Revenue Act of 1934. When Harrison had said
that the three-cent tax "was bad faith to the naked negroes of the
Philippines, he had forgotten naked white children" in Mississippi
cotton fields. Harrison's sins against the farmers were further compounded, Conner argued, by his ten-year effort during the 1920s to
turn Muscle Shoals over to the power trust and his "sulking" refusal
to vote either way on Senator George W. Norris's TVA bill. Claiming
that Harrison cared more for the respect of Wall Street than of Mississippians, Conner pointed to tax laws containing loopholes which
siphoned away millions of dollars in refunds. Harrison's companion-
ship on the golf course with the financial titans of the country proved
that he had been totally corrupted by eastern money. As a "me too"
senator, Harrison had never originated a single constructive policy in
twenty-six years in Washington. So ran the Conner message.[34]

Harrison arrived in Mississippi on July 1 at the same time that the
new sales tax tokens were released for circulation and a drought-
breaking rain covered the state, a pair of events that permitted Harrison to take a slap at Conner's sales tax and to joke with the farmers
that he had ended the dry spell. The latter playful boast prompted a
retort from Conner that the senator "was wet enough to have brought
you a flood." Conner blamed Harrison for the Democratic administration's repeal of the Eighteenth Amendment and the passage of successive beer and liquor legalization measures.

A crowd of some 15,000 braved a thunderstorm at Crystal Springs
to hear Harrison open the first campaign that he had conducted in
twelve years. Within three weeks he had spoken in more than fifty of
the state's eighty-two counties. One by one Harrison responded to
Conner's charges. If rubber-stamping meant standing "shoulder to
shoulder" with the president, then he was happy to do so. If he spent
too much time in Washington, it was because he was elected to represent Mississippi there. In a slap at Bilbo, who had already hit the
hustings, Harrison declared that he had never projected himself into
anyone else's campaign in the state. His speeches were all cut from
the same cloth. He defended his golfing as a physician-prescribed
exercise, while charging that Conner had never taken up the game
because a golf club "looks something like a gun and some people don't

like to get too close to guns," a reference to Conner's World War I deferment. As for Bilbo, he never played golf although he "plays a lot of other things." Refuting the claim that Conner had never opposed a bonus, Harrison pointed to the governor's vote at Chicago in 1932 against the plan for immediate payment. Citing Conner's early opposition to Roosevelt, the senator drove home the point repeatedly that support of the administration was the only real issue in the race. In contrast to his own closeness to the president and his inclusion in numerous White House conferences, Harrison predicted that Conner "could be in Washington for 40 years and not find his way to the White House."[35]

As far as Mississippi campaigns went, the Harrison-Conner exchange was rather mild in the early weeks of the contest. *Newsweek* thought that the race offered all the decorum of a chautauqua circuit, but Bilbo's rhetoric added a new flavor. Both Conner and Harrison dropped their early restraint, and the fur began to fly at the courthouse steps, county fairgrounds, and municipal parks around the state. "Conner is getting nasty and Pat is having to start skinning a skunk before he gets taken for a ride," Paul J. Miller, a Harrison aide, wrote to Edwin Halsey, the secretary-treasurer of the Senate Democratic Campaign Committee. Most of the fighting was reserved by Harrison and Bilbo for each other. Harrison waved before his listeners Bilbo's letter of appreciation for the 1933 "meal ticket"; Bilbo retorted that Harrison's attempt to export him to Puerto Rico in 1934 warranted his entry into the race. Bilbo charged that Harrison had gone so eastern and high hat that he "had to put his picture on telegraph poles so folks will know who he is." Moreover, the "our Pat" stickers on Ford automobiles throughout the state were entirely appropriate because, indeed, the senator was "Their Pat." Bilbo brought out his version of Harrison's "wreck" of the Gulfport bank, an attack elaborated upon in the speeches of Harrison's Gulf Coast enemy Bidwell Adam, who tagged the senator "Promissory Pat." Harrison readily responded that "if all who are in debt will vote for me, then I have no doubt as to the outcome."

Harrison's battery of speakers included two raconteurs who could match Bilbo phrase for phrase. S. C. ("Sweep Clean") Broom, a former law partner of Bilbo who had broken with him, drew mammoth audiences. Reproving Bilbo for having troubled Harrison with a bothersome campaign, Broom quoted from the book of "Duteronimy" [*sic*] that Jonah had said to the whale, "If you had kept your damned mouth shut, this never would have happened." From several counties came calls to Harrison headquarters to send Marion Reily, a popular Meridian lawyer whose reputation on the stump was as well known as his former alliance with Bilbo. Reily's forte was a jesting description of Bilbo's social life in Washington. The junior senator had learned to dance; furthermore, Reily deplored in mocking tones, he "dances with his eyes closed." As former Bilboites, Broom and Reily drew delighted crowds, but they held no monopoly on crowd-pleasing antics. Bilbo's showmanship, Miller complained, "the ruralities swallow like a bass swallows a fly."[36]

Early in the race both Harrison and Bilbo committed blunders that each should have known would lead to reprisals on the campaign trail. Bilbo drew so many taunts over his new political affection for Conner that he felt compelled to say that he had never basically disagreed with Conner's politics. "Conner's always been my baby," Bilbo bragged. That rather foolhardy remark invited Harrison to ridicule Conner as "Mother Bilbo's Tootsie-Wootsie." Harrison rallies now opened with the local band's rousing rendition of "Yessir, That's My Baby." The high-spirited Broom enlivened many a rally by trundling a doll buggy about the platform while crooning the song.[37] Although Conner had canvassed the state four years earlier as a gubernatorial candidate free from the taint of "Bilboism," he was reluctant to renounce his new political patron. The match of the "Yale man and the jail man" was indeed one of the strangest alliances that a populace accustomed to peculiar liaisons had seen in a long time.

Harrison's mistake, out of keeping with his customary political acumen, was to employ his campaign manager, Judge Norfleet R. Sledge, as majority expert for the Finance Committee. Two days after Sledge resigned his position as county chancellor his name was entered on the federal payroll at an annual salary of $3,000. Unnoticed at the time, the appointment was discovered by Bilbo who happened to be reading the records of the Senate. Perhaps, he decided, he could make enough of the Sledge appointment to drag Harrison down on a charge of payroll corruption. When Harrison countered that senators commonly used their salaried committee aides during campaigns, both Senator Joseph Robinson and the financial clerk of the Senate,

Charles F. Pace, concurred. Since Bilbo had raised the issue of federally paid campaign assistants, Harrison in turn questioned Conner's use of a $10,000-a-year man, namely Bilbo. Despite his jests at Bilbo's role in Conner's campaign, Harrison's image was tarnished by the Sledge appointment. A supporter later wrote to the senator's manager, "It was a very unwise move . . . in that it gave the opposition something to muddy the waters about."[38]

Harrison's headquarters directed the activities of the numerous county organizations that had been formed in the late spring, schooled county leaders on campaign pointers, and blanketed the state with thousands of leaflets, including a weekly publication called *The Truth*, a rebuttal to Conner's organ, *The Record*. Speakers were urged to praise the administration's relief and recovery programs, all the while pointing to Senator Harrison as the "keystone in the arch of Southern leadership." According to the promotional literature, Harrison's preeminence in party and administration circles had netted every section of the state resettlement communities, highways, CCC camps, reforestation and soil erosion projects, and a myriad of public buildings. Through the summer the headquarters released news of the approval by the Washington WPA office of additional projects for Mississippi. (In one instance, thirteen new projects were designated on one day.) When the Conner team tried to show to the contrary that earlier PWA programs had gotten a slow start in Mississippi, Harrison laid the blame on Conner's inability to get along with his highway commission and with federal relief officials. Governor White, the former state PWA chief, echoed that "had it not been for Pat Harrison . . . the $15,000,000 grant for highways would not be available today."[39] There was no question that the incumbent held the advantage in what was the only real issue—the continuation of a New Deal for Mississippi. Conner could scarcely hope to win the support of the powerful interest groups that had already reaped the benefits of Harrison's power in Washington—the veterans, the farmers, and organized labor.

Mississippi ex-soldiers, who had once looked circumspectly at Harrison's bonus record, joined his camp after the bonus bill passed in 1936. A bonus victory supplement of the Jackson *Daily News* as well as a special issue of the *Mississippi Veteran* carried full-page endorsements from the national commanders of the Veterans of Foreign

CHAIRMAN ‗FINANCE COMMITTEE‗ U.S. SENATE

Courtesy: Senate Historical Office, Washington, D.C.

Wars and the Disabled American Veterans.[40] The farmers of Mississippi were ready to stand behind Harrison also. Edward O'Neal, the head of the American Farm Bureau, appealed to the Mississippi bureau in July to endorse the senator, while Chester H. Gray, the Washington representative of the AFB, softened the criticism on the coconut oil matter by stating that the three-cent tax on imported oils was the best the farmers could have gotten. Probably the most effective farm spokesman for Harrison was the state commissioner of agriculture, J. C. Holton, who instructed his full force to "get busy." Holton forwarded to the principal newspapers in the state a mimeographed sheet that catalogued all the farm measures the senator had supported since 1929. In a letter printed in *The Truth*, Holton told the senator that his department had never before taken an active part in any campaign. "Our personal esteem for you warranted our actions," he concluded.[41]

Harrison was particularly anxious to have the support of organized labor. Because he had crossed the AFL on prevailing wages, his opponents hoped to paint him as the oppressor of the working man. Forgiving Harrison for that one vote in view of his efforts to pass relief measures, public works programs, and social security, William Green endorsed the senator. An additional coup came with the personal visit to the Harrison headquarters of the Atlanta representative of the AFL who announced that "organized labor is in cordial sympathy with Senator Harrison's campaign." Subsequently, numerous national and state affiliates fell in line. Harrison's campaign media played to the hilt endorsements from the Order of Railway Conductors and twenty other railway labor groups. One week before the first primary the Mississippi Federation of Labor with its 150 locals endorsed the senator. When Harrison spoke at McComb, a railroad center in south Mississippi, prominent railway labor leaders, several of them longtime Bilbo partisans, joined him on the platform.[42] On the other hand, Conner had alienated labor when he had called out the national guard in the textile strike of 1934, urged the repeal of an absentee voter law that had permitted the laboring man away from home to vote, vetoed homestead exemption, and "fathered" the sales tax.[43]

The strongest backing that Harrison could possibly receive was that of a single man in Washington. Throughout June and July Franklin D. Roosevelt said little on Harrison's behalf. In June, while he was in Arkansas to attend the state's centennial celebration (and incidentally to back Joe Robinson), the president had asked Hugh White to gather the Mississippi editors in attendance. "Senator Harrison has been one of the most valuable assets of the nation and the Democratic Party," FDR told the journalists. Bilbo, afraid that Roosevelt would intervene in the Mississippi primary, reminded Farley that the president had assured him that he would "not take any part" in the race and warned the postmaster general that the "Democracy in Mississippi would bitterly resent" outside interference. Although the president apparently intended to avoid involvement in the Mississippi race and refused a request from Congressman Aubert

Dunn to send a statement that Dunn could use in his support of
Harrison, by mid-August Roosevelt had been convinced that Harrison's opposition was real and potent.[44]

The Washington law partner of ex-senator Stephens had written to
Marvin McIntyre that in Mississippi "the one big issue is Franklin
D. Roosevelt." He described Conner's organization as "hardworking,
alive [and] smart" and reminded McIntyre that Bilbo had always
reached a large group of "gullible and ignorant voters." Stephens had
already written to Roosevelt of the "vicious and dirty" campaign
against Harrison and warned the president that a marginal Harrison
victory in August would provide excellent grist for the Republican
presidential campaign. What concerned Roosevelt more than anything else, however, was the certain elevation of the conservative
William H. King to the chairmanship of the Finance Committee in
the event of Harrison's defeat. Such a consequence of a Conner
victory was also on the mind of a Franklin County farmer who wrote
his local editor, "I understand that if Mr. Harrison goes back to the
Senate, he will have the purse strings of the nation, and if Mr. Conner goes to the Senate, a man named King from Idaho [*sic*] will have
the little old pocket book in his jeans."[45]

Roosevelt finally decided to come to Harrison's aid. According to
Morgenthau, FDR contrived a scheme to identify Harrison with an
anticipated treasury drive against tax evasion. Two weeks before the
first primary, the president summoned the senator to the White
House for an "important conference," and Harrison flew to
Washington for a day. Arthur Krock observed that the gesture would
not be lost on Mississippi voters "who have a habit of requiring that
Congress back the President." In the estimation of the columnist
Harrison was "New Deal Leader No. 2" ("Number 1" was majority
leader Robinson). Krock hardly saw how, with such credentials, Harrison could be defeated. While Harrison employed the president's assistance to its best advantage, he also arranged behind the scenes to
have his friend Louis Jiggits receive from James Farley a telegram,
actually composed by the senator, that concluded, "No Democratic
leader is held in higher esteem and affection by President Roosevelt."
Joseph Guffey, Pennsylvania's New Dealer, concurred that such a
telegram would be crucial for Harrison.[46]

Harrison returned from the White House conference to spend a

furious two weeks winding up his campaign. He made his last appearance in north Mississippi at a mammoth rally in Stephens's
hometown of New Albany where his listeners partook of 12,500
pounds of barbecued beef and lamb. Both Stephens and Dennis Murphree spoke for Harrison before the large audience that had come
from several nearby counties. Since the northeastern section of the
state was Bilbo country, it was generally conceded that the real battle
of the ballot would be fought in the hills. The New Albany rally
helped Harrison's cause immensely. Then, in the final days, Harrison returned to his Gulf Coast home to host another giant supper,
this time of boiled shrimp and crab to be consumed to the music of six
bands which entertained the crowd until midnight. He then remained at home to await the returns of the August 25 primary. [47]

By the time of the election, predictions were that Harrison would
win the race by no more than ten thousand votes, the smallest majority given him in eighteen years. Catherine Blanton, Harrison's secretary, deplored to Halsey that it had been a "damn campaign, filled
with lies"; but even so, her boss was "going to lick the devil out of
them." As it turned out, he carried all but two counties; the final
count ran 128,729 for Harrison and 65,296 for Conner. Conner won
only his home county of Covington and small, rural Benton County
on the Tennessee line. An exuberant Harrison backer telegraphed
manager Sledge, "Sen-nett and his Mother Bilbo said you were expert
for the majority, but lawdy, what a majority." Election analysts attributed the victory to the credit the electorate gave Harrison for the
largesse which the New Deal had showered upon Mississippi. Conner, it was said, lost more than he had gained by "too much Bilbo."
Moreover, he had hurt himself by his old fight with the highway
commission, his reputed inaccessibility as governor, and the unpopu-
larity of the sales tax. Thousands of voters probably cast their votes
more against the sales tax than against Conner. From a national
perspective, Harrison's two-to-one majority, Byrnes's seven-to-one
win, and victories for Robinson in Arkansas, John Bankhead in
Alabama, and Morris Sheppard in Texas were indicative of the popularity of the New Deal in the South. [48]

Conflicting evidence precludes an adequate assessment of two significant factors in Harrison's victory—the extent of financial backing
from his friends and the political advantages of a large constituency

carried on the federal payroll. "The Man" Bilbo was one of the few Mississippi politicians who could run a campaign on a shoestring and win. Unquestionably, Harrison conducted his 1936 race on more than a bank account of goodwill and personality. Reports circulated at the time and have since been repeated that Bernard Baruch aided the senator substantially, both in the 1936 campaign and earlier in meeting other financial obligations following the crash of 1929.[49] Baruch was said to hold a "stable of senators," which included Robinson and Byrnes as well as Harrison, and it was generally known that he had purchased memberships for Harrison, Byrnes, and eight other friends when the Jefferson Island Club was short of money.[50] It is unlikely that anyone will ever know how much Baruch offered in gifts and loans from his cashbox. Other friends of Harrison, notably George E. Allen and Eugene Fly, contributed money in 1936, and it is probable that labor unions, cotton cooperatives, lumber associations, and trade groups whose policies the senator had supported provided aid. A campaign assistant long after the election recalled that Harrison "never asked anybody for money" and ran his campaign on $32,000 volunteered by friends. For whatever aid Harrison received there was never any scandal. Years later Henry Wallace recalled, "I don't know that Pat ever did anything that was wrong."[51]

Both Harrison and Bilbo denied holding the reins on public employees, notably WPA employees; but any reading of their correspondence leaves the definite impression that they actively vied for the votes of government workers. Harrison always seemed to know who his friends and enemies were, county by county, and he bragged of his "little black book" of opponents. At a victory rally in Jackson he warned, "We are going down the line to do some purging. I haven't lost my red book [of friends] and my black book." In extant correspondence there are broad hints of post-election shenanigans of rewards and reprisals. "I have been unable to check up on the WPA workers but will do so and let you know in regard to that matter later but am satisfied there were some who voted against us," wrote one campaign worker to Harrison two weeks after the primary. Another reported a Resettlement Administration manager who "lined his clients up," a man whose job Bilbo boasted that he would "get."[52]

Victory for Harrison in 1936 led to a furious jostling for jobs reminiscent of the early days of the New Deal. "The situation [is] more trying than even during the campaign with hundreds of people even into the late hours of the night having conferences regarding employment," Sledge wrote to his wife. Judge Sledge himself hoped to be named to the Interstate Commerce Commission, but more realistically he expected to be given employment in some legal capacity. In the end he became an assistant to Attorney General Cummings in the claims division of the Justice Department.[53]

Mississippians still faced the general balloting in November, when the only real election would be that of a president. The campaign was of little consequence in Mississippi. The only question was the state's maintenance of its distinction as the most Democratic state in the nation. Senator Harrison had long been certain that his president would return to office. The Republicans had no candidate in sight who "could do more than wobble around in the job," he had said in the fall of 1935.[54]

Despite a temperature of 96°, the Democratic convention at Jackson's city auditorium in mid-June of 1936 had been the most harmonious in thirty years. To his followers, who were in complete control, Harrison telegraphed a request that the convention instruct its delegates to nominate Roosevelt and Garner. Departing from its time-honored custom of sending uninstructed delegates to the national convention, the Mississippi Democrats asked their Philadelphia-bound contingent to cast its full vote for FDR. In Washington, Harrison was said to be the White House spokesman to avert the threat of a bolt of former candidate Al Smith and his conservatives allies. From the portico of the White House the Mississippian pledged, "We are going to give them such a good platform that there will be no cause for them to leave the party." Harrison attended the Philadelphia convention for only one day. The old sinus complaint which had forced him to abandon the tax bill flared up again and he was not well. He declined service on the platform committee, thinking that he was not needed since "there isn't any scrap on anything." Besides, he wanted to conserve his strength for his own vigorous campaign which would begin a week later.[55]

The Young Democrats of Mississippi sponsored a giant rally in Jackson to hear Roosevelt's acceptance speech by radio. The event, chaired by a young Jackson attorney named Ross Barnett, drew a crowd that came to town by wagon, automobile, and mule. During the same week an American Institute of Public Opinion poll revealed that 83 percent of the Mississippians who were asked "Are the acts of the present Administration helping or hindering recovery?" responded in favor of the New Deal. A further endorsement of Roosevelt came in September when the state legislature adopted a resolution applauding the Democratic administration. Harrison did not even campaign for the ticket in his home state. Instead, he left Washington for a two-week speaking tour during the latter part of October that carried him into seven Middle Atlantic and Midwestern states. To his audiences he predicted that "when the smoke of political controversy fades, future generations will more fully appreciate the fact that Franklin D. Roosevelt is the GREATEST HUMANITARIAN that this country has ever seen."[56]

Pollsters working for the Democratic National Committee determined that South Carolina, and not Mississippi, would return the greatest percentage of votes for Roosevelt. Herbert Holmes, the state chairman, refused to concede the lead; nor would Lieutenant Governor Snider. The two decided to wager with their South Carolina counterparts "one live Democratic Mississippi donkey against one Democratic South Carolina donkey" that Mississippi would poll the greater percentage for FDR. The returns in November proved the Mississippi braggarts wrong. Roosevelt voters gave the state a percentage of only 97.5, while South Carolina came through with 98.3 percent for the Democracy. Consequently, "Queenie" rode the train to Washington that carried Governor White and several hundred Mississippians to the inaugural festivities. In a ceremony held in the lobby of the Mayflower Hotel, Snider turned the four-footed Mississippi Democrat over to the South Carolina lieutenant governor, who promptly put her under the watchcare of Farley.[57]

In the summer of 1936 Mississippians had seen more political horseplay than in any other year of the decade. Pat Harrison won what *Newsweek* called "the most raucous, name-calling, hair-pulling campaign in recent Mississippi history."[58] His stature among Mississippians was directly related to his image as a New Dealer *par excellence*. Whatever disagreements he may have had with President Roosevelt over taxation or lesser questions seemed to be of little consequence. At the year's end there were no indications that within a year the Harrison-Roosevelt accord would be seriously strained and that the two would reach a point of mutual distrust.

CHAPTER VIII

"By God . . . This Thing Goes Deeper Than You Think"

1937

THE DEMOCRATIC VICTORY in 1936 was an amazing personal triumph for Franklin D. Roosevelt. The president carried all but two states, and his influence figured significantly in the congressional races that left the party completely dominant on Capitol Hill. Seemingly, FDR was in a position to get anything that he wanted from the Seventy-fifth Congress. "Why, if the President asked Congress to commit suicide tomorrow, they'd do it," discouraged old Carter Glass complained. Roosevelt's battery of Senate leaders had all been returned by overwhelming victories of their own. There seemed to be little question that the party leaders could not easily lord over the small group of unenthusiastic and unreliable Senate Democrats. Congress was expected to "have the courage of the President's convictions," political scientist O. R. Altman later wrote. [1]

While a head count indicated that Roosevelt should be able to have whatever he willed from his Congress, there were a few mischievous qualities inherent in the great Democratic victory. Did not many of the Senate Democrats harbor a feeling of independence since the president was in his second term and another name would head the ticket in four years? Would the behemoth size of the Democratic majority destroy the cohesiveness that comes when smaller numbers must huddle under the cloak of partisan loyalty? And what could be the portent of the new "Roosevelt coalition" of Negro, urban, and eastern voters? [2] If the president requested for the one-third of the nation he lamented as ill-clad, ill-housed, and ill-nourished programs incompatible with the economic and social views of his congressional leaders, would he have to turn elsewhere for counsel and support? After all, there had been earlier suggestions that his Senate coadjutors resented the intrusion of the eastern liberals who were all but contemptuous of the legislative process.

Less than a month after the inaugural ceremonies, a disconcerting mood fell over the Democratic legislative leadership. The president asked for a farm act, a wages and hours law, a measure to dot the nation with "little TVAs," and an executive reorganization statute so extensive that Congress would be stripped of virtually all its powers over the executive except that of appropriation. To journalists Joseph Alsop and Turner Catledge "the President was suffering from an attack of political folies de grandeur" in his belief that he could have all of his program.[3] The fact that Pat Harrison maintained a quietude on the new proposals suggested dissatisfaction. Along with other leaders so accustomed to being called to the White House for consultation, he resented the fact that few invitations were issued in that January of 1937.

If the "Big Four," as the press called Garner, Robinson, Byrnes, and Harrison, had known of the plan which the president had been quietly contemplating for some time, they might well have been troubled. Only Attorney General Cummings was privy to a court plan that Roosevelt had had the Justice Department working on for almost two years. Without any warning, FDR unveiled his plan to reorganize the judiciary at a brief White House cabinet meeting to which only Speaker William Bankhead, majority leaders Robinson and Rayburn, and the two judiciary committee chairmen, Hatton Summers and Henry Ashurst, were invited from the Congress. It was a case of "telling and not asking" when the president disclosed his plan which, in essence, called for as many as six additional justices for the Supreme Court. Speaker Bankhead expressed the shock of the congressional captains when he asked a friend, "Wouldn't you have thought that the President would have told his own party leaders what he was going to do? He didn't because he knew that hell would break loose."[4]

Bankhead's prediction was correct. The court-packing plan played havoc directly or indirectly with every measure that came before Congress from February 5, the day of the message, until its eventual defeat in late July. As William E. Leuchtenburg has said, "To explain the rupture of 1937 and ignore the Supreme Court donnybrook is like accounting for the coming of the Civil War without reference to slavery." The congressional leaders, whom Roosevelt had snubbed in his formulation of the plan but upon whom he would have to depend to get the bill passed, did not divulge their real thoughts in the platitudinous public statements they made. Robinson, who actually considered the plan "pretty raw," told reporters that it would pass.[5] Observers found it significant that Harrison, Tom Connally, and Walter George initially refused to make any comments. A week after the message Harrison finally broke his silence and offered a modest but qualified endorsement of "the general idea." He hoped it would be possible to maintain the Court at nine, but he supposed that some good might come of the president's plan if a few justices would retire. Harrison's ambiguity was enough to put him on the list of senators invited to the White House for the presidential pep talks that went on until the bill went to the Judiciary Committee. After a White House consultation on February 13 Byrnes announced that he was "a little stronger" than he had been and Harrison finally stated, "Of course I am for the proposition." Turner Catledge, writing for the New York *Times*, referred to the two as "stalwarts in this as in all former battles for the administration," but the statement, if accurate then, would need modification later.[6]

A week later Harrison, in the company of Robinson, Ashurst, Barkley, Byrnes, and Black, returned to the White House for a conference to decide upon an uncompromising drive to force the court plan through Congress. By then, of the Mississippians in Congress, only Representatives Wall Doxey and Aaron Ford openly opposed the president. Rankin, who had heatedly defended Roosevelt, was preparing a constitutional amendment limiting the terms of all federal judges. The seven Mississippians in Congress who now backed judicial reorganization with varying degrees of commitment were sustained by the Mississippi Bar Association, which approved FDR's court reform program at a called meeting held in Jackson. Former governor Earl Brewer, who steered the resolution to victory, declared that the court struggle pitted the "Mills, the Hoovers, Wall Street, and predatory wealth" against the "white plume of the President." Before March was out, Bilbo inserted into the *Congressional Record* a favorable resolution from the state's farm organizations. The American Institute of Public Opinion weekly survey released at the end of March indicated that Mississippi, one of twenty states in favor of the plan, backed the measure by 67 percent.[7]

If the depth and sincerity of Harrison's support of the court plan was suspect during February and March, by April he had clearly come to have second doubts. Two issues repeatedly linked with the plan bobbed to the surface in April and converted reluctants such as Harrison into opponents. It was Senator Byrnes, generally believed in 1937 to be closer to FDR than either Harrison or Robinson, who took the initiative in calling for Senate condemnation of sit-down strikes and further large-scale relief spending. On April 1, without any warning, Byrnes suddenly rose to offer an amendment to the Guffey-Vinson coal bill then under debate.[8] Gravely concerned over the filtering of John L. Lewis's textile organizing teams into South Carolina, Byrnes threw the Senate into turmoil when he called for a public declaration against all sit-down strikes. The strikes, which had begun in late 1936 and finally succeeded in defeating General Motors, seemed to be invincible. Southern senators, sensitive to the section's alarm at the prospect of unchecked unionism, were on the spot. Privately supporting Byrnes, they were reluctant to force the president's hand by sending him a coal bill that included the embarrassing amendment.

When the Committee for Industrial Organization launched a drive on textile mills on April 4, sending forty-five agents into eight southern states, the vote on Byrnes's amendment was all the more crucial. Byrnes hoped to have the support of his two closest friends in the Senate, but neither was willing to accept the stricture on labor drafted by the South Carolinian. Robinson privately told him, "I am for it, Jim, but I will have to oppose it." Reportedly, the Democrats who released their president from the trap acted under White House inspiration. The Mississippi senator made his own position clear, however, in a statement to the Senate and in a press release dispatched to Mississippi papers as well as to the Memphis *Commercial Appeal*. His vote had not reflected sympathy for the strikes, he demurred. He opposed the amendment because it dealt exclusively with coal miners; any sense-of-the-Senate condemnation of sit-down strikes should be in the form of a separate resolution applicable to all industries. "I have no sympathy with sit-down strikes," he insisted. When the matter came before the Senate on April 7 in the form of an innocuous concurrent resolution condemning both the strikes and industrial espionage, the solons accepted it by a 75 to 3 vote.[9] Harri-

President Franklin D. Roosevelt, Governor Hugh L. White, and Harrison, during presidential visit to Mississippi, April, 1937

Louisiana Governor Richard Leche, Harrison, President Roosevelt, and Governor White during April, 1937 presidential visit to Mississippi

Senators James F. Byrnes (S.C.), Robert J. Bulkley (Ohio), and Harrison on Jefferson Island outing (1937)

Senator Alben Barkley (Ken.), Key Pittman (Nev.), and Harrison, probably during Majority Leadership contest (1937)

Senators Walter F. George (Ga.), Harrison, and Robert M. LaFollette, Jr. (Wis.) (1937)

Harrison (1938)

Harrison and Labor Secretary Frances Perkins on February 28, 1939 at Senate Finance Committee hearings on Social Security amendments

Secretary of Agriculture Henry A. Wallace and Harrison at Senate Finance Committee hearings in 1939

Harrison and SEC Commissioner Martin Sennett (Mike) Conner at Mississippi
State-Ole Miss football game (1940)

Senators William H. King (Utah) and Harrison (Carter Glass, Va., in background) 1940

Harrison and Secretary of State Cordell Hull (Arthur Capper, Kan., and Arthur Vandenberg in background) at Finance Committee hearings on reciprocal trade agreements extension, February 26, 1940

Senators Alben Barkley, Harrison, Pittman, and Byrnes after the three-vote defeat of Pittman's amendment on the reciprocal trade agreements extension, February 30, 1940

son's own quick shuffle had been a display of his facile political tight-
rope artistry. Presidential foes, chagrined that the Senate's sidestep-
ping motion had not forced administration leaders to break with the
president, quickened when Byrnes made his second move, this time
against relief spending.

Harrison had been encouraged by the president's January message
on the 1938 budget which presented a balanced slate except for
statutory contributions to debt retirement. Three years earlier Harrison had stated that the government could not stand a spending spree
of more than three years duration. When, on April 20, 1937,
Roosevelt requested $1.5 billion for the WPA, his trio of Senate lead-
ers, now firmly backed by Vice-President Garner, set about to cut the
president's request by half a billion dollars. Harrison, perturbed over
the expansive relief appropriations, was critical of the executive message. When Harrison, Robinson, and Byrnes met with Roosevelt
along with Garner, Bankhead, and Rayburn, the entire congressional
delegation demanded that the relief figure be set at no more than one
billion dollars. In FDR's presence, and to his obvious chagrin, the
group polled itself to prove to him that Congress was unwilling to go
along with the presidential figure. [10]

Actually Roosevelt himself was disturbed by mounting federal expenditures. When Harrison joined him in April on the presidential
train carrying FDR to a Gulf Coast vacation, the chief executive
pressed upon the senator his desire for economy. At the heart of the
executive-congressional disagreement over economy was Roosevelt's
refusal to make budgetary allowances for pet projects proposed by
several legislative leaders. Harrison was annoyed because the president spurned his aid to education bill, and Bankhead feared a short-
age of funds for the farm tenancy program. Hence, the congressional
economy drive was precipitated not only by Roosevelt's relief requests
but also by his refusal to allow his leaders a piece of the spending
pie. [11]

A House rebellion in May temporarily slashed the $1.5 billion fig-
ure to $1 billion. Restored shortly afterward, the presidential request
found opposition in the Senate. Harry L. Hopkins, who had done
missionary work among the rebellious representatives, went to work
upon individual senators. In mid-June he called Governor Hugh
White to discuss how Harrison might be prodded to support the WPA

appropriation bill. The two concluded, however, that since Bilbo would deliberately move to cancel Harrison's vote, however it went, it would be best to leave both alone.[12] Hopkins's intercession, which further irritated congressional critics of his spending propensities, would not have bothered Harrison. The two men had always gotten along well, but Harrison's difficulties with Bilbo over WPA politics in Mississippi had soured him on the agency. Passage of the WPA appropriation without a roll call spared Harrison the embarrassment of a recorded vote on relief. The battle over relief cuts ended just as Byrnes thought that it would. "You cannot hope to beat a Santa Claus that comes every day," he wrote a constituent.[13]

The stirrings over sit-down strikes and relief spending subsided, but they had intensified congressional feeling against the court plan. Moreover, just when it began to appear that Roosevelt's chances of winning over Congress were growing dimmer, the justices further weakened the president's hand in their reversal of earlier decisions against the New Deal. Roosevelt's difficulty with the Court seemed to have solved itself, and Byrnes wondered, "Why run for a train after you've caught it?"[14] Harrison had the same thought. While the president was still away on his southern vacation a remarkable little episode occurred in the private office of Edwin A. Halsey, secretary of the Senate. Invited there to lunch, James Roosevelt, the president's son and sometime legislative liaison, found Harrison, Barkley, and Robinson waiting. The trio told the younger Roosevelt that the best thing to do was to capitulate on the demand for six additional justices and leave the court bill in their hands. Warning that the bill was wrecking the Democratic party, the group advised Roosevelt's son to relay their advice to his father before he returned to Washington. As spokesman for the group, Robinson suggested, "You tell your poppa that he'd better leave this whole thing to us to get what we can out of it. We'll do our best for him." When the inner council of White House advisers, consisting of, among others, Cummings and Democratic party publicist Charles Michelson, heard of the senators' mandate, even they agreed with the congressional leaders. Roosevelt, who never liked losing skirmishes to his senators, doggedly rejected any compromise.[15]

A short time later Harrison and Byrnes were at the White House on a matter which meant more to them than any other they had ever

carried to the president. Two hours after Willis Van Devanter resigned from the Supreme Court on May 18, Joe Robinson's two
closest friends reminded FDR that he was expected to name their
associate to the bench. Roosevelt was peeved at being reminded of the
promised appointment (it had gained wide currency), for he was
aware of all the talk that Robinson's appointment would replace one
conservative with another. Neither did he like the senators' repeated
advice that still another opportunity for compromise had opened.[16]

By June Harrison was fed up with the court business. In surveying
the issues still before Congress—a promised tax inquiry, farm tenancy, flood control, and relief funds—he remarked, "That bill is the
key to the situation."[17] The Senate was in a shambles. Garner had
"gone fishing" in Texas, Robinson was reluctant to go to the White
House on any matter whatsoever, and the Senate Democrats were
badly divided, at least half of them resentful that the president had
rejected the advice of Harrison and Byrnes, described by Catledge as
"his wily, immensely knowledgeable lieutenants in past battles."[18]
When the final debate began on the court plan, the Senate was deadlocked. Robinson, who held the key to any hope of a compromise
acceptable to FDR, was obviously near physical collapse. On the
morning of July 13, pain forced him to turn his duties over to Barkley
and to retire to his apartment. At noon that day, when Senators
Harry S. Truman and Harrison had lunch with Halsey in the Senate
secretary's private office, the discussion centered upon the disastrous
party fight over the court plan. Halsey asked the Mississippian, who
had not said a word about the plan on the Senate floor and little
elsewhere, to make one of his good-natured, conciliatory speeches.
Harrison pushed his chair away, slammed a balled fist upon the table,
and hotly replied, "By God, no, I won't do it. This thing goes deeper
than you think, and I won't have any part of it."[19]

On July 14 the man whom Harrison considered to be "the most
useful, the most influential man [he had] ever seen in public life"
was found dead. Joseph T. Robinson's death meant the end of the
court fight, for the votes crucial to any sort of a presidential victory
were no more than personal pledges given to the popular majority
leader. Less than a week later, Harrison did assume a conciliatory
role, but it was no more than futile gesture. Knowing that court reform would be limited to procedural changes involving the lower

courts only, Roosevelt agreed to Harrison's proposal that an arbitration committee, composed of five administration and five opposition senators, be created to work out a substitute bill. Although Roosevelt was amenable to the idea, opposition leaders Wheeler and Bailey objected, for they were not willing to have the court plan lifted from the Judiciary Committee.[20] Even when it became apparent that the court bill faced recommittal and certain death, Harrison was unwilling to do anything more to save the president's pride or position. At a White House luncheon on July 21 Roosevelt sought the Mississippian's help in the approaching showdown over recommital, but Harrison declined. On the next day the bill was returned to the hostile Judiciary Committee. Harrison's vote was one of the seventy that sent it there.[21]

Harrison's attitude and virtual inaction through the five-month controversy over the president's court plan was similar to that of many other Southerners in Congress. Initially he had offered unenthusiastic support, followed by silence marked by little to no aid. As were most Southerners, he was apprehensive about the executive power that might ensue from a handsome presidential victory—power to be exercised at the expense of Congress. There is no doubt that the southern bloc resented the influence of the inner council presided over by Thomas Corcoran that encouraged the president to resist capitulation to the senatorial compromisers. And, even in the absence of concrete evidence, particularly where Harrison is concerned, Southerners feared that a liberalized court would move to disrupt the state of race relations in the South.[22]

Interwoven with the troublesome disposal of the court bill was an issue that created additional fractiousness within the Senate Democracy and heightened Harrison's personal estrangement from the president. The question of Robinson's successor as majority leader had risen long before his death. As early as 1934, Washington *Evening Star* columnist Frederic Wile had predicted that Robinson would be elevated to the Supreme Court and that his successor would be Harrison or Byrnes. When Van Devanter resigned in 1937 immediate attention focused upon four candidates whose names were bantered about in cloakrooms and corridors as Robinson's successor: Harrison, Byrnes, Barkley, and Pittman. Harrison withdrew from the speculated race on May 19 and Pittman followed suit the next day, leaving as the principal contender Byrnes who had the open support of Garner. Within a day Harrison was back in the race at the insistence of friends when Byrnes's associates circulated talk that he would withdraw in deference to his Mississippi friend. The rumor mill that May manufactured considerable talk that the administration was alarmed at the possibility that Harrison's promotion to majority leadership would leave the Finance Committee in the hands of the arch-conservative King. At the same time Harrison's supporters maintained that he could retain his chairmanship if both Barkley and Byrnes were appointed as assistant leaders to help shoulder the duties.[23]

Robinson's death compelled the Senate Democrats to shift from conjecture to action. For a second time Byrnes removed himself from the field, leaving the contest to Harrison and Barkley. As the assistant leader, Barkley had more of an official claim on the post than did Harrison, but it was clear that a majority of the Senate Democrats favored Harrison, who was looked upon as less subservient to the White House. Openly backed by the senators who opposed the court plan, Harrison also drew support from court plan proponents who simply thought that the election of the congenial and popular Mississippian would serve to heal party wounds. But there was no question that White House objections to Harrison went beyond FDR's reluctance to have the Finance Committee chairmanship go to King who, he told Farley, was "just impossible to deal with." Roosevelt, who considered Barkley to be a better friend of the New Deal than Harrison, was particularly vexed over Harrison's tax philosophy, which he thought to be only slightly more liberal than King's. Aware of the Mississippian's rumblings over the Revenue Act of 1936, Roosevelt confided to Farley, "Barkley must win. Harrison would repeal the capital gains tax. He would do it now if he could."[24]

On July 15, the day following Robinson's death, the campaign for the selection of his successor began in earnest. The day was remarkably full of controversial moves. While Byrnes continued to marshal votes for Harrison, an approximate dozen first-term "Young Turks" met to promote Barkley, whose campaign was to be headed by Pennsylvania's Joseph F. Guffey. Iowa's Clyde Herring, in whose office the meeting was held, made it clear that the group favored Barkley because of his "liberal" views. Not all the freshmen senators favored Barkley. After four of the new senators (Prentiss M. Brown of Michigan, Edwin C. Johnson of Colorado, Charles O. Andrews of Florida, and Guy M. Gillette of Iowa) met with the president and pleaded for withdrawal of the court plan, an alarmed Roosevelt addressed a public letter to Barkley regretting that a "decent respect" for the memory of Robinson had not deferred discussion of politics and legislation. Bearing the salutation "Dear Alben," the letter deplored that "advantage is being taken of what, in all decency, should be a period of mourning." Aware that such an expression could have been made just as well to Key Pittman, the president *pro tempore*, Roosevelt was careful to say to Barkley that he had been the recipient on the basis of his status as acting majority leader. The letter, which transparently made the court bill the symbol of the contest between Harrison and Barkley, added another ingredient to the leadership contest—that of legislative independence from the executive. Indiana's Frederick Van Nuys spoke the defiance of FDR's critics: "We'll elect our own leader and dispose of the Court bill in our own way without any dictation by any source whatsoever." Minority leader Charles McNary, who had always been personally close to Harrison, took exception to FDR. "If there's been any political activity, it's been at the White House," he decided.[25]

Circumstances dictated that Harrison and Byrnes maintain a semblance of calm over the letter. Privately they were furious. On July 16, the day of Robinson's state funeral, Roosevelt conferred first with Byrnes and then with Harrison, the latter summoned late in the day. An eager press corps awaiting his emergence from the White House learned that the president had given his "absolute assurance" that no executive action would be taken "under any circumstances" in the contest. When Turner Catledge privately asked the senator if he trusted Roosevelt, Harrison answered, "Why, he's into it up to here," drawing an index finger across his throat just below his chin. Harrison knew that the "Dear Alben" letter was costly, for an hour after its publication Morris Sheppard told him that he could no longer support him. "I am sorry, Pat, but the President's wishes come first with me," the Texas senator explained.[26]

The dozens of subdued washroom and cloakroom discussions on the leadership vote, now set for July 21, that took place on the two days following Robinson's death were transferred to the funeral train.

Aboard were thirty-eight senators (of whom twenty-three were Democrats), party chairman Farley, Assistant Attorney General Joseph B. Keenan, and the White House legislative liaison officer Charles West, the latter two on hand more to monitor discussions on the court bill than to pay their last respects to Robinson. Farley refused to inject himself in the continual discussions, which did not cease even for the more solemn aspects of the occasion. Train attendants were careful about how they quartered Democrats, and funeral managers were advised on how to group the senators en route to the church lest opponents be cast together. Even in the relaxed atmosphere of the local country club, where the delegation lunched before the service, the senators gathered in factional groups. Vice-President Garner, who joined the delegation in Little Rock, studiously avoided taking sides, although it was common knowledge that he preferred that Harrison win. Not even his faithful "Ettie" could pry a word from him. "There isn't a human being who has heard me express myself," he told his wife, "and that includes you."[27]

The journey to and from Little Rock was little more than a rolling caucus as battle lines were formed for what would be the most acrimonious leadership election since 1923, when Robinson had won over Furnifold M. Simmons of North Carolina in a contest which Harrison had managed for his Arkansas friend. In many ways the careers of the two contestants in 1937 ran parallel in their long continuous service in public office. Harrison had entered the House of Representatives in the Sixty-second Congress, Barkley in the Sixty-third. Both had been national convention keynoters. Harrison had been a senator since 1919 and Barkley since 1927. Harrison merited the post on terms of seniority; but on the basis of loyalty to the administration Barkley appeared to have the edge. On only a single issue, the soldier bonus, had the Kentuckian left the reservation, and he had publicly identified himself with the court plan. While Harrison's supporters in the Senate and in the press argued that he would appoint Byrnes as assistant leader and that the two would be as loyal to Roosevelt as Robinson had been (an argument that caused some senators to smile), others concurred with columnist Heywood Broun that "the selection of Pat Harrison will mean a 99.78 per cent sabotaging" of all the president's plans.[28]

Neither Harrison nor Barkley mingled openly with their colleagues on the return to Washington, both keeping to their private quarters, from which senators came and went singly or in small groups. Harrison was at his usual ease. In fact, when one reporter attempted to determine if the Mississippian were nervous over what by ordinary standards could be the most exciting contest of a senator's lifetime, Harrison assured him that the coming election was not his greatest thrill in life. "Barring romance," he drawled, "it was when I went to my first baseball game."[29]

The senators were back in Washington on Monday, July 19, a day in which the leadership contest dropped into the background while New York Governor Herbert Lehman's letter to Senator Wagner attacking the court plan became the leading topic of Senate buzz groups. Tuesday, the eve of the election, however, was consumed almost entirely by intense conferences. In the morning the president fielded a battery of questions from reporters and cavalierly denied that he had interceded in any way in the contest. His neutrality, he insisted, was "very obvious and [had] been from the very beginning." Later in the day FDR summoned both contenders to the White House to join Pittman and Garner in a conference of general legislation.[30] The ploy, an outward show of presidential neutrality, concealed manipulations which had occurred during the past few days and continued through Tuesday night.

Working through two powerful Democratic bosses at Roosevelt's behest, administration aides attempted to detach two promised votes from Harrison. With Harry Truman they were unsuccessful, for when Tom Pendergast, the Missouri boss, informed the senator that the White House had called for his help in getting Truman to switch to Barkley, the answer came, "I can't do it, Tom. . . . I've given my word to Pat Harrison." The flinty Missourian was so piqued that he telephoned Steve Early and left a message for FDR: "Tell him to stop treating me like an office boy." In the case of William Dieterich, the administration scored. When a Chicago *Tribune* reporter filed a bulletin from the funeral train that the Illinois senator intended to vote for Harrison, the wheels were set in motion to change that vote. Dieterich's original commitment to Harrison was so strong that he had told Byrnes that he would second Harrison's caucus nomination. Nevertheless, one hour before the caucus met, Dieterich informed

Harrison that he could not honor his pledge since the screw had been
turned the night before. In a three-cornered telephone conversation
among the senator, a White House representative, and boss Edward
Kelly of Chicago, it was made clear to the two Illinoisans that WPA
funds for Chicago (and Mayor Kelly) were at stake. Dieterich, whose
reelection was dependent upon Kelly, had little recourse but to
capitulate. Roosevelt had intended that the Chicago call be made by
Farley, but when FDR contacted the postmaster general late in the
night of July 20, Farley refused. "Very well," the president replied,
"I'll get Harry Hopkins to do it." Whether it was Hopkins or Tom
Corcoran who became the White House conduit is debatable. Ickes
later wrote that Corcoran took care of the call and volunteered his
efforts at defeating Harrison in a manner which would not involve the
chief executive. "It was Tom," he wrote, "who squeezed out the vote
necessary to elect Barkley. . . .and he believes that he pulled it off
without anyone's knowing just how it was done."[31]

Roosevelt persistently denied that he had entered the fray and
Barkley never acknowledged FDR's aid, long maintaining that the
White House had kept "hands off." Two years later, when the president told Farley at a Hyde Park session that he had wanted Barkley to
win because of Harrison's opposition to his taxation and spending
policies, Farley bluntly informed FDR that the intervention was a
mistake. To Farley it seemed that Harrison's work for Roosevelt at
the Chicago convention warranted at least Roosevelt's neutrality. "I
told you before and I repeat now that . . . his action placed you under
everlasting obligation to him," Farley told his "Boss," who said nothing in reply but became "frigid."[32]

Harrison well knew of one vote that he would not get—that of his
colleague Bilbo, who claimed that he had pledged his vote to Barkley
at the time when Robinson was expected to become a Supreme Court
justice. When Byrnes approached him on behalf of Harrison after the
Dieterich vote was known to be lost, Bilbo declared that he would
vote for Harrison if the senator would ask for it. The two senators had
not spoken to each other since the Harrison-Conner primary, and
Harrison refused to humble himself before Bilbo. After mulling over
Bilbo's terms, Harrison told his campaign manager, "Tell the son of a
bitch I wouldn't speak to him if it meant the Presidency of the United

States." It was a costly decision. "When I hitch, I stay hitched," Bilbo boasted in defense of one of the sweetest morsels of revenge that he enjoyed in his long career.[33]

Both of the contestants claimed enough pledges to win. The Barkley forces boasted of forty definite votes, while Harrison's managers claimed thirty-eight. Since there were only seventy-five Democrats in the Senate, it was obvious that one of the contenders was either overly optimistic or the victim of duplicity. Realistic observers believed that Byrnes's figures were the more accurate. Even when Dieterich confessed at zero hour that his vote would go to Barkley, the Harrison supporters entered the caucus room assured of a one-vote margin; they knew that the Kentuckian's list contained definite Harrison men. The atmosphere of the large chamber on the third floor of the Senate office building crackled with excitement as the Democrats gathered on the morning of July 21. All were present except John Bankhead, who was home in Alabama, his proxy having been sent for Harrison. Carl Hayden, a patient at the Naval Hospital, came on the arm of Leslie Biffle, the majority party secretary. Pittman presided over the forty-five-minute session and Black recorded the votes as they were lifted from Carter Glass's battered Panama hat, which served as a ballot box, a circumstance that caused William Smathers to remark on the inconsistency of conducting a secret ballot in a Glass hat! In alphabetical order the senators marched to the front and cast their votes. When the voting ended, the two tellers (Kenneth D. McKellar for Barkley, Richard B. Russell for Harrison) opened the ballots and called them off. Barkley took an early lead but then Harrison overtook him; for the remainder of the count the two were never more than a vote apart. At the moment of the last vote, the count stood 37 to 37. "That last ballot looked like a bed quilt," Barkley later recalled. "I bit my pipe stem in two." The last vote went to Barkley, who was immediately surrounded by congratulating senators. His friends later said that if all who rushed him and claimed to have voted for him had done so, he would have netted 59 votes instead of 38. Harrison broke through the large circle and promised his support "for the success of the country . . . and the Democratic Party."[34]

A postmortem quickly followed when approximately a dozen Harrison supporters joined Byrnes in his office to determine who had reneged on a promised vote. Even after the Dieterich decision, Byrnes had been certain of a majority of one. In checking over the list of Democrats the group paused at a name halfway down and agreed that it "was useless to read further." When Walter George questioned Byrnes as to why the senator in question had been counted as a supporter at all, Byrnes replied, "Pat Harrison told me he was the first senator who asked him to be a candidate and that he would answer for that vote." According to Drew Pearson the crucial vote was cast by King, who was angered that the Missippian had promised FDR that he would remain as chairman of the Finance Committee if elected. There is no question that the seventy-four-year-old Utah senator longed to become chairman and that on several previous occasions his jealousy of Harrison had been overt. Of equal weight in the eventual loss was the vote of Tennessee's new senator, George L. Berry, who had been appointed in April by Governor Gordon Browning at the death of Nathan Bachman. Although it is hard to conceive how Harrison could have expected a vote from Berry, a former head of Labor's Non-Partisan League, he had counted upon Berry's support because of the latter's obligation to heed Browning's wishes as well as those of Fred Sullens, whose newspaper associations with Berry reached back to the turn of the century. "Our friend did not stick," Harrison telegraphed Browning on the day of the defeat. [35]

Common talk had it that Harrison had won the votes of some twenty-five conservative senators plus the votes of a dozen staunch New Dealers who were simply too fond of "Old Pat" to desert him. Florida's Claude Pepper was one of the latter. On the other hand, Barkley won the votes of a few of Harrison's closest associates. Pittman apologized to the Mississippian, explaining that he was obligated to support Barkley on the basis of his previous efforts to have the Kentuckian named as the permanent assistant leader. [36]

One thing was crystal clear in the closeness of the vote. The Democracy was deeply divided. Speaking for the delighted Republicans, Arthur Vandenberg chortled that the "Democratic leadership isn't in the bag—it's in two bags." The president tried to gloss over the division within his party but his overtures fooled no one. His invitiation to Barkley and Harrison for lunch at the White House immediately after the caucus was a vacuous gesture which did nothing to dispel the notion that he had been an active party in the contest. Most of the journalists who analyzed the election concluded that in terms of political reality Roosevelt was the loser. "There is precious little czardom in a majority of one," Hugh Johnson, the disillusioned former New Dealer, concluded. Conservative writers, such as David Lawrence and Mark Sullivan, surmised that the administration would have fared much better had Harrison become the leader. His harmonizing personality and his influence with the conservative insurgents were valuable assets lost to the White House by its thoughtless interference. The official party publicist, Charles Michelson, later wrote that the Senate had actually preferred Harrison, "probably the most popular member of the body," and deeply resented the President's "meddling."[37]

There was ample proof that White House intervention in the leadership contest was ill-advised. By his duplicitous manipulations through Corcoran and others, Roosevelt had stepped upon sensitive senatorial toes. Moreover, as James Patterson has explained, Roosevelt had diverted Senate leadership from the personal style of Robinson, Harrison, and Byrnes to that of "an errand boy" who would leave Roosevelt dependent upon factors and pressures outside the Senate.[38] The old team of Robinson, Harrison, and Byrnes as White House coadjutors could no longer be relied upon. One of the last memories of the two still living was that their friend "Joe" was never certain of the promised Supreme Court appointment. Now that Harrison was also the victim of a broken White House pledge, the bond of loyalty appeared to have snapped in two. Besides the unshackling of Harrison through the events of the majority leader contest, there was another reason why Harrison was freer to be himself. Much of his loyalty to the administration had in essence been loyalty to Joe Robinson, whom Harrison had followed through thick and thin. Now Robinson was gone, and in the future Harrison would bear watching. As one Washington *Evening Star* columnist wrote, the Mississippian "will be politely invited to decide whether he'll kiss, make up and play ball, or get out of his uniform." Fred Sullens, who knew Harrison perhaps as well as any newspaperman did, predicted, "Pat is going to enjoy his present political freedom."[39]

With twelve of his Democratic colleagues holding a Senate longevity record of four or more years over Barkley, the Kentuckian was looked upon as something of an upstart. Almost immediately his leadership and holding power were found wanting. In his first act as leader he suffered a thorough defeat in rallying votes to support the president's veto of a bill continuing farm loan interest rates. Rebuffing FDR, the Senate overrode the veto by a vote of 71 to 19 and followed that action on the same day by recommiting the court bill on a 70 to 20 count. Sans any public statement, Harrison voted against the administration on both counts, but then neither vote was much of a test of his anticipated "liberation."

During the hostility that peaked against still another New Deal measure in July, 1937, Harrison finally took an open stand against the president. In May, Hugo Black had introduced a fair labor standards bill to guarantee minimum wages and maximum hours through a five-man board to be named by the president. After revisions were made to satisfy organized labor's William Green and John L. Lewis, the controversial bill came under Barkley's tutelage only five days after his assumption of Senate leadership. He had the support of neither Harrison nor Byrnes.

In the days of his early ardor for the New Deal in 1933, Harrison had voted for Black's thirty-hour bill (Stephens had opposed it), but circumstances had changed and now he was alarmed by the growing threat of unions. In fact, the *New Republic* reported that the CIO was the chief cause of the widening breach between Roosevelt and the southern conservatives in Congress. In the spring of 1937, representatives of the International Ladies' Garment Workers had appeared in Tupelo to organize the garment plants, the principal local industry. Prolonged friction resulted in an attempt by management to liquidate the plants, an action opposed by the National Labor Relations Board. In July Harrison conferred with J. Warren Madden, the NLRB chairman, to reconcile the differences between labor and management in Tupelo. Representative Rankin, whose home was in the town, was vehemently opposed to the NLRB and even more to the pending program. The labor board, he was convinced, was "conspiring with communistic influences to destroy Southern industries."[40] Most of the southern delegation were more alarmed by the potential destruction of wage differentials, which permitted southern industries both to attract industry from the North and compete against the East.

Debate on the bill began in late July. Harrison, named as leader of the assault, finally rose on July 30 to deliver his first anti-New Deal speech. The day before he had told a Mississippi friend, "I'm going to give Franklin Roosevelt a licking tomorrow. . . . I just can't take any more." It was an angry and candid revelation of much that lay upon his mind. "I have at times been accused of being a conservative," he said. "Well suppose I accept that encomium," he continued, adding that he had been as progressive or conservative as the administration had been, for he believed that he had followed the Rooseveltian trend whatever it was. Now he concluded, "I sometimes think I have traveled so fast that I like to get under the shade and rest a little while." He frankly confessed that one of his principal objections to the bill was that "Ma-dam" Perkins would have "a great deal of say" in its administration and he did not care to pass legislation to be executed by persons having an idea that "our women wear no shoes, and who have various impressions about my people which are not true." (His reference was to an unfortunate remark made by Miss Perkins in 1933 that southern women could provide a market for the northern shoe industry.) The senator's attack was an open admission that he had never cared for the labor secretary.[41] Nor, for that matter, had most of his southern colleagues.

Harrison reminded the Senate that wage differentials had been permitted under the National Recovery Administration to protect southern industries; he warned that the so-called "good wages" of the Black bill would "strike down business that is on its last legs." The speech was reminiscent of his vitriolic sallies of the gadfly days. Aware that he had displayed a mood not seen in recent years, Harrison admitted, "I have said perhaps more than I should have said." Republicans sat back smiling, hoping that the senator from Mississippi would be heard more frequently in the future. Fred Sullens observed that "Senator Harrison has definitely parted company with President Roosevelt," while a surprised Roosevelt told Ickes, "Pat Harrison has gone off the deep end."[42]

The wages and hours bill died in the House in August when a hostile Rules Committee discarded it. During the fall recess Harrison carried his battle against wage and hour legislation to Mississippi, where he found a receptive audience. Speaking in Jackson in September, he predicted that the expected passage at the next session would "bind the South in industrial shackles." He recognized that many southern industries, including "some" in Mississippi, did not pay reasonable wages, but a forty cents an hour wage would force the closing of many small industries that provided jobs for workers driven from the farm and those taken from WPA rolls. "I have no doubt such a law will injure labor, add to unemployment and result in the continuation of the WPA, of course which I vigorously oppose," he argued. [43]

Of the nine Mississippians in Congress only Bilbo supported the drive for a wages and hours law. Ross Collins and William Colmer were noncommittal; the other five representatives were hostile. To the president Bilbo wrote of his "missionary work" for the bill and passed along the rumor that his Senate colleague was "trying to line up the boys in the House" to join the opposition. When Congress reassembled in the fall in a special session called by Roosevelt, House opponents of the fair labor standards bill had their way. In December a 216 to 198 vote crushed the bill and returned it to committee as rebel yells echoed through the chamber. Not one of the seven Mississippians voted for the bill. [44]

In August of 1937, just when Harrison was beginning to exert his independence of the White House, the Jones-Costigan Sugar Act came up for renewal, and its extension was expected to provoke a lively debate. Columnist Jay Franklin reported that "America's sweet tooth is one of the biggest headaches of the Roosevelt administration." A "liberated" Senator Harrison had no inclination to buffer the president from the demands of the domestic sugar interests that they be given a larger share of the sugar market at the expense of island growers and refiners. Supported by cabinet members Ickes, Hull, and Wallace, Roosevelt insisted that the House sugar bill unfairly established a colonial system contrary to traditional American policy. Harrison, anxious to get the sugar bill out of the way before the Senate bogged down on a tax loophole measure, produced a compromise to freeze refining activities in the continental United States and the insular possessions at their previous maximum levels. It was not likely that the president would approve the so-called "Harrison Compromise" after Ickes, who suspected that domestic sugar refiners would use the system to restrain trade, convinced Roosevelt that Harrison's quotas were "unconscionable and unfair and rotten." [45]

Meanwhile Harrison had conferred with the president and gotten the impression that his compromise was acceptable. Hearing from its chairman that no veto was anticipated, the Finance Committee promptly adopted Harrison's plan by a vote of 15 to 2. Harrison was mistaken in his assessment of FDR's position. Whether the error was due to another instance of presidential indecision and ambiguity or whether Harrison simply heard what he wanted to hear is a matter of conjecture. Whatever the case, Roosevelt wrote Harrison that the inclusion in the sugar bill of restrictive refining quotas was not acceptable, while Secretary Wallace reinforced administration objections that the changes made by the committee granted an "airtight monopoly" for continental sugar refiners. In apparent defiance of Roosevelt's letter, the Finance Committee reaffirmed its earlier action by a second vote, this time backing the freeze on refining by a vote of 16 to 1. The committee's action proved that the president was no match for either the forceful sugar lobby or the determination of Congress to write its own sugar bill without White House direction. Passed by the Senate without a record vote, the bill was rushed to conference in order that time could remain before adjournment to act upon the anticipated veto.[46]

Roosevelt was still undecided about a sugar bill that violated one of his major precepts. Maryland's Representative David J. Lewis counseled that few of the "faithful friends" of FDR's "welfare program" would be alienated by a veto while "all" of the bill's principal supporters "have already shown their hostility to a general democratic program." At the same time the staunch administration backer from Indiana, Sherman Minton, warned that the bill was "vital to the political life" of FDR's warm friends Senators James Pope of Idaho and Elbert Thomas of Utah.[47] Annoyed in making a concession to the senators who had followed Harrison's leadership, Roosevelt delayed his decision to capitulate as long as possible, signing the bill exactly ten days after passage. Furthermore, the president had seen the House leadership abandon the wages and hours bill and the Senate refuse to consider his request for reorganization of the executive department. Altogether, the 1937 session had been replete with frustrations for Roosevelt in the face of a growing congressional independence.

There were those who blamed men like Harrison and Byrnes for the president's reverses, but not all Capitol observers laid the blame at those particular senatorial feet. "T.R.B." of the *New Republic*, who generally wrote caustically of the two senators, admitted that Roosevelt's apologists had to look elsewhere to explain his defeats than at the "otiose mass of Southern bourbonism." "Who are these vicious red-jawed reactionaries waiting to gobble up the little liberals?" T.R.B. asked. One could scarcely point to Harrison and Byrnes, he answered. They both had nearly flawless New Deal voting records. To a great extent Roosevelt himself was responsible for his difficulties with Congress. He had alienated many members of the legislature by his court-packing scheme and his role in the majority leadership contest. But, as James Patterson has concluded, the president's real dilemma was the peculiar result of his own successes. He had gained the support of a liberal coalition that wanted to push ahead on the road to reform, while at the same time the economic recovery which the nation was just beginning to enjoy led many former New Deal supporters to believe that retrenchment was now possible. [48]

As matters stood at the end of the 1937 regular session, Pat Harrison's future actions were a matter of speculation. Frank Kent, the acerbic witness of "the great game of politics," was convinced that for the first time in five years the senator was a free man, destined to become "a greater force in the Senate and in the country than would have been possible for him as Senate leader." [49] Never known by his colleagues to be a vindictive person, Harrison was not expected to set himself against the president out of spite. Yet his independent action on the labor standards and sugar control measures served notice that he no longer would do the president's bidding, as he had done in the past.

CHAPTER IX

"The President . . . Was Just Misinformed"

1937–39

AFTER THE LATE SUMMER OF 1937, when Pat Harrison began to assert his independence from the White House, there was to be no real reconcilation between the senator and the president until domestic issues were submerged by international questions in 1940. Latent differences between Roosevelt and his Senate taxmaster over New Deal lending and spending and an omnipresent need for higher levels of revenue finally surfaced in the debates over the revenue measures of 1938 and 1939. In the protracted bitterness that stirred congressional furies against New Deal fiscal policy during those two years, the fact became abundantly clear that Harrison, despite his defeat in the majority leadership contest, was at the zenith of his power in the Senate. In the struggle over the continuation of taxes on capital gains and undistributed profits, a close relationship with Vice-President John Nance Garner enabled the Mississippi senator to maintain a commanding position in the enactment of tax legislation. Furthermore, through a personal friendship and political partnership of long standing, Senators Harrison and Byrnes worked in tandem to reduce relief spending when the president again requested funds for the Works Progress Administration.

The Roosevelt-Harrison accord on tax legislation, it will be remembered, was always somewhat tenuous. Only his loyalty to the president had stayed Harrison's hand from writing *finis* to the presidential program of wealth taxation in 1935 and 1936. And of the perennial White House requests for tax measures during the years 1935–1940, only the tax message of 1937 entirely suited the chairman. Not since 1934 had Harrison been so amenable to a tax program pressed upon Congress by the White House. Although the revenue bill of 1937 did not come to the Senate until after the summer fissure within the Democratic leadership, Harrison quite willingly sped the bill to passage, for it dealt with a subject—tax evasion—which roused his ire as much as it stirred the president.

In early 1937 Roswell Magill, the new under-secretary of the treasury, conducted an investigation of tax evasion and found a bag of tricks that defied the imagination of all but the cleverest of tax lawyers. Incorporation of yachts, country estates, hobbies, and personal talents, along with the formation of foreign corporations and personal holding companies, had grown to shocking proportions. [1] The revelation of such blatant "tax bracketeering," as presidential confidant Samuel I. Rosenman called the schemes, pricked the moral sensibilities of Roosevelt, who had already formulated a set of notions about "economic royalists." On May 28, 1937, when the president indignantly described to the press the "immoral inventions" of "high-priced lawyers," he reported that he had already talked to Harrison and Doughton about the wholesale evasions and that they were willing to launch an immediate crackdown. What he did not share with the press was the fact that he had appealed to the political animal in his tax chieftains by estimating that quick action was worth ten million votes. Harrison, thereupon, had agreed to "expose the whole damn thing." [2]

On June 1 Roosevelt sent a message to Congress on taxes, a summer ritual Congress had grown accustomed to; but this time what he had to say fell on receptive ears. Emphasizing that he was calling for neither new taxes nor rates, the president asked for legislation to close the loopholes. Immediately after the message was read Harrison offered a joint resolution, drafted by Magill, calling for the creation of a Joint Committee on Tax Evasion and Avoidance. Supported by McNary and the Republicans, the resolution met with little opposition in Congress. The public outcry from the wealthy served only to point out the necessity for legislation; J. P. Morgan intemperately scoffed, "Congress should know how to levy taxes. It is not up to us taxpayers to repair the mistakes of Congress." [3]

Smarting from the Morgan manner, the Joint Committee on Tax Evasion conducted public hearings which ran for six weeks. Roosevelt temporarily assigned Thurman Arnold from the Justice

Department to the treasury to assist in the investigation. Arnold joined Abe Fortas of the Yale Law School and Randolph Paul, a treasury tax analyst, in assembling and preparing testimony. Morgenthau, who as the first witness complained that "tax ethics generally today are where business ethics and trade practices were in the Nineties," was followed by other treasury personnel who named names and described practices that clinched an open-and-shut case against the tax dodgers. As a chairman who had done his homework, Harrison was already familiar with the testimony likely to be given by the private individuals who came before the committee to defend their artful dodging, and he succeeded in nailing them under cross-examination.[4]

On August 5 Harrison submitted a voluminous report on the Joint Committee's findings and recommended legislation plugging eight loopholes. Doughton's committee hurried the bill to the House floor, where a vote of 173 to 0 dispatched it to the Senate within two hours. As Congressman Thomas A. Jenkins, an Ohio Republican, admitted, "This is a different kind of a tax bill—one that nearly every fair-minded member will vote for." Going on to the Finance Committee, the bill was quickly adopted after a three-hour session with treasury experts. Had it not been for the requests of two business firms for a hearing, Harrison, anxious to get the measure passed before the customary hurly-burly of the final days of the session could jeopardize the bill, would have dispensed with Finance Committee hearings altogether. The hearing, held August 18, lasted no more than one hour; only four witnesses appeared.[5]

The speed with which the Senate acted upon the proposed legislation was due to Harrison. Late in the afternoon of August 18 he sauntered into the Senate chamber with his committee members in tow. Seeing that Garner was not then presiding, he retired to the cloakroom and returned momentarily with the smiling vice-president. Harrison, a past master at Senate maneuvering, spoke briefly to Barkley and then ambled over to the Republican side to confer with leaders there. While Barkley whispered a word to Kenneth D. McKellar, who was blasting away at the Interstate Commerce Commission over an airlines bill, Harrison went to La Follette's desk. Someone in the press gallery quipped, "Watch close, boys, you're about to see how to run a railroad."[6] In a lightning burst of speed, for which he had to drop his customary drawl, Harrison gave a one-minute coverage of the bill, and Garner set the clerk to a reading which jumped and skipped over the provisions. At three different times the vice-president almost gaveled the bill to passage while Harrison stood at his desk with a fistful of amendments trying to find where they went in the bill. The Senate passed the measure without a record vote, but it had seen in operation the well-oiled senatorial machine, which Garner was suspected of running with the cooperation of the Senate conservatives whom he reportedly had returned to Washington to command.[7]

The Revenue Act of 1937 imposed a virtual death sentence upon domestic and foreign personal holding companies and struck at the use of foreign corporations, multiple trusts, and the incorporation of personal talents to avoid the payment of taxes. Morgenthau was extremely pleased at the outcome of his department's sortie against the tax dodgers; Harrison was happy over the prospects of added revenue.[8]

The unanimity with which Roosevelt and Harrison worked to produce the Revenue Act of 1937 was the last display of harmony over New Deal taxation. Even before 1937 Harrison had lost whatever enchantment he may once have had with the undistributed and capital gains provisions of the Revenue Act of 1936, subjected now to mounting criticism. As early as November, 1936, Arthur Krock had written of Harrison's "open mind" toward capital gains revisions. Both Roswell Magill and Lovell Parker, a Joint Committee staffer, were known to be out of sympathy with the capital gains provision, and by February, 1937, Morgenthau clearly knew of Harrison's sensitivity to the complaints of businessmen. Advice from the Treasury Department that the revisions which the senator had in mind would result in a $167 million loss in revenue persuaded Harrison to do nothing for the time being.[9]

By the autumn of 1937 the move within the business community for modification of the Revenue Act of 1936 had gained momentum. Obviously annoyed by recurring news stories that the two taxes in question were to be modified, the president found it "rather interesting" that the press neglected to write of "that portion of the population [with] nothing to live on," whose purchasing power was practically nil. Undoubtedly he was piqued when former New Dealer Hugh

S. Johnson wrote of the "enterprise-destroying, unemployment-making taxes" and Thomas L. Stokes charged that the capital gains tax intensified stock market booms and busts. Furthermore, ordinarily sympathetic observers like Walter Lippmann and John Maynard Keynes warned the president that his tax reforms were irritants to recovery.[10]

Actually the new economic debate encompassed much more than tax policy. By August, 1937, the nation had slumped into a recession. As a prime remedy Harold Ickes, Harry Hopkins, and Federal Reserve Board Governor Marriner Eccles pressed increased spending upon the president. Eccles, moreover, was an ardent defender of the profits tax as a vital element in a program of compensatory fiscal policy intended to divert corporate income into consumer spending. An increasing number of congressional leaders, on the other hand, responded to the pleas of businessmen that a modified tax structure would permit them to take up the slack in unemployment. Otherwise, the industrialists claimed, there was no incentive to convert profits into payrolls.

Conservative critics of the Revenue Act of 1936 scored a measurable victory when Secretary Morgenthau made what was viewed as an administration policy address before the Academy of Political Science in November, 1937. The secretary announced that Roosevelt would make a determined effort to balance the budget through reductions in relief and public works expenditures and would encourage the expansion of private business through the revision of inequitable taxes. Widely applauded by his audience, Morgenthau won immediate plaudits from Doughton and Harrison. Doughton was encouraged by the realization by "those in highest places" that businessmen were "to have more consideration in the future than has been accorded them in the past." Harrison telegraphed the treasury head that his "courageous expressions" confirmed his own determination that extreme emergency expenditures should be checked, the budget balanced, and some modification made in the undistributed profits tax. Aware that the president was apt to take umbrage at his accord with Morgenthau and convinced that FDR's past behavior had not been altogether fair, Harrison added: "The Administration must appreciate that honest differences of opinion may arise as to policies but that it cannot permit those differences to influence insinuations and charges of party disloyalty."[11]

According to the general interpretations given to Harrison's message to Morgenthau, the senator had plainly demanded a revision of the profits tax. Hugh Johnson opined that Morgenthau's statement had been "warily weasel," but Harrison's response was the most forthright fiscal statement since Salmon P. Chase's "The way to resumption is to resume." Harrison's mail ran heavy with congratulations. Herbert Bayard Swope, onetime economic diplomat at the London Conference and a business associate of Bernard Baruch, wrote Harrison that the telegram was "well thought out." If translated into action, Swope predicted, "Your country's opinion of you will be high." The editor of *Textile World*, Douglas C. Woolf, wrote that managers in his field were withholding plant modernization programs because of the profits tax. Similar sentiments arrived from other industrialists eager for tax revisions and relief. "I would want nothing better than to have you be the Pat Harrison of old," wrote a Chicagoan.[12]

The expressions of Morgenthau and Harrison were particularly provocative in light of FDR's call for a special congressional session to begin on November 15, 1937. Even though Roosevelt sent Congress a message promising an activation of private capital, viewed as the most conciliatory overture made to business in five years, there was little thought that the legislators would tackle a major tax measure at that time. Certainly Harrison and Doughton did not intend to place a tax bill before the special session. Actually, the session proved to be a political Jonah for Roosevelt. Many members of both houses were annoyed at having been called back to Washington, and by the end of December all that an unenthusiastic Senate had done was to pass a revised farm bill. Harrison, convinced of the futility of the session, spent most of his time in his office writing letters to constituents, and he spoke only once on the floor, merely reiterating what he had said to the press on the necessity for some sort of tax modification.[13] It appeared that he intended to keep his powder dry for more important battles.

If the special session did not produce any significant legislation, it did provide an opportunity for conservative senators to coalesce upon a program planned to strengthen the congressional independence from the White House which had become so noticeable in the summer of 1937. Senator Bailey's attempts to block any further plans of administration liberals through a "Conservative Manifesto" were thwarted. While the manifesto died aborning and powerful Democrats such as Harrison and Byrnes shunned participation, it was not really crucial to the growing vitality of congressional conservatism. For the manifesto's call for "immediate revision of taxes on capital gains and undistributed profits in order to free investment funds" there was already ample support from senators who never signed Bailey's round robin. That oldline Democratic spines were stiffening was clear enough when one after another of the congressional patriarchs spoke up. John J. O'Connor, the House Rules Committee chairman, called for action "now" to modify the profits tax, and Key Pittman concurred. The Nevadan, long a critic of the Revenue Act of 1936, remonstrated, "When you shoot at a bandit, you don't shoot into the crowd." In fact, a later November polling of the Senate disclosed that ninety senators were in favor of revisions or repeal of the undistributed profits tax. Reportedly, eighteen Finance Committee members favored modification in some form. [14]

Harrison was reluctant to launch a tax bill in the special session. He knew that the session could scarcely do justice to a major tax measure, and he feared that the momentum of opposition would stampede the Senate into repealing the taxes on profits and capital gains without repairing the damage done to the treasury's income. He made his position clear to his Senate colleagues when a number of the more eager repealers laid plans to attach riders to various unrelated measures pending before the body. Repeal sentiment from such former administration loyalists as Byrnes, who belittled the idea that a longer period of time was needed to prepare a bill ("I could do it myself in 12 hours," he scoffed), alarmed Roosevelt, who called Harrison to the White House to lay plans to check any hasty congressional action. Subsequently, the senator, who was holding his own committee in reserve, reviewed with Doughton tentative decisions of the Ways and Means Committee to grant exemptions and concessions in levying the profits tax. [15]

In the fall of 1937 both Harrison and Doughton were showered with correspondence from industrialists who warned that the reces-

sion would deepen unless more liberal exemptions were made to allow
for reinvestments and debt retirement. Walter Parker of the New
Orleans Interior Bureau of Economics wrote Harrison that in the
South "the unhappy economic effect" of the profits and capital gains
taxes prevented industry from absorbing workers thrown into unemployment, while a Gulf, Mobile and Northern railroad executive
complained that the railroad had been forced to declare a dividend
unwarranted by business conditions because the "penalties for not
doing so were so great that there was nothing else to do." "Businessmen are apprehensive of the deepening depression and the imminent danger that the whole business structure will go down in an
uncontrollable tail spin," warned James F. Bell of General Mills.
Meanwhile *Business Week* reported widespread business practices of
either abandoning or deferring industrial expenditures for equipment
and improvements because of the mandatory distribution of profits
through dividends.[16]

Crucial to Harrison's thought was the conference he had in late
November with Joseph P. Kennedy, who came to Washington to "talk
taxes" with the senator. Later, after Harrison conferred with Roswell
Magill, the latter told Morgenthau that the senator was "clearly influenced by what he got from Kennedy," who had reported that the
profits tax had affected large corporations but little while compelling
smaller companies to borrow from banks, thus resulting in banking
control of the small-scale companies. Harrison confided to Magill that
he knew of no one in the Senate, except possibly La Follette and
Norris, who opposed repeal or drastic modification of the tax, and he
was having great difficulty in preventing the Senate from taking up a
revenue bill immediately. The Finance Committee chairman had
concluded that business conditions demanded that either there be
quick action on taxes by the special session or else a simultaneous
announcement should be made by Roosevelt and congressional leaders that the business taxes would be revised. The president, however,
was reluctant to make any statement beyond the generalities of his
message to Congress.[17]

As he usually did whenever a major tax measure was in the making, Harrison went on the air on the *Evening Star* forum on November
19, 1937. Speaking on "Our Tax Problems," he delivered one of the
most significant speeches of his long career. Because "an incentive

should be given to business to take up as much as possible of the slack on unemployment," and because of the "fear and uncertainty" occasioned by tax laws, Harrison now favored "substantial" modification of the undistributed profits tax. He endorsed the plan of the Ways and Means Committee to exempt from the tax all corporations with net incomes of less than $25,000, an exemption he noted that would relieve 88 percent of all corporations of the strictures on profits retention. In addition, Harrison pointed to the effects of the capital gains tax in discouraging the trade in stocks, securities, and property holdings and in "freezing credits and preventing the flow of capital into new enterprises." Capital gains, he now believed, should be removed as a segment of ordinary income and placed in a tax category to itself. The speech substantially implied that the Revenue Act of 1936, which Harrison acknowledged to have had his support, had been a mistake. "However high and laudable may be the purpose of certain policies, and however attractive they may appear theoretically sometimes, as a practical matter, the injurious effects are greater than the benefits sought," he concluded.[18]

Although low-keyed and placid, Harrison's speech nevertheless left the press certain that he had declared his independence from the White House. *Newsweek* recorded that the radio talk had dramatized a new phase in Harrison's five-year evolution from the status of "a Roosevelt errand boy." Representative of a "score of semi-conservative Southerners" in Congress, Harrison had emerged as an outspoken Democrat "willing to go along with the New Deal only if it meets him halfway." Harrison's "repentence seems final," Arthur Krock observed, pointing to the marked dissimilarity in Harrison's willingness to admit a mistake in policy and Roosevelt's refusal to confess to a capitulation to one of Herman Oliphant's "quick sales." *Business Week* reported that Roosevelt had lost all hope of continuing the undistributed profits tax.[19]

Businessmen were jubilant over Harrison's speech. "You set the example of the spirit . . . and the method of dealing with our difficult economic situation which I hope may be followed elsewhere," Owen D. Young, the former economic diplomat of debt reparations, wrote Harrison. Herbert Swope praised the senator's "frankness" and "essential democracy," while railroad executives from Minneapolis and Kansas City were grateful that he had expressed a confidence that

"business is safe and worth promoting." Small businessmen from
Mississippi chorused their approval of their senator's stand and cited
sit-down strikes and unbalanced budgets as other causes of the recession. It was, of course, expected that the business community would
castigate the administration's guiding tax principles, but far more
damaging testimony came from another source. In early December
the Brookings Institution released a report which concluded from a
study of 1,560 corporations that the undistributed profits tax had
limited the possibility of "prompt and flexible capital developments."
Furthermore, it was impossible to administer the tax fairly in any
form, the Brookings economists declared. [20]

While the House committee engaged in fratricidal strife over the
new revenue bill soon after the new session began in January, 1938,
over in the Senate the special Committee on Unemployment and Relief headed by Byrnes heard from Bernard Baruch. "The single missing element in a great forward movement is . . . the belief that money
can be spent or invested without confiscation of reasonable profits by
inordinate taxation," the financier asserted. His testaments, some
administration supporters charged, were no more than the result of
collusion between Byrnes and Harrison aimed at giving a final impetus to a Senate overhaul of the House tax bill. Morgenthau telephoned Roosevelt that columnist Joseph Alsop had said to him at a
private dinner that "Harrison and Baruch have put their heads together." When Harrison went to work, the bill would be "exactly
what Baruch wanted," Alsop predicted. In fact, on the day that
Baruch completed his testimony before Byrnes's committee, a poll of
the Finance Committee showed that thirteen of the twenty-one
members favored a complete repeal of the profits tax. Apparently, the
tax would be viscerated once the bill reached the Senate. [21]

As passed by the House on March 11, the revenue bill of 1938
carried corporate levies ranging from 16 to 20 percent on incomes of
over $25,000; it retained only a modest 4 percent tax on undistributed
profits. The House defeat of the so-called "third basket" surtax on
family held corporations was a severe blow to the administration.
Harrison had maintained all along that the penalty did not have "a
tinker's chance in hell." With the tax revision measure now in his
committee, the chairman wasted no time in releasing a statement of
his position. He wanted to "improve" the capital gains provision of the

House bill by taking that category of income out of the general income area and applying a flat rate of approximately 15 percent. He believed that the "skeleton" undistributed profits tax retained by the House would "haunt" business; he preferred instead the return to a flat corporation tax. He reemphasized his belief that "tax laws should be written for revenue purposes," an aim unachievable when surtaxes ranged so high as to have led to diminishing treasury income. When Magill insisted that Harrison's rates would not result in needed revenue, the Mississippian retreated from his customary stand for revenue only and acknowledged that it was "better to help business and lose a little revenue."[22]

When the Finance Committee opened to a weeklong public hearing in mid-March, almost to a man the more than sixty witnesses confirmed the decisions already made by the committee to repeal the profits tax and modify the capital gains levy. An unhappy Roosevelt conferred with Morgenthau, Magill, and La Follette on means to stem the growing sentiment within the Finance Committee for outright repeal of the profits tax, but Harrison's influence was much too strong. In two executive sessions the committee scuttled the House bill, eliminating the profits tax by a vote of 17 to 4 and substituting a flat 18 percent tax on corporate income while exempting corporations earning less than $25,000 a year. The stampede against the profits tax was so unbridled that even Pennsylvania's Joseph Guffey, who had prided himself on his 100 percent administration record, joined the repealers. When the committee reported its work on March 31, Harrison was thoroughly satisfied on two counts. The undistributed profits tax had been eliminated, and he estimated that his bill would bring in 11.4 percent more revenue than the House version would have produced.[23]

The stage was set for a swift Senate vote, and Barkley could do no more than stand by helplessly on April 7 when Harrison took command of the Senate. After only a little more than two hours of debate, the clerk, John C. Crockett, who had mastered the knack for rapid delivery over a period of twenty years service, began to tick off the provisions of the bill at the command of Garner, who punctuated the proceedings with "No objections—amendment agreed to." Now and then a senator half arose to offer an objection, but before it could be voiced the clerk and the vice-president were a page or two beyond the

Washington *Evening Star,* April 5, 1938
Courtesy: Archives and Special Collections, University of Mississippi

senator struggling for recognition. Within forty minutes the clerk had
"read" the 370-page bill, interrupted by only one roll call. With only
four senators (Barkley, La Follette, Connally, and Robert J. Bulkley
of Ohio) known to oppose the elimination of the profits tax, only a few
minutes were spent on discussion of the subject. Without a record
vote or any audible "nays" the revenue bill of 1938 was passed on
April 9.[24]

Joseph Alsop and Robert Kintner wrote, "The rebellion on the tax
bill was tantamount to a public humiliation for Senator Barkley, but
it is a true symbol of the situation." Barkley's efforts had been limited
merely to an impotent "no" vote while the bill was in committee.
Roosevelt's defeat on the tax bill of 1938 was a stunning setback since
a near unanimous Senate had turned its back on a treasured New

Deal principle and gone down the line with Harrison and Byrnes, who had both fallen from White House favor. [25]

While the eventual outcome of Harrison's bout with FDR over the tax bill was never in doubt, the affair ran on for nearly two more months. Garner aided his Mississippi friend by appointing a strong group of Harrison men as Senate conferees. The president, privately infuriated by Harrison's contention that concessions to business were necessary to encourage recovery, mulled over ways by which he could publicly answer the senator and finally decided to write a letter to the conference committee in terms so plain that they could be understood by "the man in the street." In spite of warnings from Steve Early and James Roosevelt that such an approach would antagonize the Senate and accomplish nothing, Roosevelt insisted on writing the letter. Drafted by Magill and signed by FDR, the letter, dated April 13, reached the committee after its deliberations had begun. Calling the bill a "strike at the roots of the fundamental principles of taxation," Roosevelt appeared to be lecturing the committee on its duties, an action not likely to set well with a Congress already feeding on the oats of independence. Early and the younger Roosevelt were correct. Harrison was annoyed and laid his plans to have the last word in what had turned into a contest between the president and the senator to win a public debate. [26]

During the brief recess that followed a week-long conference deadlock, Byrnes moved to bolster the position of the Senate conferees when he released the result of a seven-month study made by his Committee on Unemployment and Relief. The report called for an immediate repeal of the undistributed profits tax and stringent modification of the capital gains levy. The strong wording of the report surprised even those who were accustomed to seeing Harrison and Byrnes in action, "as wily a set of Democrats," Alsop and Kintner wrote, "as you would find in a very long walk around Washington." Obviously vexed by Byrnes's action, Roosevelt asked a press conference the next day, "Now what do I do? Do I say again, 'Oh well, let us encourage business, to Hell with principle'?"[27]

Contrary to expectations, it was a difference over capital gains and not undistributed profits which was at the core of the secret conference tussle. The Senate won when the House conferees finally agreed to tax long-term capital gains at a separate, flat rate of 20 percent rather than as ordinary income. In return Harrison dropped his insistence upon the repeal of the profits tax and agreed upon the retention of a 2½ percent levy to be in effect for 1938 and 1939 only. Actually the senators conceded very little, for the House bill had reduced the tax to 4 percent.[28]

Now the final decision in the long struggle was up to the president. To sign the bill, columnist Jay Franklin wrote, would be a confession that "the New Deal has no program, no policy, no national economic design." But Roosevelt had told Morgenthau and Magill that he could not very well veto the measure. After mulling over the dilemma, the president, without disclosing his plan to Morgenthau or Harrison, made his decision. He chose to address his remarks to thirteen bewildered children who graduated on May 27 from the little school at Arthurdale, West Virginia, the subsistence homestead community closest to Mrs. Roosevelt's heart. Regretting that "some people" had abandoned the principle of progressive taxation, the president claimed that under the new bill the man who made $5,000 and the man who cleared $500,000 in stock profits would both pay the same 15 percent. Furthermore, he insisted, 80 percent of all reported capital gains were not made by investments in new, developing companies but through market ventures in old established firms. Too, he doubted that the nominal tax on undistributed profits would eliminate the tax avoidance practices of the past. Therefore, he announced that for the first time since becoming president he was going to permit a bill to become law without affixing his signature. At midnight that night the bill would become law.[29]

Roosevelt's surprise attack stung Harrison into a quick and bitter retaliation before a Saturday session swelled by members from the House who stood against the walls of the Senate chamber to hear the Mississippian's expected reply. Waving a copy of the president's speech and slamming it against his desk, Harrison denied that the Senate had abandoned the principle of progressive taxation. Resentful of the president's implication that all closely held corporations were evil, he contended, "In my section of the country, closely held corporations built up many communities." What irritated him the most about the Arthurdale speech was Roosevelt's oversimplification of the effect of the tax levies. The chief executive "was just misinformed" in stating that there was no progressive taxation on capital gains because he had failed to note that short-term gains were taxed as ordinary income at normal rates. Harrison even wished that the president had vetoed the bill because the senator had no doubt what Congress would have then done. The bill had been approved by 90 percent of the representatives in the House and without dissent from a single Democratic senator. [30]

Although Roosevelt had named no names at Arthurdale, Harrison believed that his own loyalty had been questioned, if not in the speech at least in private presidential conversations. "I grew up in that atmosphere of Democracy in which party disloyalty was considered to be almost treason," he told the Senate. "I concede to none of my Democratic brethren a greater degree of loyalty to the President than I. God knows I have shown it. I do not know many other Democratic Senators who have faced the breastworks and the fire of battle to carry out administration policies more often than I." Apparently Roosevelt was not convinced of Harrison's fidelity. Three days later, when a reporter asked him at a press conference to comment on Harrison's statement, FDR replied that he had not read the speech. [31]

Nonetheless, Roosevelt was shaken by Harrison's speech; no leading Democrat had ever before taken the Senate floor to question the accuracy of a specific statement of the president. Nettled by the senator's charge that he had been "misinformed" (a euphemism, some members of the press said, for "lied"), Roosevelt turned to Morgenthau's department for clarification of the point over the capital gains tax. Asked by FDR if any of Harrison's charges on the Arthurdale speech were correct, Morgenthau directed Magill to prepare a memorandum on which to base a reply. Magill wrote that the president's remarks *were* erroneous in regard to individuals with small incomes and that progressive rates still applied to short-term capital gains. At a treasury staff meeting even Herman Oliphant, who among all the treasury advisers had given the strongest backing to the president, admitted that the statement had contained errors. Morgenthau transcribed the conversation:

> Morgenthau: Well, were any of the statements he made wrong?
> Magill: Yes.
> Morgenthau: They were?
> Magill: His statement on capital gains is wrong. It's a—well, I would say it's 50 percent wrong.

Washington *Evening Star,* May 31, 1938
Courtesy: Washington *Star*

Oliphant: Tommy Corcoran called me and he read the statement and I said, "That's wrong."[32]

The estrangement between Harrison and Roosevelt, which had begun in the summer of 1937 and was now heightened by their major differences over the Revenue Act of 1938, would continue for at least another year. As a matter of fact, Harrison did not again call at the White House until August, 1938, following the president's friendly reference to him in a radio speech as one of the fathers of social security. Harrison's pique extended to Morgenthau as well as to FDR, but the spat with Morgenthau was short-lived. While Harrison went for a few months without speaking to the treasury head, a basic agreement on tax policies brought them together before the year had ended. Never able fully to accept continuing unbalanced budgets and ceaseless expenditures for public works, Morgenthau grew more inclined to count as Harrison did upon private capital rather than government spending to spur the economy. He was now amenable to further reductions on business taxes, including the removal of the remaining stub of the undistributed profits tax. [33]

In the latter half of 1938, Harrison remained a publicist for the removal of taxes that he considered to be deterrents to recovery. The June issue of *Nation's Business* carried his article on a "streamlined tax program," which, in essence, was an overture to the private sector to carry the burden for recovery now that the new tax law offered greater incentives. The man "walking the streets" could now look to business for a job. "Money is what makes the mare go," he told the Mississippi state Democratic committee in late August. Then in December in a widely publicized speech made to the Detroit Economic Club, Harrison declared that the government had not yet done all that it could in formulating tax policies to encourage industry to hire the unemployed. He intended to turn his efforts toward reducing surtaxes in the higher brackets of individual income taxation, where, he said, the 79 percent maximum had reached the point of diminishing returns. [34]

As the new session opened in 1939, Congressional watchers predicted a showdown between the two groups expounding conflicting tax theories. The protagonists were presumed to be Roosevelt (schooled by Marriner Eccles, Leon Henderson of the Securities and Exchange Commission, and the New Deal team of Thomas Corcoran and Benjamin Cohen) and Harrison's battalion of conservative Republicans and Democrats, the latter bolstered by a stinging rebuke of FDR in his abortive "purge" of the party in 1938. In fact, one survivor of the president's foray against his enemies was Walter George, one of Harrison's senior lieutenants on the Finance Committee. Harrison had been deeply disturbed by the president's entry into the Democratic primaries, and, while he was happy to see his old friends return unscathed, he was anxious to bind the party wounds. Essential for that, Harrison believed, was a moderation of Roosevelt's approach to spending and taxation. In a memorandum to Morgenthau, Magill illuminated Harrison's position. Recounting a conversation, Magill wrote: "The Senator also said he was very blue about the political situation. He had had it out with the President . . . on the tax bill last spring. The President had told him that he ought to be more cooperative. Senator Harrison had said that there was no man more cooperative than he, but that his tax philosophy and the President's tax philosophy were entirely different and no amount of discussion could bring them together. He said that Senator George is one of the best men in the Senate and if George is a conservative, he is too."[35]

There were no surface harbingers of another tax battle. Behind the scenes, however, a tug-of-war had developed between the president and his treasury secretary over the measure of agreement between Morgenthau and Harrison on the removal of the so-called "tax irritants." The secretary took his stand at a February press conference: "Of course we must have additional revenue, but in my opinion the way to make it is for businessmen to make more money." Meanwhile Morgenthau and Harrison gained an unexpected ally in Harry Hopkins, who had left the WPA to become the secretary of commerce, when he told a group of businessmen in his home state of Iowa that he favored a change in any federal taxes that "tend to freeze the necessary flow of capital."[36]

Morgenthau and Hopkins had said their piece while Roosevelt was away on a three-week cruise inspecting the navy. Upon his return, the chief executive engaged Morgenthau in a series of discussions that left the secretary confused and torn between a president, to whom he had always been intensely loyal, and the congressional team of Harrison and Doughton, who had eagerly backed the treasury head in a public letter on March 2 asking for treasury recommendations for removing tax deterrents. "We stand ready to cooperate," the letter concluded. Roosevelt was alarmed about what Congress might do to a tax program outlined by the treasury to repeal the capital stock and profits tax, reduce the surtaxes on higher individual income brackets, and reduce corporate income levies. Opposed on economic grounds to the scheme, which he termed a "Mellon plan of taxation," the president also feared the political consequences in 1940 of any kind of business appeasement. He was also determined not to permit Congress to run away with a tax bill as it had done in 1938. "The people on the Hill want to put us in the hole," he told Morgenthau.[37]

Determined to divorce himself from any rumored move to repeal the tax deterrents, Roosevelt tried to convince the press that the pro-

posal for removing the taxes on undistributed profits and excess profits had come from Senator Harrison. As for the president and the
senator, the struggle over a pending tax program resolved into a "paper war" as letters were shot back and forth. When FDR wrote Harrison on March 21 to remind him that they had agreed that any revision should not result in a loss of revenue, Harrison replied that it
was only through newspaper rumors that he had learned of the Treasury Department's new tax plans. Throwing the burden of responsibility back to the administration, the senator concluded, "I assure you
of my sincere desire to cooperate wholeheartedly in effectuating the
purposes announced by the Secretary of the Treasury—to aid business through the modification or elimination of any provisions of our
tax laws which act as a deterrent to business." To Jere Cooper, a
Tennessean who had become the chairman of the Ways and Means
taxation subcommittee, Harrison wrote that he had not made public
either the president's letter or his reply, since "it would just result in
exaggerating the situation."[38]

Needless to say, the press was well aware of the efforts of both the
administration and the senator to saddle each other with the responsibility for initiating a new tax bill. Roosevelt wrote Morgenthau that
he hardly knew how to answer Harrison's letter. To eliminate what
was left of the undistributed profits tax would violate "a matter of
fundamental principle." He did not want Morgenthau to appear as
the originator of the changes. "It seems perfectly clear that the origin
of the proposed changes was Senator Harrison himself," Roosevelt
insisted. "Frankly, the political mistake, made while I was with the
Fleet, was in falling into Senator Harrison's trap," he added. It was
just too bad, it seemed to FDR, that "we did not pin this thing on
Senator Harrison."[39]

Morgenthau was not willing to take the blame himself, nor could
he agree that Harrison was culpable. In a March 27 conversation
with John W. Hanes, Morgenthau's new under-secretary, the two
treasury officials exonerated the senator:

> Morgenthau: Of course, I can't agree with the President that Pat is as
> deep-dyed [a] villain as he tries to paint him.
>
> Hanes: No. (Laughter) No, I can't myself, because I think un-
> less Pat is deceiving you, which I don't believe he would
> do. . . . He has been as fair and as open about the thing as
> anybody could possibly be.

Morgenthau: Because if he was such a deep-dyed villain, he could have jumped on the President with both feet the other day.

Hanes: Yes. Yes, and he could have made this letter that he has written the President public too.

Morgenthau: Yeah. Which he hasn't done.

Hanes: Which he's not going to do, I am sure. Pat wouldn't do that because he—he wouldn't be keeping faith with us if he did.

Morgenthau: Now, you see, where the President, I think, left himself unnecessarily open was he never gave us a chance to go over the letter he wrote to Pat in advance.

Faced with a presidential request for aid in drafting a reply to Harrison, Morgenthau was disturbed. "This is a duel between the President and Pat Harrison, and I'm not going to get caught in the crossfire," he told Hanes.[40]

When Hanes studied the exchange of correspondence, he could find no indication that Harrison had originated the new tax proposals. To him it was apparent that "the President had fixed in his mind the thought that Senator Harrison has set a trap and that these suggestions are his instead of ours." In fairness to the senator, Hanes thought that both he and Morgenthau should assume whatever responsibility rested with them for having initiated the drive for tax revision. Hence, when the secretary wrote the president on March 30, he pointed out that Harrison's tax statements had been merely repetitions of what he had heard from the Treasury Department and from Hopkins. "I should not myself want to avoid responsibility for initiating the suggestion that the corporate tax structure be revised. It was not done at Pat Harrison's suggestions," Morgenthau concluded.[41]

One thing must have been apparent to Roosevelt. He was not dealing with the Pat Harrison of 1935 who had "taken the rap," as the press so often put it, for an idea which had come from within the official family. Now, with Morgenthau so obviously on Harrison's side, the president modestly admitted to Harrison that he had no desire "to confuse the record" and that the origin of the tax amendments did appear "to have come from a variety of sources."[42]

Roosevelt's position was understandable. He was uneasy over the treasury's willing acknowledgment that some New Deal taxes had become deterrents, and he shared certain of his advisers' sudden un-

easiness over business appeasement. Too, he did not relish losing face
as a result of a congressional victory over the executive, which the
columnists now freely predicted. Both the president and Harrison
were particularly edgy during a long White House conference on May
15. The senator plainly told the president that he could expect the
repeal of the undistributed profits tax with or without White House
aid and that he was ready to push ahead as it was growing late in the
congressional session. Reporters noted that Harrison emerged from
the unpleasant conference with a flushed face and a cigar tilted upward. Manifestly, he had taken the initiative after more than two
months of White House dallying. The senator had concluded that the
1939 revenue bill should retain the excess profits and capital stock
taxes needed for revenue, but that it should repeal the undistributed
profits stump while substituting a flat 18 percent corporate income
tax. Roosevelt was cool to the proposals but reconciled to the fact that
Congress was about to start the bill on its way. The next day
Morgenthau reported to Hopkins that he had told the president, "Pat
has been very patient." Hopkins would do well to "go over there today
and get the President to treat Harrison gently."[43]

It was not Hopkins but Senator Byrnes who stepped into the
breach as peacemaker. Following a weekend cruise with the president, Harrison's congenial South Carolina friend arranged for the
Mississippi senator to have lunch at the White House on May 24, a
week after the stormy conference at which Harrison had been bluntly
rebellious. Finally recognizing the determination of a powerful congressional bloc insistent upon tax revisions favorable to business,
FDR agreed to permit the treasury secretaries to initiate legislative
proceedings. In deference to Roosevelt's sensibilities over losing face,
the two senators told only a few colleagues of their White House
"coup," but within two hours there were so many rumors of
Roosevelt's defeat that Harrison called a press conference to dispel
such talk. Still, the report was widespread that Roosevelt's submis-
sion to a tax measure had saved his loss of both Hanes and
Morgenthau through resignation. Morgenthau told Harrison that
day, "I congratulate you and myself."[44] Two days later the secretary
went before the Ways and Means Committee, and on June 16 the
committee reported to the full House a bill which, at the core, carried
an 18 percent tax on corporate incomes of over $25,000. The undis-
tributed profits tax was conspicuously absent.

From then on legislative action on the revenue bill of 1939 was miraculously swift. On June 19 the measure passed the House after only six hours of quiet discussion and one dissenting vote. A day later the Finance Committee held a two-hour executive session and on June 22, during a four-hour truce in a filibuster being waged by the silverites, Harrison wedged in his report on the revenue bill, which sailed to passage without a roll call.[45]

The passage of the 1939 revenue bill set a congressional speed record for a major tax measure. Within three weeks the measure had gone from House hearings to Senate passage, whereas in the past twenty-two years thirteen major revenue bills had consumed an average of ninety days each. Roosevelt routinely signed the bill on June 30. Given to some sort of mental gymnastics that enabled him to rationalize a victory where none existed, he told Morgenthau, "You and I started in one corner and Pat Harrison started in the other extreme corner and each, by giving a little bit, we finally by a preconceived plan arrived at exactly the point we had in mind at the beginning." For Morgenthau it took restraint to "keep from saying 'Ha!— Ha!—Ha!'"[46]

Defeated by the growing power of the congressional conservatives on taxation in 1938 and 1939, Roosevelt fared little better in his requests for a renewed spending program. After months of advice from "spenders and lenders" within administration inner circles that the recession had been caused to a great extent by cutbacks in the PWA and WPA, the president agreed in the spring of 1938 to turn once again to the panaceas of outlays for relief. With the recession in its seventh month, FDR in April spoke from his "fireside" to prepare for his request that Congress release nearly $4.5 billion to turn the economy upward through Reconstruction Finance Corporation loans and injections into five New Deal agencies including the WPA and PWA. When reporters asked Harrison for a comment on the chat, it was obvious from his answer that he had little sympathy for another spending spree. "I didn't hear it," he retorted. "I am busy on other things now."[47]

With an election year hardly the time to oppose relief spending, the House Democrats quickly honored their president by a vote of 329 to 70, virtually all of the opposition coming from the minority party. While there were highly vocal Senate Democrats who opposed the bill in theory, their opposition withered as the measure wound its way through the Appropriations Committee and onto the floor. Harrison remained silent. His favorable vote was not particularly meaningful since only six Democrats failed to support the administration.[48]

Harrison dropped his silence on the subject of relief by the end of the summer of 1938. In Mississippi before the state Democratic committee he attacked the WPA as a shelter of "thousands . . . that have no business there." "There are just too many people in America who think the government exists just to take care of them," he added. In October he predicted that one of the "paramount" issues before the next session would be the reduction of relief expenditures, and in a late December lecture tour of the Midwest he concentrated on the twin issues of taxation and spending. Before the Detroit Economic Club he deplored the fact that $18 billion had been spent on relief during the five previous years; in spite of "whatever benefit may have come, there are tens of thousands of our citizens whose rugged characters have been affected and whose views on life and government have been transformed." Aware that such opinions marked him as a conservative, he told the Masonic Consistory at South Bend that it did not matter to him whether he was called a conservative or a liberal. Meanwhile, Byrnes spoke publicly along the same lines. Arthur Krock, reporting that the speeches of both senators were drafted after conferences with Democrats who were determined to curb the New Deal, surmised that the protests marked the "formal intention of a powerful Democratic group to restore the functions of Congress."[49]

Harrison was one of the senators known to favor the earmarking of WPA funds and the decentralization of relief administration, the latter particularly popular among the survivors of the purge of 1938 who now wished to prevent the executive branch from using relief funds as political rewards. As one of the four Democrats on the interim Committee on Campaign Expenditures to investigate widespread reports that WPA funds had been diverted to political ends in Kentucky, Tennessee, and Pennsylvania, Harrison subscribed to the findings of the committee substantiating the charges that indeed funds had been used for political profiteering.[50] The report was hardly an attractive backdrop for Roosevelt's January call for a supplemental $875 million to run the WPA until July 1, 1939. Furthermore, the president wanted the money to be distributed at the discretion of the WPA officialdom. While the House conservatives lopped off $150 million, a movement got underway in the Senate under Byrnes to write a formula by which the funds could be allocated on the basis of population, a proposal which Harrison had urged upon Ickes as early as 1936. They were unable to make any headway on the move, however, and nothing came of it. Determined that the House cut be maintained by the Senate, Byrnes and Harrison worked as members of a coalition that buttonholed senators for support. "We have got to make a start somewhere on cutting down these huge governmental expenditures," Harrison argued. With the Senate vote on the relief cut imminent, Garner, Byrnes, Harrison, and McNary, the Republican leader, spent a large part of January 25 seeking pledges for votes. There was no question but that the senators would be won over by corridor and cloakroom maneuvers and not by the Senate debate, which ran for only two days. In this initial test of the chief executive's control of Congress in 1939, the administration forces sustained a blow when the Senate voted 47 to 46 to retain the House cut. According to Alsop and Kintner, the twenty-six Democrats who spurned Roosevelt's relief request included men "whose ancient power in their party is threatened by the President." Harrison and Byrnes were specifically named. [51]

Two weeks later, when FDR threw the relief issue back to Congress in asking for a restoration of the $150 million, Harrison remarked, "It seems to me that the WPA ought to make the garment according to the pattern that Congress laid down." In a statement to the Senate press corps, viewed as a bugle call for a renewed drive against government spending, Harrison asserted: "I have no confidence in the economic philosophy that we must spend ourselves out of this economic disaster." Moreover, he contended that the government should make an overall slash of 10 percent in its 1939 expenditures, thus effecting a savings of nearly $900 million to apply against a recently indicated deficit of over $3 billion for the fiscal year 1939–1940. According to *Time* magazine, the senator had said that "a lot of this emergency stuff could be cut to hell." His attitude was perfectly understandable to the Cleveland *Plain Dealer*, for "down in Mississippi men don't lift themselves by their bootstraps or get their vehicles started by loading them down more heavily." [52]

Harrison's disputations were not limited to the liberal-minded

Swing It, Pat!

Baltimore *Sun*, March 4, 1939
Courtesy: Baltimore *Sun*

spenders who moved within the White House orbit. When the United States Chamber of Commerce converged on Washington in early May, the senator addressed the group at its final dinner and bluntly censured those local delegations that had spent much of their convention time lobbying for funds to continue hometown projects. "There isn't a project desired at Squeduck or Yellow Rabbit or Vinegar Bend . . . that your local Chamber of Commerce does not meet and resolute and frighten [Congress] with the fire of your influence." Such pressures, Harrison charged, were one of the greatest forces in the demand for government funds. Quoting a message that had come to him on a postcard, he insisted, "You can no more spend yourself into prosperity than you can drink yourself sober."[53]

Although Harrison and Roosevelt were basically irreconcilable on the issues of taxation and spending in 1938 and 1939, there was one presidential request the senator could honor—executive reorganization. Ever since he had been a member of a joint committee on reorganization under Warren G. Harding, Harrison had been keen to the coordination of governmental operations. Presidential heavyhandedness had killed executive reorganization in 1937, but in 1938 Roosevelt resubmitted to Congress a plan based upon the recommendations of a study committee headed by Louis Brownlow.[54] Floor manager for the bill in the Senate was Byrnes, who had succeeded Robinson as the chairman of the Senate Select Committee on Reorganization. As one of the nine senators on the committee from its beginning in January, 1937, Harrison was in a position to serve first one and then the other of his two closest Senate comrades.[55] The influence of their leadership as well as his belief that the plan would result in economy led him to back the president: "The task must be placed in the hands of some one official. The President is the proper one." The Senate passed the bill by a narrow margin, but the House killed it less than two weeks later. Executive reorganization thus became a victim of the president's opponents in the House. "It was a case of any stick being a good one to use on the dog," Lindsay Rogers wrote at the end of the session.[56] In 1939 a blander version of the bill, permitting the president to propose rather than to order executive reorganization, reached Congress. Harrison supported Byrnes, who was again the Senate manager. As James Patterson has pointed out, the vote on reorganization demonstrated the shifting nature of the Senate conservatives. Both Harrison and Byrnes were at the moment bitter-enders against Roosevelt's relief plan, but they went down the line for him on reorganization.[57]

By the middle of 1939 it was apparent that the real leader of the Senate was Pat Harrison and not Alben Barkley. Harrison had become the idol of a number of Senate Democrats who had once been willing White House wheelhorses but who had gone unwatered after they had kicked over the traces in the court battle of 1937. Barkley, it was said, consulted the White House even before "salting his soup."[58] In March, 1939, when fifty-three Washington correspondents named the ten ablest men in the Senate, they omitted Barkley altogether. Instead, they determined that the most influential senator was Pat Harrison; second to him was James F. Byrnes.[59]

In 1938 and 1939 these two had served as the field marshals in checking the spending proclivities of the New Dealers. Moreover, Senator
Harrison had established beyond the shadow of a doubt that he was
indeed the taxmaster of the entire Congress.

Washington *Evening Star,* April 14, 1939
Courtesy: Archives and Special Collections, University of Mississippi

CHAPTER X

"If the Agitators & Reformers Don't Come In"

1938–40

"WE DON'T NEED and we won't tolerate agitators from other sections," explained the angry Mississippi Democrat, Louis Jiggitts, early in 1939. "In the first place, we have our own crackpots and rainbow chasers to contend with, to say nothing of our uplifters."[1] Although Jiggitts at the time was annoyed by the picture of farm tenancy in Arkansas given by the Southern Tenant Farmers' Union, his complaints were not unlike those which led many southern Democrats, including Pat Harrison, to bristle at the slightest criticism leveled at the social, economic, and political habits of the South. During the latter years of the New Deal, attacks, real or imagined, upon the region evoked prompt and sharp responses from the Mississippian. Quick to defend the South against wage and hour legislation, successive antilynching bills, and anti-poll tax strictures, Harrison was an active leader of the southern defense corps. At the same time, however, it was somewhat anomalous that it was Senator Harrison whose name would be carried on successive bills to allocate federal aid to education, a realm of activity for which the shibboleth traditionally had been "states' rights."

It was the wages and hours bill of 1937 that had first led Harrison to speak out against the New Deal. While the bill had been shelved in the House, it was only a matter of time before its advocates would renew their efforts. The Mississippi senator, meanwhile, took the case of the southern industrialists to the nation. For a January, 1938, issue of *Collier's* he prepared an article on "The Wages of Dixie," which catalogued the arguments of the South against a wages and hours law.[2] The region, he militantly stated, "has been the object of unjustified criticism, receiving from the invective tongue of the social uplifter and prejudiced journalists a castigation of misrepresentation." The South's position, he explained, was grounded upon its belief that the federal government should interfere as little as possible in "private freedom, management, and control," and it was under that philosophy that the South had made giant industrial strides since the Civil War. Now that southern industries had increased their national markets through the advantages of climate, hydroelectric power, natural resources, and a labor force whose cost of living was lower than that of northern workers, it was unfair that the region should "be held up to rebuke." Regional wage differentials had been written into the policies of the WPA, PWA, and the NRA in recognition of sectional differences. Admittedly, many workers in the South were paid too little, but it boiled down to a choice between insufficient wages or no wages at all, since many locally promoted plants lacked credit or reserves with which to pay more. Under the circumstances, he argued, it was best to permit these smaller industries to pay wages only slightly above relief scales than to force them out of business through proclamations from Washington.

"Local labor in the South," Harrison continued, "where uncontaminated by outside influence, is, generally speaking, very well satisfied." Southern laborers, anxious to retain their jobs, were, he said, not interested in "this agitation." Harrison must have realized that he was fighting a lost cause, for he concluded that, if regulatory wages had to come, they should come gradually and without "such a shock as to shatter industry."[3] As events turned out in the renewed battle for federal legislation, it was on the issue of gradualism that the senator made his last futile stand.

Heartened by the primary victories in the spring of 1938 of two southern liberals, Florida's Claude Pepper and Alabama's Lister Hill, the administration decided to revive the wages and hours bill. Brought out of the House Committee on Rules in May by a petition not signed by any Mississippi representative, the new bill had been revised to placate organized labor. It passed the House on May 24 by a vote of 314 to 97 (one converted Mississippian, William Colmer, cast a "yea"). The measure carried provisions for neither the five-man labor board nor the regional wage differentials that had made the Senate version of 1937 at least partially palatable to its southern critics. As soon as the tax conference committee completed its work, Harrison began lining up southern colleagues for the inclusion of geo-

graphical differentials on wages. Although he did not speak of a
filibuster as such, he intimated that "Congress will be here until
August" if the differentials were not granted.[4]

Few senators cared to spend an election year summer in
Washington, and by early June even Harrison had become resigned to
the fact that some kind of a wages and hours bill would be enacted.
After protracted conference sessions over House and Senate differences, the conferees finally agreed upon a compromise whereby a
wage floor of 25 cents an hour was set for the first operative year, to
be advanced within seven years to 40 cents an hour. From a
maximum 44-hour work week a 40-hour week was to become effective within two years. A wages and hours administrator was to
monitor the provisions with the consent of industrial advisory committees. Thus, while regional wage differentials were not written
into the report as such, a way was left open to accord to the South
something of the protection that opponents of the measure had demanded. On June 14 the Senate adopted the report without a roll
call. Thus the two-year fight for a minimum wage and maximum
hour law was concluded.[5]

Harrison kept a wary eye open to protect the South in the administration of the new law. In early 1939 he was afraid that regulations
emanating from the office of the new wage administrator, Elmer F.
Andrews, would call for wages to be paid during a worker's training
period at a rate that would prevent the location of new industries.
The senator informed Andrews that he knew of "at least" seven Mississippi communities where garment plants would either locate or
increase their labor force if "a reasonable modification" could be
made for training wages. Harrison's complaint was worded so strongly
that Andrews rushed to Washington for an hour's conference with
the senator on May 2. Evidently Andrews gave little satisfaction to
southern protestors, for in July the governors of Mississippi and
Alabama, Hugh L. White and Frank M. Dixon, testified in hearings
conducted by Andrews in Atlanta that the proposed 33½ cents
minimum wage for the textile industry was an attempt to keep the
South in "economic thralldom" to the North.[6]

Southerners found competition from northern industries to be
double-edged. Southern apologists for low wage levels seldom argued
against the wage bill without bringing up the matter of freight rate

differentials.[7] At Warm Springs in November, 1937, nine southern governors, including White, confronted Roosevelt with an appeal for relief from what they charged were blatant discriminatory rates. White bitterly complained, "We have too long been a mercantilist colony." Jiggitts, who as an official of the Democratic party often penned long chronicles to Roosevelt concerning Mississippi, wrote that if the freight rate differentials were abolished, a great deal of opposition to the wages and hours bill would "evaporate." Jiggitts complained to Roosevelt, "We in the South are beginning to wonder whether we are to continue to be the milch cow of the nation."[8]

The campaign for lower rates continued throughout the balance of the Roosevelt administration. Harrison supported the crusade principally through attempts to retain Southerners on the Interstate Commerce Commission. He endorsed the appointment of a former Alabama Public Commission official, J. Haden Alldredge, who had edited a TVA study of freight rate structures which had become a virtual bible for the South's public campaign. Alldredge, appointed in 1939, joined another Alabamian, Marion M. Caskie, on the commission. When the latter resigned in 1940, Harrison again counseled the president that a Southerner should be appointed.[9] The freight rate controversy simmered down after the ICC began to grant relief along the lines laid down by the southern governors, actions attributed largely to the presence of Alldredge.[10]

Roosevelt was not deaf to the pleas of his southern intelligence gatherers. In the summer of 1938 he commissioned a study of the problems and needs of the South. Although he intended the study to be an overture of good will, FDR jeopardized the acceptance of the *Report on Economic Conditions of the South* through his charge to the commission. "It is my conviction that the South presents right now the nation's No. 1 economic problem" he wrote, thus provoking cries of anguish from Southerners who resented what they thought to be a slur.[11]

If, in releasing the report, the president had the best of intentions, other statements seemed to indicate that he was antagonistic toward the South's leadership. Critics charged that the President was bent upon destroying a substantial segment of the senatorial Democracy. In August Roosevelt timed his public announcement of the recently completed report on the South with his endorsement of a candidate seeking to oust Walter F. George. George could not "be classified as belonging to the liberal school of thought," Roosevelt declared. [12] The report on the South should have gained a favorable currency with senators such as Harrison since it supported much of what they had long argued regarding the debilitating effects of high tariffs and freight rates. But the president's use of the report as a basis for a political "purge" negated its acceptance in many southern quarters. [13]

Four days after Roosevelt spurned Senator George, Harrison denounced the southern economic report. "I think that the people who live in the South know that certain things that have been blasted to the country are not true," he said. The fact that the report was prepared by Southerners, among them Lucius O. Crosby, a prominent Mississippi lumberman, did not alter the senator's view that the summary was a blatant misrepresentation of the region. Southerners, he explained, "have a hard row to hoe because of certain conditions which were put upon them, but I think they know what they are up against." The real cause of his resentment surfaced: "As everyone knows, I have always been a warm admirer of Senator George." [14]

Pat Harrison did not throw himself into the congressional campaign of 1938 as he had done in previous years when he had canvassed the North and West in the interest of his colleagues. He explained his reluctance to a party leader in Missouri: "I find that this is a very peculiar campaign . . . due to the criminations and recriminations and the drawn issues around the President's speaking engagements in several of the states." Because the legislative battles of recent years had complicated every senator's campaign, it was "a delicate problem as to which Senators can be helpful to some other Senator." [15] Harrison honored one request, that of Bennett Champ Clark of Missouri. Clark, who had left the New Deal reservation on a number of crucial issues, was never in any serious trouble in his home state. In fact, his position was so strong that Roosevelt had considered it unwise to oppose him; and Harrison, who discussed the Missouri situation with Clark's colleague Truman, concluded that Clark could win hands down. Nevertheless, because both Clark and Edwin Halsey, the majority party secretary, wanted Harrison in Missouri, the Mississippian agreed to speak at Kirksville in early November in the closing week of the campaign. [16]

The advocacy of Clark's reelection was a secondary purpose of Harrison's Kirksville address. Halsey, who it will be remembered had wanted Harrison to smooth ruffled party feathers at the height of the animosity over the president's Supreme Court plan, now wanted the senator to give a speech with "an old time ring" suitable for national publicity. Harrison complied, although he was guarded in his praise of Roosevelt. While predicting that "Franklin D. Roosevelt will rank in history as the great progressive President of all time," Harrison faulted him with one political offense, "an extreme position" on labor and relief. Defensive of his friends under attack from Roosevelt, Harrison noted that "sharp differences of opinion" on issues and policies had always been part of the nation's history. "It is only when action becomes intimidated and independence becomes shackled" that the nation would be endangered, he added. [17]

Roosevelt probably paid no attention to what Harrison said in Missouri. On the next night, November 4, he warned of what "an ill-advised shift from liberal to conservative leadership can do to an incompleted liberal program." After only one of FDR's targets, John O'Connor of New York, had been turned out of office, the New York *Times* reported that Harrison, Byrnes, and Garner all agreed that the conservative victories were signals from the middle class for the administration to slow up and consolidate the gains already made. When the new Congress met, Harrison hoped to see "every element of the party represented at the council table—the purged and the unpurged." [18]

There is no extant evidence that Senator Harrison's resentment of the report on the South and of Roosevelt's intervention in the primaries of 1938 was based upon an uneasiness over the growing criticism of the South's racial patterns. But Harrison would have been too astute to make public statements about such matters. Granted the president himself made no direct reference to race in the summer campaign or in his remarks in transmitting the report, but there is no question that his call for a liberalization of the Democratic party gave encouragement to the increasing number of liberals disturbed by racial discrimination in the South. [19] Under the impetus of the Southern Conference for Human Welfare, an organization to which Harrison vigorously objected, fresh attention would be drawn to the South's old problems including that of lynching, a barbarism that increased with the onset of the depression. And, in Mississippi, the most rural southern state, lynching occurred most frequently. [20]

The National Association for the Advancement of Colored People under the direction of Walter F. White had determined that the time had come for the renewal of its crusade for a federal antilynching law. Drafted by the NAACP and sponsored by Senators Robert F. Wagner of New York and Edward P. Costigan of Colorado, an antilynching bill was introduced in 1934. [21] As a deterrent against the crime, the bill defined a mob as three or more persons acting in concert without the authority of law for the purpose of killing or injuring any person in the custody of a peace officer. [22] Furthermore, the bill provided for fines and imprisonment for a law officer who failed or refused to make diligent efforts to protect an accused person or failed to prosecute persons participating in mobs. Federal district court jurisdiction extended to such cases.

The bill was never espoused by President Roosevelt, who was wary of challenging the southern wing of the Democratic party and the powerful chairmen whose committees held the key to crucial New Deal legislation. [23] In fact, just at the time that the Wagner-Costigan bill reached the Senate floor in April, 1935, the Finance Committee was readying the social security bill and the measure extending the NRA. The Wagner-Costigan bill ran into the expected stone wall of southern opposition and a six-day filibuster ensued. Harrison never spoke on the bill but instead spent his time preparing his veterans' bonus bill substitute, knowing that his colleagues would be happy to switch from the antilynching bill to the more popular bonus. [24] The Wagner-Costigan bill, which never came to a vote upon its own merits, was killed by a parliamentary ploy engineered by majority leader Robinson, none too soon for Roosevelt who rebuked for laggardness in passing administration measures a group of senators that included Harrison and Wagner. [25]

Editor Fred Sullens, who admitted that the Mississippi senators were silent while the short-lived debate took place, was certain that "it is tolerably well known by their constituents how they stand on the subject." Governor Conner boasted at the death of the bill that Mississippi had numerous laws against lynching and that the state's chief executives had tried to enforce them. He contended that the enactment of the Wagner-Costigan bill would have "destroyed the last vestige of state rights" and would have violated the fundamental principles of the federal constitution. A year later during their senatorial race, when Conner criticized Harrison's silence during the filibuster, the senator retorted, "I do not chase windmills." He claimed that the Democratic steering committee, of which he was a member, had upbraided Wagner and Costigan for bringing up their bill. "They were sort of playing for the colored vote. . . .We picked out a man who wasn't busy and let him talk on it," Harrison explained.[26]

In 1936 congressional antilynching activity took a holiday, but more than fifty antilynching bills were pending before the new session in 1937. Of them the measure sponsored by Representative Joseph Gavagan of New York, Senator Wagner, and Indiana's Senator Frederick Van Nuys was brought to the floor of the House in April, 1938, by a discharge petition. Debate had scarcely begun on the bill, a reincarnation of the Wagner-Costigan measure, when news reached the chamber that a lynching had occurred at Duck Hill, Mississippi. Two Negroes, accused of murdering a rural white storekeeper, were seized from an apathetic sheriff, chained to trees, and put to death by a blowtorch. A caravan of forty automobiles had followed the doomed pair to the piney woods spot where five hundred spectators waited. Horror was combined with irony, for on that afternoon of April 13 Governor White had just told a farm conference meeting in Jackson that "We are justly proud of the fact that Mississippi has not had a lynching in fifteen months."[27]

Organized women's groups in Mississippi favored the antilynching proposal. The state's chapter of the Southern Association for Women for the Prevention of Lynching endorsed the bill and five thousand members of the Methodist Women's Society in north Mississippi petitioned Governor White to support federal action.[28] Mississippi men in Congress were not of like mind. The one Mississippi representative, Dan R. McGehee, who did not vote on the Gavagan bill, abstained because of sentiment in his district favorable to passage. The others agreed with Aaron Lane Ford that it was a "twentieth century force bill." The Mississippi senators also stood foursquare against the measure. When fifty members of the American Student Union at Millsaps College in Jackson petitioned Bilbo to support the bill, he branded the organization communistic and demanded an investigation of all Mississippi student organizations.[29]

Harrison said nothing on the Senate floor as the Wagner–Van

Nuys bill was maneuvered to consideration in August, 1937. With fresh memories of the majority leadership contest and of the court plan, Harrison, Byrnes, and George, it was said, harbored a secret desire that the bill come to a vote and pass, thus embarrassing the president for whom either a signature or a veto would be political dynamite. Likewise, those senators who had opposed Harrison, among them Hugo Black, would be embarrassed if forced to vote on the measure only to await the displeasure of their constituents. Black, at least, was saved from the pending dilemma when he was appointed to the Supreme Court. [30]

When Wagner agreed to let a pressing farm bill take precedence over his antilynching proposal, the latter measure lay over until the next session. While at home in Mississippi in the fall of 1937, Senator Harrison conceded that an antilynching bill would be passed when Congress reconvened. "There is no way to stop it," he said, in spite of its "complete usurpation of the police powers of the state." Such an admission of helplessness against a liberal onslaught was offered solely for political self-preservation, some critics said, in the event that the bill actually should pass. [31] Meanwhile, Governor White, whose position paralleled Harrison's, pragmatically objected that sheriffs would be reluctant to make arrests and handle prisoners without calling for a national guard escort; he did not welcome the prospect of keeping the guard in barracks for readiness at all times. "It will take a standing army to enforce a federal antilynching law," he complained. [32]

In January, 1938, the Wagner–Van Nuys bill was taken up as promised by Barkley. "Dear Alben," *Time* quipped, appeared to be rather like "a Confederate general trapped into acting as a front for a group of carpetbaggers." [33] Pat Harrison's friends spoke of his relief that the leadership defeat had spared him such a dilemma. At any rate, he was now a member of a band of filibusterers lined up by Tom Connally, which included Georgia's Russell, North Carolina's Bailey, Louisiana's Allen Ellender, and Byrnes of South Carolina. In fact, almost every southern senator slammed a few blows at the bill during the talkathon that ran from January 5 until February 21. Nonetheless, the most devastating speech came from "Big Bill" Borah of Idaho, an old enemy of federal antilynching measures, who questioned the constitutionality of the bill, its wisdom, and the reality of its enforcement. Widely applauded by Southerners in Congress and out, Borah seemed to be embarrassed by their support. Three days later, while Harrison praised him, Borah got up and left the Senate chamber.[34]

In previous filibusters against antilynching proposals, Harrison had either remained silent or employed parliamentary stratagems to prevent debate. This time he spoke for two hours. He laid his previous silence to his reluctance to discuss any subject which might raise a sectional issue or evoke the race question. Not since the Republican decade had Harrison been as saber-tongued as he was in his denunciation of the Wagner–Van Nuys bill and its northern Democratic supporters. In the bill itself Harrison criticized such things as its disregard of the "foulest crime against the fairest flower that grows" in southern soil, its "great inroads upon the police powers and sovereign rights of a State," its "rape of the Constitution," its attention solely to southern crime while neglecting northern crime, but he added nothing new to the southern line of defense. Repeating the familiar plea of a misunderstood South whose "tragic era" had been forgotten by a North that did not know "a tinker's dam about the situation that confronts the southern people," Harrison warned his colleagues to leave southern institutions alone. He was apprehensive that antilynching laws were only the beginning of a larger threat against the South, for he foresaw that laws maintaining segregated railway cars and public lodgings were an NAACP target. Moreover, other attacks would follow against miscegenation laws and white primaries. Just as much at stake as the future of the South was the future of the Democratic party if its northern leaders should weaken the faith of the South merely for the sake of retaining the support of "certain groups of Americans [who] voted the Democratic ticket in the past two campaigns."[35]

The speech was one of the rare occasions in Harrison's long Senate career when he engaged in personalities free of pretense. His targets were Alben Barkley and Robert Wagner, and after this particular philippic he would not leave the chamber arm-in-arm with his adversaries as he had once done with James Watson, his Republican friend of the gadfly days. Shaking a finger at the Kentuckian, he cast a warning of "beware" to the "aspiring gentlemen . . . who may entertain some hope" of a presidential nomination. To Wagner he thundered that the senator who expected to be appointed to the Supreme Court (Justice Sutherland had recently resigned) had "better beware."[36] Clearly, Harrison intended to lead the southern opposition to any presidential candidate or court nominee who persisted in supporting the antilynching bill. Having formerly pled silence for the sake of unity, he had now deliberately and bluntly sought to drive a wedge in the Senate leadership.

At January's end the filibuster was still droning on. Bilbo, who had fortified himself with the complete run of Vardaman's newspaper, *The Issue*, asked permission to address the Senate for thirty days. Finally, after the failure of two moves to invoke cloture, the Senate set aside the Wagner–Van Nuys bill in late February to take up an emergency relief resolution; even Wagner and Van Nuys voted to drop the measure in order to proceed with other legislation. When Wagner took the floor on the last day of debate and pledged to go into the states of the cloture opponents, Harrison asked if he would include Mississippi. No, the New Yorker replied, he was enough of a "realist" not to go into Mississippi.[37]

Few senators were as candid about the dictates of politics as Harry Truman, who told the Southerners, "You know I'm against this bill . . . but the Negro vote in Kansas City and St. Louis is too important." Doubtless his Dixie colleagues studied the political credit and debit columns as they fretted over the prospects of the Wagner bill's coming to a vote. Although Harrison held a lien on his Senate seat until 1943, there is little question that his response to the measure was due to his desire to add a little more to his political stock in Mississippi. The state legislature had given him a strong reading when it passed a joint resolution against the Wagner bill, calling it "a violation of the Constitution of the United States and an insult to the Southern states." Indicative of the attitude of many Mississippians was the statement made by the city attorney of Grenada following a mass meeting in that town. "Call us anything you like, we would rather be sleeping in the bed with Senator Borah, Republican, than in the bed of Senator Wagner."[38]

By January, 1940, another Gavagan–Wagner–Van Nuys bill had been prepared. Governor White accused northern congressmen of vote-angling; editor Sullens aroused himself to say it was a "rotten measure"; the Mississippi legislature unanimously passed another resolution of censure; Bilbo pledged to "give them everything I've got in my shop"; and Harrison said nothing to be found on record.[39] Passed by the House, the bill was never called up for Senate debate. It was the last antilynching bill that Senator Harrison would face.

Just as Harrison had linked the fear of an antilynching law with the threat of strictures upon southern voting procedures, the southern crusade against an antilynching law was closely kin to the larger issue of Negro disfranchisement. Harrison had reason enough to be sensitive about the poll tax. At a time when Mississippi held the dubious record for lynching, it also had the lowest rate of voter participation in the nation. By 1938 the poll tax was under siege by a number of groups and individuals, none of them popular in the South. In March, Howard Kester of the Southern Tenant Farmers' Union, in testifying before the Senate Committee on Unemployment, urged abolition of the tax. In November the Southern Conference for Human Welfare took a similar stand, and in January, 1939, the Southern Policy Committee included the death of the tax as part of a program to advance the South's economic position.[40]

Roosevelt was as reluctant to challenge the southern Democrats on the poll tax as he had been to espouse the antilynching bills. It was probably not until the summer of 1938, when he hoped to broaden the base of his southern support at the expense of the conservative senators whom he sought to defeat, that FDR gave serious thought to the tax. In September at an informal press conference at Hyde Park, he revealed that in a personal letter to Brooks Hays, Arkansas Democratic national committeeman, he had endorsed an Arkansas amendment to abolish the poll tax. At home in Mississippi, Harrison read of the president's statement and was angered. An audience at Hazlehurst provided a forum for the senator's denunciation of Roosevelt and his own defense of the tax. After someone (not Harrison) sent the president a news clipping of the speech, FDR promptly forwarded the item to the senator expressing a hope that Harrison had been misquoted in his statement that the president intended to support federal legislation to abolish the tax. "You doubtless . . . know that at no time and in no manner did I ever suggest Federal legislation of any kind," the president reminded the senator, adding a request that Harrison clarify the statements made at Hazlehurst.[41]

In answer Harrison quoted the Associated Press story that had led him to believe the president would lend support to the states directly or to federal legislation to kill the tax. After closer study of the news dispatches, the senator admitted that he found no suggestion, after all, that the chief executive had called for federal action. Moreover, he found the recent letter from Hyde Park a reassurance that there was no executive intent to deprive states of their poll tax rights. Did Roosevelt think that Harrison's misrepresentation to the press and the president's clarification were of "sufficient importance" to be made public? Evidently Roosevelt was not willing to have his views aired publicly (it was only three weeks before the November congressional elections), for Harrison's secretary shortly telegraphed that Marvin McIntyre's office had relayed the message "in re poll tax letter Mac says for you to forget it." Thus ended the brief contest between Harrison and Roosevelt over the poll tax. [42]

Harrison's alarm over the tax shifted from Washington to Mississippi and the coming gubernatorial race in 1939, a new chapter in the continuing saga of the Harrison-Bilbo feud. Should a Bilboite win, the junior senator's chances of obtaining a second term in 1940 would be measurably enhanced. Also at stake was the question of which senator would have an amenable governor as a partner in controlling the Mississippi delegation to the 1940 Democratic convention. It was no secret that Bilbo was backing his old adversary, Paul B. Johnson. He had wanted Attorney General Cummings to appoint Johnson to Thurman Arnold's legal staff engaged in combatting monopolies. As a legal consultant to the cotton seed trust investigators, Johnson could remain in Mississippi to wage his campaign for governor while enjoying recognition from the administration in Washington. Nothing came of the request, but Bilbo continued to promote Johnson's candidacy in other and more conspicuous ways. In the late summer of 1938 Harrison conferred at length with the incumbent governor, his friend Hugh White, and then broke a long-standing precedent in predicting that, before the ballots were counted in 1938, "I will be in it with both feet." [43]

As the inscrutable ways of Mississippi politics would have it, Harrison ended up backing the candidacy of his onetime bitter foe, Mike Conner, who hit the comeback trail in 1939. Conner, who had opposed FDR in 1932, was described as still anti-Roosevelt in 1939; he was expected to remain so in 1940. In the first primary Johnson led the seven-man field of candidates, but was forced into the second primary with Conner. In the interval Conner picked up the public support not only of Harrison but also of White and Ellen Woodward, now a member of the Social Security Board. All three shared the platform with Conner at his final rally in Jackson, and ex-senator Hubert Stephens made his first public appearance in three years when he joined Conner's team. At the campaign's end the Washington "Merry-Go-Round" gleefully reported "one of the most significant political upsets in recent southern history." Johnson had "soundly trounced" Conner. To Pearson and Allen it meant the cracking of Harrison's "long bossism." With Johnson slated for the governor's chair it did indeed seem that the bottom rail was on top. [44]

Johnson had won the election on the advocacy of a social program for Mississippi that included free textbooks, a dollar a day pension for the needy aged, and the establishment of a department of labor. [45] On inaugural day he came out in opposition to the poll tax, an "oppression [which] should not be tolerated in a free state any longer." Reported to be at the head of the repeal movement, Bilbo argued that the tax burdened persons on relief and others hard hit financially. Quick to point out that there were ways enough to keep blacks from voting, he had no intention that his crusade should enfranchise them. [46]

By 1940 the anti-poll tax drive had gained momentum on at least two fronts. California's Congressman Lee H. Geyer, who had seen his first bill outlawing the tax wither away in the House Judiciary Committee in 1939, again introduced the measure in early 1940; and the Mississippi legislature that greeted the new governor contained a number of Bilbo followers who pushed for repeal. Early in the session Harrison wrote his own personal friends in the legislature that he was opposed to the extraction of any "teeth" from the electoral code, particularly the requirement that voters produce receipts to show payment of the tax for two preceding years. To a constituent he wrote that the tax had the salutary effect of providing substantial revenue for the maintenance of the public school system. Moreover, when one read of the "dark, tragic, and unjustified era . . . known as the carpet-bag days . . . he cannot but glory in the fine work of the men who composed the Convention of 1890." In view of the fact that in many Mississippi counties Negroes greatly outnumbered whites, Harrison was convinced that to repeal the requirements in effect since 1890 would be a "tremendous mistake." [47]

The same week that Harrison wrote to the Mississippian who had inquired about his poll tax views, the senator was interviewed by a researcher gathering material for Dr. Ralph J. Bunche's study on the political status of the southern Negro. Bunche, disheartened by the widespread political apathy of southern Negroes, believed that southern officials rationalized their own positions on the basis of that apathy. Harrison seemed to prove the point, for he told the interviewer that the Negro "is satisfied down there" and had "played no part in politics for forty years and has no desire to do so." He continued, "Right now, so far as the people of my state are concerned, if the status quo was maintained and agitators and reformers don't come in and try to cause trouble, there is mighty little to fear of the Negro." (He had particular reference to John L. Lewis, Mrs. Roosevelt, and the Southern Conference for Human Welfare.) In calling attention to the "lax" laws in northern states where residence and tax laws were nil and to difficulties in Louisiana where the poll tax had been abolished, Harrison boasted that "we have fine and clean election laws and elections now in my state." Because Mississippians believed in the tax as their contribution to the public schools, Harrison thought that there was "no chance of its repeal."[48]

From interviews with the few Negro political leaders to be found in Mississippi, Bunche's field workers found a mass of evidence to contradict Senator Harrison's assurance that blacks could vote in Mississippi if they met the constitutional qualifications. The chairman of the Republican central committee in the state, a Negro doctor, countered that the Negro's status in southern politics was "dark as Hell and smells like cheese." Bunche concluded that Harrison was no different from the other "Bourbons" of the South, men like Garner, Byrd, and Glass. They were economic oligarchs who represented middle and upper class property holders. Fearful to "risk the uncertainty of a political contest in which thousands of new voters would participate," the southern senators for the most part held on to the poll tax as the last bastion of protection.[49]

There were holes in the fabric of Harrison's political ideology regarding Mississippi Negroes. His statement that they had no real desire for voter rights must have been nothing more than a rubric expressing a pious hope. Harrison was too aware of political currents to dismiss the Negro in his home state. His statement regarding the Negro's contentment with his lot were like those in reference to the low wage earner's satisfaction with his pay. Harrison's behavior relative to both classes was based on a perception of his constituency that was comfortable and politically profitable and a contradiction of his usual awareness of reality. It would appear that he simply blocked his conscience for political expediency.

According to George C. Stoney, a free-lance journalist who participated in the SCHW crusade for poll tax repeal in 1940, both of Mississippi's senators were the beneficiaries of the tax. Stoney charged that both men ran "machines" which paid the tax for their regular followers and had them kept on file to be issued on election day, recollected, and reissued for subsequent elections.[50] To gather substantiating evidence for such an indictment forty years after the fact would be difficult. It is not going far afield, however, to suggest that Harrison's primary concern over Bilbo's repeal activities was based on a fear that repeal would vastly increase voting among roving tenants and other dislocated whites who were potential Bilbo voters.

By the summer of 1940 the poll tax issue had died down in Mississippi. The legislature had taken no action, and endorsements from Mrs. Roosevelt and John L. Lewis weakened the movement in the state. No more popular were the SCHW organizers who appeared on the scene along with a Negro lobbyist who attempted to influence legislators in the halls of the state capitol. Harrison learned that Bilbo was the object of "furious criticism" for his advocacy of repeal. In fact, by the time certain members of Congress, among them the liberal senator from Florida, renewed the drive for repeal, Harrison and Bilbo were in accord in their opposition, the latter promising to "take the heat out of a pod of Pepper."[51] The final resolution of the poll tax question would come years after the era of both senators had ended.

All the while that Senator Harrison defended his state from the domination that he saw inherent in federal legislation relative to wages and hours, voting, and lynching, he seems to have had no qualms over federal aid to education. For five years he sponsored a series of education bills. Although he did not offer his own bill until 1936, he had striven, as an administration leader, to secure federal grants for schools in the Seventy-third Congress (1933–1934), when thirty or more bills were introduced in each session to provide such aid in one form or another. Few of the proposals were passed, and none of them provided for a permanent policy of federal grants-in-aid.

Harrison's own particular concern was, of course, the Mississippi school system, financially weak in the best of times. In April, 1934, the senator and Mississippi Congressman Russell Ellzey, a member of the House subcommittee on education, pled with Roosevelt for a large allocation of the relief budget toward alleviating the school crisis. They were successful in aiding state superintendent Willard F. Bond in acquiring funds on an *ad hoc* basis to keep the schools in session for the remainder of the 1933–1934 term. When many schools faced a shutdown again in 1935, the senator went once more to the White House and came away with assurances that no school terms would have to be curtailed in Mississippi that year, for funds would come from the new work relief budget. For the FERA administrator, who had met with Harrison and Bond on several occasions, the senator had nothing but praise. He told the Senate, "I do not know of any public official who has measured up to the duties of his office more than has Harry Hopkins."[52]

When Mississippi rural schools faced a closure in still a third year, the legislature appropriated a million dollars, an act that alarmed Harrison, who feared that it would wreck the state's social security program. This time his appeal to Hopkins and his deputy, Aubrey Williams, was unavailing. The rebuff, in February, 1936, convinced Harrison that a permanent policy was necessary. Such a program had long been in a formative stage under the auspices of the National Education Association, whose leaders selected as a sponsor Senator Harrison since his previous successes in securing funds were impressive. The NEA executive secretary, Dr. Willard Givens, who addressed the Jackson meeting of the Mississippi Education Association in late April, 1936, told the teachers that their senator was one of their best friends. "There are two men in Washington to go to when you want anything done," Dr. Givens said. "One of them is Senator Pat Harrison and the other is Senator Joe Robinson. Both have the ear of the President." At the same time, Harrison was readily available to Howard A. Dawson, an Arkansas school official who was called to Washington by the commissioner of education to assist in the administration of relief funds for rural education. The senator once told Dawson, "If money cannot be found for education there is something wrong with the ruling power."[53]

In June, Harrison introduced a bill, cosponsored in the House by

Brooks Fletcher of Ohio, providing for an initial appropriation of $100 million with annual increases of $50 million until a maximum of $300 million was reached. Designed to equalize educational expenditures by the states, the funds were to be appropriated to states and territories according to the number of persons in the age group five to twenty, with the manner of expenditure left wholly to the states. Harrison pointed to the fact that in the United States over 100,000 schools had been forced into a practical state of bankruptcy, that many closed schools had reopened on a tuition basis, thus barring poor students, and that school district indebtedness had increased by nearly a billion dollars. Pointing to the long established policy of federal aid to education dating back to the Morrill Act of 1862, he argued that public education was the greatest investment in citizenship that a government could make. The growing mobility of population and the incidence of more children of educable age living in the less wealthy states made federal assistance imperative. Harrison denied that any state that cared to support its schools adequately could divert its own funds to education by pointing to his own state, which ranked forty-eighth in wealth, forty-sixth in the amount spent for education, yet seventh on the basis of the percentage of state income spent for education. Well aware of the widespread fear that federal aid would mean federal control, he dismissed such criticism as a "fabricated bogeyman" and a "flimsy excuse for failure to admit squarely the economic and social justice of Federal assistance to the States."[54]

Endorsed by both the NEA and the American Federation of Teachers, the Harrison-Fletcher bill lay in committee for the balance of the 1936 session. In January, 1937, Harrison again offered the public education bill with Hugo Black as the Senate cosponsor and Fletcher again the House pilot. During the Senate hearings before Black's Committee on Education and Labor, representatives and petitions from some seventy organizations, particularly NEA and AFT affiliates, called for enactment. The bill carried the endorsement also of the NAACP with the qualification that safeguards be included for the protection of Negro school children. The organization inaugurated a campaign through its National Coordinating Committee which eventually secured amendments to provide a measure of protection in the proposed distribution of funds. In a letter to the Washington *Evening Star* the eminent Negro educator Kelly Miller of

Howard University lauded the proposal as "the reincarnation of the Blair education bill," updated in the "new, national, liberal spirit . . . to stamp out the widespread curse of ignorance."[55]

Reported unanimously from the Senate committee, the bill was predicted by the New York *Times* to face "hard sledding" in Congress. Harrison had no sooner brought the measure up for discussion than William Borah cogently asked if its passage would necessitate new taxes. When Robinson concurred with the Idahoan that "we cannot go on extending federal activities into new fields [and] increasing expenditures without making some provisions for meeting them," congressional observers were shocked that Harrison's Arkansas friend was prepared to oppose the bill. "It was as if Damon had struck Pythias," columnist Paul Mallon wrote, adding that some spectators nearly "fell out of the gallery" when Robinson spoke up. Actually Harrison knew exactly what bothered his friend, for Roosevelt had just ordered a resurvey of all departmental expenditures. In spite of the fact that Harrison had never yet left the administration fold on budgetary matters, he was ready to do so on education. Moreover, he was privy to information from White House aides that FDR would veto the bill because it failed to give him a hand in the distribution of the funds.[56]

Behind the scenes the White House worked to prevent the Harrison-Black-Fletcher bill from coming to a vote. When agriculturalist Clarence Poe strongly urged his senator, Josiah Bailey, to support the bill, Bailey replied that the bill would pass if brought to a vote. The only force to prevent that, Bailey wrote, was "the influence of the President." Representative Braswell Dean of Georgia, a member of the House Committee on Education who personally opposed the measure, privately informed Marvin McIntyre that the bill would be difficult to defeat on the House floor; therefore, if the bill should be quietly killed in committee, Dean wanted to be so advised. Publicly Roosevelt said nothing in opposition, but at a White House conference held on the same day that Dean contacted McIntyre, the president told congressional finance leaders and Treasury Department officials that his coming budget message would call for no new taxes and a relief request of $4.5 billion. Thus it was clear that he had shoved aside the request that relief be pared to $1 billion to leave funds for the education bill.[57]

Roosevelt's budget message in April, 1937, carried his strongest demand for governmental economy since 1933. Clearly he had set himself against extraordinary projects and his legislative adjutants were thus directed to reject Harrison's bill. On April 17 the House committee sidetracked the bill by a vote of 12 to 5. Nevertheless, the bill remained on the Senate calendar, and educational leaders continued to manifest a lively interest in its passage. [58]

Roosevelt's stand prompted criticism from education and labor leaders. In an open letter the AFL chided Roosevelt's opposition as "an attempt to balance the budget at the expense of the school children of America," and in its official journal the NEA demanded to know what the president had meant when he had said at Kansas City in October, 1936, "The school is the last expenditure upon which America should be willing to economize." While the bill gained in popularity among educators, it began to lose ground with other groups. Senator Bailey's remark to a constituent that the government would be constitutionally obligated "to provide equally for all groups, classes and individuals" indicated that race was one of the unspoken factors of opposition among some of the Southerners. And, at the annual governor's conference held at Atlantic City in September, the South Carolina executive, Olin D. Johnston, set forth a view that had the tacit backing of other governors when he declared that his state would "always demand its right to segregate the whites and blacks." [59]

In order to await the report of a special presidential advisory committee on education created in 1936, Harrison decided not to try to push the Senate to a vote on his bill in 1937. When Roosevelt expanded the duties of his executive committee on the day before he sent his budget message to Congress, it appeared that he intended to stall passage of the Harrison bill. The committee must have disappointed the president, for when it concluded its work in February of 1938, it came out strongly for "general aid to the States for elementary and secondary education" to be initiated with a six-year program of grants beginning on July 1, 1939. [60] The report seemed to insure that the bill would pass. In addition, it now had the backing of major agricultural organizations. Clarence Poe of the *Progressive Farmer* had been "delighted" to learn from an interview with Harrison that he was "ready to renew the fight . . . in spite of all obstacles." Harrison's bill was now cosponsored by Elbert Thomas of Utah, who had replaced Black as the chairman of the Education and Labor Committee. The Utah senator succeeded in bringing out a favorable report. [61]

When the Senate began its election year drive in 1938 for a June adjournment without taking any action on education, Harrison became impatient. The bill faced the same obstacles that had doomed it on two previous occasions. Administration loyalists still stood in place for Roosevelt, whose position was unchanged. Some of Harrison's oldest Senate associates spurned his bill. Tom Connally told the Senate that he had "never regarded [Harrison] as one of our leading educational authorities," and Alben Barkley was determined that the bill not come to a vote. By June 7 the Mississippian could suppress his irritation with the administration no longer, and he took the floor to plead for his proposal. Harrison thought it deplorable that the bill had been on the calendar for more than a year, especially since it now carried the approval of one of the president's special committees. "I have brought it to the attention of the highest authority in the country. I did not get anywhere," he lamented. Could Senator Barkley "conjure in his mind" any explanation of why the administration should refute its own committee? When the majority leader replied that he had "no idea," Harrison retorted, "I am the easiest person in the world to get along with, but I do not like to be kicked around too much." [62]

Knowing that Barkley would not allow a vote on the bill, Harrison sought a promise that the measure would be taken up at the next session. But Barkley would not commit himself to even that "whisper of assurance," as Harrison put it. Thomas also made a strong plea for Barkley's aid. The Utah senator dreaded facing his constituents with the fact that Congress could spend a billion and a half on battleships and refuse to give children thirty-six weeks of schooling. Only William Gibbs McAdoo, the aging Californian, offered any floor support to Harrison and Thomas, while J. Hamilton Lewis of Illinois raised the question of discrimination against parochial schools and Nebraska's Edward R. Burke, who had turned into an irretractable conservative, warned that federal control would follow federal aid to education. [63]

A third, but still weaker, round over a general education bill began with the Seventy-sixth Congress in 1939. Harrison, in cataloguing his case for federal aid in the January issue of *State Government*, announced that he and Thomas would renew their bill.[64] Thomas introduced the bill in February. This time the various titles called for an appropriation of $889,705,000 to be disbursed over a six-year period from 1940 through 1945. When Floyd W. Reeves, the chairman of the educational advisory committee, sought to learn the administration position prior to his scheduled appearance before the Senate committee, his request stirred Daniel W. Bell of the Budget Bureau to contact the president. "It seems to me," Bell wrote to FDR, "that S. 1305 should be considered as not in accord with your program." Thomas was able to bring out a favorable report, but it was weakened by a minority report submitted by Ohio's Republican senator, Robert A. Taft.[65] In May, James Davis of New York spoke for the proposal, but no one else offered to extend the discussion. Thus the bill faded away.

Federal aid to education was virtually dead. In 1940 Roosevelt was more unwilling than ever to have the subject discussed even in congressional hearings. When the new House sponsor, William H. Larrabee of Indiana, began to inform educational circles that the House at the president's request would hold no hearings, Mrs. Roosevelt asked Lauchlin Currie, one of her husband's close advisers, to remind FDR that, since the Senate committee had reported the bill favorably during the previous session, the House should at least hold a hearing. Roosevelt wrote Currie, "I think frankly in view of the political situation, it is best to defer any education grant at this session."[66] Hence there was no bill in 1940.

When Thomas introduced an education bill again, this time in April, 1941, the nation, already on the eve of World War II, had begun to make preparations for defense. Rather than calling for the general grants which the previous bills had proposed, the new Harrison-Thomas measure provided funds for states that had gained a sudden influx of population as a result of defense installations. The bill called for a five-member board under the Federal Security Agency to administer an annual appropriation of $300 million. The Thomas committee conducted hearings, but beyond that nothing came of the proposal. Harrison was a sponsor only by proxy, for he had become seriously ill and had left Washington in March for an extended rest. At Harrison's death in June, Thomas referred to him as the chief spon-

sor of the aid-to-education bills over a period of five years. The NEA
in its annual meeting in June memorialized the Mississippi senator as
"a splendid American and a true friend of education." The loss of his
friendship, the organization recorded, was a "severe blow to the
schools of the United States."[67]

Harrison's role in the battle for federal school funds during the
New Deal is indeed interesting in view of the fact that twenty years
earlier he had vowed that he would never vote for federal aid to education. Just as he had been led by Dr. Felix Underwood of Mississippi
to consider the medical needs of the aged during the formulation of
social security legislation, Harrison was won over to the needs of
school-age youth by a bevy of outstanding schoolmen of his state,
among them J. S. Vandiver, the state superintendent of schools; H.
M. Ivy, the head of the Meridian school system and one time chairman of the NEA's committee on federal legislation; and two Gulf
Coast school superintendents, B. Frank Brown of Gulfport and Fred
Young of Pass Christian. The Mississippi school leaders, all active in
the work of the NEA, worked closely in convincing Harrison of the
needs of education. Perhaps the senator's early years as a smalltown
principal had left a mark, and it may be noted that as a young teacher
Harrison had once attended a summer institute conducted by W. F.
Bond. Aware of the obstacles to his program, he once told Dawson
that new and desirable objectives take a long time to accomplish and
suggested that perhaps it would take twenty-five years to win support
for a comprehensive federal education program.[68]

Regardless of who or what changed Harrison's mind in the interval
of twenty years (and it may have been the devastation of schools by
the depression), his convictions on education were productive and his
arguments cogent. "Areas that now have good schools need not think
they can in the future escape the consequences of poor schools in poor
areas today," he wrote in 1939.[69] He was, of course, completely correct, but it would be a quarter of a century before both the president
and the Congress would join forces in behalf of elementary and secondary education, long after the Harrison bills had become a forgotten chapter in the history of federal aid to education.

Harrison failed because obstacles were too formidable. He was
fully aware of congressional qualms over the issues of local control
and parochial schools. Also, within the executive department federal

aid was a controversial subject and none of the officials who could have spoken for it was inclined to do so. Harry Hopkins, who looked upon the crisis as one of unemployment, advocated the hiring of unpaid teachers for rural schools and adult education services, while Aubrey Williams was jealous of funds for the aid of needy students through his National Youth Administration.[70] Daniel Bell was budget-minded. The president supported them in their desire to administer funds through agencies operated from Washington rather than to dissipate both money and authority through decentralized school districts. Moreover, Roosevelt did not relish the loss of the political advantages which accrued to him from the control of educational relief programs by the executive department. He was no more willing to relinquish control of federal activities in the realm of education, as the Harrison bills would have meant, than the senator was willing to allow greater authority to the administration in Washington. In the final analysis the common denominator in the issues of wages and hours legislation, antilynching bills, poll tax repeal, and federal aid to education was the growth of power for the government in Washington. Deeply concerned by the centralizing tendencies of the latter New Deal, Harrison was unable to reconcile his differences with Franklin D. Roosevelt until the advent of a crisis in national defense.

CHAPTER XI

"We Cannot Afford to Make a Change of Leaders"

1940

ALTHOUGH PAT HARRISON was the ranking Democrat on the Senate Foreign Relations Committee throughout the New Deal, he preferred to concentrate his efforts upon the committee that he chaired. Hence his role in foreign affairs was insignificant until after the great European powers went to war in 1939. And even then his "service to country" came under the aegis of his major committee assignment. Once again taxation, this time for the collection of a national purse to begin defense preparations, consumed his energies, which by 1939 began to give way to minor health problems and a final terminal illness. From the summer of 1939, when FDR desperately sought the repeal of an earlier neutrality law that tied his hands, until the summer of 1941, when Harrison died, the Mississippi senator was at peace with Roosevelt. After all, the great surge of New Deal reformism was over, and there were no great issues that divided the president and the senator. The debates were now on foreign policy and the kinship of Roosevelt with southern congressmen was deeply based in their mutual Wilsonian ancestry. When James T. Patterson concluded his work on the conservatives and the New Deal, he remarked that "on most questions of foreign policy through 1941 the conservative coalition failed to function."[1]

There is little to record of Harrison's role in foreign affairs from 1933 until the effusive debate on the neutrality bill of 1939. In 1933, when Frances Perkins had wanted the United States to join the International Labor Organization, an affiliate of the League of Nations, Roosevelt, remembering that Woodrow Wilson had committed a major blunder in not seeking senatorial counsel, told her to consult with members of the Foreign Relations Committee. After her "pleasant talk" with several members, including Harrison, the president asked Miss Perkins to prepare a resolution that the United States apply for membership in the ILO. "Get Pat Harrison to introduce it and go ahead," he told her. The resolution went through without opposition. Two years later, when Roosevelt urged that the United States join the World Court, he suffered one of the most significant defeats of his first term. Twelve years of patient negotiations were flung aside when the Senate vote fell short by seven of the needed two-thirds. Twenty Democrats voted against the World Court, but neither Bilbo nor Harrison deserted the president. [2]

In 1935 the Senate placed a mandatory embargo upon the shipment of war implements to belligerents. Harrison supported both the embargo, which expired in February, 1936, and its extension until May 1, 1937. In March, 1937, Harrison defended neutrality legislation: "Whenever we permit anything to be done in the matter of carrying guns on ships even for defensive purposes, we are likely to get into trouble. Little things provoke wars," he said, "and we should follow, therefore, a policy of absolute neutrality which will guarantee the United States not becoming embroiled in another war." In late April, when Congress adopted a "permanent" neutrality policy which added to the arms embargo a discretionary cash-and-carry feature in order that the nation might trade non-armaments with belligerents, no southern senator cast a dissenting vote. [3] It had been Harrison's good friend Bernard Baruch who had advanced the "cash-on-the-barrel-head and come-and-get-it" compromise; thus the Mississippi senator found it easy to support the policy.

Although the arms embargo of 1937 was intended to avoid involvement in just such a crisis as the civil war in Spain, by early 1938 there was growing pressure on the administration to revise its neutrality policy. Ironically, it was the arch-isolationist Gerald P. Nye who led the movement to repeal the embargo. His resolution to lift the ban put the president and Secretary of State Cordell Hull in a bind, since any change of policy was bound to alienate diverse groups within the Roosevelt coalition. Finally Roosevelt and Hull decided to oppose repeal. On May 13 chairman Key Pittman produced a letter to that effect from Hull, shortly before the Foreign Relations Committee was to take up the Nye resolution. Columnists Pearson and Allen reported that it was Harrison who acted by "prearrangement," supposedly with Hull, to defeat the Nye proposal. Although he had not attended a meeting of the committee in weeks, Harrison was present "in all his wise-cracking glory" so that he might "jump in" to move for an indefinite postponement of the Nye resolution. Harrison's motion carried by a vote of 17 to 1. The truth of the matter was that Harrison had attended few sessions of the committee because he had been tied up with the revenue bill of 1938 during most of April. Nevertheless, Harrison's action on the resolution fitted into his earlier role of administration "fixer."[4]

While both the House and Senate committees conducted lengthy hearings on neutrality revision in 1939, the administration attempted without success to settle upon a coherent program. Finally, in the face of Pittman's faltering leadership, the White House in late May determined to assume direction of revision and to push for repeal of the arms embargo and retention of a modified cash-and-carry prescription. Defeated when the House voted in late June to retain the arms embargo, Roosevelt concentrated upon the Senate Foreign Relations Committee in the hope that he could reverse the action of the House. With Pittman procrastinating still, the president was alarmed to hear that Senator Harrison had made plans to leave Washington temporarily. Knowing that the Mississippian now favored abolition of the mandatory arms embargo, Roosevelt wrote on July 6: "Pat, old dear: What is this I hear about your going home ahead of time? Do please don't! I need you here on lots of things, including the next big thing on the calendar—the neutrality bill." Harrison stayed.[5] Heavy isolationist pressure to postpone neutrality repeal took its toll in the Senate committee and the anti-administration senators carried the vote 12 to 11, Harrison voting with the minority. A week later the president announced his decision to abandon neutrality revision until 1940.[6]

Hitler's invasion of Poland in September changed Roosevelt's mind, and he called Congress into special session to tackle neutrality revision for a second time in 1939. Congress was to reassemble on September 21, but it was not likely that Harrison could attend for he had been ordered by his Gulfport doctor to rest three weeks following the removal of two badly abscessed teeth. In the course of two lengthy telephone conversations with the president, Harrison pledged his "100 percent" support and promised to return to Washington to join the fight to repeal the neutrality law. According to Alsop and Kint-

ner, Harrison was Roosevelt's first choice to assist the ineffectual
Pittman, but Harrison's illness forced Roosevelt to turn to others.
The senator was not yet back from Mississippi when the Foreign
Relations Committee met to draft a repeal measure. When the com-
mittee reported out an arms embargo repeal bill on September 28,
Harrison's "yea" came by proxy. [7]

Harrison left for Washington on October 1, the day before the
Senate debate began, and met with Roosevelt two days later. Although he had not yet fully recovered, he intended to remain in his
home during the neutrality debate and attend only those sessions
when crucial votes would be taken. Pittman would hold his proxy.
Harrison was, however, present to support the president's opposition
to an amendment that would have separated the cash-and-carry provision from the arms embargo. He was also present to cast votes on
three other occasions when anti-repeal senators sought to limit the
sweep of the bill, and he cast his "yea" when the repeal resolution
cleared the Senate on October 27. When Pittman named Harrison as
a conferee, the latter declined in favor of Connally since he had spent
most of the four weeks during which the bill was under consideration
at home under doctor's orders. [8]

Harrison's health had improved by the time Congress reassembled
on January 3, 1940. The administration faced its first testing of the
Neutrality Act, for Russia had invaded "brave little Finland" in late
December. While the American public was pro-Finland, Roosevelt
vacillated for he was reluctant to antagonize Soviet Russia in spite of
his genuine sympathy for the underdog nation. The State Department, too, was unwilling to take a strong stand or to encourage private groups to supply the military aid that the Finns needed so desperately. When a bill offered by Michigan's Prentiss Brown to extend
loans to Finland to purchase non-military supplies under the aegis of
the Export-Import Bank reached the Foreign Relations Committee,
Harrison objected that even food loans would be a violation of the
"letter and spirit" of neutrality. Also, he opposed an increased
capitalization of the bank for reasons of economy. When the committee voted to increase the lending funds of the bank, Harrison voted
"nay." At the same time he offered a "sense of the Senate" resolution
that the Securities and Exchange Commission expedite the flotation
of any privately subscribed loans that would enable Finland to buy the

military supplies forbidden her through any public funds she might
acquire from the United States. Supported by Secretary of War
Frank Knox and adopted by the committee without opposition, Harrison's resolution passed the Senate by a vote of 65 to 3.[9]

The resolution meant little because Finnish bonds had already depreciated to such a point that it was unlikely that any new issue could
be sold to private investors. Two historians of United States foreign
affairs, Whitney S. Shepardson and William O. Scruggs, have
criticized Harrison's move and have mused that the Foreign Relations
Committee adopted the proposals for "reasons which cannot even be
conjectured." The senator's own objections to Finnish aid were
clarified in the Senate hearings dominated by Hiram Johnson,
California's longtime isolationist. While Johnson predicted his opposition to aid on the strict grounds of neutrality, the Mississippian
argued that the additional $100 million for foreign loans was needed
to finance the domestic farm parity program. Moreover, he feared
that Finnish aid would probably force an increase in both taxes and
the national debt limit. When the Senate approved the Brown bill in
February, Southerners Harrison, Connally, George, and Russell
were among the sixteen Democratic opponents. Over in the House,
John E. Rankin of Mississippi argued that credit to Finland would
"plunge" the United States into a foreign war at the cost of millions of
men and billions of dollars, "losing what few friends we have abroad,
and then having us called Shylocks again when it is over." But in both
the House and Senate the overwhelming public popularity of aid to
Finland carried the day, and on March 2 Roosevelt signed the Brown
bill.[10]

In the early spring of 1940 Harrison's greatest concern was a
three-year extension of the Hull trade agreements program. So many
western Democrats had announced their opposition to the reciprocal
tariff program that close observers predicted that the law would be
permitted to expire on June 12. The real danger, it was said, would
come from active Westerners such as Pat McCarran of Nevada and
Henry Ashurst of Arizona, who claimed to have enough votes to add
to any trade agreements extension measure an amendment that would
call for Senate ratification of the executive trade agreements by the
two-thirds vote normally required for treaties. The amendment
would, of course, virtually kill the entire trade program initiated in

1934 by Secretary Hull. Extension won an easy partisan victory in the House in February, and the battle shifted to the Senate Finance Committee. Hearings opened with Hull's testimony that a worldwide wave of totalitarianism would follow any abandonment of the trade agreements and Henry Wallace's insistence that the agreements had greatly augmented domestic purchasing power. With the Democrats in control, the committee reported the House extension measure without amendment.[11]

Behind a move by Key Pittman to treat the trade agreements as treaties subject to ratification were the western cattle and mining senators. A survey made by Harrison and his floor assistant, "Jimmie" Byrnes, indicated that unless Argentine beef and Chilean copper were excluded from the trade agreements that Secretary Hull was then negotiating, the extension bill would be defeated by western defectors. After Hull heeded their warnings, Harrison and Byrnes were reported to have rounded up a dependable majority of eight votes with four more pocketed in reserve. Still, when debate began on March 25, the Mississippi senator admitted that a "real fight" was in store.[12]

Harrison's opening speech registered all the historic Democratic arguments for a low tariff policy. Moreover, he argued that the emergencies of the European war compelled an extension of the reciprocal agreements. If the United States should fail to continue the program, he maintained, "We shall throw to the winds an opportunity in the future to help the peoples of the world along rational, unselfish, and just principles of international trade. . . .We shall invite our foreign neighbors at the close of this war to begin . . . a trade war." Harrison had no more than completed his speech when Pittman offered his amendment calling for Senate ratification of any trade agreement. James J. Davis, a Pennsylvania Republican true to form, complained that the twenty-two agreements negotiated under the 1934 act had sharply reduced tariffs on over a thousand products affecting 42 percent of the dutiable imports. The act had constituted a "guerilla attack on American trade protection."[13]

As the debate continued, the Democrats favorable to extension adhered to their customary procedure of sitting out opposition speeches. Except for the remarks of Thomas, George, and McKellar, all warm admirers of Cordell Hull, the Democratic case was closed.

Arthur Vandenberg, Michigan's effective Republican spokesman, based his party's condemnation on the grounds that the trade agreements were an unconstitutional delegation of authority to the president and that negotiations were conducted by the State Department in "despotic secrecy." Western Democrats McCarran and Edwin C. Johnson of Colorado claimed that presidential tariff-making prevented a senator from protecting his home state, and Johnson particularly was upset by the sugar quota arrangements with Cuba. Johnson, who acted as opposition whip in the tariff debate, reluctantly admitted to reporters that Harrison appeared to have a two-vote margin. When asked his advice on placing bets on the chances of the Pittman amendment, Johnson replied, "Well, I wouldn't advise anyone to bet a lead nickel against Pat Harrison." Meanwhile, Harrison with the assistance of majority whip Sherman Minton circulated the word to all Democratic senators to remain in Washington. When Truman was grounded at Pittsburgh on a return from Kansas City to vote against the Pittman amendment, Harrison laid plans to send an army plane. The weather cleared and Truman reached the Capitol one hour before the voting. [14]

Johnson had correctly sized up the strength of the Mississippi "fox." On March 29 the vote went 44 to 41 against ratification as an Easter holiday crowd looked on. Not a single Republican voted against the amendment. Of the eighteen Democrats who supported Pittman, two were Southerners—Connally and Glass. [15] Pittman's amendment posed the only real threat to Harrison's hope for an unfettered trade agreements extension. Other amendments that would have crippled the bill went down in ballots on which the administration margin never fell below six votes. On April 5 the trade agreements extension resolution passed by a vote of 42 to 37. All twenty Republicans who were present voted "nay" as did fifteen Democrats, all of whom were western protectionists except the "sugar" senators from Florida. [16]

"Your leadership throughout the battle and your final success combined to make the President a very happy man," Steve Early wrote to Harrison on the day after the resolution cleared the Senate, thus winning for the administration the major battle of the session. When Roosevelt signed the measure on April 12, he handed the signature pens to Harrison, Doughton, and Hull. The rapprochement between Harrison and Roosevelt led to speculation that the senator would now "go down the line" for FDR on a third term. [17] Indeed, the president's generous praise of Harrison did much to restore a great measure of goodwill between the two. Even though the senator held no reservations at all about reciprocal trade agreements, his enthusiasm for a major administration program drew considerable comment in view of his earlier opposition to portions of the president's program.

Concurrent with his engagements over the renewal of reciprocity, Harrison was absorbed by the usual questions of budget and taxes. He was not happy over continued domestic spending in 1940, and he was alarmed by the mounting demands that national defense programs would make upon the treasury. Immediately after the chief executive presented a "bedrock" budget of nearly $8.5 billion in his January message to Congress, Harrison announced that he would introduce a resolution calling for a temporary joint congressional committee to study the twin problems of taxation and spending. It had been Henry Morgenthau who originally proposed such a study in the spring of 1939, when House reaction had been cool. Now, in 1940, the lower house was not expected to be any warmer. Harrison left a White House conference on January 6 under the impression that Roosevelt had endorsed his committee. "The administration will not be shooting at this plan," he told reporters. The president, however, had no intention of pressing for such a study. The matter was entirely up to Congress, and Congress proved to be divided on the joint budget committee idea. Harrison's Senate colleagues approved it without a record vote, but the House greeted the idea stiffly. Jealous of its prerogatives and alarmed over the political pitfalls of slashing the budget in an election year, the House was in no mood to risk holding up the five bills which its appropriation committee had ready for floor action. When the House refused to act upon Harrison's plan, his supporters simply had to admit that it was a dead issue. As a result, the senator had no recourse but to turn to the alternative of spending decreases— taxation increases. [18]

In the absence of any pending new tax program, Harrison and other congressional leaders maintained that the anticipated half-billion dollars in defense spending could be offset by curtailment in domestic programs. Secretary Morgenthau, now thoroughly commit-

THE NATIONAL BUDGET AND PROPOSED INCREASE IN TAXES

COME ON, BOYS. LET'S TAKE A LOOK!

Washington *Evening Star*, January 8, 1940
Courtesy: Archives and Special Collections, University of Mississippi

ted to business appeasement and opposed to new taxes, was determined to interpret existing tax laws so as to curb the anticipated and
politically dangerous accumulation of excess profits certain to accrue
to industry as defense production accelerated. The picture changed
in May when disturbing events in Europe prompted Roosevelt to call
for an additional $1,182,000,000 for national defense. Although
business recovery would result in a larger revenue yield, the
additional taxes could not possibly match increased spending. Something had to give, and it was apparent that, first of all, the national
debt ceiling could not be held to its existing legal limit of $45 billion.
Previously opposed to an increase in the debt ceiling, Harrison now
consented to lifting the limit provided that the president share the
responsibility. As for new taxes, Harrison was still of the opinion that

none were necessary and the matter could go over until the next session.[19]

Harrison soon reversed his stand against a new tax bill in the face of congressional clamor that the defense program be adequately financed. At the same time that Morgenthau's department conducted a tax study, the secretary reluctantly submitted to Harrison's insistence that the $3 billion increase in the debt ceiling be offset by an issue of national defense bonds to be liquidated by new taxes producing from six to seven billion dollars annually over a period of five years. The short-term bonds would raise the cost of borrowing; when Roosevelt approved the program on May 28, Harrison announced the new scheme to a highly receptive Senate. The Finance Committee chairman had already conferred with McNary, who pledged Republican cooperation. There were few politicians who were "more practical than the old Mississippi fox," Alsop and Kintner wrote.[20]

Meanwhile, Roosevelt, who had been quietly studying the subject of excess profits taxation for nearly six months, suddenly fixed upon a tax scheme worked out by Randolph Paul, a private tax lawyer. Alarmed by the possibility that the Republicans would make capital of any Democratic failure to go at potential "war millionaires," the president told Morgenthau to have Harrison work excess profits taxation into the bill. "You just tell Pat I will give him the first crack at it," Roosevelt told his treasury head. "We will make him the most famous senator in Washington." Neither Harrison nor Doughton believed that an equitable taxation of excess profits could be worked into a bill to be passed so late in the session. It was now June, Roosevelt's favorite month for tax surprises. Nor was Morgenthau happy over the president's plan. "This is the way we start every year," he complained, "only this is starting late." But he was willing to go along for the sake of Roosevelt. "I am sick and tired of the President giving orders and the people giving him the run around. . . .God damn it, I am going to give it to Pat just the way I got it and old Doughton too, and we will have to shout it four times," he told his staff.[21]

Harrison thought it best to delay excess profits taxation until after the presidential election. Also, as Morgenthau told Roosevelt, "Pat says if we are going to get into a war . . . we would have to do it, but the thing he is afraid of at this time, is that it sounds as though we are going to get into a war." Thus persuaded, Roosevelt agreed to postpone a war profits tax on condition that "there will be no war millionaires." Morgenthau then instructed his assistant, John M. Sullivan, to have Jere Cooper of the House subcommittee announce that the Ways and Means Committee would make a recommendation in the fall: "If they don't by God! the President is going through with one of those letters that upset Pat a couple of years ago," Morgenthau told Sullivan. [22]

After Harrison informed Doughton that the Senate was willing to broaden the tax base considerably, Doughton's committee produced a bill that added more than two million taxpayers to the rolls by reducing exemptions along the lines that Senator La Follette had suggested for years. The bill also boosted corporation taxes by 1 percent and excise taxes by 10 percent, while raising surtaxes on individual incomes between $6,000 and $100,000. [23] Expecting to hear news of the fall of France any day, few congressmen cared even to discuss the measure, and, after a single day of debate, the House on June 11 passed the first revenue bill of 1940 by a striking vote of 396 to 6. Its take in additional taxes was set at just over one billion dollars. After the Finance Committee reported out the bill unanimously, the chairman told the nation via radio on June 16, "We must all tighten our belts." [24]

Senate debate, which began immediately after the surrender of the French army, lasted only three days. The Republicans offered their usual remonstrances against Rooseveltian extravagance, with Vandenberg warning that the "defense" argument was only a delusion. He protested that the bill was intended to cover for the "accumulated deficit spending of seven long, extravagant years in which Santa Claus was the administration's perpetual patron saint." His remarks set off nearly a day of sparring over various attempts led by the Senate economizers to cut domestic appropriations. The most striking Senate change was the addition of an excess profits tax, a favorite tax idea of La Follette. Although Harrison denied that the bill was "makeshift," as La Follette described it, he argued that there had not been enough time to devise an excess profits tax. In spite of the fact that administration supporters Harrison, Barkley, and Byrnes all opposed La Follette's amendment, it carried by a vote of 41 to 31. Against his wishes Harrison also agreed to carry into conference Connally's proposition to replace all normal individual and corporation taxes with a war profits tax to become effective immediately upon the declaration of war. In the end the completed bill won a 75 to 5 passage. Conference action removed both the La Follette and Connally amendments as Harrison knew it would. Roosevelt signed the bill on June 24, the day that the Republican convention began. [25]

Convinced that excess profits were still untouched, Roosevelt continued to talk of a stronger measure; he was particularly attentive to the political angles pointed out by Harold Ickes, who advised that it was unwise to increase the tax burden upon the middle income brackets, as the Revenue Act of 1940 did, without making provisions for taxing industry's excess profits. Following a June cabinet meeting that urged the president to press for an excess profits bill ("it would be bad politics for us to wait until the next session"), Ickes recorded that Vice-President Garner had taken him by the lapels and said, "Pat Harrison is against an excess profits tax and so was Simmons ahead of him. Doughton is opposed to an excess profits tax." In fact, Garner could not recall any fiscal chairman "who has had personal contacts with big business" who had not been opposed to the tax. [26]

Roosevelt told Morgenthau only a week later that he wanted an excess profits tax bill, and he directed the secretary to have his staff draft a message on the subject. At a meeting of the congressional chairmen and Treasury Department officials on July 1, Harrison complained that if he had known that the president was going to demand a new bill within a week of the enactment of a tax law, he would have "gone on and accepted Mr. La Follette's ideas because he seems to have a good part in the forces that move the Administration." But the Mississippian had not thought that La Follette's plan was "well thought out." Furthermore, Harrison maintained, there was no need to "put a big excess profits on all corporations in the country simply because they have one good year." He thought that the bill only recently passed had amply taken care of most businesses, but he conceded that, in the case of airplane industries or other plants "making enormous profits by virtue of this national defense thing," Congress could "jack them up." Nevertheless, Harrison was not happy over turning right around and putting through another revenue bill. He told the high level conferees that day, "Wendell Willkie will be elected if we lose our heads." Harrison warned his colleagues that La Follette would "make plumb fools out of us—you can't go in there

on the floor and take one position one week and another position
another week." The president wanted a tax bill in a week, and Harrison thought that Congress needed two or three weeks to "work out a
plan."[27]

While the Mississippi senator saw no political advantage in a preconvention message (the Democrats were scheduled to convene in
Chicago in mid-July), the president did. On July 1 he sent eighty-
nine words to Congress asking for a "steeply graduated excess profits
tax." Harrison, not at all happy, announced that the measure would
be introduced within ten days. One may wonder if he could have been
the unnamed Democrat "who must assume many of the burdens of
managing tax legislation" whom Arthur Krock quoted as saying the
president's message was a "case of the Philadelphia jitters."[28]

Both Harrison and Doughton were less sensitive to Morgenthau's
pleas for a profits tax than they were to the advice of Secretary of War
Henry L. Stimson that an amortization plan should be enacted apart
from the tax bill in order to stimulate production. When Ickes
warned the president that Harrison and Doughton did not like the
Treasury Department's demand that a tax bill accompany amortization, the secretary was disappointed to learn that Roosevelt's attitude
was "we ought to get the best bill that Congress is willing to give us
without exercising too much pressure." Roosevelt told Daniel Bell
that he was willing to leave the excess profits schedule to Harrison
and Doughton, and if "there were any mistakes in it, they could be
corrected at the next session." On August 5 Morgenthau told his staff
that the president had told him, "I want a tax bill; I want one damn
quick; I don't care what is in it; I don't want to know." Morgenthau
was in a quandary. He knew that if Roosevelt, in the end, disap-
proved of whatever bill was passed, he would "say what he thinks."
At the same time the secretary had the Finance Committee chairman
to deal with. "I went through this once before with Harrison, as a
result of which he didn't talk to me for two years, so it is a very
ticklish situation," Morgenthau moaned.[29]

To please the preparedness-minded secretary of war, Morgenthau
agreed to go along with the congressional committees in drafting a bill
suitable for the needs of the War Department. Before the Ways and
Means Committee he played down the tax features of the treasury
plan and emphasized the amortization proposals. Haste was the order

of the day. The Finance Committee sat with the House committee and heard a galaxy of defense industry officials urge speedy legislation in order to clear up tax uncertainties. Stimson testified that contracts had been signed for the construction of only thirty-three of the four thousand airplanes for which Congress had appropriated funds nearly two months previously. The bill that the committee reported out in late August allowed corporations a period of five years in which to recover the fresh capital invested in new plants by deducting the building costs from that portion of corporate income subject to excess profits taxation. It also levied an excess profits tax of 25 to 50 percent but permitted corporations some leeway in arriving at a base for tax computation.[30]

Few House members understood the bill, and even its supporters admitted that it was an imperfect measure. Congressman Wesley E. Disney of Oklahoma suggested that the committee had presented the bill in the spirit of an old Dodge City dance hall sign, "Don't shoot the piano player; he is doing the best he can." The House passed the bill by a voice vote and dispatched it to the Senate, where tax leaders greeted it cooly. As expected, they immediately said that the bill would have to be rewritten because the House had converted a revenue measure into a "penalty" plan. Even so, La Follette was already talking of higher excess profits taxes than those imposed by the House.[31]

Business spokesmen before the Finance Committee complained that the bill had translated a tax on excess profits into a general levy on corporations. "We will try to formulate a bill, not to please everybody, but in the hope of pleasing somebody," Harrison remarked as executive sessions began in which the committee cut away much of the highly legalistic language of the bill. In line with his customary simplistic approach to taxation, Harrison led his colleagues into substituting a flat corporate income levy for a graduated schedule and raising the normal corporate rate by 3.1 percent, a move that alarmed the Treasury Department, which believed that the increase in normal corporation income taxation abandoned the principle of ability to pay inherent in the graduated profits tax. Moreover, Morgenthau thought that the Senate bill would not raise more than $100 million.[32]

La Follette prevailed upon the two treasury secretaries to appear once again before the committee to "say something pointing out that this is a very bad bill," thus laying the groundwork for him to introduce a measure on the floor embodying the treasury principles. [33] Reporting on their second committee appearance, Morgenthau told Roosevelt that he and Sullivan had gone to the Hill "and we did our Boy Scout deed and they tore us limb from limb." [34] The Finance Committee refused to act upon the treasury objections, reporting its own version by a vote of 14 to 7. Harrison concluded that his committee had gotten "the best bill that they could get from what came to them from the House." The Senate would approve the committee report just as soon as he could "get a little steam behind it." [35]

Harrison confessed to the full Senate that the bill was complicated. It "beat anything [he had] countered in all [his] experience—which had not been so short" to confine an excess profits tax to only those corporations engaged in national defense production. Vociferous protests followed his speech. Vandenberg called the bill "an imponderable mess" and complained that the committee had permitted each witness only ten minutes in which "to tell why the bill would all but ruin him." La Follette added that the proposed legislation had been considered in haste "under the genial driving of the Senator from Mississippi who was behind the wheel." Six days after the initial discussion on the second revenue bill of 1940 had begun, the Senate passed it by a vote of 46 to 22. [36] Once again Harrison's stature as the Senate tax expert had carried the day.

The conferees were deadlocked for a week over their sharp differences. The week-long logjam continued through a Saturday afternoon session called by Doughton in spite of the fact that a doubleheader was scheduled at Griffith Stadium. Ruffled over that and anxious to have a completed report ready for a vote on Monday, Harrison called a session for Sunday morning. Reminded by the more pious House chairman that the Sabbath was a holy day, Harrison retorted, "The better the day, the better the deed." In the stillness of the hour the conferees accepted the Senate bill virtually intact. [37]

Still, the bill was far short of what treasury experts thought to be adequate from both the standpoint of fairness to small corporations and as a revenue-producer. No one doubted that there would be another revenue bill before the next session; it was possible that the provisions of the pending bill would be effective for only a few months. Thus, the conference report elicited little interest in either wing of the Capitol. The House approved the report by a voice vote on September 1, and two hours later, with only twenty senators on the floor, the Senate accepted it in like manner. Only Vandenberg was heard to say a "nay."[38]

Roosevelt signed the bill late on October 8 without comment, even though Lauchlin Currie suggested that the occasion would be apt for a "little dig" that excess profits would have been automatically taxed at higher rates and the new legislation "with its numerous inequities" would have been unnecessary had the undistributed profits tax been retained. The fact remains that FDR had wanted any kind of an excess profits tax that would encourage defense production and deflect the rebuke expected from the Republican party at the height of a presidental campaign.[39]

Both Harrison and the Mississippi Democrats had begun to give serious attention to the 1940 campaign in early 1939, while the groundwork was being laid for the state convention to be held in the early summer of 1940. The quadrennial decision over whether the state should send an instructed delegation was complicated by the mystery surrounding Roosevelt's third-term intentions. When Herbert Holmes, the state chairman, wrote Harrison in February, 1939, that the "seeds are being sown" for an instructed delegation, the senator replied, "It would be suicidal for the delegation to go there instructed for Mr. Roosevelt or to start any plans at this time." Because of the general talk of a Harrison-Roosevelt break, friends of Paul V. McNutt, an exceedingly popular former Indiana governor, approached Harrison seeking his support. The Mississippian, who was much too smart to show his hand prematurely, refused to commit himself in any way. "I have given no intimation whatsoever to what I think on the subject," Harrison told one man, while Miss Blanton wrote a Michigan Democrat, "The Senator has refrained from getting into any of these presidential controversies." The editorial columns of Harrison's intimate, Fred Sullens, plumped for McNutt, who had made a host of friends in Mississippi when he addressed the teachers of the state. McNutt and the senator were old friends and golfing companions, Sullens was happy to report.[40]

Mississippi's two senators approached the third-term issue differently. Bilbo considered himself as one of the "original third-

termers." "Just because George Washington got old and sick and
wanted to retire was no reason to set up a precedent against a third
term," Bilbo contended. Harrison, on the other hand, bided his time.
When a Georgia woman wrote for an assurance that "there is no hope
of a third term," the senator replied that he had no idea what
Roosevelt planned to do. He told a Mississippian that he would make
no public statement about the matter until the president announced
what he intended to do.[41] Obviously, Harrison was playing his cards
close to his chest.

Democratic party leaders in Mississippi were likewise divided on a
third term. In the last week of his administration, Governor White
assured Roosevelt that "it is the hope of the people of Mississippi that
you will accept a third term nomination." The state senate, however,
was unwilling to take a stand. When Senator Evon Ford, the former
state NRA administrator, introduced a resolution "urgently requesting" that FDR permit his name to be presented to the convention, the
Senate refused to take action. As the time neared for official action by
the state executive committee, Harrison and Holmes were again in
touch. The senator advised Holmes in February, 1940, that the beat,
county, and state meetings should be put off as long as possible in
order to take advantage of the "confusion as to what is going to happen here."[42]

Even though he did not like the third-term notion, in March,
1940, Harrison confided to a state committeeman in Mississippi that
the president would be the strongest possible candidate: "If he should
be nominated I would be strongly for him." Finally, one week before
the state convention met, Harrison endorsed a third term. In a telegram to Holmes, obviously meant for public consumption, Harrison
asked that the "Democracy of Mississippi" unanimously endorse
Roosevelt. "Because of his thorough grasp of the international situation, his masterful handling of our foreign affairs . . . and the accom-
plishments of his administration," the senator thought that
Roosevelt's reelection was imperative and assured. Because the Mississippian had made no previous revelation of his third-term views,
his statement was rather surprising to his fellow senators. Claude
Pepper remarked that it went to show "all questions regarding a third
term idea had disappeared," and Sherman Minton, another liberal,
now thought that "all shades of opinion in the Democratic party will

be heartily behind the President." The Washington *Post* editorialized
that the draft drive had gained its "most influential conservative re-
cruit," while *Newsweek* called Harrison's statement the "highlight" of
the Democratic week. [43]

To some extent Harrison was following and not leading the Mississippi Democrats. Eighteen county conventions had already instructed
their delegates to the state convention to support Roosevelt. Harrison,
unable to leave Washington because of the tax bill, sent his proxy to a
Gulfport friend with instructions to see that Louis Jiggitts was kept as
the national committeeman. His more immediate concern was to protect his influence against inroads from the Johnson-Bilbo "crowd."
Roosevelt's endorsement seemed assured by the time the state convention met on June 12. Breaking a long precedent, the convention
instructed its delegation to give first-ballot support to the president,
and it endorsed Harrison for vice-president. In spite of the political
gossip abroad since 1939 that Governor Johnson and Senator Bilbo
would capture the party in Mississippi, the convention was organized
on a pro-Harrison basis with the nomination of Herbert Holmes as
state chairman. [44]

At the peak of his estrangement from Roosevelt in early 1938, Harrison was approached by a few party dissidents who wanted him to
announce for the presidency. Former candidate James M. Cox wrote
in his Miami *Daily News* that Harrison's candidacy was a possibility.
The senator, however, did not have the least ambition to be president. Aware of the utter impossibility that a Deep Southerner could
secure the nomination, he knew that his own chances were nil. "Circumstances attaching to much important legislation having some sectional feeling and differences would handicap me," he wrote a Flo-
ridian. The Mississippi state executive committee in June, 1938,
endorsed him, but to Harrison it meant nothing more than friendly
praise of a favorite son. To Bilbo, who was asked if he could support
Harrison, it was an affront. "Hell no," he snapped, "my campaign in
1936 is a full answer." [45]

When a small Harrison boom reappeared in 1940, the senator completely discounted its strength. To an ardently pro-Harrison Mississippian Catherine Blanton wrote, "The presidential bee hasn't stung
him, and he hopes to God it never will." After Harrison joined the
third-term movement in June, a Washington columnist wrote that a

Roosevelt-Harrison ticket was no longer "the height of the improbable." The senator was gaining favor at the Senate luncheon tables, he reported. When Holmes wrote Harrison that some of his friends were anxious to begin a financial campaign to support his candidacy for the vice-presidency, Harrison moved quickly to check the drive. He wrote two of his boosters that he preferred to remain as chairman of the Finance Committee and would refuse a vice-presidential nomination if one were made.⁴⁶ When viewed from a perspective broader than the confines of his home state, it is pretty clear that Harrison's candidacy was hardly more than a figment of a few imaginative Mississippi minds.

Harrison went to Chicago with his boon companions, George E. Allen, CBS executive Harry Butcher, and Holly Stover, a railroad director. The senator told reporters there that Roosevelt would be nominated. "We cannot afford to make a change of leaders at this time," he stated at the same time that such other Democrats as Walter George, "Cotton Ed" Smith, Edward Burke, and Carter Glass inveighed against a third term. There were, nonetheless, a few intimates who believed that Harrison's ebullience ("Why mention any other man for President except Roosevelt?") was an act of political expediency and not one of the heart. James Farley, who had broken with "The Boss" and thrown his own hat into the ring, later recalled that "Pat didn't say much, but what he did say made it unmistakable that he was not in sympathy with the drift of events." Farley was convinced that "Genial Pat," one of his "Democratic idols," still nursed the wounds of the leadership contest. Farley's supporters could have been correct, but now that the bitterness of the past two years had diminished, Harrison had reverted to his political deportment of the early New Deal era. While he may have shared with confidants such as Byrnes and Garner private reservations that went unrecorded, his public statements supported the third-term bid that Roosevelt won on the first ballot.⁴⁷

When the Mississippians held their caucus in Harrison's room at the Hotel Stevens, the senator asked that his name not be placed in nomination for the vice-presidency. It would be nothing more than a gesture and the matter of a running mate for FDR was serious business. The president supposedly had left the choice open to the delegates, but his convention emissary, Harry Hopkins, was expected to reveal Roosevelt's choice. On the morning of July 18, when a group which called upon the president in Washington advised him to name James F. Byrnes, Roosevelt instead tapped Henry Wallace. Many of the delegates were openly rebellious over the choice of Wallace. Byrnes later wrote a constitutent that Harrison had told him that he intended to nominate Byrnes. When the South Carolinian told his friend that he would immediately decline and announce his commitment to Wallace, Harrison retreated. Byrnes had been present in Hopkins's hotel room when the Wallace choice was announced; Harrison was not.[48] There was little that the Mississippi Democrat could do but curb his anger and present a front to his delegation. It was to be Wallace on the first ballot, he told them. The Mississippians, however, rejected the New Deal mystic from Iowa. When the convention voted in a stormy early morning session, Wallace got only four Mississippi votes, while William Bankhead, the House speaker from neighboring Alabama who genuinely wanted the nomination, won 13½ votes, and "Jim" Farley the remaining one-half vote.[49]

Within a week after the convention, Senator Harrison was the central figure in a post-convention party harmony movement at the Capitol. Supposedly, Harrison, whose "gifts for oiling waters [were] the Senate's best," would persuade disaffected southern Democrats not to bolt. Edward J. Flynn, who assumed the party chairmanship at Farley's resignation, asked Harrison to work at the national headquarters for a week in August,[50] but Harrison did not leave Washington during the late summer. If he could have gotten away, he would not have gone north to Gotham but south to Mississippi, where his close friend, Hugh White, was campaigning against Bilbo for the Senate.

The Bilbo-Johnson alliance was enough to bring combatants of earlier Mississippi contests together in the common cause of Hugh White, and Mike Conner joined Harrison in backing him. Although the senior senator issued a statement that he would take no part in the campaign, he intended to go home to vote for White if the congressional calendar cleared. When Bilbo reported that Harrison had confided that he had tried to keep White out of the race, Harrison telegraphed White, "I made no such statement to Bilbo." Probably Harrison warned White of Bilbo's strength and advised him not to make the race. At any rate, Harrison found it impossible to leave

Washington because the Senate was slated to vote on crucial amendments to a selective service bill right at the time of the Mississippi
primary.[51]

Senator Bilbo defeated White by a vote of 91,334 to 62,631. Even if
Harrison had returned to Mississippi and put in a week of hard campaigning, it is doubtful that White could have won. The truth is that
Harrison's following was entirely personal and he seemed unable, and
sometimes unwilling, to sway his supporters except when he himself
was a candidate. Of course, the same was true of other prominent
officeholders in the state. Although Harrison made no public statements about White's defeat, it is safe to say that he was a worried
man now that Mississippi political breezes seemed to blow the way of
Theodore G. Bilbo and Paul B. Johnson. In the most recent Mississippi elections, Harrison's candidates had gone down in defeat, and
the next major race in Mississippi would be his own bid for reelection
in 1942.

Senator Harrison had made certain the fact that his support of
Roosevelt in 1940 was largely based on a belief that trends in international affairs left the Democrats no other choice. Likewise, he had no
reservations about supporting to the hilt the preparedness program as
it evolved in 1940. The presidential campaign was scarcely under way
when Congress was asked to make a far graver commitment to national defense than mere money. In August debate began on what
became the first peacetime selective service act in the nation's history. Senator Edward Burke and Representative James Wadsworth
proposed the registration for military service of all men between the
ages of twenty-one and thirty-six. Harrison could scarcely have been
more in line with public opinion in Mississippi than he was in his
ardent support of the Burke-Wadsworth bill. A Gallup poll showed
that the nation's strongest conscription sentiment was in Mississippi,
where 87 percent of those polled favored the drafting of men between
the ages of eighteen and thirty-two for service of one year. On August
26 the American Legion held a mass meeting in Jackson to protest
congressional complacency in delaying the passage of a compulsory
military service bill. When the group telegraphed its position, Harrison answered, "Am here on the job doing everything possible to expedite the enactment of the selective service program." His vote bore
him out. He voted to reject an amendment to limit compulsory train-

ing to a time of war or threatened invasion; and then, on August 28, he helped push the bill to passage on a 58 to 31 vote.[52]

By 1940, Harrison had returned to the administration fold. The reconciliation between the senator and the chief executive did not come through the surrender of either to the other on any principle of taxation, spending, relief, or on any other difference on the New Deal, which had virtually ended anyway. The domestic quarrels of the past decade had now been replaced by the threat of war. Pat Harrison's Senate career had come full circle, returning to the point at which it had begun. Once again, the energies of his president were consumed by defense preparations, and the senator intended to perform his own duties free of animosity.

CHAPTER XII

"He Was Square, Approachable, & Intensely Human"

1941

IN MANY WAYS THE new year of 1941 marked the high
point of Senator Pat Harrison's thirty years in Congress. He became
the president *pro tempore* of the Senate and had his choice of two
powerful committee chairmanships. He once again enjoyed an association with Franklin D. Roosevelt somewhat like that of a decade earlier, and he was now even on speaking terms with his old adversary,
Senator Bilbo. But there was one serious problem which would mar
the picture. Harrison was a very sick man and, although no one
seemed to be aware of just how ill he was, he had less than six months
to live.

Key Pittman, who had been both the chief elected officer of the
Senate and the chairman of the Foreign Relations Committee, died in
November, 1940. As the ranking Democrat, Harrison was the logical
successor to Pittman, but he had no desire to give up the Finance
Committee for another chairmanship. He thought that his own committee was the more important of the two, and he held the highest
regard for Walter F. George, who was next in line to head Foreign
Relations. Moreover, Harrison had no interest in the social mingling
of the diplomatic set. In all his years in the nation's capitol, he had
attended only two Washington ambassadorial functions. "I hate dressing and undressing, buttoning and unbuttoning the kind of clothes
required for big social occasions," he once complained. [1]

The *pro tempore* post was, of course, little more than an honor
customarily bestowed upon a majority party senator on the basis of
seniority. Only three Democrats had been in the Senate longer than
had the senator from Mississippi—Cotton Ed Smith, Morris Sheppard, and Kenneth D. McKellar. As soon as Pittman's death on
November 10 became known, Senator Byrnes told another old friend,

Joseph P. Tumulty, that he was anxious to have Harrison as the Senate presiding officer. "I think by all means you should take it. It would be very helpful to you in Mississippi and elsewhere," Tumulty advised the senator, who was resting in Gulfport. [2]

The Democratic caucus on January 4 was something of a love feast. The two Mississippi senators had buried the hatchet a year earlier on a January day of 1940 when Harrison had entered an elevator in which there were no other persons but Bilbo and the operator. "How do you do, Senator Bilbo. How's your health?" Harrison had asked. "Fine," Bilbo replied. The third occupant, the operator, was so shocked that he had "nearly collapsed," he later said. After leaving the elevator the two senators had then chatted for a while about means of defeating the antilynching bill. Since then their relationship had been amicable. The day before the Senate caucus met in 1941, Harrison and Bilbo had gone arm in arm to the Senate well for the ceremonies attending the beginning of the junior senator's second term. Now, when Byrnes nominated Harrison for president *pro tempore*, Bilbo seconded the nomination. Following his selection by the caucus, Harrison nominated Barkley for a third stint as majority leader. The display of harmony continued when the man whom Barkley had once defeated for the Senate, Albert B. ("Happy") Chandler, seconded that nomination. [3] The formal election of Harrison by the Senate two days later was merely routine. The new *pro tem* looked forward to a "harmonious session." President Roosevelt congratulated the senator. "I cannot think of anyone who has had more varieties of legislative experience than you. . . . It is not surprising therefore that your colleagues have come to lean heavily on you whenever something big is to be done." [4]

Although Harrison had avoided "tux and tail" occasions as much as possible all of his life, he now had reason to dress up without grumbling. He enjoyed the limelight thrown upon him now that he was the highest officer of the Senate. At the president's third inaugural he sat on the rotunda behind Chief Justice Charles Evans Hughes, and for the first time he made the rounds of the inaugural night festivities. At a brilliant affair given by the Mississippi Society of Washington, the senator and his wife celebrated their thirty-sixth wedding anniversary. Three weeks later the Mississippi Society engaged the Carlton Hotel for a reception honoring Harrison on the beginning of his

thirty-first year in Congress. More than 1,800 people, including
cabinet officers, Supreme Court justices, and a host of old friends,
stood in a line that reached outside the hotel lobby and into the street
to greet the senator and his wife. Seven private railroad cars brought
officials to pay their respects. It was said to be the largest affair of its
kind that Washington had ever seen. The actual anniversary day,
March 4, was marked by a crisper ceremony when Harrison and
Doughton, who had both entered the House of Representatives on the
same day in 1911, met in the president's room in the Senate wing,
shook hands with one another and with Vice-President Wallace, and
then returned to work. The Washington *Post* quipped that the happi-
ness of the occasion was overshadowed only by the fact that the
baseball season had not yet opened. [5]

Harrison was involved in only one major piece of legislation during
his last few months in the Senate—FDR's controversial request that
the United States become the "arsenal of democracy." On the first
day of the new Congress in January, 1941, the president disclosed to
Barkley, Byrnes, and Harrison, now frequently referred to as the
"triumvirate," that he would soon offer a comprehensive program of
massive aid to Britain. The Mississippian remarked, "There can be
no limitation on expenditures for our defense except what the job
requires." When Senator Glass insisted that assistance to Britain
should be sufficient to "wipe Germany off the face of the map," it was
clear that the economy bloc had disbanded. The president's message
to Congress, delivered in person on January 6, drew the highest
praise from Harrison, who was certain that the American people
overwhelmingly approved of a stronger national defense program and
mammoth aid to Britain. [6]

With the lend-lease bill completed by the Treasury Department
and cleared by Cordell Hull, the question of its congressional spon-
sorship arose. Although it seemed logical to refer the bill to the Senate Foreign Relations Committee, both Hull and Secretary of War
Henry L. Stimson thought that the wisest move would be to send the
measure to Harrison's Finance Committee because the senator was
such an ardent supporter of aid to Britain. Roosevelt agreed. When
Morgenthau took the document to the White House on January 7, the
president told him to have Harrison handle it in the Senate. The
Cabinet officers involved in drafting the measure were all convinced

that Garner, before leaving office, had packed the Foreign Relations
Committee with isolationists like himself. When House Speaker Sam
Rayburn expressed a fear that referral to any group other than the
normally appropriate Foreign Relations Committee would irritate
Congress, Barkley agreed. Therefore the final decision was to send
the bill to Senator George's committee. [7]

Hearings began in the House committee on January 15; by the time
of the hearings in the Senate committee two weeks later both George
and Harrison were convinced that they had the votes to report the bill
favorably. Events bore them out when the committee reported the bill
by a vote of 15 to 8 on February 13, five days after the House had
passed lend-lease 260 to 165. If Harrison's attendance record at previous hearings before the Committee on Foreign Relations had been
spotty, he was present on each of the thirteen days of the lend-lease
hearings. Although his health was rapidly failing and he made no
remarks in the long and acrimonious debate which ran for three
weeks, he attended Senate sessions to join the Democratic majority in
turning back a plethora of amendments intended to curb the president's use of American armed and naval forces beyond the limits of
the western hemisphere. When the Senate finally passed the lend-
lease bill, Harrison, of course, stood with the majority. Appointed a
conferee, he was not called upon to serve since the House accepted
the Senate amendments without contest. [8]

Although the official records show that Harrison was silent in the
committee room and on the Senate floor from January through mid-
March of 1941, he steadily worked the cloakroom area on behalf of
lend-lease, spending much of his time with the newer senators. His
colleagues credited him with having prevented a filibuster which
could have killed the lend-lease program; and, after his death in June,
the New York *Times* attributed to him a major role in putting through
the bill. When some of his closest friends appealed to him to take an
extended rest, he refused to do so because he thought that he was
needed "around the boys." When a leading isolationist, unnamed by
the *Times*, pleaded with Harrison to slacken his pace, the Mississippi
Democrat answered that he would not go away for a rest until the bill
was passed. Since it was inevitable that the Democrats would enact
the measure, the isolationist reportedly told his opposition colleagues,

"Boys, old Pat won't go away until the bill is acted upon. We've got to bring this thing to an end."[9]

To Turner Catledge, who saw Harrison routinely, the declining health of both the senator and President Roosevelt appeared to be similar. Of the president, Catledge wrote, "He would start talking about something, then in midsentence he would stop and his mouth would drop open and he'd sit staring at me in silence. I knew I was looking at a terribly sick man." Harrison, he found "in almost the same condition." Mississippians who saw the senator on his visit home in the late fall of 1940 noticed that he was easily fatigued, and Washington columnists had observed from time to time in 1940 that Harrison did not appear to be well.[10] The senator and the members of his family knew that he was troubled by some physical disorder, but they all believed that an extended rest would restore his health. On March 14, 1941, Harrison entered the Army and Navy Hospital at Hot Springs, Arkansas, for what was described as general fatigue. Three weeks later the hospital's chief officer reported that Harrison's condition was "not serious," but rumors persisted that the senator was gravely ill.[11]

Harrison's friends insisted that he not worry about the tax bill which Congress received in April when Morgenthau placed before the two fiscal committees the defense needs of the government for additional revenue. Before leaving Washington, Harrison conferred with Senator George and Congressman Doughton. "I am relying on finance committee members to carry on for me in my absence," he announced from Hot Springs at the same time that Miss Blanton informed Steve Early that the doctors "turned the heat on him a plenty" when the senator told the hospital that he was ready to return to Washington. Harrison was forced to reconcile himself to an indefinite stay in the Arkansas hospital. "It has not been easy to walk away from things, but I know it is what I should do," he wrote Byrnes, who replied that the Senate was "doing very little here now, and you need not fear your missing anything of importance." Roosevelt wrote that he was "much down at the mouth" at the thought that Harrison could not handle the tax bill, but he wanted the senator to think of the "many years of usefulness ahead" if the Mississippian would give attention to his health for the moment.[12]

Harrison left the Army and Navy Hospital on June 8 and returned to his Washington home to continue his rest. News releases reported that he would gradually resume his Senate duties as the family doctor advised, but privately it was well known that the senator could never return to work. The doctors in Hot Springs had found that he had cancer of the lower colon, and they knew that there was no hope without an operation and very little with one. A final examination revealed a lump in the abdomen. On Sunday, June 15, Harrison entered the Emergency Hospital in Washington for major surgery to remove the intestinal obstruction. The operation revealed that the cancer had spread to other vital organs to such an extent that it could not be removed. The incision was closed, and the family was told that there was no hope for recovery. Following the operation Harrison was reported to be "doing nicely," but as the week went on, the hospital bulletins indicated a rapid decline. On Friday he took a turn for the worse, and the day's hospital release reported restlessness, a high temperature, poor circulation, and an inability to take sufficient nourishment. Late in the afternoon his doctor authorized the senator's office to report his condition as "very grave." Harrison had fallen into a comatose state and was able to recognize only his wife, his son, and Miss Blanton. By Saturday his family realized that death was only a matter of hours. At 6:35 A.M., on Sunday, June 22, Harrison died from what the doctor termed "exhaustion." He was not quite sixty years old.[13]

Members of the family declined the honor of a state funeral because they did not think that he would have wanted one. On Monday afternoon Senator Harrison lay in state in the Senate chamber while his colleagues made preparations for a special train to convey his body to Gulfport. All senators who could arrange to leave Washington were designated as members of the funeral committee. On Monday night, when the train began its trip down through the countryside to Gulfport, its passengers included Vice-President Wallace, thirty senators, including Byrnes (now a Supreme Court nominee), and twenty representatives. Attached to the train was the special car of John J. Pelley, president of the Association of Railroads, which carried many of Harrison's personal friends, including, of course, Bernard Baruch. Probably never again would such a large body of old friends accompany a member of Congress to his final rest. There was scarcely a person on the train who did not retell a story that the senator would have delighted in hearing retold, for he had always been, as Henry Wallace recalled, "a very joyous kind of person."[14]

On June 25 a simple service was conducted at the Gulfport First Methodist Church, Harrison's home church, with graveside services at the Evergreen Cemetery in Gulfport. Steve Early attended as a representative of the president, and the Treasury Department secretaries, Morgenthau and Sullivan, accompanied by James M. Landis, dean of the Harvard Law School, arrived by amphibian plane. Swelling the crowd of 10,000 persons who heard the services by loudspeaker outside the church were members of the Mississippi Bar Association, then holding its annual session on the coast, and a large number of state officials who had come by special train from Jackson. It was the greatest assemblage of national and state dignitaries in Mississippi's history.[15]

In spite of the unspoken injunction to say nothing but good of the dead, the eulogies offered to Pat Harrison appeared to be genuine. President Roosevelt recalled on the basis of a thirty-year friendship that the senator had been "keen of intellect, sound in principle, shrewd in judgment [with] rare gifts of kindly wit, humor, and irony which delighted all," and former president Herbert Hoover remarked that Harrison had been "everything a United States Senator should be." Secretary of Treasury Morgenthau stated that he would "sorely miss his clear head, his hearty spirit, and the happy gusto" with which Harrison had always approached his tasks. Former Mississippi governor Hugh White believed that the senator had "done more to put Mississippi right with the people of the country" than had any other man in the history of the state. He had been, as the Sunflower *Toscin* judged, the "most powerful, at the same time the most diplomatic and practical" senator whom the state had had in its 124 years. Scarcely an editorial eulogy failed to mention that the greatest single factor in Harrison's success had been his personality. He had taught by example, the Washington *Evening Star* said, "the efficacy of sweet reasonableness." The *Nation*, which had often been critical of Harrison's conservatism, recalled his "humor and unfailing good nature" and reminded its readers of Harrison's political ability and his "years of useful service."[16] Democratic party chairman Edward Flynn thought that no senator of Harrison's generation "ever contributed as much to the smoothing out of differences and the reconciling of controversies." Nearly thirty years later someone asked Everett M. Dirksen, a powerful Republican titan, which senator in the long range of the Senate's history he most admired. "Pat Harrison," Dirksen instantly answered. "I had great admiration of his ability to handle about anything."[17]

Harrison was above all a man whose engaging warmth and friendliness filled his life with the loyal friendships of a wide range of people whose politics cut across party lines. The perfect ease with which he closed the door on partisanship when he left the Senate chamber to join the social company of the so-called "economic royalists" led many New Deal purists to look upon him as a "Bourbon." The label did not bother him at all. Clad in his B.V.D.s in warm weather and his long red underwear on cooler days, Harrison was a familiar figure on the greens of the Burning Tree Country Club.[18] Politics was adjourned at the club, where his partners were as likely to be the Republican senators James Couzens of Michigan, Frederick Hale of Maine, or McNary of Oregon, as they were his Democratic colleague Burton K. Wheeler. He played the game as congenially and non-ideologically with his good friend Merle Thorpe, the conservative editor of *Nation's Business*, as with Joseph E. Davies, an enthusiastic New Dealer who was for a time an assistant secretary of state. Football and baseball companions might be Harry Butcher of the Columbia Broadcasting System, Judge Kennesaw Mountain Landis, the czar of baseball, or the Russian ambassador. An avid sportsman, Harrison could be found at Hobcaw, Baruch's South Carolina estate, hunting with Senators Pittman, Byrnes, and Byrd, as well as in the fields of Tippah County, Mississippi, birdshooting with smalltown friends.

One facet of Harrison's charm was his homespun manner and his unaffected lifestyle. The few columnists who saw him as the archetype of a species of southern senator later known as Claghorn were predisposed by their dislike of his politics and his wealthy friends. The remarkable thing about the seantor was that he never did go "high hat," as Bilbo liked to say. His dislike of large social functions led him to seek relaxation through a bridge game at home or at a sentimental movie, preferably in the company of Senator Henry Ashurst who shared his love of sad films. Harrison went to see

"Suwannee River" three times! His tastes were southern and simple. He breakfasted daily on griddlecakes and blackstrap molasses, and his favorite dessert (in season) was watermelon or the sweet potato pie baked for him daily at the Senate cafeteria. After his death one of his Senate protégés reflected: "Here was a man . . . associated in his work with the great financial barons of the country [with] many opportunities presented to him, but he died with a modest home and a very modest fortune."[19]

Harrison's two closest friends and political partners of long standing were, as an examination of almost any New Deal legislation reveals, Joseph T. Robinson and James F. Byrnes. Harrison shared with them the political arts common to the southern senator whose political habitat enabled him to return session after session until his skills were polished to a gloss. Byrnes and Harrison, who had entered Congress together in 1911, complemented one another from the beginning in their powers of shrewdly judging men and their acute perception of the Senate's mood. On the night of Byrnes's first day in the Senate, Harrison held a dinner for his South Carolina friend in order that he might quickly become acquainted with his new Senate colleagues. From the beginning both Robinson and Harrison assigned Byrnes responsible tasks. Having known them both in the House and the Senate, Bennett Clark declared that "there was never in either body a more effective team than Pat Harrison and Jimmy Byrnes." Whenever Harrison entered the Senate chamber and Byrnes walked up to join him, the members of the press knew that some legislative move was under way. "Both of them were born manipulators," Turner Catledge recalls, "and between them they could con the pants off almost anyone in Washington." In one of Harrison's last visits to the White House, he led a delegation of senators to press for the appointment of Byrnes to the Supreme Court upon the resignation of Justice James C. McReynolds. The honor, never given to Robinson, went to Byrnes.[20]

In 1935 a writer in *Fortune* declared that Senator Harrison "knows men and he knows legislators. And he knows how to turn legislators into men and vice versa." At the same time that Harrison worked in harness with seasoned senators, he cultivated the talents of the younger men who came to the Senate, although they did not always subscribe to his political views. One such freshman was Florida's

Claude Pepper, whose Tallahassee law partner had been Harrison's first secretary. "I never failed to go to him for counsel," Pepper later said, remembering that Harrison had aided him in obtaining preferred committee assignments. When Prentiss Brown became a member of the Finance Committee, Harrison went out of his way to induct the freshman from Michigan into the legislative process through special assignments, and during Harrison's last illness Brown sat at his bedside to receive committee instructions. In Brown's opinion, Harrison was "the greatest senator of our time." Harrison also left his mark on a younger set of Mississippi men. Congressman William Colmer had revered Harrison as his "youthful idol" and later recognized the senator as "the ablest man in Mississippi during his era."[21]

Sketches of Pat Harrison in the 1930s never failed to mention that he seldom joined in floor debate as he had done in the "gadfly days." He appeared far less buoyant in conducting the business of the Finance Committee than he had been when engaged in the lighthearted role of the minority jester. Senator Harrison, the Washington *Post* observed, "hasn't been quite happy since the sun set for Smoot of Utah." The levity of the newsmen masked the convictions which Harrison held on the process of lawmaking. A firm believer that laws should be drafted by legislative committee and threshed out in committee executive sessions, he once told the Senate, "I think it is bad practice in the first place to legislate upon the floor of the Senate. These matters [an amendment to the "pink slip" income tax publicity measure] should have been brought to the attention of the committee considering the bill." Consistently opposed to the attachment of unrelated riders to revenue bills, Harrison objected to the same procedure where other measures were concerned. When the Senate added a TVA bond issue to a liberty bond bill in 1939, he objected. "I am still one of the rare specimens who believe in orderly legislation," he said.[22]

The largest single component of Harrison's success was his ability to cajole others to retreat from their demands in order that the Senate could pass the only bill that seemed achievable at the moment. In an exchange with Frederick Steiwar over a bonus bill, the Oregon senator insisted, "I think that the sound thing for courageous men to do is to stand for things which they think are right." "And get nothing," Harrison retorted. As a matter of routine, he carried bills to the conferees from the Ways and Means Committee, having purposely added amendments that he could bargain away. His closely observed cloakroom prowls usually netted a trade which would result in the passage of a measure fervently wanted by the administration. According to Turner Catledge, Harrison literally "horse-traded" the National Recovery bill through a dubious Senate. The *Life* panel of Washington correspondents agreed that Harrison was the "best wrangler in the Senate," a man who had "elevated horse-trading to statecraft."[23] Crucial to the success of his bargains was the certainty that they were always good. The senator from Mississippi was never known to welsh on a trade and he was never accused of cynically manipulating men.

Admired as a virtue by his Senate friends, Harrison's belief that "politics is the art of the possible" was regarded as a vice by the recruits from the eastern universities and legal firms who entered the service of Franklin Roosevelt. The only protracted conflict between Harrison and any group of Washingtonians was with the New Dealers, represented best by Rexford G. Tugwell and Thomas Corcoran. Part of the trouble was the constant sense of insecurity harbored by the idealistic coterie of White House advisers. A suspicious Tugwell once recorded in his diary, after a Democratic dinner in early 1934 with the senators whom he referred to as the "Old Guard": "These are our real enemies and will get rid of us if they can. . . .It is working inside an organization whose senior places are in such hands that makes life discouraging."[24] Eventually Tugwell was bested by his Senate critics and their allies in the Department of Agriculture, but within a year of his leave-taking, the White House circle of liberals scored a limited victory when Corcoran intervened in the majority leadership contest to defeat "Harrison and Friends."

The senator from Mississippi did not find all of the president's inner council to be deceptive and intractable. It might seem surprising that Harrison should hold Harry Hopkins in such high regard since Hopkins's manner alienated many people and Hopkins had been, after all, one of the White House handymen who had helped defeat Harrison in the 1937 leadership struggle. But to Harrison, Hopkins was different. The difference may have been that the relief administrator and WPA chief was a man of practical field experience, and one of those fields had been Mississippi and the South. As the director first of the Gulf division of the Red Cross and later of all the agency's activities in the Southeast in the postwar years, Hopkins had come to know the South. "I know Mississippi," he once said. "I've been to almost every county in the state."[25] Hopkins's selection of a soft-spoken Alabamian, Aubrey Williams, to be his deputy director of the WPA as well as his appointment of a Mississippian, Ellen Woodward, to his staff did much to advance the Harrison-Hopkins friendship. That the senator found Hopkins to be the right kind of a New Dealer may reflect a certain regional bias which he and many other southern senators held against White House counselors who did not know the South firsthand.

More than anything else, the conflict between Pat Harrison and the New Dealers was a consequence of differences in their personalities and manner of operation. While Harrison was, as his Republican friend Charles McNary once said, "square, approachable, and intensely human," the senator and his close colleagues regarded the New Dealers as devious, aloof, and calculatingly cold. It would be hard to imagine any statement so unlike Harrison as Corcoran's reputed quip, "Fighting with a businessman is like fighting with a Polack. You can give no quarter." Raymond Moley, a disillusioned New Dealer, later ruminated that the "lawyer-minded New Dealers" believed that government functioned "not through the process of consultation, compromise, and harmonious adjustment [the hallmarks of Senator Harrison] but rather through the litigious process." The modus operandi of the bright young men who drafted many of the major New Deal laws was antithetical to the political style of the congressional patriarchs. The Harrisons and Robinsons, who had long ruled the Senate, resented the way in which the presidential inner circle attempted to short-circuit the traditional legislative process. Thinking ahead to the days when the New Deal would be over, the Senate oligarchs feared that they would be unable to reclaim their former prerogatives. Harrison consistently resisted advice from the interlopers. His trust was in the judgment of his committee's own aides, men like Lovell H. Parker and Colin Stam, rather than in theorists from the Treasury Department such as Herman Oliphant. "I would rather have the estimates of the staff of the joint committee than the estimates of the gentlemen in the Treasury," he once told the Senate. [26]

The Washington *Evening Star* reported within a month of Roosevelt's first inauguration, "Dixie is in the saddle on Capitol Hill, all right."[27] That was nothing new, of course, since Democratic administrations had often recruited their strength from the South, and it had been the South that had often provided the party with its dominant point of view. But, as time went on, the southern congressional leaders began to sense that Roosevelt intended to change the tone of the party and enlarge its political base to include new blood, an alteration made manifest after the election of 1936. The Robinsons, Garners, and Harrisons began to feel threatened by the liberalism injected by the urban East and the progressive West. Moreover, despite the fact that the southern voter continued to give the president handsome electoral majorities, there was an undercurrent of opposition to the New Deal within certain powerful economic constituencies of the Southerners in Congress. Senator Harrison was aware of the uneasiness of his old friends in Mississippi, one of whom, the balanced budget advocate Alfred H. Stone, grumbled that Chancellorsville could not have been fought in 1935 because the South "would have to secure from Washington thirty days' rations and a permit to fight."[28] Harrison, too, was concerned that the South was threatened by the directions which the New Deal was taking in the realm of economic control, particularly in the matter of wages and hours legislation. It is not surprising that the Mississippi senator and his longtime Senate partners were alarmed to see a Democratic president influenced by a strain of thinking alien to the South.

Any attempt to pin an ideological label upon Pat Harrison is difficult because he was not given to public revelations of his political and economic philosophy. Except for a few short topical articles that appeared from time to time on various pieces of legislation, he left no body of writings which articulated his views. In only a few instances did he ever wander from a subject germane to Senate debate to shed any light on his true opinions. His colleagues often suspected that he did not approve of certain measures that issued from the Finance Committee, and Roosevelt's advisers warned him so often that Harrison was basically a conservative that the president became convinced that Harrison was not a New Dealer. Newspaper columnists wrote that the senator's performances were characteristically only perfunctory acts undertaken to advance the political fortunes of the Democratic party and a Democratic president, since Harrison was, above all, a devoted party man. *Fortune* characterized him more aptly than any other journal. He was, the magazine surmised, "a New Deal wheelhorse . . . suspicious of his load."[29]

After Harrison became disenchanted with the New Deal, disillusioned by the treatment accorded him by the president in 1937, and convinced that the economic emergency was over, his attitudinal modification was obvious.[30] Subsequently, his refusal to support the administration, his open leadership of the Finance Committee in diminishing the effect of administration measures, and his evident affection for senators cast off by the president all began to indicate that he was ready to match his Senate performance with the beliefs that he probably had always had. Alarmed by a request for an appropriation for the inspection of coal mines in 1940, Harrison told the Senate, "It seems to me that we ought to proceed as conservatively as possible. I so often hear that word that I like to use it, because I sometimes feel honored when it is said that I am somewhat conservative."[31] But then, he had once said that was as conservative as the president and as liberal.

Harrison embodied a curious blend of conservatism and liberalism that defies definition. If an acceptance of the federal government as an agency for social good is a tenet of the liberal's creed, then Harrison was in some respects a liberal. Ironically, it was Frances Perkins who recalled that "Pat Harrison was a humanitarian [whose] impulse rested upon philosophical considerations." She thought that his absence of original ideas on how to cope with social problems stemmed from his background in Mississippi, where there had been little or no social experimentation. His Alabama colleague Lister Hill, whose social conscience was far more sensitive than Harrison's, recalled that, while the Mississippian was not a "wide-eyed liberal," he was "reasonably looking into the future."[32]

Essential in delineating Harrison's conservatism is James T. Patterson's study of the New Deal congressional conservatives. Through an analysis of some forty roll calls which reflected a clear distinction between administration and anti-administration members of Con-

gress, Patterson defined thirty-five senators who served between
1933 and 1939 as the "most conservative Democrats" if they opposed
the administration on at least 12 percent of the votes on which they
were recorded. By this accounting Harrison appears to be the least
conservative of "the most conservative." His 12 percent anti-
administration voting record, the lowest in a range up to 81
percent—that of Carter Glass—placed him below eleven other members of his Finance Committee. (Members Barkley, Black, and Guffey did not make the list.) Furthermore, of the entire Mississippi
congressional delegation, with the exception of Bilbo, Harrison was
the least conservative (or if one prefers a more positive outlook, the
most liberal). [33] As Patterson points out, figures cannot reveal how
Harrison may have diluted administration bills in committee, but
neither can they disclose the extent to which Harrison's party loyalty
robbed him of the courage of his convictions and led him into protecting administration bills from the clutches of his more conservative
committee colleagues. Harrison was remarkably successful in dealing
with his committee associates, many of whom were his match in
adroitness and drive, some of them his intellectual superiors (certainly
the non-Democrats La Follette and Vandenberg) and several of them
to the left or right of him in their economic views.

The shifting nature of Harrison's actions and the difficulty of assessing his true position are related to the fact that Roosevelt himself
was often ambivalent and indirect. Confusing White House economic
policy made loyalty a difficult matter. At times the chairman of the
Finance Committee found it impossible to learn the administration
position on a bill. That was true in the case of the extension of the
NRA in 1935, the bonus bill compromise in 1936, the sugar control
bill in 1938, and even in the instance of the repeal of the undistributed profits tax in 1939. The president so often left Harrison and
the Finance Committee to flounder in a morass of conflicting instructions from the White House and the Treasury Department that it is
difficult to determine whether Harrison was loyal or disloyal to the
president on many issues.

Harrison's disappointment with the president probably began in
1935, when the White House blamed him for suggesting that the
wealth tax be passed in haste. He was certainly aware of other times
when the president devised schemes to have his Senate leaders held

responsible for unpopular orders that issued from the White House. Harrison found Roosevelt to be devious and sometimes blatantly dishonest, as he was in his insistence that he had not intervened in the majority leadership contest. Harrison was deeply disturbed by the president's actions in 1937, because they showed that the White House would not brook criticism and was determined to punish dissenters. The senator, too, was hurt that his past record of service seemed to mean little to Roosevelt. Harrison sensed that the same was true in the case of his faithful friend Joe Robinson. Three years later Hugh Johnson, now crustily bitter about the New Deal, told a Jackson Day gathering of Democrats, "It is these veteran Democrats who have borne the heat and burden of all these close contests . . . and all too often gotten kicks in the pants for their pains."[34]

Harrison could never really understand why Roosevelt had turned against him. "My record here shows that I have been a more consistent cooperator from the time the President went into office than almost any other Senator," he wrote a Mississippian in 1939.[35] What the senator either could not realize or was unwilling to accept was the fact that the Democratic party whose services he had entered under Woodrow Wilson was not the Democratic party of Franklin D. Roosevelt. Like Josiah Bailey, Harrison was a Wilsonian liberal in another era.[36] Those men who had been Wilson liberals had become Roosevelt conservatives and their once ready response to the New Deal ended when the immediate crisis had been met. Just when it appeared that Pat Harrison had made his peace with the new Democracy and was at the threshold of commitment to assist a Democratic president during another great national crisis, the senator's death removed him from that service.

Harrison's essential importance during the New Deal lies in more than the fact that he was the persuasive chairman of a key Senate committee and a master tactician of fiscal legislation. As a member of a small corps of Democratic senators whose collective position on legislation often served as a bellwether for scores of uncommitted colleagues, Harrison's power in the Senate was extensive. Moreover, in the drafting of new legislation and the administration of enacted measures, Harrison's influence was often sought by administration officials. "He and Robinson and Byrnes controlled the Senate," William O. Douglas, chairman of the Securities and Exchange

Commission, later wrote. "They were the ones with whom I
negotiated on the Hill," he added. [37] In the early years of the New
Deal Harrison's power stemmed from his closeness to both the president and the majority leader. Ironically, in the post-1937 years when
conservative opposition coalesced against the New Deal, Harrison's
popularity and power issued from the very fact that he was no longer a
confidant of the president and a political twin of the majority leader.

Harrison's influence on the measures that came from his committee was immense. The public record reveals that the senator stayed
the hands of the reformers who would have used taxation as a greater
social force in the redistribution of wealth. Successive tax bills
adhered to his basic belief that tax laws should be as simple as possible and directed above all to the collection of revenue. Because he had
no philosophical bent toward remolding society or restructuring the
economy, Harrison viewed the New Deal as an approach to the
exigencies of extreme depression. He was not interested in adding
provisions for social control to any of the bills which his committee
handled. Thus the architects of social reform who attempted to prod
the president into supporting more liberal measures were critical of
Harrison's conservatism and, like William O. Douglas, were disappointed that Roosevelt could work through the Mississippian and his
associates "only by trimming his sails." In the opinion of Douglas,
Harrison, Robinson, and Byrnes were "the real reason why FDR
soft-pedaled all racial issues." [38] On the other hand, it is possible that
Roosevelt got as much from the Senate as he did because Harrison
and a few other skillful party leaders exerted themselves to enact a
substantial part of the president's programs.

The Washington correspondents who named Harrison the most
influential senator in 1939 gave him the lowest marks in "integrity"
and "intelligence." Defining the former as a devotion to personal principles and an independence of party politics, the journalists awarded
their highest plaudits to Senators Glass and Norris, their lowest to
Harrison, Vandenberg, McNary, and Byrnes. Harrison's loyalty to
his party, "right or wrong," was both a weakness and a strength. On
the surface, blind loyalty to party can be unattractive, but in Harrison's case his fealty to his party and its candidates added to his stature
among his Democratic colleagues, whose own inclinations to rise
above party could have meant administration defeats.

By his own admission Harrison was not an intellectual in the academic sense of the word. He never cared to spend his time in scholarly pursuits, did not maintain his study or practice of law, and had no private library. He studied people, not books, and while he never gained a reputation for scholarship, observers found him to possess a certain native shrewdness. "Birddog sense, he had it," Happy Chandler recalled. He was, the newsmen agreed, as "smart as the devil."[39] Unoriginal in his own thinking, he listened to other men and, brokering the ideas of businessmen, educators, and others, he transformed these into legislation.

In the rush of events that have occurred since 1941, Senator Harrison has been largely forgotten. Today it is only the older generation in Mississippi that remembers him. Few young Mississippians even know the name of Pat Harrison; but neither do the younger Mississippians know much of the New Deal nor of the political controversies spawned by its programs. In Harrison's case, his death coincided with the end of an era that many people wanted to forget, and he has been forgotten with it. Much of what he provided for the state in the days when his popularity and influence brought vast financial relief to the state and the careful attention of men like Harry Hopkins has been overshadowed by the effects of the war and the monumental economic growth of the state that came in the postwar decades.

No political figure in Mississippi since the New Deal has achieved the stature Pat Harrison had as a powerful Senate leader who was both a Democratic party chieftain prominent at the national convention podium and on the biennial congressional campaign trail as well as a working associate of the president. To a great extent Harrison's successors have been of more limited use to the Democratic administrations, since their own provincial views on social issues and federal-state relations have become the foci of national debates. Harrison's death denied to his state the services of a political sage who perhaps could have given Mississippi the moderate voice that it lacked in the years that followed 1941.

Notes

NOTES TO CHAPTER I

1. "Taxmaster," *Time,* June 1, 1936, p. 10.

2. For biographical data, some of which is inaccurate, see Albert D. Kirwan's sketch of Harrison in the *Dictionary of American Biography*, Supplement Three: *1941–1945* (New York, 1973), 334. Numerous references were made in magazine vignettes on the senator to his ancestors among the Harrison family of Virginia which produced two presidents. Senator Harrison once stated, "I have never traced my ancestry, and . . . have no personal knowledge as to the authenticity or foundation for any such statement." Pat Harrison to Floyd I. McMurray, May 18, 1938, in Harrison Papers, University of Mississippi, Oxford.

3. Louis Cochran, "The Gadfly in the Senate," *Outlook* (August 5, 1931), 430; Jackson (Miss.) *Daily News*, May 14, 1938, p. 2.

4. Interview with Pat Harrison, Jr., Gulfport, August 9, 1970. For further biographical data, see Catherine Blanton to Gene Holcomb, April 1, 1940, in Harrison Papers, and numerous clippings in the Harrison Scrapbook in the possession of Pat Harrison, Jr.

5. Carlisle Bargeron, "Old Man River," New York *Herald Tribune*, March 30, 1941, Sec. X, p. 6.

6. Albert D. Kirwan, *Revolt of the Rednecks: Mississippi Politics, 1876–1925* (Harper Torchbook, New York, 1965), 191–210; Summit (Miss.) *Sun,* June 26, 1941, and Poplarville (Miss.) *Weekly Democrat,* June 26, 1941, in Harrison Scrapbook.

7. Quoted by William S. Coker, "Pat Harrison—Strategy for Victory," *Journal of Mississippi History,* XXVIII (November, 1966), 268.

8. New York *Times,* July 9, 1922, Sec. VII, p. 2.

9. "Pat Reminisces Over 28-Year Term," Jackson *Daily News,* March 4, 1939, p. 8. Harrison enjoyed a social intimacy with Wilson during the president's Christmas vacation on the Mississippi coast in 1913. George C. Osborn, "Pass Christian, the Winter White House: Christmas, 1913," *Journal of Mississippi History,* XXII (January, 1960), 3, 11, 22. Harrison later said that the idea of running for the Senate first came from Wilson's physician, Dr. Cary Grayson.

10. For Harrison's career in the House, the author has relied extensively upon William S. Coker, "Pat Harrison: The Formative Years," *Journal of Mississippi History,* XXV (October, 1963), 251–78.

11. *Congressional Record,* 63 Cong., 2 Sess., 3919–20 (February 25, 1914), 64 Cong., 1 Sess., 1599 (January 26, 1916), 10916 (July 12, 1916).

12. Coker, "The Formative Years," 254; William S. Coker, "Pat Harrison's Efforts to Reopen the Choctaw Citizenship Rolls," *Southern Quarterly*, III (October, 1964), 36–41; Russell D. Buhite, *Patrick J. Hurley and American Foreign Policy* (Ithaca, 1973), 19. Harrison was no more successful in defending Choctaw claims in 1938.

13. Arthur S. Link, "The South and the 'New Freedom': An Interpretation," *American Scholar*, XX (Summer, 1951), 316; Richard M. Abrams, "Woodrow Wilson and the Southern Congressmen, 1913–1916," *Journal of Southern History*, XXII (November, 1956), 437.

14. Coker, "Pat Harrison—Strategy for Victory," 269–70.

15. *Congressional Record*, 63 Cong., 2 Sess., 2821 (February 3, 1914).

16. Coker, "The Formative Years," 260–62, 263–67, 274.

17. Dewey W. Grantham, "The Southern Senators and the League of Nations, 1918–1920," *North Carolina Historical Review*, XXVI (April, 1949), 199.

18. Kirwan, *Revolt of the Rednecks*, 284. Wilson's letter to Harrison was quoted by Cochran, "Gadfly in the Senate," 432.

19. "Pat Harrison," *Current Opinion*, LXXVII (July, 1924), 28.

20. Jackson *Daily News*, July 2, 1918, p. 8.

21. Kirwan, *Revolt of the Rednecks*, 286; Coker, "Pat Harrison—Strategy for Victory," 270; Jackson *Daily News*, July 10, 1918, p. 4, July 18, 1918, p. 6, July 23, 1918, p. 4.

22. New York *Times*, August 11, 1918, p. 6.

23. Quoted by Kirwan, *Revolt of the Rednecks*, 289. Wilson also supported Harrison by diverting Vardaman's patronage to him. In spite of Harrison's popularity in Mississippi, the congressman's victory was considered in the capital to be "something of a long shot at best." Seward W. Livermore, *Politics Is Adjourned: Woodrow Wilson and the War Congress, 1916–1918* (Middleton, Conn., 1966), 139.

24. Kirwan, *Revolt of the Rednecks*, 289–91. The fullest account of the campaign is found in William F. Holmes, *The White Chief: James Kimble Vardaman* (Baton Rouge, 1970), 338–59.

25. In 1922 Vardaman lost an attempt to return to the Senate, and in 1923 Bilbo was defeated in a comeback try for the governor's chair. Harrison was on the chautauqua circuit during the summer of 1923 and missed "the fun in Mississippi," as he called the campaign. Senator Williams wrote to Harrison from retirement, "Well, we beat the d - d little crook. . . . Looks like we are going to have a 'clean stable.' " Williams to Harrison, August 30, 1923; Harrison to Williams, September 23, 1923, both in Harrison Papers.

26. For Harrison's role in the Democratic conventions and campaigns from 1920 through 1932, see Chapter II of this volume.

27. *Congressional Record*, 66 Cong., 1 Sess., 2940 (July 21, 1919), 8786 (November 19, 1919), 66 Cong., 2 Sess., 4599 (March 19, 1920), 67 Cong., 1 Sess., 865 (April 30, 1921), 69 Cong., 1 Sess., 2568 (January 22, 1926).
After Wilson left the Capitol upon the completion of the inaugural ceremonies for Warren G. Harding, Harrison and James F. Byrnes called upon the Democratic leader at his home on S Street. James F. Byrnes, *All in One Lifetime* (New York, 1958), 48.

28. Gompers to Harrison, December 20, 1923, Harrison's speech on "Restrictive Immigration," both in Harrison Papers.

29. *Congressional Record*, 69 Cong., 1 Sess., 6622–25 (March 31, 1926); Harrison

speeches to private groups on January 27, 1925, and March 26, 1926, in Harrison Papers; Jackson *Daily Clarion-Ledger*, February 21, 1926, p. 1.

30. New York *Times*, June 24, 1931, p. 16, November 29, 1932, p. 3; *Time*, July 6, 1931, p. 11; Jordan A. Schwarz, *The Interregnum of Despair: Hoover, Congress, and the Depression* (Urbana, 1970), 79–80.

31. Quoted by Randolph E. Paul, *Taxation in the United States* (Boston, 1954), 137.

32. Harrison to John J. Jones, January 18, 1924; Harrison to Carl Marshall, January 23, 1926, both in Harrison Papers; *Congressional Record*, 68 Cong., 1 Sess., 939–40 (January 14, 1924), 2804–2807 (February 20, 1924), 69 Cong., 2 Sess., 2410–12 (January 28, 1927).

David B. Burner has described the evolution of the Democratic party's tax policy in the 1920s from its resistance to early Mellon proposals to its call for a reduction of corporate taxes as an adaptation to "the business temperament of the decade." Burner, *The Politics of Provincialism: The Democratic Party in Transition, 1918–1932* (New York, 1968), 165.

33. For Harrison's role in 1932, see Jordan A. Schwarz, "John Nance Garner and the Sales Tax Rebellion of 1932," *Journal of Southern History*, XXX (May, 1964), 173, 178–79.

34. *Congressional Record*, 67 Cong., 2 Sess., 8235 (June 6, 1922). For evidence of Harrison's consistent opposition to tariff duties, see Charles M. Dollar, "The South and the Fordney-McCumber Tariff of 1922: A Study in Regional Politics," *Journal of Southern History*, XXXIX (February, 1973), 48–49.

35. *Congressional Record*, 67 Cong., 4 Sess., 2688 (January 30, 1923). For Harrison's standard arguments against McNary-Haugenism, see the *Congressional Record*, 69 Cong., 1 Sess., 11954–55 (June 25, 1926). For a limited analysis of Harrison's role call voting on agricultural bloc legislation, see Patrick G. O'Brien, "A Reexamination of the Senate Farm Bloc, 1921–1933," *Agricultural History*, XLVII (July, 1973), 254–57.

36. *Congressional Record*, 67 Cong., 1 Sess., 4444 (July 29, 1921), 68 Cong., 1 Sess., 10280–81 (June 3, 1924), 68 Cong., 2 Sess., 182–85 (December 5, 1924), 70 Cong., 1 Sess., 4635 (March 13, 1928), 9842 (May 25, 1928).

37. See the Harrison brochure circulated by the Thomas Brady Speakers Bureau, Harrison Papers.

38. *Congressional Record*, 71 Cong., 3 Sess., 426 (December 9, 1932), 72 Cong., 1 Sess., 13768 (June 23, 1932), 14957 (July 9, 1932); Harrison to F. C. Bryan, February 13, 1932, in Harrison Papers.

39. See the conclusions of Ben G. Edmonson, "Pat Harrison: The Gadfly of the Senate, 1918–1932" (M.A. thesis, University of Mississippi, 1967), 23.

40. Cochran, "Gadfly in the Senate," 430. Sullivan was quoted in the Brady brochure on Harrison.

41. Memphis *Commercial Appeal*, March 5, 1939, p. 11.

NOTES TO CHAPTER II

1. Jackson *Daily News*, June 20, 1920, p. 8; James G. Hoffman (comp.), *Official Report of the Proceedings of the Democratic National Convention held in San Francisco, California, June 28 . . . July 6, 1920* (Indianapolis, n.d.), 134–35.

2. *Review of Reviews*, LXII (August, 1920), 121; James M. Cox, *Journey Through My*

Years (New York, 1946), 114; Arthur F. Mullen, *Western Democrat* (New York, 1940), 255. Senator Thomas Connally later referred to Harrison as Cox's "floor leader"; see Connally, *My Name is Tom Connally* (New York, 1954), 105.

3. Frank Freidel, *Franklin D. Roosevelt: The Ordeal* (Boston, 1954), 67.

4. New York *Times,* July 31, 1920, p. 2, September 1, 1920, p. 3.

5. John M. Blum, *Joe Tumulty and the Wilsonian Era* (Boston, 1951), 248; Cox, *Journey Through My Years,* 114. For some insight into the nature of Harrison's work as director of the Speakers' Bureau, see the Harrison correspondence with Irving Fisher between October 20 and 26, 1920, in the Fisher Papers, Yale University Library. Unimportant in detail, they are useful in revealing the petty intricacies of scheduling speeches, making lodging and travel arrangements, and pacifying local party nabobs.

6. New York *Times,* November 7, 1920, p. 6; Harrison to Mrs. Henrietta Mitchell, February 11, 1921, Mitchell Papers, Mississippi Department of Archives and History, Jackson, Box 1.

7. New York *Times,* April 8, 1924, p. 20, May 18, 1924, p. 1.

8. New York *Times,* June 18, 1924, p. 2; Ben G. Edmonson, "Pat Harrison and Mississippi in the Presidential Elections of 1924 and 1928," *Journal of Mississippi History,* XXXIII (November, 1971), 333–37.

9. Claude G. Bowers Memoir, Columbia Oral History Collection, Columbia University (hereinafter cited as COHC), 57.

10. New York *Times,* June 25, 1924, p. 5.

11. Daniel C. Roper, *Fifty Years of Public Service* (Durham, 1941), 224; New York *Times,* June 25, 1924, p. 1.

12. Harrison to Williams, December 31, 1923, in Harrison Papers.

13. Charles A. Greathouse (comp.), *Official Report of the Proceedings of the Democratic Convention held in Madison Square Garden, New York City, June 24 . . . July 9, 1924* (Indianapolis, n.d.), *passim.* See Claude G. Bowers, *My Life: The Memoirs of Claude Bowers* (New York, 1962), 117. Harrison on Underwood is in the Jackson *Daily News,* March 4, 1939, p. 8.

14. New York *Times,* July 10, 1924, p. 10, October 26, 1924, p. 16, November 19, 1924, p. 1.

15. Edmonson, "Pat Harrison and Mississippi in the Presidential Elections of 1924 and 1928," 342.

16. Louis M. Jiggitts, "Al's Chances in Dixie," *Independent,* October 15, 1927, pp. 377–78. A New York *Times* editorial surmised, "When we remember that MR. HARRISON has a reasonable interest in the preservation of his own political bacon, we may be tempted to see in his admission an indication that political judgment and sagacity are getting the better of passionate dogmatisms" (July 27, 1927, p. 22).

17. Richard C. Ethridge, "Mississippi and the 1928 Presidential Campaign" (M.A. thesis, Mississippi State University, 1961), 26. Harrison doused the plans of the Mississippi delegation to wage a serious campaign for his nomination because "we are still a part of the section against which the presidential quarantine has not been lifted." Speech in Harrison Papers.

18. Bowers, *My Life,* 228; Byrnes, *All in One Lifetime,* 220; Roy V. Peel and Thomas C. Donnelly, *The 1928 Campaign: An Analysis* (New York, 1939), 34.

19. Williams to Harrison, February 21, 1928, in Harrison Papers. Williams added, "However I am a Democrat and take my medicine and hope for the best."

20. For evidence of Harrison's role see: Herbert L. Lehman Memoir, COHC,

227–28; Jouett Shouse to Paul Jones, January 14, 1940; Shouse to Al Smith, October 4, 1937, both in Shouse Papers, University of Kentucky Library. Shouse wrote Jones, "As a matter of fact, Pat Harrison and I were the primary factors in the New York headquarters."

21. Harrison to John McDuffie, August 7 and 11, 1928 in McDuffie Papers, University of Alabama Library, Folder 156; Harrison to Reuben Dean Bowen, September 13, 1928, in Bowen Papers, Duke University Library, Box 74; and Harrison to Alben Barkley, September 21, 1928, in Barkley Papers, University of Kentucky Library. A rather prolific correspondence between Harrison and Carter Glass on 1928 matters remains in the Glass Papers in the University of Virginia Library. The Harrison statement to Glass was made on August 17, 1928; see Box 4.

22. New York *Times*, August 2, 1928, p. 3, August 3, 1928, p. 3, October 7, 1928, p. 5.

23. A copy of Harrison's circular, dated October 30, 1928, is in the McDuffie Papers, Folder 156. His speech is in the Harrison Papers.

24. This is the conclusion of Donald Brooks Kelly in "Of God, Liquor and Politics: The Mississippi Press in the Presidential Election of 1928" (M.A. thesis, University of Mississippi, 1962), 50.

25. Williams is quoted in Ethridge, "Mississippi and the 1928 Presidential Campaign," 83. For evidence of the racial factor in the South's vote, see Edmund A. Moore, *A Catholic Runs for President: The Campaign of 1928* (New York, 1956), 157–58, and David Burner, *The Politics of Provincialism*, 224–25.

26. This March 17, 1932 speech is in the Harrison Papers.

27. Actually Harrison was no factor in the choice of a vacation spot. "Mr. Kenny [Smith's friend, William F. Kenny] telephoned the weather bureau and asked what part of the country had the mildest climate on that particular day and the reply was 'Biloxi' where it was 78° in the shade. That is how I happened to go to Biloxi." Alfred E. Smith, *Up to Now: An Autobiography* (New York, 1929), 419.

28. Chellis O'Neal Gregory, "Pat Harrison and the New Deal" (M.A. thesis, University of Mississippi, 1960), 15. Shortly after the election when Harrison was involved in a minor accident at a New York City traffic light, the investigating officer inquired, "Are you the Senator Harrison who supported Al Smith?" Upon learning that he was, the officer marched to the driver of the front car and barked, "Lady, what the hell do you mean backing into this fellow?" Told to the author by Burton K. Wheeler, Washington, D.C., November 24, 1970, and James W. Cummings (Harrison's son-in-law), Bethesda, Maryland, November 22, 1970.

29. Harrison to R. D. Bowen, October 30, 1929, in Bowen Papers.

30. Harrison to FDR, December 24, 1928 and February 23, 1929, in Roosevelt Papers, Franklin D. Roosevelt Library, Hyde Park, Group 12; Lehman to Harrison, March 5, 1929, in Harrison Papers.

31. FDR to Harrison, November 15, 1930; FDR to Butler, November 15, 1930, in Elliot Roosevelt, *FDR: His Personal Letters, 1928–1945*, Vol. I (New York, 1950), 153; Sargeant Prentiss Knut to FDR, May 2, 1932, in Roosevelt Papers, Democratic National Committee (DNC), 1932, District of Columbia.

32. S. R. Bertron to FDR, February 24, 1931, in Roosevelt Papers, President's Personal File (PPF) 907; FDR telegram to Harrison, March 11, 1931, in Harrison Papers.

33. Harrison to FDR, March 19, 1931; Louis M. Howe to Harrison, May 4, 1931, in Roosevelt Papers, DNC, 1932, Miss. Raskob was exceedingly unpopular in Mis-

sissippi. The editor of the Jackson *Daily News* wrote, "They're still talking about what the Democratic Party owes John J. Raskob. And there are those who say that regardless of what the amount is, it is small compared to what the Republicans owe him" (May 14, 1932, p. 6).

34. Charles Michelson, *The Ghost Talks* (New York, 1944), 137.

35. Adolphis Ragan to FDR, March 26, 1931; Harrison to Philip Lowenthal, July 3, 1931, in Roosevelt Papers, DNC, 1932, Miss.

36. Gerald Fitzgerald to House, July 16, 1931, in Roosevelt Papers, DNC, 1932, Miss. House wrote to Harrison, "I hope the South will not be barred much longer from furnishing the candidates for President. Were it not for the inhibition you and Cordell Hull would today be the outstanding candidates of our Party" (July 31, 1931, in Edward M. House Papers, Yale University Library).

37. Tampa *Morning Tribune*, September 8, 1931, clipping in Harrison Papers.

38. Ellen S. Woodward to Harrison, January 26, 1932; FDR to Harrison, January 25, 1932; Harrison to Howe, January 29, 1932, all in Roosevelt Papers, DNC, 1932, Miss.

39. Harlee Branch to unidentified addressee (n.d.), in Roosevelt Papers, DNC, 1932, Miss.; Clarence N. Goodwin to FDR, February 6, 1932, PPF 1869; S. R. Bertron to FDR, March 15, 1932, PPF 907, both in Roosevelt Papers.

40. Jackson *Daily News*, May 18, 1932, p. 7, May 25, 1932, p. 1, June 5, 1932, p. 1; John E. Rankin to FDR, May 28, 1932, in Roosevelt Papers, DNC, 1932, Miss.

41. FDR to Harrison, June 2 and 7, 1932, E. A. Fitzgerald to FDR, June 10, 1932, in Roosevelt Papers, DNC, 1932, Miss.

42. Jackson *Daily News*, June 27, 1932, pp. 1, 6, June 29, 1932, pp. 1, 10, June 30, 1932, p. 1. Harrison voted against seating the Long delegation and in favor of the regularly elected Jared Y. Sanders group. When he told Long of his opposition, Long retorted, "Well, you are at least frank." Jackson *Daily News*, June 30, 1932, p. 14.

43. Jackson *Daily Clarion-Ledger*, July 1, 1932, p. 14; Jackson *Daily News*, July 1, 1932, p. 1; New York *Times*, July 2, 1932, p. 5. The accounts of the taxi ride are legion. See James A. Farley, *Behind the Ballots: The Personal History of a Politician* (New York, 1938), 143; Mullen, *Western Democrat*, 336; and Byrnes, *All in One Lifetime*, 63.

44. Interview with Wheeler, November 24, 1970; Edward J. Flynn, *You're the Boss* (New York, 1947), 100–101; T. Harry Williams, *Huey Long* (Bantam ed., New York, 1970), 611. Alfred B. Rollins, Jr., has written that Judge Leon C. McCord, an old-line Alabama Democrat and one of the original Roosevelt leaders, also worked to keep the mutinous Mississippi delegation in line. Rollins, *Roosevelt and Howe* (New York, 1962), 343.

45. Arthur Krock Memoir, COHC, 7.

46. C. Dwight Dorough, *Mr. Sam* (New York, 1962), 107–109; George E. Allen, *Presidents Who Have Known Me* (New York, 1950), 55–56; Farley, *Behind the Ballots*, 144–45; Creed Black, "Parsonage to Publisher: The Life of Silliman Evans, 1894–1955" (unpublished manuscript in the possession of John Seigenthaler, Nashville), 104; Douglas to the author, April 24, 1973.

47. Grayson to FDR, July 5, 1932, in Roosevelt Papers, DNC, 1932, Miss. For representative Mississippi sentiment, see James M. Alford to FDR, July 7, 1932, DNC, 1932, Miss.; New York *Times*, July 1, 1932, p. 4. Editor Fred Sullens grumbled, "Our delegation narrowly escaped making a clump of itself on several occasions." Jackson *Daily News*, July 14, 1932, p. 8.

48. Jackson *Daily News*, July 7, 1932, p. 1; Conner to Ralph Hayes, July 15, 1932, in Newton D. Baker Papers, Library of Congress, Box 116. The author is grateful to Elliot A. Rosen for providing a copy of the correspondence.

49. J. R. Abrams to Baker, December 15, 1931, in Baker Papers, Container 16. Thomas D. Clark and Albert D. Kirwan, in *The South Since Appomattox: A Century of Regional Change* (New York, 1967), 236, state that Harrison opposed Roosevelt's nomination.

50. Pittman to FDR, July 19, 1932, in Pittman Papers, Library of Congress, Box 149; Catherine Blanton to Fred Sullens, July 26, 1932, in Harrison Papers; New York *Times*, July 30, 1932, p. 3; Jackson *Daily News*, August 7, 1932, p. 15, August 9, 1932, p. 1, August 12, 1932, p. 1.

51. Harrison to Linton M. Collins, September 19, 1932; Harrison to W. J. Meininger, September 30, 1932; Harrison to Fautleroy, October 7, 1932, all in Harrison Papers; Harrison to Howe, October 5, 1932, in Roosevelt Papers, DNC, 1932, Miss.

52. Harrison to S. R. Bertron, September 26, 1932, in Harrison Papers; New York *Times*, October 9, 1932, p. 25; October 12, 1932, p. 19; undated memorandum from McAdoo in Harrison Papers.

53. Frank Freidel, *Franklin D. Roosevelt: The Triumph* (Boston, 1956), 362.

54. C. P. Perkins to FDR, November 3, 1932, in Roosevelt Papers, DNC, 1932, Miss.

NOTES TO CHAPTER III

1. New York *Times*, December 3, 1932, p. 6; FDR to Harrison, December 21, 1932, in Harrison Papers.

2. Baruch to Harrison, January 11, 1933, in Baruch Papers, Firestone Library, Princeton University; E. Pendleton Herring, "Second Session of the Seventy-second Congress," *American Political Science Review*, XXVII (June, 1933), 404. For an assessment of Baruch's influence on Harrison and Robinson, see Schwarz, *The Interregnum of Despair*, 68–70.

3. New York *Times*, December 28, 1932, p. 2; January 1, 1933, Sec. IV, p. 5; I, p. 5; George Cook to Harrison, December 31, 1932, in Harrison Papers. The William Hard quotation is from an NBC speech in the Harrison Papers.

4. Washington *Evening Star*, January 6, 1933, p. 1; New York *Times*, January 8, 1933, p. 2, January 11, 1933, p. 10.

5. Washington *Post*, February 14, 1933, p. 3; Washington *Evening Star*, February 15, 1933, p. 8; *Hearings before the Committee on Finance on Investigation of Economic Problems, February 13–28, 1933*, 72 Cong., 2 Sess., 7–9; *Business Week*, February 22, 1933, p. 3.

6. Washington *Post*, March 25, 1933, p. 4.

7. Jackson *Daily News*, March 4, 1933, pp. 1, 8; Washington *Evening Star*, March 5, 1933, p. 4.

8. "Taxmaster," *Time*, June 1, 1936, pp. 10–11. Also see "Pat Harrison: The Portrait of a Politician from Jokes to Taxes," *Newsweek*, December 13, 1937, pp. 14–15.

9. Francis Gloyd Aswalt, "Recollections of the Banking Crisis in 1933," *Business History Review*, XLIII (Autumn, 1969), 349; Arthur L. Rogers, Jr., "Mississippi Banking During Depression and Recovery" (M.A. thesis, George Washington University, 1938), 40, 55–56; J. F. T. O'Connor, *The Banking Crisis and Recovery Under*

the Roosevelt Administration (New York, 1971), 53; Washington *Post*, March 2, 1933, p. 2.

10. New York *Times*, March 11, 1933, p. 1; Washington *Evening Star*, March 10, 1933, p. 2.

11. *Congressional Record*, 73 Cong., 1 Sess., 252–56 (March 13, 1933).

12. *Ibid.*, 350–51 (March 14, 1933), 471 (March 15, 1933).

13. Washington *Evening Star*, March 21, 1933, p. 10.

14. Washington *Times*, November 26, 1933, clipping in Harrison Papers.

15. *Congressional Record*, 72 Cong., 1 Sess., 15448 (July 15, 1932); New York *Times*, November 10, 1932, p. 9, November 19, 1932, p. 2.

16. New York *Times*, January 25, 1933, p. 3; Tom S. Hines, Jr., "Mississippi and the Repeal of Prohibition," *Journal of Mississippi History*, XXII (January, 1962), 15.

17. Washington *Evening Star*, March 13, 1933, p. 1; *Congressional Record*, 73 Cong., 1 Sess., 314 (March 14, 1933).

18. Washington *Post*, March 16, 1933, p. 1; New York *Times*, March 16, 1933, p. 1; *Congressional Record*, 73 Cong., 1 Sess., 531, 537, 539 (March 16, 1933). Thomas H. Cullen was a New York representative from Brooklyn.

19. *Congressional Record*, 73 Cong., 1 Sess., 625 (March 20, 1933); New York *Times*, March 21, 1933, p. 1; Washington *Post*, March 23, 1933, p. 2. Although Harrison was no longer reticent about his defense of the beer bill, his failure to appear in the news picture of that historic moment may have been an intentional ·avoidance of public recognition of his role in bringing back beer.

20. New York *Times*, March 15, 1933, p. 1.

21. The quip on Smith is in J. T. Salter (ed.), *Public Men In and Out of Office* (Chapel Hill, 1946), 350. Harrison's good relationship with Peek is described in Peek's diary entry for March 22, 1933. Harrison blamed Louis Howe for helping thwart the selection of Peek as secretary of agriculture. George N. Peek Diary, University of Missouri Library, 41.

22. Milburn L. Wilson Memoir, COHC, 771–73.

23. Peek Diary, 41–42.

24. Washington *Post*, April 18, 1933, pp. 1, 3; *Congressional Record*, 72 Cong., 1 Sess., 7756 (April 8, 1932); Washington *Evening Star*, April 20, 1933, p.1.

25. Washington *Post*, April 26, 1933, pp. 1, 3; *Congressional Record*, 73 Cong., 1 Sess., 2320–21 (April 25, 1933), 2552, 2562 (April 28, 1933).

26. Jackson *Daily News*, March 21, 1933, p. 1; Washington *Evening Star*, July 22, 1933, p. 1; Harrison to FDR, May 29, 1933; Wallace to FDR, July 10, 1933, in Roosevelt Papers, Official File (OF) 149. In the nine years of CCC operations in Mississippi 12 percent of the young Mississippi men between the ages of seventeen and twenty-four worked in CCC camps. Larry F. Whatley, "The New Deal Public Works Program in Mississippi" (M.A. thesis, Mississippi State University, 1965), 45.

27. Washington *Post*, May 23, 1933, p. 2; Jackson *Daily News*, May 1, 1933, p. 12, June 18, 1933, p. 6. From July, 1932, through March, 1933, the RFC disbursed to Mississippi the sum of $3,233,054, some of which went for garden tools and seed for persons on direct relief. Whatley, "New Deal Public Works Program," 11.

28. "One-fourth of a State Sold for Taxes," *Literary Digest*, May 7, 1932, p. 10; *Congressional Record*, 72 Cong., 2 Sess., 62 (December 6, 1932); Washington *Evening Star*, January 8, 1933, p. 4; New York *Times*, January 15, 1933, p. 3; Jackson *Daily News*, April 14, 1933, p. 12, November 16, 1934, p. 12.

29. *Congressional Record*, 73 Cong., 1 Sess., 3108 (May 10, 1933), 3329 (May 12, 1933); New York *Times*, May 9, 1933, p. 3, May 13, 1933, p.4.

30. For the drafting process see Arthur M. Schlesinger, Jr., *The Age of Roosevelt*, Vol. II: *The Coming of the New Deal* (Sentry ed., Boston, 1958), 95–99, and Roy G. and Gladys C. Blakey, *The Federal Income Tax* (London, 1940), 339–40.

31. Washington *Sunday Star*, May 14, 1933, p. 1; New York *Times*, May 16, 1933, p. 1, May 21, 1933, p. 5.

32. *Time*, June 19, 1933, p. 14; New York *Times*, May 23, 1933, p. 16, May 24, 1933, p. 1; Washington *Evening Star*, June 2, 1933, p. 1.

33. New York *Times*, June 3, 1933, p. 1; Washington *Evening Star*, June 3, 1933, p. 1. The Senate grapevine reported that the insurgents were miffed over Roosevelt's failure to confer with senators over appointments. New York *Times*, June 4, 1933, p. 1; *Time*, June 12, 1933, p. 16.

34. Washington *Post*, June 6, 1933, p. 1; New York *Times*, June 6, 1933, p. 1; *Congressional Record*, 73 Cong., 1 Sess., 4996 (June 5, 1933).

35. *Congressional Record*, 73 Cong., 1 Sess., 5152, 5162, 5182 (June 7, 1933), 5416, 5424 (June 9, 1933); New York *Times*, June 10, 1933, p. 1.

36. New York *Times*, June 11, 1933, p. 3; *Congressional Record*, 73 Cong., 1 Sess., 5765–66 (June 12, 1933).

37. *Congressional Record*, 73 Cong., 1 Sess., 5859 (June 13, 1933).

38. Hard quoted the late Senator Thomas J. Walsh, who had once defined a Democrat as "a man who gets into office on Jeffersonian principles and sometimes stays there on Hamiltonian ones." Washington *Sunday Star*, March 19, 1933, Sec. II, p. 2. See Doughton to L. A. Carriher, March 25, 1933, in Doughton Papers, University of North Carolina Library; *Congressional Record*, 73 Cong., 1 Sess., 2330 (April 15, 1933).

39. Jackson *Daily News*, July 26, 1933, p. 6.

40. E. Pendleton Herring, "First Session of the Seventy-third Congress," *American Political Science Review*, XXVIII (February, 1934), 82; Jackson *Daily News*, January 5, 1933, p. 1; Harrison to Samuel E. Lumpkin, June 23, 1933, in Harrison Papers. Raymond Clapper recorded that Long's reference to FDR as "that crippled son-of-a-bitch" provoked Farley's patronage knifing of Long (Clapper Diary, 1932–39, Library of Congress).

41. Jackson *Daily News*, June 13, 1933, p. 1, June 24, 1933, p. 3, August 31, 1933, p. 1. For Long's patronage interview with Roosevelt, see Williams, *Huey Long*, 668–69.

42. *Congressional Record*, 73 Cong., 2 Sess., 3898 (March 7, 1934); Marvin McIntyre to FDR, March 16, 1933, in Roosevelt Papers, OF 259; Washington *Evening Star*, March 23, 1933, p. 2. Collier died of a sudden heart attack in September, 1933, after only six months of service on the commission.

43. Fly, who had managed the Mississippi gubernatorial campaign of Hugh White in 1931 and the Stephens 1928 senatorial campaign, became Harrison's political manager in Mississippi. As the commissioner in charge of relief and public works in the district, Allen was given a vast amount of correspondence which came to Harrison from Mississippians who hoped to find work in Washington. The records were later lost in a flood that damaged Allen's office building basement. Author's interview with Allen, Washington, D.C., April 7, 1972.

44. Harrison to Louis M. Howe, January 10, 1933, in Roosevelt Papers, PPF 4069; Harrison to Roosevelt, April 20, 1933, in Roosevelt Papers, OF 51-A;

Washington *Evening Star*, November 14, 1933, p. 1. The endorsement of White is found in Harrison and Stephens to Farley, June 19, 1933, in Emil Hurja Papers, Franklin D. Roosevelt Library, Hyde Park.

45. Jackson *Daily News*, June 16, 1933, p. 1.

46. Harrison to E. W. Wood, June 14, 1933; Harrison to I. W. Cooper, June 27, 1933, in Harrison Papers; Jackson *Daily News*, June 7, 1933, p. 4. His Meridian friend, Martin Miller, wired Harrison on June 26: "Call me. Our enemies [are] trying to put something over." Wire in Harrison Papers.

47. Jackson *Daily News*, March 22, 1933, p. 1, April 2, 1933, p. 8, July 26, 1933, p. 1, August 20, 1933, p. 2; Washington *Post*, August 13, 1933, p. 2. The Mississippian who testified that he had drunk twenty-seven bottles of 3.2 percent beer in one day and then driven his wife to Jackson without feeling intoxicated offered living proof to Harrison's statement! The judge acquitted the man. Washington *Sunday Star,* July 2, 1933, Sec. IV, p. 2.

48. New York *Times*, September 15, 1933, p. 5; Jackson *Daily News*, September 20, 1933, p. 8; Washington *Sunday Star*, October 15, 1933, Sec. IV, p. 2. Mississippians rejected the Twenty-first Amendment by a two-to-one vote in July, 1934.

49. Louis J. Alber to Harrison, July 29, 1933; Ellen Woodward to Harrison, August 8, 1933; Hugh S. Johnson to Harrison, August 9, 1933, all in Harrison Papers; Jackson *Daily News*, July 28, 1933, p. 9, August 11, 1933, p. 16, September 8, 1933, p. 10.

50. F. W. Foote to Harrison, September 20, 1933, in Harrison Papers; Jackson *Daily News*, October 17, 1933, p. 3; October 20, 1933, p. 11.

51. Washington *Sunday Star*, November 5, 1933, Sec. IV, p. 2; Jackson *Daily News*, December 7, 1933, p. 1. It can be added that probably the most dastardly of all attacks on the NRA occurred at McComb when a large chicken hawk swooped down to slay the Blue Eagle insignia on a local barbershop window. The eagle remained in good health; the hawk died of a broken neck. Jackson *Daily News*, September 1, 1933, p. 7.

52. Jackson *Daily News*, June 20, 1933, p. 1, August 7, 1933, pp. 1, 9, August 8, 1933, p. 10; October 15, 1933, p. 5. By the beginning of 1934 the value of Mississippi farm crops exceeded that of January, 1933, by 52 percent. Washington *Sunday Star*, January 7, 1934, Sec. IV, p. 1.

53. Jackson *Daily News*, September 9, 1933, p. 24, October 10, 1933, p. 1; Washington *Evening Star*, October 3, 1933, p. 2; D. B. Cooley to Harrison, September 29, 1933, in Harrison Papers.

54. Jackson *Daily News,* August 26, 1933, p. 1, August 28, 1933, p. 1. By December, Hopkins's Civil Works Administration had 60,000 people at work in Mississippi and funds expended had gone past the $3 million figure.

55. Washington *Sunday Star*, August 27, 1933, Sec. IV, p. 2; October 22, 1933, Sec. IV, p. 2; Harrison to Hopkins, November 27, 1933, in Harrison Papers.

56. Jackson *Daily News*, August 4, 1933, p. 1, August 25, 1933, p. 16, August 30, 1933, p. 8; Harrison to McIntyre, August 6, 1933, in Roosevelt Papers, PPF 4069.

57. E. G. Williams to Harrison, August 15, 1933; D. B. Cooley to Harrison, October 9, 1933; Ashton Toomer to Harrison, August 22, 1933, all in Harrison Papers. A Lee County friend added an extra enticement to an invitation: "I have a good supply of cold bottles, not the Mike Conner brand." Jim Redus to Harrison, September 28, 1933, in Harrison Papers.

58. Jackson *Daily News*, October 19, 1933, p. 1.

NOTES TO CHAPTER IV

1. Jackson *Daily News*, September 10, 1933, p. 1; Washington *Post*, September 10, 1933, p. 2; New York *Times*, September 13, 1933, p. 3. Carlisle Bargeron, a *Post* columnist, wrote, "The truth is that Pat has been down among his Mississippi cotton growers and they are asking where are those high prices for cotton which were being quoted a couple of months ago" (September 17, 1933, p. 6).

2. *Franklin D. Roosevelt Press Conferences* (25 vols., Roosevelt Library, 1956–57), II, 262 (September 13, 1933); James P. Warburg Memoir, COHC, 1441; Washington *Evening Star*, September 14, 1933, p. 2; New York *Times*, September 15, 1933, p. 5; *Time*, September 15, 1933, p. 9; Schlesinger, *The Coming of the New Deal*, 237.

3. Washington *Post*, September 16, 1933, p. 1, September 17, 1933, p. 6; *Washington Evening Star*, September 21, 1933, p. 1; John A. Brenan, *Silver and the First New Deal* (Reno, 1969), 97–99; "Inflation Finessed," *Time*, October 2, 1933, p. 9.

4. Oscar McGough to McN. McGough, no date, copy in Harrison Papers. The Minneapolis *Journal* correspondent is quoted by Van L. Perkins, "The AAA and the Politics of Argriculture: Agricultural Policy Formation in the Fall of 1933," *Agricultural History*, XXXIX (October, 1965), 222–23. See also Jeannette P. Nichols, "Silver Inflation and the Senate in 1933," *Social Studies*, XXV (January, 1934), 17.

5. Schlesinger, *The Coming of the New Deal*, 244–45; New York *Times*, October 5, 1933, p. 36, November 14, 1933, p. 3; Washington *Post*, October 20, 1933, p. 3; Early to McIntyre, November 25, 1933, in Roosevelt Papers, PPF 4069.

6. New York *Times*, November 18, 1933, p. 10; Bernard Baruch, "The Dangers of Inflation," *Saturday Evening Post*, November 25, 1933, p. 5. Harriss wrote to Harrison on April 6, 1932, "Senator Thomas spent last weekend . . . with me and I think you would find it *most interesting* if you had a conference with [him] at an early date." Letter in Harrison Papers.

7. Washington *Sunday Star*, December 3, 1933, Sec. II, p. 1; New York *Times*, December 31, 1933, Sec. IV, p. 7.

8. New York *Times*, January 16, 1934, p. 4, January 28, 1934, p. 1; Washington *Evening Star*, January 18, 1934, p. 12.

9. New York *Times*, April 22, 1934, p. 1; Brennan, *Silver and the First New Deal*, 124. "Pat Harrison . . . is a delightful fellow, but none of his personal friends . . . would think of proposing him as a financial expert," a Washington feature columnist had written in 1933. (Washington *Post*, October 1, 1933, p. 12.) The same was often said of FDR, particularly after the zaniness of the gold-buying became public knowledge. There is one item on record suggesting that both were somewhat taken with Professor Irving Fisher's unorthodox theories. In 1934, FDR prepared a memorandum for Morgenthau: "Pat Harrison is really interested in the plan which Fisher also advocates to issue scrip which must be turned over once a week, or else be subject to a 2¢ tax—you know the plan. Will you please look into [it] further." FDR to Morgenthau, September 13, 1934, in Roosevelt Papers, OF 21.

10. New York *Times*, January 2, 1934, p. 1, February 21, 1934, p. 1.

11. Jackson *Daily News*, March 6, 1934, p. 10, March 10, 1934, p. 1; Washington *Post*, March 13, 1934, p. 9; Henry Morgenthau Diary, Roosevelt Library, Book 1, p. 17; *Congressional Record*, 73 Cong., 2 Sess., 10556 (June 6, 1934).

12. Jackson *Daily News*, March 3, 1934, p. 1; New York *Times*, February 28, 1934, p. 1.

13. *Congressional Record*, 73 Cong., 2 Sess., 5544 (March 27, 1934), 5585, 5587, 5606 (March 28, 1934); Washington *Post*, March 30, 1934, p. 2.

14. New York *Times*, March 30, 1934, pp. 2, 20, April 2, 1934, p. 6.

15. Washington *Sunday Star*, September 24, 1933, p. 1; Washington *Evening Star*, November 10, 1933, p. 1.

16. Washington *Post*, December 12, 1933, p. 1, December 21, 1933, p. 1, December 28, 1933, p. 5; *Joint Hearings before the Committee on Ways and Means and the Committee on Finance on the Tax on Intoxicating Liquors, December 11–14, 1933*, 73 Cong., Interim, 65–70, 91–92.

17. *Congressional Record*, 73 Cong., 2 Sess., 159 (January 5, 1934), 337 (January 10, 1934); New York *Times*, January 7, 1934, p. 6, January 9, 1934, p. 7, January 13, 1934, p. 2; Sidney Ratner, *American Taxation: Its History as a Social Force in Democracy* (New York, 1942), 464–65.

18. Washington *Sunday Star*, July 2, 1933, p. 1; Washington *Post*, September 15, 1933, p. 1; Washington *Evening Star*, January 18, 1934, p. 12.

19. Washington *Evening Star*, February 21, 1934, p. 1, March 22, 1934, p. 3; New York *Times*, March 30, 1934, p. 1.

20. Morgenthau Diary, Book 1, pp. 25–28.

21. *Congressional Record*, 73 Cong., 2 Sess., 5845–48 (April 2, 1934); 5971–72 (April 4, 1933), 6091 (April 5, 1934). The Harrison-Long argument had begun in a Finance Committee hearing on the confirmation of Daniel O. Moore as internal revenue collector for Louisiana. Long was furious over Harrison's refusal to permit some foul language directed at Long to go into the report of the hearing. The conflict is described in Williams, *Huey Long*, 724–25.

22. Washington *Evening Star*, April 6, 1934, p. 1; New York *Times*, April 12, 1934, p. 24; *Congressional Record*, 73 Cong., 2 Sess., 6553–54 (April 13, 1934).

23. *Congressional Record*, 73 Cong., 2 Sess., 5965–66 (April 4, 1934), 6316 (April 10, 1934), 6392 (April 11, 1934); L. J. Taber, Edward O'Neal, et al. to FDR, April 17, 1934, in Roosevelt Papers, OF 400.

24. New York *Times*, April 15, 1934, p. 1; Washington *Sunday Star*, April 15, 1934, p. 1.

25. Washington *Post*, April 15, 1934, p. 2; Washington *Sunday Star*, April 15, 1934, p. 4; New York *Times*, April 18, 1934, p. 4, April 26, 1934, p. 1; Washington *Evening Star*, May 10, 1934, p. 2.

26. Fred Greenbaum, *Fighting Progressive: A Biography of Edward P. Costigan* (Washington, 1971), 145–47; author's interview with Felton M. Johnston, Washington, D.C., April 6, 1972. Mr. Johnston was assistant clerk of the Finance Committee from 1933 to 1935 and clerk from 1935 to 1941.

27. *Roosevelt Press Conferences*, III, 237 (March 14, 1934); Stephen Early memorandum to FDR, March 16, 1934, in Roosevelt Papers, OF 241; Morgenthau Diary, Book 1, p. 27.

28. New York *Times*, April 5, 1934, p. 7; Memphis *Commercial Appeal*, July 1, 1934, Sec. II, p. 7; *Congressional Record*, 73 Cong., 2 Sess., 6737 (April 17, 1934), 6794–95 (April 18, 1934).

29. Rexford G. Tugwell Diary, Roosevelt Library, April 8, 1934; clipping from the Washington "Merry-Go-Round" for March 28, 1935, Harrison Papers. See *Congressional Record*, 74 Cong., 1 Sess., 4618 (March 28, 1936) for Harrison's reply to Pearson.

30. New York *Times*, March 1, 1934, p. 1; Washington *Post*, March 3, 1934, p.

1; *Congressional Record*, 74 Cong., 2 Sess., 3580 (March 2, 1934); Schlesinger, *The Coming of the New Deal*, 254.

31. Washington *Post*, March 30, 1934, p. 1.

32. Washington *Evening Star*, April 24, 1934, p. 10; New York *Times*, April 30, 1934, p. 1; *Hearings before the Committee on Finance on An Act to Amend the Tariff Act of 1930*, 73 Cong., 2 Sess., 8–24; *Congressional Record*, 73 Cong., 2 Sess., 8992 (May 17, 1934).

33. New York *Times*, May 1, 1934, p. 1, May 2, 1934, p. 6; *Congressional Record*, 73 Cong., 2 Sess., 8987–9001 (May 17, 1934).

34. Jefferson Frazier, "The Southerner as American: A Political Biography of James Francis Byrnes" (honors thesis, Harvard College, 1964), 121; Memphis *Commercial Appeal*, July 1, 1934, Sec. II, p. 7; *Congressional Record*, 73 Cong., 2 Sess., 9604 (May 25, 1934).

35. New York *Times*, June 2, 1934, p. 1; Washington *Post*, June 4, 1934, p. 1; *Congressional Record*, 73 Cong., 2 Sess., 10363, 10395 (June 4, 1934).

36. *Congressional Record*, 73 Cong., 2 Sess., 10371 (June 4, 1934). A copy of Harrison's radio talk is in the Harrison Papers.

37. Cordell Hull, *The Memoirs of Cordell Hull* (New York, 1948), I, 217.

38. *Congressional Record*, 73 Cong., 2 Sess., 4475 (March 14, 1934), 8714 (May 12, 1934), 11489 (June 14, 1934), 12013 (June 16, 1934); Jackson *Daily News*, April 3, 1934, p. 6.

39. William E. Leuchtenburg, *Franklin D. Roosevelt and the New Deal, 1932–1940* (Harper Torchbooks, New York, 1963), 75; *Congressional Record*, 73 Cong., 2 Sess., 5712 (March 29, 1934).

40. *Congressional Record*, 73 Cong., 2 Sess., 6096 (April 5, 1934); Tugwell Diary, 1934, p. 4; Ernest K. Lindley, "A Review of President Roosevelt and Congress," *Literary Digest* (June 2, 1934), 42.

41. Bilbo to Harrison, January 9, February 13, 1933, in Harrison Papers; Jackson *Daily News*, March 13, 1933, p. 1.

42. Allen, *Presidents Who Have Known Me*, 68; Peek Diary, 41 (March 22, 1933).

43. Joseph and Stewart Alsop, *The Reporter's Trade* (New York, 1958), 21; Allen, *Presidents Who Have Known Me*, 69; Henry A. Wallace Memoir, COHC, II, 273–74; Chester C. Davis Memoir, COHC, 296–98; Jesse W. Tapp Memoir, COHC, 107–108. Tapp recalled that Bilbo went to see "everybody" about an automobile parking space and ended up in the office of Paul Appleby, a high echelon assistant to Wallace. Appleby, feigning seriousness, explained that the request was difficult to handle and that perhaps Bilbo should see Albert Einstein, to which the new appointee quickly replied, "What's his number, I'll call him up."

44. Jackson *Daily New*, June 22, 1933, p. 1; Washington *Evening Star*, June 23, 1933, p. 1; Washington *Post*, June 25, 1933, p. 7, July 9, 1933, p. 10. Tugwell later said that Bilbo's job was "useless" and condemned as "immoral" the arrangement by which the administration placated Harrison through Bilbo's appointment. The only justification that Tugwell could see in the affair was that it gained needed support from Harrison to pass legislation which he found "objectionable." Rexford G. Tugwell, *In Search of Roosevelt* (Cambridge, 1972), 275–76.

45. Chester Davis Memoir, COHC, 298–300.

46. Bilbo to Harrison, February 23, 1934, in Harrison Papers.

47. Jackson *Daily News*, June 13, 1934, p. 14; New York *Times*, August 15, 1934, p. 9.

48. Jackson *Daily News*, March 10, 1934, p. 8, May 15, 1934, p. 1, August 29, 1934, p. 1; unidentified Pearson column, dated August 21, 1934, in Harrison Papers.

49. Washington *Post*, May 9, 1934, p. 9; Jackson *Daily News*, April 15, 1934, p. 1, July 2, 1934, p. 1, August 3, 1934, p. 1, January 8, 1935, p. 6; Marvin McIntyre to Stephens, August 7, 1934, in Roosevelt Papers, PPF 1665.

For background on factionalism in Mississippi politics, see V. O. Key, *Southern Politics in State and Nation*, (New York, 1949), 230–38, and the statements made to Alexander Heard in the interviews conducted for the Key book which are on deposit in the Southern Politics Collection in the Special Collections of the Joint University Libraries, Nashville, Mississippi Folders. One interviewee stated that the Vardaman-Bilbo faction consisted of "unpropertied rednecks . . . not so respectable people" and the Williams-Harrison faction of "wealthy, conservative, respectable people."

50. Jackson *Daily News*, August 31, 1934, p. 1, September 7, 1934, p. 6, September 20, 1934, p. 1; Memphis *Commercial Appeal*, September 17, 1934, p. 1; Robert J. Bailey, "Theodore G. Bilbo and the Senatorial Election of 1934," *Southern Quarterly*, X (October, 1971), 95, 100.

51. Jackson *Daily News*, August 29, 1934, p. 1, September 6, 1934, p. 1, September 14, 1934, p. 39, September 21, 1934, p. 6, October 8, 1934, p. 1, October 9, 1934, p. 8. The critical comment appears in an unidentified clipping dated October 15, 1934, in the Harrison Papers.

52. Jackson *Daily News*, November 4, 1934, p. 6, November 8, 1934, p. 1.

53. *Ibid.*, November 16, 1934, p. 13, November 18, 1934, p. 1, November 19, 1934, p. 1.

54. Wallace Memoir, COHC, II, 227; see also Jay Franklin in Nashville *Tennessean*, September 20, 1938, p. 5.

55. New York *Times*, November 27, 1934, p. 1; Searle F. Charles, *Minister of Relief: Harry Hopkins and the Depression* (Syracuse, 1963), 96; Tugwell Diary, November 26, 1934; M. L. Wilson Memoir, COHC, 1439.

NOTES TO CHAPTER V

1. Arthur M. Schlesinger, Jr., *The Age of Roosevelt*, Vol. III: *The Politics of Upheaval* (Boston, 1960), 409–15. Tugwell is quoted by Schlesinger.

2. Arthur J. Altmeyer, *The Formative Years of Social Security* (Madison, 1966), 30; Edwin E. Witte, *The Development of the Social Security Act* (Madison, 1962), 80. Frances Perkins remembered that FDR had said that the measure was to be a Harrison-Doughton bill and curiously remarks that years later "the President erroneously referred to the Social Security Act as the 'Wagner-Lewis bill.'" Perkins, *The Roosevelt I Knew* (New York, 1946), 296.

3. Jackson *Daily News*, June 20, 1935, p. 6.

4. New York *Times*, January 18, 1935, p. 1, January 19, 1935, p. 1; Wilbur J. Cohen, "From Dream to Reality," *LithOpinion* (Fall, 1970), 74.

5. Washington *Post*, February 17, 1935, p. 7; Jackson *Daily News*, February 17, 1935, p. 1; Morgenthau Diary, Book 3, pp. 412–19.

6. Marion B. Folsom Memoir, COHC, 30–32; Witte, *Development of the Social Security Act*, 89. Folsom, who later served as secretary of health, education, and welfare (1955–1958), was a friend of Walter F. George. His Georgia origins pleased Harrison.

7. Thomas H. Eliot, "The Social Security Bill: 25 Years After," *Atlantic Monthly* (August, 1960), 74.

8. Witte, *Development of the Social Security Act*, 95, 103. Witte personally told his young assistant, Wilbur J. Cohen, that without Harrison's help the old age annuities (i.e., what is commonly called "social security") would not have been approved by the committee. Cohen to Felton M. Johnston, April 18, 1972, copy in possession of the author. See the Joseph P. Harris Memoir, COHC, 30, for another laudatory description of Harrison's chairmanship.

9. Paul H. Douglas, *Social Security in the United States: An Analysis and Appraisal of the Federal Social Security Act* (New York, 1936), 110–12; Witte, *Development of the Social Security Act*, 102; Altmeyer, *Formative Years of Social Security*, 40–41. Harrison's coolness toward Miss Perkins stemmed in part from his initial treatment when he went on her second day in office in 1933 to pay a courtesy call. The front office secretary did not announce his presence to Miss Perkins. After a twenty-minute wait, and still unannounced, he asked the secretary to tell the new cabinet member of his call "when you get around to it." Then he left. Shocked when she learned of the matter, Miss Perkins asked Frank Bane to smooth things over with the senator. (Bane was a native Virginian who had become director of the American Public Welfare Association.) Harrison was only partially mollified. He told Bane that he understood Miss Perkins had not been responsible for her secretary's action, but he added, "You go back and tell Miss Perkins . . . I forgive her. You don't have to tell her this, but you could add that I ain't agoin' to love her." Maurine Mulliner Memoir, COHC, 44–45. Miss Perkins later discounted the newspaper stories of the office blunder: "There was no ill will on Harrison's part; he perfectly understood the situation." Perkins Memoir, COHC, IV, 377.

10. Altmeyer, *Formative Years of Social Security*, 33; Robert J. Myers Memoir, COHC, 92–93; *Hearings before the Finance Committee on the Economic Security Act*, 74 Cong., 1 Sess., 415 (February 4, 1935).

11. Washington *Post*, May 18, 1935, p. 1, May 31, 1935, p. 4.

12. *Congressional Record*, 74 Cong., 1 Sess., 9267–73, 9283–94 (June 14, 1935).

13. *Ibid.*, 9521 (June 18, 1935), 9628, 9631 (June 19, 1935). Leonard Calhoun was a Mississippi lawyer who did legislative liaison work for Harrison. According to Dr. Bernice Bernstein, another of Witte's assistants, Calhoun possessed a "sharp mind" and an effective approach. Pleading, "I'm a poor country boy [and] I don't know what this is really all about" in a southern drawl enabled him to find out how certain individuals actually stood on various issues. The information he garnered was relayed to Harrison who used it to determine appropriate strategies useful in getting around objections to legislative proposals. Bernstein Memoir, COHC, 95–96.

14. Frances Perkins to Marvin McIntyre, June 21, 1935, in Roosevelt Papers, OF 121-A.

15. *Congressional Record*, 74 Cong., 1 Sess., 12793 (August 9, 1935), 13078 (August 14, 1935).

16. Cohen, "From Dream to Reality," 73, 75; Paul K. Conkin, *The New Deal* (New York, 1967), 60–62; Barton J. Bernstein (ed.), *Towards a New Past: Dissenting Essays in American History* (New York, 1968), 274; Roy G. and Gladys C. Blakey, *The Federal Income Tax*, 390–92, 394; Schlesinger, *The Coming of the New Deal*, 313–14.

17. John M. Blum, *From the Morgenthau Diaries*, Vol. I: *Years of Crisis: 1928–1938* (Boston, 1959), 300. Roosevelt is quoted in Leuchtenburg, *Franklin D. Roosevelt and the New Deal*, 133.

18. Abraham Epstein, *Insecurity: A Challenge to America* (Second rev. ed., New York, 1938), 744; Eliot, "The Social Security Bill," 75.

19. *Congressional Record*, 74 Cong., 1 Sess., 9440 (June 17, 1935); Jackson *Daily News*, January 17, 1935, p. 7, September 28, 1935, p. 1.

20. *Congressional Record*, 74 Cong., 1 Sess., 95 (January 4, 1935).

21. Jackson *Daily News*, January 25, 1935, p. 1, January 27, 1935, p. 1; New York *Times*, March 2, 1935, p. 2. The relief psychology was so pervasive in Mississippi that when Superintendent Bond asked a Perry County child, "Who were the Three Musketeers?" the pupil answered, "The CWA, CCC, and PWA." Jackson *Daily News*, March 11, 1934, p. 5.

22. Miller to Aubrey Williams, October 1, 1934, in Harry Hopkins Papers, Roosevelt Library; New York *Times*, October 30, 1934, p. 8; clipping in the Kemper *County News*, dated November 14, 1935, in Harrison Papers.

23. *Congressional Record*, 74 Cong., 1 Sess., 2396 (February 21, 1935), 3724 (March 15, 1934).

24. Jackson *Daily News*, July 20, 1935, p. 6, September 19, 1935, p. 14; New York *Times*, September 24, 1935, p. 3, July 9, 1936, p. 11; Ellen Woodward to Harrison, October 8, 1935, in Woodward Papers, Mississippi Department of Archives, Box 3.

25. Harold L. Ickes, *The Secret Diary of Harold L. Ickes*, Vol. I: *The First Thousand Days, 1933-1936* (New York, 1954), 302; Schlesinger, *The Politics of Upheaval*, 270-71; *Congressional Record*, 73 Cong., 2 Sess., 2839 (February 20, 1934).

26. Washington *Post*, February 15, 1935, p. 1; New York *Times*, February 21, 1935, p. 2; *Congressional Record*, 74 Cong., 1 Sess., 2003-2004 (February 15, 1935).

27. Washington *Evening Star*, February 22, 1935, p. 2; New York *Times*, March 1, 1935, p. 18; *Time*, March 18, 1935, pp. 16-17.

28. Washington *Post*, March 12, 1935, p. 3, March 30, 1935, p. 1; New York *Times*, March 14, 1935, p. 1, March 31, 1935, Sec. IV, p. 1; *Newsweek*, April 6, 1935, p. 1.

29. Washington *Post*, April 19, 1935, p. 1, April 21, 1935, p. 1; Washington *Evening Star*, April 22, 1935, p. 2; *Hearings before the Committee on Finance Investigation of the National Recovery Administration, March 7 . . . April 18, 1935*, 74 Cong., 1 Sess., 299, 301, 2454; Josiah Bailey to H. R. Stowe, March 25, 1935, in Bailey Papers, Duke University Library, Box 169.

30. Washington *Post*, May 1, 1935, p. 1; Washington *Evening Star*, April 28, 1935, p. 1; New York *Times*, May 5, 1935, Sec. IV, p. 1; *Newsweek*, May 11, 1935, p. 7.

31. Washington *Post*, May 2, 1935, p. 1; Richberg to Marvin McIntyre, May 1, 1935, in Roosevelt Papers, OF 466; *Congressional Record*, 74 Cong., 1 Sess., 7471, 7480 (May 14, 1935).

32. Washington *Post*, May 15, 1935, p. 1, May 28, 1935, pp. 1, 14; Washington *Evening Star*, May 31, 1935, p. 9.

33. Washington *Evening Star*, May 30, 1935, p. 8, June 5, 1935, p. 1; Washington *Post*, May 29, 1935, p. 5, June 5, 1935, p. 1. On May 30 Evon Ford, Mississippi's NRA compliance officer, appealed to the state's businessmen to continue observance of the code agreements on wages and hours until a new course was determined. Jackson *Daily News*, May 30, 1935, p. 1.

34. New York *Times*, June 10, 1935, p. 1, June 11, 1935, p. 1, June 12, 1935, p. 1; New York *Herald Tribune*, June 11, 1935, p. 6; *Newsweek*, June 15, 1935, p. 4; *Congressional Record*, 74 Cong., 1 Sess., 9190 (June 12, 1935).

35. "The United States Senate," *Fortune*, XI (February, 1935), 134.

36. Hugh S. Johnson, "Where Do We Go From Here," supplement to *The Blue Eagle from Egg to Earth* (Garden City, 1935), 4–6; Max Freedman, *Roosevelt and Frankfurter: Their Correspondence, 1928–1945* (Boston, 1967), 276; Perkins, *The Roosevelt I Knew*, 252. McKnight was quoted by the Washington *Evening Star*, May 4, 1935, p. 1.

37. Irving Bernstein, *Turbulent Years: A History of the American Worker, 1933–1941* (Boston, 1970), 340; Leon Keyserling to the author, September 18, 1973. Harrison's apathy toward the 1934 bill could have been influenced by a rash of textile strikes in Mississippi occurring in September. Workers at Kosciusko and Magnolia labored for one day under the shadow of three hundred national guardsmen sent by Governor Conner. Jackson *Daily News*, September 10, 1934, p. 1.

38. Washington *Post*, April 30, 1935, p. 15; Judge Charles E. Wyzanski, Jr. to the author, September 15, 1973. Judge Wyzanski at the time was the solicitor in the Labor Department.

39. *Newsweek*, February 16, 1935, p. 7; author's interview with Cully A. Cobb, Atlanta, September 28, 1973; Donald H. Grubbs, *Cry From the Cotton: The Southern Tenant Farmers' Union and the New Deal* (Chapel Hill, 1971), 57; Roy Scott and James G. Shoalmire, *The Public Career of Cully A. Cobb: A Study in Agricultural Leadership* (Jackson, 1973), 230–31. The author is grateful to Professors Scott and Shoalmire for making available their correspondence with Camp. H. L. Mitchell, a ranking official of the STFU, has found no correspondence with Harrison in the STFU Papers.

40. Jackson *Daily News*, February 17, 1938, p. 6.

41. James T. Patterson, *Congressional Conservatism and the New Deal: The Growth of the Conservative Coalition in Congress, 1933–1939* (Lexington, 1967), 41; *Congressional Record*, 74 Cong., 1 Sess., 9053 (June 11, 1935).

42. New York *Times*, January 27, 1935, p. 17; Washington *Post*, February 11, 1935, p. 2, March 19, 1935, p. 1, March 23, 1935, p. 1.

43. New York *Times*, April 15, 1935, p. 1; Washington *Post*, April 22, 1935, p. 2, April 24, 1935, p. 1.

44. Washington *Post*, April 26, 1935, p. 1, May 8, 1935, p. 6; *Congressional Record*, 74 Cong., 1 Sess., 6762 (May 2, 1935), 6871–72 (May 3, 1935), 7068 (May 7, 1935).

45. *Newsweek*, May 18, 1935, p. 6; Jackson *Daily News*, May 11, 1935, p. 7; Washington *Post*, May 10, 1935, p. 2; Louis M. Jiggitts to FDR, December 28, 1934, in Roosevelt Papers, PPF 2405.

46. Washington *Post*, May 20, 1935, p. 1, May 24, 1935, p. 2, May 26, 1935, Sec. II, p. 1; *Time*, June 3, 1935, p. 13; *Congressional Record*, 74 Cong., 1 Sess., 8061, 8067 (May 22, 1935).

47. New York *Times*, June 9, 1935, Sec. IV, p. 10; Jackson *Daily News*, October 2, 1935, p. 1; Washington *Post*, December 27, 1935, p. 1.

48. New York *Times*, January 11, 1936, p. 1; Washington *Evening Star*, January 13, 1936, p. 5; *Congressional Record*, 74 Cong., 2 Sess., 303 (January 13, 1936). Three representatives of the Mississippi Disabled American Veterans, who were in the gallery when Harrison introduced the bill, asserted: "We are for Senator Harrison one hundred percent." Jackson *Daily News*, January 14, 1936, p. 1.

49. *Congressional Record*, 74 Cong., 2 Sess., 561 (January 17, 1936), 703 (January 20, 1936).

50. New York *Times*, January 25, 1936, p. 1; *Congressional Record*, 74 Cong., 2

Sess., 1015 (January 27, 1936); O. R. Altman, "Second Session of the Seventy-fourth Congress," *American Political Science Review*, XXX (December, 1936), 1095. The only Mississippian to support the president was Will Whittington. Within a week after the issuance of the "baby bonds" on June 15, Mississippi veterans collected $8.7 million on some 174,000 bonds delivered to the state's ex-soldiers. Jackson *Daily News*, June 21, 1936, p. 14.

51. Washington *Evening Star*, May 10, 1935, p. 2; New York *Herald Tribune*, June 9, 1935, Sec. II, p. 2; Washington *Post*, August 3, 1935, p. 2.

NOTES TO CHAPTER VI

1. Walter K. Lambert, "New Deal Revenue Acts: The Politics of Taxation" (Ph.D. dissertation, University of Texas, 1970), 104, 109, 149; Ratner, *American Taxation,* 467.

2. Washington *Post*, March 12, 1935, p. 1; *Time*, April 8, 1935, pp. 15–16.

3. Morgenthau Diary, Book 3, p. 415; Washington *Post*, March 7, 1935, p. 1.

4. Washington *Post*, March 14, 1935, p. 1; *Congressional Record*, 74 Cong., 1 Sess., 4584, 4614 (March 28, 1935).

5. Morgenthau Diary, Book 2, p. 277. Lambert concludes that Morgenthau thought primarily in terms of revenue; see "New Deal Revenue Acts," 175.

6. Morgenthau Diary, Book 2, pp. 176–80.

7. *Roosevelt Press Conferences*, V, 33 (January 5, 1935).

8. Raymond Moley, *After Seven Years* (New York, 1939), 308, 310, 367. "Do let Pat Harrison have his kittens," Frankfurter wired on June 10 to Marguerite LeHand (Roosevelt Papers, PPF 140).

9. Morgenthau Diary, Book 6, p. 81, Book 7, p. 140.

10. Paul Mallon, *Evening Star* columnist, wrote that the senator "who is supposed to be in charge of such legislation [Pat Harrison?] confided in friends that he did not know about the message until two hours before it was delivered" (June 22, 1935, p. 2).

11. *Congressional Record*, 74 Cong., 1 Sess., 9657 (June 19, 1935); New York *Times*, June 20, 1935, p. 2. One reporter quipped that the message called for "a play from the New Dealers' Long suit." "The New Deal Deals Taxes," *Business Week*, June 22, 1935, p. 1. Will Rogers remarked, "I would sure liked to have seen Huey's face when he was woke up in the middle of the night by the President who said, 'Lay over Huey, I want to get in with you.' " *Time*, July 1, 1935, p. 13.

12. New York *Herald Tribune*, June 20, 1935, p. 1.

13. The "nuisance taxes" provided some $500 million in revenue and accounted for the largest single portion of federal revenue.

14. Morgenthau Diary, Book 6, p. 81.

15. Washington *Post*, April 29, 1935, p. 1; Raymond Clapper, "Is Roosevelt Changing," *Review of Reviews*, XCII (August, 1935), 19; New York *Times*, June 21, 1935, p. 1. Bilbo signed the round robin; Long did not since he had his own ideas of procedure.

16. New York *Times*, June 23, 1935, p. 1, June 25, 1935, p. 1; New York *Herald Tribune*, June 25, 1935, p. 6, June 27, 1935, p. 8.

17. *Congressional Record*, 74 Cong., 1 Sess., 10032–33 (June 25, 1935); New York *Herald Tribune*, June 26, 1935, p. 19; New York *Times*, June 26, 1935, p. 1; Washington *Post*, June 27, 1935, p. 5.

18. *Roosevelt Press Conferences*, V, 385, 388 (June 26, 1935). Roosevelt privately

explained that the news media had made statements based on "surmise" and two days later attempted a "cover up." FDR to Hugh A. Murrill, June 29, 1935, in Roosevelt Papers, PPF 200-A. The letter apparently was not sent.

19. *Time*, July 8, 1935, p. 10; *Newsweek*, July 6, 1935, p. 5.

20. Freedman, *Roosevelt and Frankfurter*, 280.

21. *Congressional Record*, 74 Cong., 1 Sess., 10152, 10156–57 (June 26, 1935); New York *Times*, June 27, 1935, p. 1; Washington *Post*, June 27, 1935, p. 4; *Literary Digest*, July 6, 1935, p. 4.

22. New York *Times*, June 27, 1935, p. 20; *Congressional Record*, 74 Cong., 1 Sess., 10273–74, 10276 (June 27, 1935); Blum, *From the Morgenthau Diaries*, I, 304.

23. New York *Herald Tribune*, June 30, 1935. Sec. II. p. 2. *Business Week* called Harrison Roosevelt's "mouthpiece" and charged that he was dependent upon White House support against his Mississippi enemies and Huey Long (August 3, 1935). The "deference" speculation is that of James MacGregor Burns, *Roosevelt: The Lion and the Fox* (New York, 1956), 348. Harrison was quoted by the New York *American*, August 28, 1935, p. 14.

24. New York *Times*, June 30, 1935, p. 23.

25. Washington *Evening Star*, June 28, 1935, p. 1; Washington *Post*, June 26, 1935, p. 5; Ernest K. Lindley, *Half Way With Roosevelt* (Rev. ed., New York, 1937), 254; Morgenthau Diary, Book 7, pp. 165–66.

26. Washington *Evening Star*, July 6, 1935, p. 1, July 10, 1935, p. 2; New York *Times*, July 17, 1935, p. 12; Morgenthau Diary, Book 8, p. 1.

27. New York *Times*, July 30, 1935, p. 12, July 31, 1935, p. 1; *Hearings before the Committee on Finance on the Revenue Act of 1935, July 30–August 8*, 74 Cong., 1 Sess., 96–99.

28. Washington *Post*, August 11, 1935, pp. 1, 7; Morgenthau Diary, Book 9, p.
28. Daniel Hastings filled the Senate in on Harrison's out-maneuvering of La Follette in committee sessions. *Congressional Record*, 74 Cong., 1 Sess., 13056 (August 14, 1935).

29. New York *Times*, August 15, 1935, p. 1; *Congressional Record*, 74 Cong., 1 Sess., 13041–42, 13044, 13057 (August 14, 1935). *Business Week* pointed out that the new revenue yield would be just about "10 days' rations" at the current rate of spending (August 24, 1935, p. 9).

30. *Congressional Record*, 74 Cong., 1 Sess., 13210, 13213, 13254 (August 15, 1935). Josiah W. Bailey wrote an apt summary to C. A. Cannon on August 15, "The present bill was drawn very hurriedly and I do not think it can be said to represent any special theory. One group wished to please the President, another group wished to soak the rich and another group wished to expand the base." See Bailey Papers, Box 547.

31. Moley, *After Seven Years*, 312; Raymond Moley, *The First New Deal* (New York, 1966), 531. See also Mark Sullivan in Washington *Evening Star*, June 9, 1935, Sec. II, p. 3; Arthur Krock in the New York *Times*, July 16, 1935, p. 18; Harold L. Ickes, *Secret Diary*, I, 363; Freedman, *Roosevelt and Frankfurter*, 282.

32. Paul K. Conkin, *The New Deal* (New York, 1967), 65; *Business Week*, August 17, 1935, p. 7; George Terborgh, "Soaking the Rich," *Nation*, CXLII (April 15, 1936), 480; Leuchtenburg, *Franklin D. Roosevelt and the New Deal*, 154.

33. George Wolfskill and John A. Hudson, *All But the People: Franklin D. Roosevelt and His Critics, 1933–1939* (London, 1969), 235. *Nation's Business*, October, 1935, is representative of the business press.

34. New York *Times*, February 29, 1936, p. 8.

35. Ellis W. Hawley, *The New Deal and the Problem of Monopoly: A Study in Economic Ambivalence* (Princeton, 1966), 350–51; Schlesinger, *The Politics of Upheaval*, 505–507; Bernard Sternsher, *Rexford Tugwell and the New Deal* (New Brunswick, 1964), 316, 319.

36. New York *Times*, March 4, 1936, p. 3. In a reply to a constituent who wrote, "When the party is turned over to a lot of professors . . . it is not to our liking," Doughton replied, "I also agree with you that we have had too many theories in key places under this Administration." Alex Howard to Doughton, June 26, 1936; Doughton to Howard, June 27, 1936, in Doughton Papers, Folder 561. See also Joseph Alsop and Robert Kintner, "'Henny Penny': Farmer at the Treasury," *Saturday Evening Post*, April 1, 1939, pp. 8–9.

37. *Congressional Record*, 74 Cong., 2 Sess., 6367 (April 29, 1936); Washington *Evening Star*, April 24, 1936, p. 2.

38. See the testimony of George O. May, senior partner of Price, Waterhouse accountants and a former treasury adviser, in *Hearings before the Committee on Finance on the Revenue Act of 1936, April 30–May 12*, 74 Cong., 2 Sess., 538–42. For business thought, see the *Commerical and Financial Chronicle*, March 14, 1936, p. 1692; "Taxing and Destroying," *Business Week*, May 9, 1936, p. 48; and Joseph S. Lawrence, "A Death Sentence for Thrift," *Review of Reviews*, XCIII (May, 1936), 40–43.

39. Morgenthau Diary, Book 23, pp. 148–50.

40. *Ibid.*, Book 24, pp. 18, 56, 111; Washington *Post*, May 10, 1936, p. 1; New York *Times*, May 22, 1936, pp. 1, 6; Washington *Evening Star*, May 21, 1936, p. 1; "Senate Listens to Reason," *Business Week*, May 16, 1936, p. 15.

41. New York *Times*, May 29, 1936, p. 1; "Tax Headaches," *Literary Digest*, June 13, 1936, p. 38; Max Lerner, "The Corporate Tax Battle," *Nation*, May 27, 1936, p. 669.

42. *Congressional Record*, 74 Cong., 2 Sess., 9110 (June 5, 1936), 10476 (June 20, 1936); Paul, *Taxation in the United States*, 198; *Newsweek*, June 13, 1936, p. 8; New York *Times*, June 21, 1936, p. 1.

43. Blum, *From the Morgenthau Diaries*, I, 318; George L. Lent, *The Impact of the Undistributed Profits Tax, 1936–1937* (New York, 1948), 21, 33, 71, 154–55, 161. Eccles is quoted in Hawley, *The New Deal and the Problem of Monopoly*, 356.

44. Otis L. Graham, *The New Deal: The Critical Issues* (Boston, 1971), 38. See also E. Cary Brown, "Fiscal Policy in the Thirties: A Reappraisal," *American Economic Review*, XLVI (December, 1956), 868.

45. Pat Harrison, "A Streamlined Tax Program," *Nation's Business*, XXVI (June, 1938), 16. Italics are this author's.

46. Baruch wrote Harrison on November 5, 1936, "I thought [it] a very good suggestion . . . that in addition to the Treasury experts there ought to be an outsider who understood the relation of business and industrial activity to the problems involved. I think that fellow Parker is about as good as I have seen." Letter in Baruch Papers. Oliphant, however, warned Morgenthau in May, 1936, that Parker, "appointed under the old regime," was too much opposed to higher surtaxes. Morgenthau Diary, Book 24, p. 45. The author is grateful to the late Felton M. Johnston, former clerk of the Finance Committee, for valuable insights given through interviews in Washington, D.C., on November 23, 1970, and April 6, 1972.

NOTES TO CHAPTER VII

1. "United States Senate," *Fortune*, XI (February, 1935), 134.

2. Gordon K. Lewis, *The Virgin Islands: A Caribbean Lilliput* (Evanston, 1972), 69–72; *Time*, July 15, 1935, p. 21.

3. Lewis, *The Virgin Islands*, 79; *Time*, July 15, 1935, p. 21; Washington *Post*, June 2, 1935, II, 7.

4. LeHand to McIntyre, January 16, 1935, in Roosevelt Papers, PPF 4069; Raymond Swing, "Justice in the Virgin Islands," *Nation*, January 23, 1935, pp. 95–96; Ickes Diary, Reel I, 829 (Library of Congress).

5. Washington *Post*, January 25, 1935, p. 1; New York *Times*, January 26, 1935, p. 11. See also *Time*, February 4, 1935, pp. 22–23; Ickes to Harrison, January 23, 1935, in Ickes Papers, Library of Congress, Box 369.

6. Ickes, *Secret Diary*, I, 301; Ickes Diary, Reel I, 830. (The "unexpurgated" diary was opened long after Ickes wrote his book.)

7. *Congressional Record*, 74 Cong., 1 Sess., 4618 (March 28, 1935); James F. Byrnes to Joseph P. Kennedy, November 2, 1938, in Byrnes Papers, Clemson University Library. Byrnes added, "About a year ago they [Pearson and Allen] decided to put me on their preferred list, and devoted a lot of space to criticism of me."

8. Washington *Post*, April 2, 1935, p. 2, July 10, 1935, p. 1; Joseph M. Price to FDR, April 15, 1935, and Mrs. James Longstreet to Harrison, April 20, 1935, in Roosevelt Papers, OF 6-Q; Freedman, *Roosevelt and Frankfurter*, 282. Drew Pearson was so firmly convinced that Harrison was against his father that he harked back to the affair in the diary that he later kept. In 1949 he still remembered Harrison and Tydings as "Democratic die-hards" who "desperately" tried to remove the governor. Tyler Abell (ed.), *Drew Pearson Diaries, 1949–1959* (New York, 1974), 93.

9. Washington *Post*, July 12, 1935, p. 1, July 24, 1935, p. 1; Washington *Evening Star*, July 12, 1935, p. 2; Dutcher in Jackson *Daily News*, August 13, 1935, p. 6; Steve Early memorandum to Marvin McIntyre, July 18, 1935, in Roosevelt Papers, OF 6-Q; Raymond Swing, "Storm over the Virgin Islands," *Nation*, July 24, 1935, p. 96.

A year later the Circuit Court of Appeals in Philadelphia upheld Wilson's ruling. In the opinion of the court there had been no "ill will, prejudice, or unfair conduct" in Wilson's actions. *Federal Reporter*, 2d Series, 83 (June–July, 1936, 382–83.

10. Ickes, *Secret Diary*, Vol. II: *The Inside Struggle, 1936–1939* (New York, 1954), 131, 188.

11. For the Mississippi political picture in the 1930s, see William C. Havard, *The Changing Politics of the South* (Baton Rouge, 1972), 475–76, and J. Oliver Emmerich, "Collapse and Recovery," in Richard A. McLemore (ed.), *A History of Mississippi* (Jackson, 1973), II, 97–119.

12. Jackson *Daily News*, May 31, 1935, p. 1; clipping from the Kemper County *Messenger*, dated July 3, 1935, in Harrison Papers; Fechner to FDR, July 25, 1935, in Roosevelt Papers, OF 268.

13. Jackson *Daily News*, August 9, 1935, p. 1, August 11, 1935, p. 1, August 13, 1935, pp. 1, 6; Washington *Evening Star*, August 14, 1935, p. 1, August 29, 1935, p. 12.

14. *Congressional Record*, 73 Cong., 1 Sess., 6081 (April 5, 1934); Jackson *Daily News*, April 6, 1934, p. 1.

15. Robinson to Harrison, September 29, 1932; Harrison to Robinson, October 1,

1932, both in W. D. Robinson Papers, Southern Historical Collection, University of North Carolina, Folder 7; Bilbo to Robinson, February 11, 1935; Robinson to Thomas F. Porter, June 7, 1935, both in Robinson Papers, Folder 12. Whatever other "intelligence" Harrison may have gathered on Long has not come to light.

16. Moley, *After Seven Years*, 305; Burton K. Wheeler with Paul F. Healy, *Yankee from the West* (Garden City, 1962), 284; Jiggitts to FDR, April 16, 1935, in Roosevelt Papers, PPF 2405; Jackson *Daily News*, September 11, 1935, p. 12.

17. Jackson *Daily News*, September 11, 1935, p. 1, September 26, 1935, p. 1, October 13, 1935, p. 21, November 6, 1935, p. 1.

18. The Catledge survey, "Mississippi Holding to New Deal's Aim," is in the Jackson *Daily News*, December 18, 1935, p. 10. In his swing around the state, the senator collected the opinions of many constituents including that of a McComb woman who reached for his hand and beamed, "I think we ought to know all our members of Congress no matter how old and ugly they are." Jackson *Daily News*, December 15, 1935, p. 6.

19. This paragraph is based on the Catledge survey.

20. Jackson *Daily News*, October 14, 1935, p. 6.

21. *Ibid.*, June 30, 1935, p. 1.

22. Washington *Post*, March 9, 1935, p. 7; *Time*, February 4, 1935, p. 23; Bilbo to FDR, February 1, 1935, in Roosevelt Papers, PPF 2184; McIntyre to Harrison, July 17, 1935, in Roosevelt Papers, PPF 4069. See also Edwin E. Meek, "Eugene Octave Sykes, Member and Chairman of the Federal Communications Commission and Federal Radio Commission, 1927–1939," *Journal of Mississippi History*, XXXVI (November, 1974), 377–86.

In March, 1935, Roosevelt named ex-senator Hubert Stephens to the board of the Reconstruction Finance Corporation. Bilbo did not contest the appointment since he had promised in his 1934 campaign that he "would see that Hubert got a good job." Jackson *Daily News*, March 7, 1935, p. 1. Two defeated Mississippi congressmen, Jeff Busby and Russell Ellzey, were named as legislative liaison representatives with the FDIC and HOLC. Presumably, they were named to the posts with the blessings of Harrison; he probably actively pursued the appointments.

23. Jackson *Daily News*, August 23, 1935, p. 1.

24. FDR to Cummings, August 23, 1935, in Roosevelt Papers, OF 208-EE; Bilbo to Cummings and FDR, August 23, 1935, PPF 2184; Jackson *Daily News*, September 28, 1935, p. 1. Bilbo's role in the Russell case is described by Kirwan, *Revolt of the Rednecks*, 298–99, 303.

25. Jackson *Daily News*, January 7, 1936, p. 1; McIntyre to FDR, January 6, 1936; Bilbo to FDR, March 2, 1936, in Roosevelt Papers, OF 208-EE.

26. *Hearings before a Subcommittee of the Judiciary on the Nomination of Judge Edwin R. Holmes*, 74 Cong., 2 Sess., 61; Jackson *Daily News*, January 24, 1936, p. 1; *Time*, June 1, 1936, p. 12; "Bilbo: 'Ex-Pastemaster General' Turns on Man Who Got Him Job," *Newsweek*, February 1, 1936, pp. 16–17.

Harrison's statement on his personal financial crisis is worth stating in full:

I may say as a personal reference that I thought in 1925, like a good many people thought, that I had done very well in a business way. I found I was mistaken. I had never had anything in my life, but in 1925 during the boom in Florida, which extended over to the coast of Mississippi, opportunities for investment seemed very promising, and I invested some money. I had to borrow in order to do it, and I put up my salary warrants to do it and to make it good. I made considerable money. I thought I did. I think in 1925 I paid something over $12,000 income tax and the following year something like $10,000 or $11,000. I thought I had made about $450,000 and was in pretty good shape for the balance of my life. But, unfortunately, the collapse came, and when it came the property that I had sold people here and there for quite large sums I had to take back, and I have had to pay taxes on it for some 10 or 12 years, and I admit that I am insolvent. When the First National Bank of Gulfport failed, I had endorsed some notes and borrowed some money there. I had done that in other banks in Mississippi. I have done everything possible to try to reduce these obligations, and have reduced them, and in time I will pay them. But I was caught like others in a trap. *(Hearings, 61)*

27. *Congressional Record*, 74 Cong., 2 Sess., 4031–32 (March 19, 1936); Jackson *Daily News*, March 20, 1936, p. 1. The three senators who supported Bilbo were Elmer A. Benson of Minnesota, Vic Donahey of Ohio, and Thomas of Oklahoma.

28. Bilbo to Harrison, March 20, 1936, and September 19, 1936; John McDuffie to R. M. Bourdeaux, September 8, 1936, all in Harrison Papers; Rudolph Forster memorandum to FDR, June 8, 1936; Bilbo to FDR, September 28, 1936; FDR to McIntyre, January 16, 1937; Joseph B. Keenan to McIntyre, January 25, 1937, all in Roosevelt Papers, OF 208-EE.

29. New York *Times*, January 25, 1936, p. 6.

30. Allen A. Michie and Frank Rhylick, *Dixie Demagogues* (New York, 1939), 76; New Orleans *Item*, July 22, 1935, p. 2; Jackson *Daily News*, July 20, 1936, pp. 3, 4.

31. Washington *Herald*, March 29, 1936, p. 10; Brandon (Miss.) *News*, April 2, 1936, p. 2; Jackson *Daily News*, May 27, 1936, p. 16; McDuffie to Rayburn, May 12, 1936, in McDuffie Papers, Folder 289.

32. Jackson *Daily News*, July 26, 1936, p. 16, August 3, 1936, p. 1, August 5, 1936, p. 3, August 23, 1936, p. 1; Harrison memorandum to Felton M. Johnston, August 8, 1936, in Harrison Papers. Of the congressional delegation only Dunn entered the fray, predicting that when the race was over, Conner could "take one of those silver-colored tax tokens and crawl through it and change his hat, coat, pants, and shirt while he is doing it." Jackson *Daily News*, July 21, 1936, p. 12.

33. When Harrison tried to get an endorsement from Senator Norris, the Nebraskan confided to his secretary that the Mississippian's opponents had pressed him to come out against Harrison on the basis of his lackadaisical role in the TVA struggle. While Norris had a "very friendly feeling" for Harrison in spite of his being "favorable to the other side" in the TVA fight, Norris declined to project himself into the Mississippi race. He concluded, however, that "Senator Harrison has been very fair in trying to help President Roosevelt carry out his policies" and had "gone along . . . sometimes against his own belief in the policies the President was advocating." Norris to John P. Roberson, July 30, 1936, in Norris Papers, Library of Congress, Tray 8. The author is grateful to Professor Richard Lowitt for providing a copy of the letter.

The Edwin Halsey Papers in the Senate Historical Office (Washington) contain evidence that Harrison tried in vain to get a statement from Norris.

34. New Orleans *Times-Picayune*, June 10, 1936, p. 2; Jackson *Daily News*, June 10, 1936, p. 16, July 13, 1936, p. 3.

35. Jackson *Daily News*, June 30, 1936, p. 1, July 3, 1936, p. 1, July 15, 1936, p. 3; Cleveland (Miss.) *Enterprise*, August 19, 1936, p. 1; Franklin *Advocate*, August 20, 1936, p. 1.

36. Paul J. Miller, Jr., to Halsey, July 25, 1936, in Halsey Papers; Jackson *Daily News*, July 21, 1936, p. 1, August 4, 1936, p. 14, August 14, 1936, p. 16, August 16,

1936, p. 17; Neshoba *Democrat*, July 31, 1936, p. 4; Port Gibson *Reveille*, August 20, 1936, p. 1; "Broom or Bilbo," *Time*, August 24, 1936, p. 23. Broom's indictment of Bilbo's new morality drew rebuttals from the Conner crowd that the incumbent senator golfed on Sunday and smoked cigars. The latter vice lost the vote of at least one moral arbiter in the state who wrote, "I can't vote for Pat Harrison because he smokes cigars." Jackson *Daily News*, July 17, 1936, p. 6.

A decade later Bilbo explained Mississippi politics: "It's always a family fight down there, and a family fight is the best of all. We're all Democrats and we have to deal in personalities because there are no issues. . . . So you don't show the other fellow is in favor of this or that. You just show he's a lowdown blankety blank." *Newsweek*, September 1, 1947, pp. 19–20.

37. Laurel *Leader-Call*, August 8, 1936, p. 1; Brandon *News*, July 23, 1936, p. 2.

38. Jackson *Daily News*, August 10, 1936, p. 8; Memphis *Commercial Appeal*, August 15, 1936, p. 4; William H. Anderson to Sledge, September 5, 1936, in Harrison Papers. The Harrison speech and the Robinson and Pace telegrams all are in the Harrison Papers.

39. Mimeographed "Suggestions for Speakers" in Harrison Papers; Jackson *Daily News*, July 28, 1936, p. 10, August 22, 1936, p. 1. In a Harrison "Summary Report of Federal Agencies in Mississippi" a "conservative approximation" of $260,784,981 was given as that distributed in the state by the federal government within the past three years.

40. Jackson *Daily News*, June 16, 1936, Special Supplement. Successive issues of the *Mississippi Veteran* are in the Harrison Papers.

41. Neshoba *Democrat*, July 31, 1936, p. 8; Gray to Catherine Blanton, August 5, 1936; Holton to Harrison, September 3, 1936, both in Harrison Papers.

42. Green to Harrison, June 11, 1936, in Harrison Papers; Jackson *Daily News*, July 7, 1936, p. 12, July 19, 1936, p. 1, August 20, 1936, p. 1; George County *Times*, August 21, 1936, p. 1; *Labor*, August 4, 1936, p. 3, August 18, 1936, p. 1.

43. Wayne Flynt, a student of the southern labor movement, concluded that labor's warm support of Harrison as well as of each of the incumbent Mississippi congressmen reflected the conservative nature of the state's unions and their abhorrence of demagoguery. According to Flynt, the return of the congressional delegation intact contributed substantially to the failure of any efforts to form a "liberal" anti-New Deal coalition of wealth sharers, Townsendites, former Populists, and union members. Flynt, "A Vignette of Southern Labor Politics—The 1936 Mississippi Senatorial Primary," *Mississippi Quarterly*, XXVI (Winter, 1972–73), 89, 99.

44. Jackson *Daily News*, June 11, 1936, p. 1; Bilbo to Farley, n.d. [1936]; Stephen Early to Dunn, August 6, 1936, both in Roosevelt Papers, OF 300, DNC, Miss., 1933–1945.

45. Paul D. Spearman to McIntyre, August 13, 1936; Stephens to FDR, August 5, 1936, both in Roosevelt Papers, OF 300, DNC, Miss., 1933–1945; Franklin *Advocate*, August 20, 1936, p. 1.

46. Harrison to Halsey, August 6, 1936; Jiggitts to Farley, n.d., and Guffey to Farley, n.d., all in Halsey Papers; Jackson *Daily News*, August 12, 1936, p. 1; New York *Times*, August 19, 1936, p. 20. John M. Blum has written, "The identification of Harrison with a drive against tax dodging was made to order for Mississippi politics." Blum, *From the Morgenthau Diaries*, I, 319.

47. New Albany *Gazette*, August 20, 1936, p. 1; leaflet for "Our Pat" Gulfport rally in Harrison Papers.

48. Blanton to Halsey, August 1, 1936, in Halsey Papers; Slim Suttle to Sledge, August 25, 1936, in Harrison Papers; Jackson *Daily News*, August 26, 1936, p. 10; New York *Times*, August 27, 1936, pp. 7, 20.

49. Raymond Moley wrote to the author on May 1, 1973, that Harrison was "an especial friend of Baruch who helped him greatly in his campaigns for reelection." James T. Patterson has cautiously stated that Harrison "probably" received support from Baruch after 1932. Patterson, *Congressional Conservatism and the New Deal*, 132.

Jay Franklin, the candid columnist for the Washington *Evening Star,* referred to Baruch's "fine collection of old masters of Southern politics [bought] at depression prices and loaned to FDR for his first term." Washington *Evening Star,* June 29, 1937, p. 1.

50. Alexander Heard interview with Henry A. Wallace, October 24, 1954, in Costs of Democracy Collection, Joint University Libraries, Nashville, Folder ; Henry Wallace Memoir, COHC, V, 870.

51. [Norfleet Sledge?] to W. T. Wynn, October 13, 1936, Harrison Papers; Wallace Memoir, COHC, VIII, 1445; Wilburn Buckley to James G. Shoalmire, April 29, 1974, Transcript in John C. Stennis Oral History Project, Mississippi State University Library. The Harrison Papers contain lists of contributors in each county which were filed with the secretary of state under the Mississippi Corrupt Practices Acts. As would be expected, they contain the details of nickel and dime collections, but provide no evidence of large sums given by individuals or industries. See Walker Wood to Norfleet Sledge, September 14, 1936, for the final (and suspiciously low) official report of the Harrison campaign collections.

52. Jackson *Daily News*, August 28, 1936, p. 1; "Purge by Computer or Little Black Book—It's All the Same," Memphis *Commercial Appeal*, February 29, 1971, Sec. VI, p. 2; A. R. Moore to Harrison, September 1, 1936; Joseph Redhead to Harrison, September 9, 1936, both in Harrison Papers.

Dissension between Harrison and Bilbo over WPA patronage in Mississippi is a story in itself and involved too many personalities and political angles to be discussed here. For the remainder of Harrison's life, Bilbo fought to have his colleague's friends removed from WPA administrative posts in Mississippi. For the most part Harrison was able to protect them through the offices of Harry Hopkins. Mississippi was never subjected to the large-scale investigations of WPA politics which other states, notably Kentucky and Pennsylvania, experienced. To avoid repetition of the 1936 fracas, before the gubernatorial election in 1939 and the Senate race in 1940, the directors of the Mississippi WPA were temporarily assigned by the Washington office to positions outside the state and returned when the political fires cooled down at home.

53. Sledge to Mrs. Sledge, September 11, 1936, September 14, 1936, both in Harrison Papers; Jackson *Daily News*, March 18, 1937, p. 4. Sledge died of a heart attack in March, 1937.

54. Jackson *Daily News*, September 29, 1935, p. 1; Washington *Post*, November 24, 1935, Sec. III, p. 1.

55. Jackson *Daily News*, June 16, 1936, p. 1; New York *Times*, June 23, 1936, p. 12, June 25, 1936, p. 1.

56. Jackson *Daily News*, June 27, 1936, p. 1, October 1, 1936, p. 12, October 15, 1936, p. 1; Washington *Post*, June 28, 1936, Sec. III, p. 1. A copy of the Mississippi resolution is in the Roosevelt Papers, PPF 3989. Harrison's speech is in his papers.

57. Roosevelt Papers, OF 300, DNC, Election Forecasts; Jackson *Daily News*,

October 16, 1936, p. 16; Washington *Post*, January 19, 1937, p. 3. "Queenie" became the official mascot of the party. She was subsequently taken from her private home on the Potomac to attend various party functions, including the South Carolina state Democratic convention in 1938 where she balked at entering any more hotel lobbies. Nashville *Tennessean*, May 18, 1938, p. 1.

58. "Pat Overwhelms Mike as Mud Flies in Mississippi," *Newsweek*, September 5, 1936, p. 9.

NOTES TO CHAPTER VIII

1. Patterson, *Congressional Conservatism and the New Deal*, 81; O. R. Altman, "First Session of the Seventy-fifth Congress," *American Political Science Review*, XXXI (December, 1937), 1071. Glass is quoted by Patterson, 95.

2. Joseph Alsop and Turner Catledge raised questions about the Democratic victory in *The 168 Days* (Garden City, 1938), 51.

3. *Ibid.*, 43.

4. Bankhead is quoted by Leuchtenburg in *Franklin D. Roosevelt and the New Deal*, 234.

5. Alsop and Catledge, *The 168 Days*, 77; William E. Leuchtenburg, "Franklin D. Roosevelt's Supreme Court Packing Plan," in Harold M. Hollingsworth and William F. Holmes (eds.), *Essays on the New Deal* (Austin, 1969), 109.

6. Washington *Post*, February 7, 1937, p. 1, February 12, 1937, p. 1, February 14, 1937, p. 1; New York *Times*, February 14, 1937, p. 1.

7. Washington *Post*, February 21, 1937, p. 1, March 7, 1937, p. 1; Jackson *Daily News*, March 12, 1937, pp. 1, 14; *Congressional Record*, 75 Cong., 1 Sess., 2735 (March 25, 1937).

There are two dozen letters in the papers of Senator Carter Glass from Mississippians who opposed the court-packing plan with the same vehemence as that of the Virginian. Many of them spoke of their disapproval of Harrison's public statements, one in particular writing. "Would like to tell you that our pan-handling Miss. senators do not . . . reflect the sentiment of the right thinking patriotic portion of the people of Miss." William H. Colohan to Glass, March 29, 1937, in Glass Papers, Box 350.

8. *Congressional Record*, 75 Cong., 1 Sess., 3017 (April 1, 1937).

9. Washington *Post*, April 5, 1937, p. 1, April 6, 1937, p. 2; *Congressional Record*, 75 Cong., 1 Sess., 3248 (April 7, 1937). Harrison's press release is in his papers. Robinson's statement to Byrnes is in Frazier, "The Southerner as American," 67.

10. New York *Herald Tribune*, January 9, 1937, p. 1; Jackson *Daily News*, August 8, 1934, p. 1; New York *Times*, April 21, 1937, p. 17; Alsop and Catledge, *The 168 Days*, 130.

11. New York *Times*, April 21, 1937, p. 1, April 29, 1937, p. 3. See Chapter X of this volume for Harrison's attempts to secure passage of successive education bills.

12. Charles, *Minister of Relief*, 165.

13. Byrnes to W. H. Beattie, July 17, 1937, in Byrnes Papers, Legislative File.

14. Alsop and Catledge, *The 168 Days*, 152.

15. *Ibid.*, 202–203; Michelson, *The Ghost Talks*, 181.

16. Washington *Post*, May 19, 1937, p. 1.

17. Jackson *Daily News*, June 5, 1937, p. 1.

18. Alsop and Catledge, *The 168 Days*, 239. Arthur Krock related a story circulating in the Senate cloakroom involving Roosevelt and an unnamed member of

Congress who attempted to tell the president of the ill feeling that the court plan had caused within the Senate. The informer described golf foursomes and other forms of friendships which had been broken up. When Roosevelt later suggested to his informer point-blank that he was only trying to defeat the bill under the guise of loyalty, the lawmaker left the White House in anger and swore that it "would be a cold day before he would volunteer any information again." While Senator Harrison was not named, the whole story suggests that he may well have been the "mediator." New York *Times,* May 2, 1937, Sec. IV, p. 3.

19. Alsop and Catledge, *The 168 Days,* 264.

20. *Congressional Record,* 75 Cong., 1 Sess., 7154 (July 14, 1937); Alsop and Catledge, *The 168 Days,* 281, 285.

21. Alsop and Catledge, *The 168 Days,* 286; *Congressional Record,* 75 Cong., 1 Sess., 7381 (July 22, 1937). Bilbo was among the twenty who voted "nay."

22. Kenneth E. Harrell, "Southern Congressional Leaders and the Supreme Court Fight of 1937" (M.A. thesis, Louisiana State University, 1959), 158–60.

23. Washington *Evening Star,* April 6, 1934, p. 8; Washington *Post,* May 20, 1937, p. 1, May 21, 1937, p. 1, May 22, 1937, p. 1. Majority leader Nelson Aldrich remained as chairman of the Finance Committee and Henry Cabot Lodge as chairman of the Foreign Relations Committee.

24. New York *Times,* July 15, 1937, p. 1; James A. Farley, *Jim Farley's Story,* 88, 125. During Barkley's Senate race in 1938, which coincided with the Senate debate over repeal of the profits tax, Roosevelt told Farley, "If Barkley loses the fight, Pat Harrison will become majority leader and I'm afraid Pat won't go along on liberal legislation." *Jim Farley's Story,* 124.

25. Washington *Post,* July 15, 1937, p. 1; New York *World-Telegram,* July 16, 1937, p. 1; New York *Times,* July 16, 1937, pp. 1, 2. The "Dear Alben" letter may be found in the Roosevelt Papers, PPF 3160. Allen and Pearson wrote in their column that Robinson had first offered the assistant leadership post to "his closest friend," Harrison, who declined for reasons of health and the pressure of committee responsibilities. Nashville *Tennessean,* July 23, 1937, p. 6.

26. New York *Times,* July 17, 1937, p. 1; "Merry-Go-Round," Nashville *Tennessean,* August 20, 1938, p. 5; author's interview with Turner Catledge, Mississippi State, Mississippi, March 25, 1971.

27. New York *Times,* July 18, 1937, p. 1, July 20, 1937, p. 3, July 21, 1937, p. 20.

28. Washington *Post,* July 21, 1937, pp. 1, 5. For Barkley's record see Polly Ann Davis, "Alben W. Barkley: Senate Majority Leader and Vice President" (Ph.D. dissertation, University of Kentucky, 1969), 15–17.

29. *United States News,* July 26, 1937, p. 5; "Caucus on Wheels," *Time,* July 26, 1937, p. 12. After Turner Catledge filed a story that the politicians who had gone to Little Rock had nearly forgotten to bury Robinson, Harrison and Byrnes called him to their private drawing room for an "upbraiding." Catledge later wrote that Harrison admonished him for writing that the two had been "button-holing" senators for votes, and then looked at Byrnes with a sly chuckle, "Jim, is there anyone we've overlooked?" Turner Catledge, *My Life and the Times* (New York, 1971), 96.

30. *Roosevelt Press Conferences,* X, 49–51 (July 20, 1937); New York *Times,* July 21, 1937, p. 1.

31. Margaret Truman, *Harry S. Truman* (New York, 1973), 111–12. Widespread news of the Pendergast move and rumors that Truman had succumbed to pressure

led the senator to show his ballot, marked for Harrison, to Senator Herring right at the moment that he cast it.

Information in this paragraph is based upon: Greenville (S.C.) *News*, July 26, 1937; Washington *Evening Star*, November 27, 1937, p. 7; Frank Kent in Nashville *Tennessean*, September 30, 1938, p. 12; Rexford G. Tugwell, *How They Became President: Thirty-five Ways to the White House* (New York, 1964), 426; Charles, *Minister of Relief*, 211–12; Farley, *Jim Farley's Story*, 92; Byrnes, *All in One Lifetime*, 99; Ickes, *Secret Diary*, II, 170, 174; Grace Tully, *F. D. R.: My Boss* (New York, 1949), 225. Miss Tully adds that Howard Hunter, a regional WPA representative, was a party to the pressure against Dieterich. Dieterich learned the hard way who his true friends were; receiving no support from either Kelly or FDR, Dieterich lost his bid for reelection.

32. Alben W. Barkley, *That Reminds Me* (Garden City, 1954), 156; Davis, "Alben W. Barkley," 30; Farley, *Jim Farley's Story*, 181.

33. Jackson *Daily News*, July 21, 1937, p. 1; New York *World-Telegram*, July 21, 1937, p. 1. Harrison's reaction to Bilbo's prerequisite is described by Allen, *Presidents Who Have Known Me*, 70. See also *Newsweek*, July 31, 1937, p. 5.

34. New York *Times*, July 22, 1937, p. 1; "38–37," *Time*, August 2, 1937, p. 10. One of Barkley's constituents wrote, "Gosh, but I became excited when I read the '38 to 37' head-lines. I first thought the President had increased the Supreme membership to 75." William Suhr to Barkley, July 25, 1937, in Barkley Papers, Political File.

35. Byrnes, *All in One Lifetime*, 100; "Merry-Go-Round," Nashville *Tennessean*, July 26, 1937, p. 4. For the conclusion on Berry's vote, see Thomas A. Early to Harrison, July 20, 1937, and Harrison to Browning, July 21, 1937, both in Harrison Papers.

In an intriguing exchange of correspondence between Byrnes and Bankhead, Byrnes wrote, "We had the votes if they had stuck—but they did not stick. . . . I am satisfied that two others included by us in the thirty-eight changed their minds but forgot to tell Pat." Bankhead questioned Neely's vote and asked Byrnes for a list on how he thought each senator had voted. When Byrnes supplied a list he wrote that, in addition to thirty-seven assured votes, the Harrisonites were promised the votes of Bone and Murray minutes before the caucus. Ashurst was scratched by Byrnes at the same time on the basis of a statement made by Mrs. Carl Hayden. Thus, Byrnes counted upon the thirty-eight needed votes. "You look over the list and when you see me you can tell me your guess," he wrote Bankhead. "I think we will agree." Byrnes to Bankhead, July 22, 1937, and August 5, 1937; Bankhead to Byrnes, July 24, 1937, all in Byrnes Papers, Folder 14. Unfortunately, the Bankhead Papers do not contain the lists Byrnes prepared.

Alsop and Kintner wrote in their column two years later that Neely's vote cost Harrison the post, and Burton K. Wheeler said the same to the author. Washington *Evening Star*, March 13, 1939, p. 9; interview with Wheeler, Washington, D.C. November 24, 1971.

36. *Time*, August 2, 1937, p. 10; Key Pittman to Harrison, July 2, 1937, in Pittman Papers, Library of Congress, Box 13. Pepper told the Senate of his support of Harrison. *Congressional Record*, 75 Cong., 1 Sess., 9341 (August 19, 1937).

37. Hugh Johnson's column quoted Vandenberg. New York *World-Telegram*, July 24, 1937, p. 17. See Johnson in the *World-Telegram*, July 22, 1937, p. 17. Lawrence is in the Washington *Evening Star*, July 22, 1937, p. 11; Sullivan is in the New York

Herald Tribune, October 31, 1937, Sec. II, p. 2; Michelson's comment is in his *The Ghost Talks*, 182.

A recent study of editorial opinion across the nation concludes that "A clear majority of the newspapers commenting on Barkley's victory over Harrison ventured the opinion that President Roosevelt's prestige had been seriously harmed by the close Senate vote." Philip A. Grant, Jr., "Editorial Reaction to the Harrison-Barkley Senate Leadership Contest, 1937," *Journal of Mississippi History*, XXVI (May, 1974), 140.

38. Patterson, *Congressional Conservatism and the New Deal*, 148. In 1962 Byrnes asked a young biographer, "How could a man with so many fine qualities tell you one thing and so often do another?" Frazier, "The Southerner as American," 72.

39. Washington *Evening Star*, August 25, 1937, p. 11; Jackson *Daily News*, November 26, 1937, p. 4.

40. Jackson *Daily News*, July 12, 1937, p. 1; Washington *Post*, July 15, 1937, p. 3; New York *Times*, July 27, 1937, p. 1; *New Republic*, July 14, 1937, p. 280.

Through Rankin and his hometown can be seen the deterioration of support for the New Deal. Rankin was recognized as the foremost House proponent of TVA, and Tupelo was known as the showplace of the whole TVA area. In late 1935 the local chamber of commerce withdrew from the national body because of the latter's "adverse attitude toward President Roosevelt, the Democratic Party [and] the TVA." By 1937 the local city leaders had undergone a change of heart. In November the city council adopted an ordinance prohibiting union organizers from talking to employees either during work hours or one hour before or after hours. Jackson *Daily News*, November 22, 1935, p. 1, November 4, 1937, p. 1; "T.R.B.," *New Republic*, August 18, 1937, p. 45.

41. *Congressional Record*, 75 Cong., 1 Sess., 7872–74 (July 30, 1937); Wilburn Buckley interview with James G. Shoalmire. After Miss Perkins's remark a number of Jackson women bundled up their shoes and mailed them to her, and Fred Sullens never referred to her again as other than "Sister-Shoeless-South Perkins." Jackson *Daily News*, September 5, 1933.

42. *Congressional Record*, 75 Cong., 1 Sess., 7874 (July 30, 1937); Jackson *Daily News*, August 1, 1937, p. 8; Ickes, *Secret Diary*, II, 182. Wilburn Buckley recalled that FDR sent a limousine for Harrison right after the speech and shortly afterwards a subdued Harried returned to his office, smiling "You know, after all, he isn't such a bad fellow." Roosevelt, Buckley remarked, "could sell an Eskimo an electric fan." (Buckley interview with Shoalmire.)

43. Nashville *Tennessean*, September 16, 1937, p. 1.

44. Bilbo to FDR, October 11, 1937, in Roosevelt Papers, PPF 2184; *Congressional Record*, 75 Cong., 2 Sess., 1835 (November 17, 1937); Washington *Post*, December 18, 1937, p. 1.

45. Washington *Evening Star*, May 29, 1937, p. 7; New York *Times*, August 7, 1937, p. 1; Ickes, *Secret Diary*, II, 189; *Newsweek*, August 21, 1937, p. 10.

46. FDR to Harrison, August 11, 1937, in Roosevelt Papers, OF 241; Washington *Post*, August 12, 1937, p. 1; New York *Times*, August 17, 1937, p. 1; *Congressional Record*, 75 Cong., 1 Sess., 8831 (August 13, 1937).

47. Washington *Evening Star*, September 2, 1937, p. 2; David J. Lewis to Marvin McIntyre, August 21, 1937; Toi Botchsheler to McIntyre, August 24, 1937, both in Roosevelt Papers, OF 241.

When the sugar act came up for renewal in 1940, the impending international crisis removed the issue from controversy. By then Roosevelt was satisfied with the workings of the measure and recommended the extension of the Sugar Act of 1937. In October, 1940, Harrison chaperoned a sugar bill to passage for a third time. *Congressional Record*, 76 Cong., 3 Sess., 4568 (April 16, 1940), 13209 (October 4, 1940).

48. *New Republic*, September 15, 1937, p. 155; Patterson, *Congressional Conservatism and the New Deal*, 162–63.

49. Baltimore *Sun*, November 19, 1937, p. 15.

NOTES TO CHAPTER IX

1. See Walter Lambert's catalogue of tax-evasion machinations in "New Deal Revenue Acts," 365–67, 389–90. At a Treasury Department conference Doughton complained that "the taxpayers' lawyers lie awake nights to cook up new schemes"; Morgenthau Diary, Book 70, p. 268.

2. *Roosevelt Press Conferences*, IX, 396–405 (May 28, 1937); Morgenthau Diary, Book 70, pp. 92–93, 268–69.

3. *Congressional Record*, 75 Cong., 1 Sess., 5126–33 (June 1, 1937); Morgan is quoted by Paul, *Taxation in the United States*, 203.

4. Paul, *Taxation in the United States*, 206–207; New York *Times*, June 18, 1937, p. 1, June 19, 1937, pp. 1, 5.

5. *Congressional Record*, 75 Cong., 1 Sess., 8246 (August 5, 1937); New York *Times*, August 17, 1937, p. 1; Washington *Post*, August 17, 1937, p. 6. The committee proceedings, *Hearings before the Committee on Finance on the Revenue Act of 1937*, 75 Cong., 1 Sess., probably set a record in brevity for a hearings document with only nine pages.

6. New York *Times*, August 19, 1937, p. 10.

7. *Congressional Record*, 75 Cong., 1 Sess., 9226–28 (August 18, 1937), 9301 (August 19, 1937); New York *Times*, August 19, 1937, p. 10; *Time*, August 30, 1937, p. 14.

8. Blum, *From the Morgenthau Diaries*, I, 337.

9. Morgenthau Diary, Book 55, pp. 104–105; New York *Times*, November 14, 1936. p. 16. Magill, as a Columbia University professor, had written *Taxable Income* (New York, 1936). See also Lovell H. Parker, "Capital Gains and Losses," *The Tax Magazine*, XIV (October, 1936), 604–10.

Roosevelt was aware of the fleeting popularity that some of the treasury experts had with Harrison and Doughton. He once told Morgenthau "Now they want Magill. They love Magill, but tell Magill not to let their love go to his head because next year they will hate him!" Morgenthau Diary, Book 70, p. 93.

10. New York *Herald Tribune*, October 22, 1937, p. 4; *Roosevelt Press Conferences*, X, 301 (October 29, 1937); Herbert Stein, *The Fiscal Revolution in America* (Chicago, 1969), 88. Johnson's column appeared in the New York *World-Telegram*, November 2, 1937, p. 13, and Stokes's column in the *World-Telegram*, October 23, 1937, p. 21.

11. New York *Times*, November 11, 1937, p. 1; Doughton to O. Max Gardner, November 11, 1937, in Doughton Papers, Folder 668; Harrison to Morgenthau, November 11, 1937, in Harrison Papers.

12. New York *World-Telegram*, November 13, 1937, p. 19; Swope to Harrison, November 16, 1937, Woolf to Harrison, November 12, 1937, Leon Gregory to Harrison, November 17, 1937, all in Harrison Papers.

13. Jackson *Daily News*, December 23, 1937, p. 4.

14. "Tax Reform," *Newsweek*, November 15, 1937, pp. 40–41; Washington *Evening Star*, November 13, 1937, pp. 1, 2; New York *World-Telegram*, November 23, 1937, p. 1; Washington *Post*, November 18, 1937, p. 2.

15. *Congressional Record*, 74 Cong., 2 Sess., 107 (November 18, 1937); Washington *Post*, November 25, 1937, p. 1.

16. "What Taxes Are Doing to Business," *Business Week*, December 11, 1937, pp. 42–49. See the letters of T. A. Finch to Doughton, November 20, 1937, and Thurmond Chatham to Doughton, November 24, 1937, in Doughton Papers, Folders 671 and 672; Parker to Harrison, November 30, 1937; V. V. Boatner to Harrison, December 1, 1937; and Bell to Harrison, November 30, 1937, all in Harrison Papers.

17. New York *Times*, November 25, 1937, p. 27, November 28, 1937, p. 1; Morgenthau Diary, Book 99, p. 161. Doughton, too, was sympathetic to the businessman's point of view. "I am in accord with Mr. Barney Baruch's statement that Government and business should work hand in hand," he wrote Parks M. King on December 3, 1937. Doughton Papers, Folder 675.

18. Harrison's speech appears in *Vital Speeches*, December 15, 1937, pp. 138–40.

19. "Pat Harrison: The Portrait of a Politician from Jokes to Taxes," *Newsweek*, December 13, 1937, pp. 14–15; *Business Week*, December 4, 1937, pp. 5–6; New York *Times*, November 30, 1937, p. 22.

20. Young to Harrison, November 30, 1937; Swope to Harrison, December 1, 1937; Matthew Sloan to Harrison, November 30, 1937; C. T. Jaffray to Harrison, December 9, 1937, all in Harrison Papers. See also the letters from Mississippians Jim Redus and J. H. Pettey, both dated December 1, 1937, in Harrison Papers; M. Slade Kendrick, *The Undistributed Profits Tax*, Brookings Institution Pamphlet Series, No. 20 (Washington, 1937), 88, 92, 95.

21. Washington *Post*, March 1, 1938, p. 1; *Business Week*, March 5, 1938, p. 5; Morgenthau Diary, Book 113, p. 98. Baruch wrote Byrnes on April 30, 1938: "Some of the gossip on how you and Pat and I connived on my testimony is amusing but I do not think it does any good. Joe Alsop's article is an effort to be funny at the expense of fact." Byrnes Papers, Folder 30.

22. New York *Times*, March 13, 1938, p. 1, March 23, 1938, p. 1.

23. Washington *Sunday Star,* March 19, 1938, p. 1; Washington *Post*, March 15, 1938, p. 6; "Senate Fights for Tax Orthodoxy," *Business Week*, April 2, 1938, p. 14.

24. *Congressional Record*, 75 Cong., 3 Sess., 4026–76 (April 7, 1938), 5183 (April 9, 1938); New York *Times*, April 8, 1938, p. 3.

25. The columnists were quoted in the Jackson *Daily News*, April 8, 1938, p. 6.

26. Rexford G. Tugwell, *The Democratic Roosevelt: A Biography of Franklin D. Roosevelt* (Garden City, 1957), 467; *Morgenthau Presidential Diary*, Book 1, p. 27 (in 1938 Morgenthau began a separate journal which is called "The Presidential Diary"); Blum, *From the Morgenthau Diaries*, I, 444; FDR to Harrison, April 13, 1938, in Roosevelt Papers, OF 962; Washington *Post*, April 14, 1938, p. 6.

27. New York *Times*, April 21, 1938, pp. 1, 4; Washington *Evening Star*, April 22, 1938, p. 11; *Roosevelt Press Conferences*, XI, 354 (April 21, 1938).

Morgenthau recorded in his diary that FDR told Doughton, "Please tell Pat Harrison for me that I have been waiting to see him for a month; that as an old friend and as a Democrat and for the sake of the Democratic Party, I beg of him to come down and see me . . . . I have been waiting for a month for him." The secretary added that he had never seen the president "plead so" over the telephone in such a quiet and forceful manner. "When he got through he said, 'Wasn't I good?' and I said, 'Mr. President, I don't see how you could have done any more and still kept your dignity as President.'" Morgenthau Presidential Diary, Book 1, p. 30.

28. Washington *Evening Star*, April 23, 1938, p. 1; "Merry-Go-Round," Nashville *Tennessean*, April 27, 1938, p. 5; "Tax Compromise Answers Business Cry for Reform," *Newsweek*, May 2, 1938, p. 31.

29. Washington *Evening Star*, May 19, 1938, p. 1; *Time*, June 6, 1938, p. 7; Blum, *From the Morgenthau Diaries*, I, 445–47; Samuel Rosenman, *Public Papers and Addresses* (New York, 1941), VII, 362–65.

30. *Congressional Record*, 75 Cong., 3 Sess., 7681–85 (May 28, 1938); Washington *Sunday Star*, May 29, 1938, p. 2; "Roosevelt and Harrison," *Business Week*, June 4, 1938, p. 52.

31. *Congressional Record*, 75 Cong., 3 Sess., 7681 (May 28, 1938); *Roosevelt Press Conferences*, XI, 440 (May 31, 1938). Bilbo remarked, "Well somebody said 'Would to God that I might be delivered from my friends.' I guess that must be the way the President feels about Pat's speech." Washington *Sunday Star*, May 29, 1938, p. 2.

32. Morgenthau Diary, Book 126, pp. 337–39, 347–48.

33. McComb (Miss.) *Journal*, June 23, 1941, p. 1; Blum, *From the Morgenthau Diaries*, I, 449–50.

34. New York *Times*, August 31, 1938, p. 5, December 20, 1938, p. 9; "A Stream-Lined Tax Program," *Nation's Business*, XXVI (June, 1938), 15–16; "Pat's Mare," *Time,* September 12, 1938, p. 28. A Macon, Mississippi, developer wrote, "It has been my job for the past 25 years to induce yankee money to come south and invest in our lands and new manufacturing plants and what has happened since Mr. Roosevelt was elected President—I make trips north and talk to investors about coming to Mississippi and they tell me to go to Washington and see Pat Harrison and President Roosevelt first—because they will not invest in any new enterprise down here, when you all take 80–90% of the profit." H. H. Hansen to Harrison, August 31, 1938, in Harrison Papers.

35. Charles W. B. Hurd, "The Coming Struggle over Taxation," *Current History*, XLIX (December, 1938), 22–23; Morgenthau Diary, Book 135, p. 147.

36. Morgenthau Diary, Book 165, p. 156.

37. Blum, *From the Mgrgenthau Diaries,* Vol. II: *Years of Urgency, 1938–1941.* (Boston, 1965), 19–21; Harrison and Doughton to Morgenthau, March 2, 1939, in Harrison Papers.

38. *Roosevelt Press Conferences*, XIII, 209–14 (March 21, 1939); FDR to Harrison, March 21, 1939, Harrison to FDR, March 24, 1939, Harrison to Cooper, March 24, 1939, all in Harrison Papers.

39. Morgenthau Diary, Book 176, pp. 169–70.

40. *Ibid.*, 162–64.

41. *Ibid.*, 146–47.

42. FDR to Harrison, April 1, 1939, in Roosevelt Papers, OF 962. Roosevelt was annoyed by a New York *Times* article that provided explicit details of his rejection of the treasury tax program. After the source of the leak came up in a treasury staff meeting, Morgenthau told one of his assistants privately, "I feel sure that Hanes told all this stuff to Senator Harrison and Senator Harrison told this to Turner Catledge." Arthur Krock exonerated Hanes, but confirmed the fact that Catledge "plentifully supplied himself from Pat Harrison and Doughton." Morgenthau Diary, Book 189, pp. 158, 184.

43. New York *Times*, May 16, 1939, p. 1; Morgenthau Presidential Diary, Book 1, p. 101; *Time*, May 22, 1939, p. 17.

44. Washington *Post*, May 25, 1939, p. 1; Paul Mallon in Nashville *Tennessean*, May 29, 1939, p. 5; "Henny Penny's Inning," *Time*, June 5, 1939, p. 15; "White House Appeasement Shift Spurs Early Adjournment Hopes," *Newsweek*, June 5, 1939, p. 11; Blum, *From the Morgenthau Diaries*, II, 29.

45. Washington *Evening Star*, June 20, 1939, p. 1; New York *Times*, June 21, 1939, p. 5, June 23, 1939, p. 1; *Congressional Record*, 76 Cong., 1 Sess., 7708 (June 22, 1939); "Mr. Morgenthau Proposes," *New Republic*, June 7, 1939, pp. 117–18.

46. Morgenthau Presidential Diary, Book 1, p. 127.

47. New York *Times*, April 15, 1938, p. 13.

48. Washington *Evening Star*, June 4, 1938, p. 13.

49. New York *Times*, August 31, 1938, p. 5, December 20, 1938, p. 9, December 25, 1938, Sec. IV, p. 3; Jackson *Daily News*, October 22, 1938, p. 1, December 21, 1938, p. 1.

50. New York *Times*, January 4, 1939, p. 1. Garner wrote Byrnes on November 25, 1938: "This way of appropriating money by Congress and leaving the expenditures to the discretion of the Executive is wrong in theory and surely doesn't work out very well in practice." Byrnes Papers, Folder 30.

51. New York *Times*, January 20, 1939, p. 1, January 26, 1939, p. 10; Washington *Post*, January 28, 1939, p. 2; Alsop and Kintner, Washington *Evening Star*, January 31, 1939, p. 9. On the Harrison-Byrnes friendship, see Alsop and Kintner, "Sly and Able," *Saturday Evening Post*, July 20, 1940, p. 41.

According to Allan A. Michie and Frank Rhylick the Senate "Republocrats" (Garner, Byrnes, Harrison, and Alva Adams of Colorado) mapped their strategy in Garner's office. Their most effective "coup" was the capture of James John ("Puddler Jim") Davis's vote through the use of pressure summoned from Joseph N. Pew, a sachem in Pennsylvania politics. "The Harrison-Byrnes combination did not overlook a bet," Michie and Rhylick wrote. *Dixie Demogogues*, 85.

52. New York *Times*, February 8, 1939, p. 10, March 12, 1939, Sec. IV, p. 3; *Time*, March 13, 1939, p. 17; "Old-Line Democrats Lead War to Curb New Deal's Spending," *Newsweek*, March 13, 1939, p. 15. The Cleveland editorial was quoted in the Jackson *Daily News*, March 13, 1939, p. 3.

53. New York *Times*, May 5, 1939, p. 7. Harrison's friend Eugene Fly wrote, "That was a good speech you gave the big wigs last night. . . . They are as unreasonable as organized labor, and you have performed a service that somebody owed society." Fly to Harrison, May 5, 1939, in Harrison Papers.

54. Richard Polenberg, *Reorganizing Roosevelt's Government: The Controversy Over Executive Reorganization, 1936–1939* (Cambridge, 1966), 42.

55. Washington *Post*, January 30, 1937, p. 2. The Harrison Papers contain a folder of letters from the directors of the various agencies advocating reorganization which were forwarded to the senator from Robinson in July, 1937.

56. Lindsay Rogers, "Reorganization: Post Mortem Notes," *Political Science Quarterly*, LIII (June, 1938), 168. It was hard for Harrison and Byrnes to do anything pleasing to the columnist Jay Franklin. He wrote that the two senators made an "unholy deal" by which "Jimmy sold out the New Deal tax program in return for enough votes to pass reorganization." Nashville *Tennessean*, April 20, 1938, p. 5.

57. Patterson, *Congressional Conservatism and the New Deal*, 302.

58. "Washington Bulletin," *Business Week*, May 30, 1939, p. 7. See also *Congressional Digest*, XVIII (June–July, 1939), 161.

59. "Washington Correspondents Name Ablest Congressmen in Life Poll," *Life*, March 20, 1939, p. 14.

NOTES TO CHAPTER X

1. Washington *Post*, March 19, 1939, Sec. III, p. 9.
2. Pat Harrison, "The Wages of Dixie," *Collier's*, January 22, 1938, pp. 11, 46.
3. *Ibid.*, 46.
4. Washington *Evening Star*, May 7, 1938, p. 8; New York *Times*, May 10, 1938, p. 1. See Paul H. Douglas and Joseph Hackman, "The Fair Labor Standards Act of 1938. I," *Political Science Quarterly*, LIII (December, 1938), 491–515.
5. New York *Times*, June 11, 1938, p. 1. Bilbo had supported the measure and told a Mississippi audience in October that the law would mean a new day for labor in the southern states. Jackson *Daily News*, October 15, 1938, p. 8.
6. Jackson *Daily News*, May 3, 1939, p. 8, July 1, 1939, p. 1.
7. Robert A. Lively, *The South in Action: A Sectional Crusade Against Freight Rate Discrimination* (Chapel Hill, 1949), 18. See also Clark and Kirwan, *The South Since Appomattox*, 270–71, and C. E. Widell, "Freight Rates with a Southern Accent," *Nation's Business*, XXVII (January, 1940), 25–27.
8. Jackson *Daily News*, November 6, 1937, p. 10; Jiggitts to FDR, January 4, 1938, in Roosevelt Papers, PPF 2405.
9. Jackson *Daily News*, March 27, 1940, p. 1. Before the southern campaign began, only five of the forty-one men who had served as ICC members had come from the rate area designated as Southern Territory. Lively, *The South in Action*, 81.
  One of Harrison's steady correspondents was D. Schrivinich, the president of a Philadelphia export corporation that marketed the sweet potato starch products of a Laurel plant fostered by Harrison, who wrote, "You have been very generous in supporting our efforts to secure lower freight rates." (August 20, 1940, Harrison Papers.)
10. A. G. Mezerik, *The Revolt of the South and West* (New York, 1946), 113.
11. National Emergency Council, *Report to the President on the Economic Conditions of the South* (Washington, 1938), 1, 58.
12. Rosenman, *Public Papers and Addresses*, VII, 468.
13. Jasper B. Shannon, "Presidential Politics in the South—1938," *Journal of Politics*, I (August, 1939), 279.
14. Jackson *Daily News*, August 15, 1938, p. 1; New York *Times*, August 16, 1938, p. 7. Harrison's sensitivity to criticism of Mississippi had been demonstrated two months earlier when he and Governor White met with Roosevelt and issued a statement that they had told him that there were no slums in Mississippi. Thereupon two United Garment Workers Association officials wired FDR to invite his attention to slums in McComb. J. L. Wilson and Mrs. Tina Kelly to FDR, June, 1938, in Roosevelt Papers, PPF 4069.
15. Harrison to M. J. Elliot, October 21, 1938, in Harrison Papers.
16. Jack Alexander, "Missouri's Dark Mule," *Saturday Evening Post*, October 8, 1938, p. 5; M. J. Elliot to Harrison, October 20, 1938, in Harrison Papers.
17. Halsey to Harrison, October 29, 1938, in Harrison Papers. The Kirksville speech is also in the Harrison Papers.
18. Rosenman, *Public Papers and Addresses*, VII, 585; New York *Times*, December 22, 1938, p. 2; Jackson *Daily News*, March 9, 1939, p. 10.
19. Thomas A. Krueger, *And Promises to Keep: The Southern Conference for Human Welfare, 1938–1948* (Nashville, 1967), 16–19.

20. Wilbur J. Cash, *The Mind of the South* (Vintage ed., New York, 1941), 313.
21. Mary White Ovington, *The Walls Came Tumbling Down* (Arno Press ed., New York, 1969), 258.
22. By definition, then, the law would not have been applicable to the fifty white men who hanged a Negro who was not in the hands of officials on March 12, 1935, at Slayden, Mississippi. New York *Times*, March 13, 1935, p. 3.
23. Louis Howe had filed the bill in 1934 with a note: "Not favored at this time—may create hostility to other crime bills." Roosevelt himself was unsure about the constitutionality of the Wagner-Costigan bill. Schlesinger, *The Politics of Upheaval*, 437–38. See also Frank Freidel, *FDR and the South* (Baton Rouge, 1965), 83–86, and Leslie H. Fishel, Jr., "The Negro and the New Deal Era," *Wisconsin Magazine of History*, XLVIII (Winter, 1964–1965), 112.
24. New York *Times*, April 26, 1935, p. 1.
25. *Ibid.*, May 1, 1935, p. 2.
26. Jackson *Daily News*, April 21, 1935, p. 6, April 28, 1935, p. 6, May 9, 1935, p. 17; speech in Harrison Papers.
27. New York *Times*, April 14, 1937, p. 52; "Lynch and Anti-Lynch," *Time*, April 26, 1937, pp. 16–17. Just when White made his boast, a large placard fell from the wall behind him. "That must have been an omen of some kind," he later said. Quoted in Robert W. Dubay, "Mississippi and the Proposed Anti-Lynching Bills of 1937–1938," *Southern Quarterly*, VII (October, 1968), 81.
28. Dubay, "Mississippi and the Proposed Anti-Lynching Bills," 83.
29. Washington *Post*, May 13, 1937, p. 2.
30. New York *Times*, August 12, 1937, p. 1, November 15, 1937, p. 1. The author has been unable to find any comment of Harrison on the Black appointment.
31. Jackson *Daily News*, September 16, 1937, p. 1; Robert L. Zangrando, "The Efforts of the National Association for the Advancement of Colored People to Secure Passage of a Federal Anti-lynching Law, 1920–1940" (Ph.D. dissertation, University of Pennsylvania, 1963), 361.
32. White was quoted in the *Literary Digest*, December 4, 1937, p. 13.
33. *Time*, January 24, 1938, p. 8.
34. *Congressional Record*, 75 Cong., 3 Sess., 138–43 (January 7, 1938); Jackson *Daily News*, January 10, 1938, p. 1. When the Meridian Chamber of Commerce later invited the Idahoan down for a "Borah Appreciation Day," he declined to go. Jackson *Daily News*, February 3, 1938, p. 3.
At the death of Borah in January, 1940, Harrison, who deeply admired the leonine senator, left his sick bed (influenza) to go to the Senate chamber ceremonies. Jackson *Daily News*, January 28, 1940, p. 2.
35. *Congressional Record*, 75 Cong., 3 Sess., 253–57 (January 10, 1938). Harrison was patently wrong in his statement that lynchings resulted from rape. Studies on lynching have shown that an assault upon a woman was the alleged cause in only one-sixth of all lynchings. Zangrando, "The NAACP and a Federal Anti-lynching Bill, 1934–1940," *Journal of Negro History*, L (April, 1965), 107.
36. New York *Times*, January 11, 1938, p. 18.
37. *Congressional Record*, 75 Cong., 3 Sess., 2203 (February 21, 1938); Jackson *Daily News*, February 3, 1938, p. 1.
38. Jackson *Daily News*, January 17, 1938, p. 1; undated clipping from the Vicksburg *Herald* in Harrison Papers. The Truman quotation is from Samuel Lubell, *The Future of American Politics* (3rd ed., New York, 1965), 26.

39. Jackson *Daily News*, January 11, 1940, pp. 1, 14; New York *Times*, March 26, 1940, p. 1.

40. New York *Times*, March 9, 1938, p. 6, November 24, 1938, p. 33, January 16, 1939, p. 1.

41. New York *Times*, September 10, 1938, p. 1; Jackson *Daily News*, September 26, 1938, p. 4; FDR to Harrison, October 6, 1938, in Harrison Papers.

42. Harrison to FDR, October 17, 1938; Catherine Blanton to Harrison, October 26, 1938, both in Harrison Papers.

43. Bilbo to FDR, October 6, 1938, in Roosevelt Papers, PPF 2084; Jackson *Daily News*, August 30, 1938, p. 1.

44. Jackson *Daily News*, August 23, 1939, p. 1, August 28, 1939, p. 5; "Merry-Go Round," Nashville *Tennessean*, September 7, 1939, p. 7.

45. Jackson *Daily News*, August 30, 1939, p. 1. Johnson once said, "Ever notice that there is usually a runt pig in every litter? Yet, these runts, if given a chance to get as much food, can grow into just as fine a hog as the others. That's what I've tried to do—help give 'runt-pig people' a chance." Quoted by John K. Bettersworth, *Mississippi: A History* (Austin, 1959), 425.

46. Jackson *Daily News*, January 16, 1940, p. 1.

47. *Ibid.*, January 9, 1940, p. 4; Harrison to V. H. Landrum, February 20, 1940, in Harrison Papers.

48. Ralph J. Bunche, *The Political Status of the Negro in the Age of FDR*, ed. by Dewey W. Grantham (Chicago, 1973), iii, 207, 380. Harrison was interviewed on February 16, 1940.

49. *Ibid.*, 24, 380, 434–35.

50. George C. Stoney, "Suffrage in the South. Part I. The Poll Tax," *Survey Graphic*, XXIX (January, 1940), 9. In another article Stoney demolished Harrison's argument that poll tax revenues supported education. He showed that in no poll tax state did the amount collected add to 5 percent of the total educational appropriations. Stoney, "Tool of State Machines," in *The Poll Tax* (Southern Conference for Human Welfare, 1940), 9.

51. Jackson *Daily News*, April 12, 1940, p. 6, December 14, 1940, p. 1; Herbert Holmes to Harrison, April 8, 1940, in Harrison Papers.

52. Jackson *Daily News*, April 20, 1934, p. 1, May 24, 1934, p. 1, January 28, 1935, p. 1; *Congressional Record*, 74 Cong., 1 Sess., 4071 (March 20, 1935).

53. Aubrey Williams to FDR, February 21, 1936, in Roosevelt Papers, OF 444-C; Howard A. Dawson to the author, October 29, 1974; Jackson *Daily News*, April 26, 1936, p. 6.

54. *Congressional Record*, 74 Cong., 2 Sess., 10360–61 (June 20, 1936); Howard A. Dawson, "The Harrison-Fletcher Bill," *Journal of the National Education Association*, XXVI (January, 1937), 2.

55. Washington *Evening Star*, March 25, 1937, p. 10; Ralph J. Bunche, "The Programs, Ideologies, Tactics and Achievements of Negro Betterment and Interracial Organizations," Book 1 (New York Public Library, Schomburg Collection), 84–85; Lyle W. Ashby and Howard Dawson, "The American Ideal of Public Education," *Journal of the NEA*, XXVI (February, 1937), 49–56.

56. New York *Times*, March 19, 1937, p. 3, April 14, 1937, p. 1; Washington *Evening Star*, April 15, 1937, p. 13; *Congressional Record*, 75 Cong., 1 Sess., 3368 (April 12, 1937).

57. Bailey to Poe, April 15, 1937, in Bailey Papers, Box 553; memorandum to

McIntyre, dated April 19, 1937, in Roosevelt Papers, OF 107; New York *Times*, April 20, 1937, p. 1.

58. New York *Times*, April 21, 1937, p. 1.

59. New York *Times*, May 10, 1937, p. 15; September 15, 1937, p. 8; "The Harrison-Black-Fletcher Bill," *Journal of the NEA*, XXVI (May, 1937), 132–33; Bailey to H. C. Perry, June 8, 1937, in Bailey Papers, Box 176.

60. *Report of the Committee* (Washington, 1938), 197; New York *Times*, February 14, 1938, pp. 1, 2. The authors of a study on federal aid to education have said that FDR "side-stepped" the education bill through his call for the extended study. Frank J. Munger and Richard F. Fenno, Jr., *National Politics and Federal Aid to Education* (Syracuse, 1962), 7.

61. Poe to Harrison, January 10, 1938, in Poe Papers, North Carolina Department of Archives and History.

62. *Congressional Record*, 75 Cong., 3 Sess., 6239 (May 4, 1938), 8351–52 (June 7, 1938).

63. *Ibid.*, 8353 (June 7, 1938). A Mississippi Mason wrote to FDR of his opposition to the committee report, for it "boldly advocates private and parochial schools should participate in these funds." Luther A. Smith to FDR, March 3, 1938, in the Roosevelt papers, OF 107.

64. Pat Harrison, "Federal Aid to Public Education," *State Government*, XII (January, 1939), 3–4. See Harrison also in *Elementary School Journal*, XXIX (April, 1939), 561–63.

In December, J. S. Vandiver, Mississippi superintendent of education, had been in Atlanta at a meeting called by the General Education Board. The South's chief education officers agreed on the need for federal support of the area's schools. Jackson *Daily News*, December 19, 1938, p. 11.

65. Bell to FDR, February 23, 1939, in Roosevelt Papers, OF 107; *Congressional Record*, 76 Cong., 1 Sess., 5807 (May 19, 1939).

66. Currie to FDR, February 5, 1940; FDR to Currie, February 13, 1940, in Roosevelt Papers, OF 107.

67. *Congressional Record*, 77 Cong., 1 Sess., 3059 (April 7, 1941), 6120 (July 3, 1941). With the nation's largest army training center near Hattiesburg, a new air corps unit at Jackson, and the Ingalls shipbuilding industry at Pascagoula, Mississippi would have benefited vastly.

68. Howard Dawson to the author, October 29, 1974; H. M. Ivy to the author, October 31, 1974; Willard F. Bond, *I Had a Friend: An Autobiography* (Kansas City, 1958), 58.

69. Harrison, "Federal Aid to Public Education," 14.

70. Dawson to the author, October 29, 1974; Munger and Fenno, *National Politics and Federal Aid*, 101.

NOTES TO CHAPTER XI

1. Patterson, *Congressional Conservatism and the New Deal*, 337. Marian D. Irish has described the disinclination of the Southerners to inject sectional controversies into international issues. Irish, "Foreign Policy and the South," in Taylor Cole and John H. Hallowell (eds.), *The Southern Political Scene, 1938–1948* (Gainesville, 1948).

2. Perkins, *The Roosevelt I Knew*, 340, 343; *Congressional Record*, 74 Cong., 1 Sess., 1147 (January 29, 1935).

3. Leuchtenburg, *Franklin D. Roosevelt and the New Deal*, 219; Robert A. Divine, *The Illusion of Neutrality* (Chicago, 1962), 166, 192; press release dated March 20, 1937, in Harrison Papers.

4. "Merry-Go-Round," Nashville *Tennessean*, May 18, 1938, p. 7; New York *Times*, May 14, 1938, p. 1; Divine, *Illusion of Neutrality*, 226.

5. Divine, *Illusion of Neutrality*, 239–76; New York *Times*, July 5, 1939, p. 1; FDR to Harrison, July 6, 1939, in Elliot Roosevelt, *FDR: His Personal Letters, 1928–1945*, II, 902.

6. Washington *Post*, July 12, 1939, p. 1.

7. Jackson *Daily News*, September 12, 1939, p. 1; Washington *Evening Star*, September 21, 1939, p. 13; New York *Times*, September 29, 1939, p. 1; *Time*, September 15, 1939, p. 12; Harrison to Leslie Biffle, September 19, 1939, in Harrison Papers.

8. Jackson *Daily News*, October 3, 1939, p. 1; *Congressional Record*, 76 Cong., 2 Sess., 1024 (October 27, 1939).

9. Robert Sobel, *The Origins of Interventionism: The United States and the Russo-Finnish War* (New York, 1960), 91–103; Blum, *From the Morgenthau Diaries*, II, 131; Washington *Post*, January 31, 1940, p. 1, February 8, 1940, p. 1; New York *Times*, February 1, 1940, p. 5; *Congressional Record*, 76 Cong., 3 Sess., 1228 (February 8, 1940).

10. Whitney H. Shepardson and William O. Scruggs, *The United States in World Affairs: An Account of American Foreign Relations* (New York, 1941), 32; *Hearings before the Committee on Finance on the Extension of the Lending Authority of the Export-Import Bank*, 76 Cong., 3 Sess., 3, 54; *Congressional Record*, 76 Cong., 3 Sess., 2102 (February 28, 1940).

11. New York *Times*, January 1, 1940, p. 1, February 27, 1940, p. 6; Washington *Post*, January 20, 1940, p. 2; Washington *Evening Star*, March 8, 1940, p. 1.

12. Alsop and Kintner, "Sly and Able," 38; Alsop and Kintner in Washington *Evening Star*, March 9, 1940, p. 11; New York *Times*, March 25, 1940, p. 1.

13. *Congressional Record*, 76 Cong., 3 Sess., 3317–19, 3321, 3341 (March 25, 1940).

14. *Ibid.*, 3412 (March 26, 1940), 3495, 3499 (March 27, 1940), 3643 (March 29, 1940); New York *Times*, March 29, 1940, p. 6; Washington *Evening Star*, March 30, 1940, p. 2; David Porter, "Senator Pat Harrison and the Reciprocal Trade Act of 1940," *Journal of Mississippi History*, XXXVI (November, 1974), 372.

15. *Congressional Record*, 76 Cong., 3 Sess., 3685 (March 29, 1940).

16. *Ibid.*, 4105 (April 5, 1940); New York *Times*, April 5, 1940, p. 1; April 6, 1940, p. 1. Frederick Van Nuys inserted into the *Congressional Record* the remarks of Joseph P. Tumulty on Harrison's "kindness, tolerance, frankness, and understanding of the other fellow's point of view [which] makes his leadership in any matter of legislation always irresistible." *Congressional Record*, 76 Cong., 3 Sess., Appendix, 1977 (April 10, 1940).

17. Early to Harrison, April 6, 1940, in Roosevelt Papers, PPF 4069; G. Gould Lincoln, Washington *Evening Star*, April 9, 1940, p. 11. The Harrison Papers contain letters from dozens of senators congratulating him.

18. New York *Times*, January 5, 1940, p. 1, January 14, 1940, p. 21; Washington *Post*, January 7, 1940, p. 1; *Roosevelt Press Conferences*, XV, 59 (January 9, 1940); "Mr. Harrison vs. the Budget," *United States News*, January 19, 1940, p. 15; *Congressional Record*, 76 Cong., 3 Sess., 213 (January 10, 1940).

19. Paul, *Taxation in the United States*, 255; Blum, *From the Morgenthau Diaries*, II, 278–85; New York *Times*, January 6, 1940, p. 1; Washington *Post*, May 18, 1940, p. 2.

20. *Congressional Record*, 76 Cong., 3 Sess., 6596 (May 22, 1940), 6975 (May 28, 1940); Morgenthau Diary, Book 266, pp. 185, 281, Book 267, pp. 1–3; Washington *Evening Star*, May 30, 1940, p. 11.

21. Morgenthau Diary, Book 268, pp. 82, 87, 219; Blum, *From the Morgenthau Diaries*, II, 287.

22. Morgenthau Presidential Diary, Book 3, pp. 569–71.

23. Washington *Evening Star*, June 8, 1940, p. 9, June 10, 1940, p. 2.

24. New York *Times*, June 17, 1940, p. 1.

25. *Congressional Record*, 76 Cong., 3 Sess., 8367 (June 18, 1940), 8598, 8613–14, 8619, 8631 (June 19, 1940). The Connally amendment was a product of a sub-committee of the Finance Committee named in 1936 following the revelations of the Nye study of the munitions industry.

26. Ickes to FDR, June 11, 1940, in Roosevelt Papers, OF 962; Ickes, *The Secret Diary*, Vol. III: *The Lowering Clouds, 1939–1941* (New York, 1954), 224, 226.

27. Morgenthau Diary, Book 278, pp. 107, 109–10. On June 28 the Republicans nominated Wendell Willkie at their Philadelphia convention.

28. Washington *Post*, July 2, 1940, p. 1; New York *Times*, July 5, 1940, p. 12.

29. Blum, *From the Morgenthau Diaries*, II, 290–93.

30. Washington *Post*, August 10, 1940, p. 1; New York *Times*, August 29, 1940, p. 1.

31. New York *Times*, August 30, 1940, p. 1. Disney is quoted by Paul, *Taxation in the United States*, 264.

32. New York *Times*, September 4, 1940, p. 10; Washington *Evening Star*, September 6, 1940, p. 3; Blum, *From the Morgenthau Diaries*, II, 294.

33. Morgenthau Presidential Diary, Book 3, p. 651. Sullivan's objections to the bill are recorded in the Morgenthau Diary, Book 305, p. 89.

34. Blum, *From the Morgenthau Diaries*, II, 295. At a staff meeting on September 12 Morgenthau said to Sullivan, "It was tough going for a while, wasn't it Johnny," to which the assistant secretary replied, "You should have been around some other times during the summer." Morgenthau Diary, Book 305, p. 145.

35. Washington *Evening Star*, September 12, 1940, p. 7; John L. Sullivan's comments on Harrison's press conference, Morgenthau Diary, Book 305, p. 100.

36. *Congressional Record*, 76 Cong., 3 Sess., 12057–71 (September 31, 1940), 12352 (September 19, 1940). Of the 46 supporters of the tax bill, 45 were Democrats. Of the objectors, 5 were Democrats including Bilbo.

37. Sullivan told the author of the Harrison-Doughton tiff over the Sunday session in an interview in Washinton, D.C., April 7, 1972.

38. *Congressional Record*, 76 Cong., 3 Sess., 12916–21, 12925 (October 1, 1940); Washington *Post*, October 2, 1940, pp. 1, 2; Roy G. and Gladys C. Blakey, "Two Revenue Acts of 1940," *American Economic Review*, XXX (December, 1940), 731.

39. Currie to FDR, October 8, 1940, in Roosevelt Papers, OF 962; Blum, *From the Morgenthau Diaries*, II, 295–96.

40. Holmes to Harrison, February 27, 1939; Harrison to Holmes, March 11, 1939; Harrison to Gus Magruder, April 19, 1939; Catherine Blanton to Howard V. Harrington, February 29, 1940, all in Harrison Papers; Jackson *Daily News*, July 16, 1939, p. 2.

41. Jackson *Daily News*, July 21, 1939, p. 9; Mrs. W. G. Moncrieff to Harrison, August 3, 1939; Harrison to Mrs. Moncrieff, August 5, 1939; Harrison to W. B. Donald, January 15, 1940, all in Harrison Papers.

42. White to FDR, January 9, 1940, in Roosevelt Papers, PPF 4535; Harrison to Holmes, February 12, 1940, in Harrison Papers; Nashville *Tennessean*, January 16, 1940, p. 1.

43. Harrison to W. C. Leonard, March 12, 1940; Harrison to Holmes, June 5, 1940, both in Harrison Papers; Nashville *Tennessean*, June 6, 1940, p. 10; *Newsweek*, June 17, 1940, p. 41. The *Post* is quoted by the Jackson *Daily News*, June 9, 1940, p. 5.

44. Harrison to Eustis McManus, June 7, 1940, in Harrison Papers; Jackson *Daily News*, June 7, 1940, p. 2, June 12, 1940, pp. 1, 10. The Mississippi resolution was inserted in the *Congressional Record* by Wall Doxey. *Congressional Record*, 76 Cong., 3 Sess., 3953, Appendix (June 17, 1940).

45. Harrison to Fred L. Sanford, February 4, 1938; Harrison to J. B. Snider, April 29, 1938, both in Harrison Papers; New York *Times*, June 28, 1938, p. 19; Jackson *Daily News*, April 15, 1938, p. 8, June 29, 1938, p. 1.

46. Catherine Blanton to E. J. Gilmore, February 13, 1940; Harrison to J. M. Alford, June 19, 1940; Holmes to Harrison, June 19, 1940; Harrison to E. J. Gilmore, June 24, 1940; Harrison to Walker Wood, June 29, 1940, all in Harrison Papers; Robert Albright in the Washington *Post*, June 9, 1940, Sec. III, p. 2.

47. Jackson *Daily News*, July 12, 1940, p. 1; Farley, *Jim Farley's Story*, 265–66. In a study of the 1940 convention, Bernard F. Donohoe wrote of Harrison as one of the Democrats of declining power represented also by men like Garner and Farley in 1940 and Al Smith, John J. Raskob, and John W. Davis of an earlier time. While he may be correct that Harrison had little influence in the Chicago convention, the senator was by no means past his prime as a power in the Senate. Donohoe, *Private Plans and Public Dangers: The Story of FDR's Third Nomination* (Notre Dame, 1965), 22, 178.

48. Jackson *Daily News*, July 15, 1940, p. 1; Washington *Evening Star*, July 18, 1940, p. 1; Byrnes, *All in One Lifetime*, 124. Byrnes later declared that the president had urged him to accept the second place on the ticket, but he had declined because he did not want to alienate Farley. Byrnes to John R. Watson, August 5, 1940, in Byrnes Papers, Legislative Folder, 1933–41.

Whether Harrison found Wallace more acceptable after Byrnes removed himself as a contender is a matter of conjecture, as is the whole business of whether Roosevelt ever really considered Byrnes as a running mate.

49. It is impossible to determine how individual delegates voted. The state sent 110 delegates to cast 18 votes. New York *Times*, July 19, 1940, p. 3.

George E. Allen has written that an agitated Louisiana delegate rushed up after the nomination and grabbed him by the coat and grumbled, "No one wanted Wallace—absolutely no one. Name me just one man that did." Allen retorted, "Brother, that I can do—and that one man was Roosevelt." Allen, *Presidents Who Have Known Me*, 130–31.

50. Albright in the Washington *Post*, July 28, 1940, Sec. III, p. 5; Flynn to Harrison, August 22, 1940, in Harrison Papers. The November election was no contest at all in Mississippi. Roosevelt won 95.7 percent of the vote.

51. Jackson *Daily News*, August 11, 1940, p. 1, August 24, 1940, p. 1.

52. *Congressional Record*, 76 Cong., 3 Sess., 11036 (August 27, 1940), 11142 (Au-

gust 28, 1940); Jackson *Daily News*, August 25, 1940, p. 1. The Gallup poll was carried in the Washington *Post*, August 11, 1940, Sec. III, p. 1.

NOTES TO CHAPTER XII

1. Jackson *Daily News*, November 13, 1940, p. 1.

2. Tumulty to Harrison, November 14, 1940, in Harrison Papers. Smith had entered the Senate in 1909, Sheppard in 1913, and McKellar in 1917. It is interesting that when Harrison began his congressional career, William Howard Taft was president and Champ Clark was speaker of the House. Now their sons, Robert A. Taft and Bennett Clark, were his Senate colleagues.

3. Jackson *Daily News*, January 12, 1940, p. 7; New York *Times*, January 5, 1941; *Time*, January 22, 1940, p. 22.

4. FDR to Harrison, February 5, 1941, in Roosevelt Papers, PPF 4069.

5. Jackson *Daily News*, January 24, 1941, p. 2, January 26, 1941, p. 5; Washington *Evening Star*, February 10, 1941, p. 3; Washington *Post*, March 4, 1941, p. 12; Ellen Woodward Papers, Mississippi Department of Archives and History, Box 1.

6. New York *Times*, January 4, 1941, pp. 1, 2; Washington *Evening Star*, January 6, 1941, p. 1.

7. Blum, *From the Morgenthau Diaries*, II, 214–16; Warren F. Kimball, *The Most Unsordid Act: Lend-Lease, 1939–1941* (Baltimore, 1969), 141, 144–46.

8. New York *Times*, January 23, 1941, p. 9, February 14, 1941, p. 1, March 8, 1941, p. 6; *Hearings before the Committee on Foreign Relations on the Bill to Promote the Defense of the United States, January 27–February 13, 1941*, 77 Cong., 1 Sess., 7; *Congressional Record*, 77 Cong., 1 Sess., 2097 (March 8, 1941).

9. New York *Times*, June 23, 1941, p. 17. The senator unnamed by the *Times* was probably Bennett Clark who told the Senate after Harrison's death that he (Harrison) had told him personally that he would not leave until legislation to which he was committed had been completed. *Byron Patton Harrison: Memorial Addresses Delivered in Congress*, 77 Cong., 2 Sess., 80–81 (May 25, 1942).

10. Catledge, *My Life and the Times*, 144. Clippings on Harrison's death in the Harrison Scrapbook describe the senator's failing health.

11. New York *Times*, April 21, 1941, p. 10. Fred Sullens insisted that Harrison had gone to the hospital merely for a checkup, and he bluntly warned that "anybody who may be planning to step in his shoes may as well forget it." Jackson *Daily News*, March 17, 1941, p. 4.

The senator's secretary attempted to discount rumors of a general illness. She informed the clerk of the Finance Committee in late April that Harrison soon would be dismissed to continue his rest elsewhere and suggested that he "check with Turner Catledge et al to see that full coverage is made." Catherine Blanton to Felton M. Johnston, April 26, 1941, in Harrison Papers.

12. Catherine Blanton to Steve Early, April 26, 1941; FDR to Harrison, April 29, 1941, both in Roosevelt Papers, PPF 4069; Harrison to Byrnes, April 26, 1941; Byrnes to Harrison, April 28, 1941, both in Byrnes Papers, Folder on "Misc., 1941."

13. New York *Times*, June 16, 1941, p. 10, June 17, 1941, p. 23, June 21, 1941, p. 19; Washington *Evening Star*, June 23, 1941, p. 1.

The news releases in Washington did not reveal the senator's true condition just as those given out in Hot Springs did not. Harrison's son, in describing his father's illness, relates that as far as the family knew he never regained consciousness following the operation. Pat Harrison, Jr., does not think that the senator was ever told he had cancer, and Mrs. Harrison did not know definitely until the operation. Pat Harrison, Jr., to the author, September 12, 1974.

Mrs. Harrison died in Gulfport on May 1, 1969, or, as the Coast now dates events, "before Camille."

14. Wallace Memoir, COHC, II, 273.

15. Washington *Evening Star*, June 23, 1941, p. 1; New York *Times*, June 23, 1941, p. 1, June 25, 1941, p. 21, June 16, 1941, p. 23. More than a hundred articles on Harrison's death and the editorial tributes that appeared in the newspapers of Mississippi and elsewhere are in the Harrison Scrapbook belonging to Pat Harrison, Jr.

16. New York *Times*, June 23, 1941, p. 17; Washington *Evening Star*, June 23, 1941, p. 3; *Nation*, June 28, 1941, pp. 739–40; Harrison Scrapbook.

17. Roosevelt Papers, DNC, 1940–1948; Neil MacNeil, *Dirksen: Portrait of a Public Man* (New York, 1971), 8.

18. *Burning Tree Club: A History, 1922–1962* (Washington, n.d.), 206–10; Memphis *Commerical Appeal*, June 23, 1941, clipping in Harrison Scrapbook.

19. *United States News*, July 26, 1937, p. 5; Jackson *Daily News*, July 16, 1939, p. 2; Catherine Blanton to Barbara Miller, April 11, 1939, in Harrison Papers; Prentiss Brown to the author, April 25, 1973.

20. Raymond Moley, *27 Masters of Political Science In a Personal Perspective* (New York, 1949), 251; Byrnes, *All in One Lifetime*, 59; Catledge, *My Life and the Times*, 71; Washington *Evening Star*, January 26, 1941, p. 3.

21. *Fortune*, XI (February, 1935), 134; *Memorial Addresses*, 70, 74; Pepper interview in Southern Oral History Project, University of North Carolina; Brown to the author, April 25, 1973; Colmer to the author, March 11, 1977.

22. Washington *Post*, April 19, 1934, p. 9; *Congressional Record*, 74 Cong., 1 Sess., 4529 (March 27, 1935), 76 Cong., 1 Sess., 6497 (June 1, 1939).

23. *Congressional Record*, 74 Cong., 1 Sess., 6872 (May 3, 1935); New York *Times*, June 23, 1941, p. 17; *Life*, March 20, 1939, p. 16.

24. Tugwell Diary, April 2, 1934.

25. Robert E. Sherwood, *Roosevelt and Hopkins: An Intimate History* (New York, 1948), 26, 106; Jackson *Daily News*, May 3, 1937, p. 7.

When Harrison read in the morning paper that Hopkins was to be sworn in as secretary of commerce in the presence of friends, he decided to go. Arriving at the White House, he found that he had "crashed" a ceremony to which only Hopkins's former staff had been invited. Hopkins, however, was delighted that the senator had thought enough of him to come. Jackson *Daily News*, January 1, 1939, p. 11.

26. *Congressional Record*, 76 Cong., 3 Sess., 12062 (September 13, 1940). Corcoran is quoted by Moley in *After Seven Years*, 290. McNary's characterization of Harrison is found in *Memorial Addresses*, 56.

27. Washington *Evening Star*, March 29, 1933, p. 8.

28. Stone was quoted in a memorandum from Lamar Hardy to Harrison, August, 1935, in Harrison Papers. For insights into the mind-set of the southern senators, see Stanley High, "Whose Party Is It?" *Saturday Evening Post*, February 6, 1937, pp. 10–11, and Joseph Alsop and Turner Catledge, "Joe Robinson, the New Deal's Old Reliable," *Saturday Evening Post*, September 26, 1936, pp. 5–6.

29. *Fortune*, XI (February, 1935), 49.

30. It is an interesting point that the Mississippi Supreme Court invalidated the

state's mortgage moratorium act of 1938 on the grounds that the state's sales tax collections and agricultural price levels proved that there was no longer an economic emergency. *Jefferson Standard Life Ins. Co. v. Noble et ux.* 185 Miss. 360, 188 So. 289 (1939).

31. *Congressional Record*, 76 Cong., 3 Sess., 486 (January 18, 1940). See John Henry on "Mississippi's Pat Harrison" (Jackson *Daily News*, April 26, 1938, p. 2) for an examination of the way in which the senator's "fundamental orthodoxy" was wrenched by the New Deal.

32. Perkins Memoir, COHC, II, 55, 60; interview with Lister Hill, December 7, 1972, Montgomery, Alabama.

33. Patterson, *Congressional Conservatism and the New Deal*, 348–49.

34. New York *Times*, April 7, 1940, p. 2. Mrs. Harrison once said that Roosevelt's failure to appoint Robinson to the Supreme Court was the one thing for which the senator never forgave the president. Gregory, "Pat Harrison and the New Deal," 162.

35. Harrison to Mrs. Grace Covert, February 22, 1939, in Harrison Papers.

36. See John Robert Moore, *Senator Josiah William Bailey of North Carolina*, (Durham, 1968), v.

37. William O. Douglas, *Go East Young Man: The Early Years. The Autobiography of William O. Douglas* (New York, 1974), 414.

38. *Ibid.*

39. Interview with Albert B. Chandler, November 9, 1972, Versailles, Kentucky; "Washington Correspondents Name Ablest Congressmen," *Life*, March 20, 1939, p. 16.

Bibliography

MANUSCRIPTS

The Harrison Papers (University of Mississippi) are terribly disappointing, for most of Harrison's personal papers were disposed of after his death. All that was retained from a thirty-five year public career were sixteen file drawers, some filled with public documents and newspapers and presenting gaps on sensitive matters and significant legislation. There was, however, a trunk of valuable photographs and an almost complete collection of the original Berryman cartoons of Harrison that appeared in the Washington *Evening Star*. The entire Harrison Collection has been processed since this study was researched.

By far the most useful sources are the Official File and President's Personal File of the Roosevelt Papers (Franklin D. Roosevelt Library, Hyde Park). An examination of many large congressional collections has turned up nothing, but scattered correspondence and peripheral items, as well as an occasional gem, are found in the papers of Josiah William Bailey and Rueben Dean Bowen (Duke University Library); Robert L. Doughton and W. D. Robinson (University of North Carolina Library, Chapel Hill); John H. Bankhead (Alabama Department of Archives); Alben W. Barkley and Jouett Shouse (University of Kentucky Library); Bernard M. Baruch (Princeton University Library); James F. Byrnes (Clemson University Library); Carter Glass (University of Virginia Library); Irving Fisher and Edward M. House (Yale University Library); John McDuffie (University of Alabama Library); Kenneth D. McKellar (Memphis Public Library); Ellen S. Woodward and Henrietta Miller (Mississippi Department of Archives and History); Key Pittman and Harold L. Ickes (Library of Congress); and Louis M. Howe and Emil Hurja (Roosevelt Library). The Edwin Halsey Papers (Senate Historical Office) are rich on the 1936 Senate race in Mississippi.

Useful diaries are those of Raymond Clapper and Harold L. Ickes (Library of Congress); George N. Peek (University of Missouri Library); and Henry Morgenthau and Rexford G. Tugwell (Roosevelt Library).

INTERVIEWS AND CORRESPONDENCE

One of the delights of research on Harrison was that his associates, remembering him fondly, were happy to share their memories. Among the most useful were the interviews with George E. Allen, Felton M. Johnston, Samuel McIlwain, John L. Sullivan, and Burton K. Wheeler (Washington); James A. Farley (New York City); Turner Catledge (Mississippi State); Cully A. Cobb (Atlanta); Pat Harrison, Jr.,

(Gulfport); Mr. and Mrs. James M. Cummings [Marianne Harrison] (Bethesda); Walter Brown (Spartanburg, South Carolina); Albert B. Chandler (Versailles, Kentucky); Wilbur Cohen (Chicago); and Lister Hill (Montgomery, Alabama). Howard A. Dawson contributed a long and productive telephone interview.

Also enlightening were the interviews with Mississippians conducted by Alexander Heard and now deposited in the Costs of Democracy and Southern Politics Collection (Joint University Libraries, Nashville) and that of James Shoalmire with Wilburn Buckley (John Stennis Collection, Mississippi State University Library).

The following Columbia Oral History Collection memoirs are rich in recollections of Harrison: Frank Bane, Bernice Bernstein, Claude B. Bowers, J. Douglas Brown, Chester C. Davis, Marion B. Folsom, Joseph P. Harris, Arthur Krock, Maurine Mulliner, Robert J. Myers, Frances Perkins, Jesse W. Tapp, Henry A. Wallace, James P. Warburg, and Milburn L. Wilson.

The following persons assisted by correspondence: Frank Bane, Prentiss M. Brown, William M. Colmer, Howard A. Dawson, Lewis W. Douglas, James A. Farley, John W. Hanes, Pat Harrison, Jr., H. M. Ivy, Leon W. Keyserling, Raymond Moley, and Charles W. Wyzanski, Jr.

GOVERNMENT PUBLICATIONS

The *Congressional Record* is, of course, the prime document for a study of this sort as well as a dozen appropriate committee hearings. The footnotes indicate the extent to which these sources were used together with reports made to Roosevelt by special executive committees. Although not a Government Printing Office publication, the microfilmed stenographic transcripts of the Roosevelt Press Conferences (Roosevelt Library, Hyde Park) were an essential aid.

NEWSPAPERS AND MAGAZINES

In the absence of suitable indices there was no recourse but to read a decade of selected newspapers on a daily basis: New York *Times,* Washington *Evening Star,* Washington *Post*, and the Jackson (Miss.) *Daily News*, the latter selected because of the editor's habit of covering Harrison extensively. Other newspapers read for certain subjects and commentaries were: Jackson (Miss.) *Daily Clarion-Ledger*, Nashville *Tennessean* (for Drew Pearson), New York *Herald Tribune* (for Mark Sullivan), New York *World-Telegram* (for Hugh Johnson), (Washington) *United States News,* and the Memphis *Commercial Appeal*. There are scrapbooks in the possession of Pat Harrison, Jr., (Gulfport) and Marianne Cummings (Bethesda) that contain hundreds of clippings and miscellaneous items.

Also productive was a weekly scanning of a decade of *Business Week, Nation, New Republic, Time, Newsweek,* and the ill-fated *Literary Digest*.

PRIMARY AND SECONDARY ACCOUNTS

Indispensable to a study of a topic such as this is James T. Patterson's *Congressional Conservatism and the New Deal: The Growth of the Conservative Coalition in Congress, 1933–1939* (Lexington, 1967). Anyone who writes on a New Deal congressional conservative can scarcely do more than fill in the pattern drawn by Patterson in his superb study. Other essential accounts of the era are the classic volumes by William E. Leuchtenburg, *Franklin D. Roosevelt and the New Deal, 1932–1940* (New York,

1963); Frank Freidel, *Franklin D. Roosevelt: The Ordeal* and *Franklin D. Roosevelt: The Triumph* (Boston, 1954, 1956) [The third volume in the series, *The Hundred Days*, is as brilliant as the others but disappointing in that Harrison is scarcely mentioned]; James M. Burns, *Roosevelt: The Lion and the Fox* (New York, 1956); and Arthur M. Schlesinger, Jr., *The Age of Roosevelt: The Coming of the New Deal* and *The Age of Roosevelt: The Politics of Upheaval* (Boston, 1958, 1960). None of these studies, with the exception of Patterson, does more than mention Harrison, but they superbly describe the milieu in which he operated.

Extremely useful in understanding the complex subject of taxation and fiscal policy are: Roy G. and Gladys C. Blakey, *The Federal Income Tax* (London, 1940); Randolph E. Paul, *Taxation in the United States* (Boston, 1954); Sidney Ratner, *American Taxation: Its History as a Social Force in Democracy* (New York, 1942); Herbert Stein, *The Fiscal Revolution in America* (Chicago, 1969); and M. Slade Kendrick, *The Undistributed Profits Tax* (Washington, 1937). The two volumes of John Morton Blum, *From the Morgenthau Diaries: Years of Crisis, 1928–1938* and *Years of Urgency, 1938–1941* (Boston, 1965) are exceptionally valuable even when one has used the diaries extensively.

Two excellent accounts of the social security act that provide favorable insights into Harrison's role are Arthur J. Altmeyer, *The Formative Years of Social Security* (Madison, 1966), and Edwin E. Witte, *The Development of the Social Security Act* (Madison, 1962). Critical of Harrison is Abraham Epstein, *Insecurity: A Challenge to America* (New York, 1938). For an understanding of the controversies spawned by the NRA see Ellis W. Hawley, *The New Deal and the Problem of Monopoly: A Study in Economic Ambivalence* (Princeton, 1968). The fullest account of Harrison and the Supreme Court struggle is Joseph Alsop and Turner Catledge, *The 168 Days* (Garden City, 1938).

New Deal contemporaries of Harrison have provided random, but always rich, insights into the personal qualities of the man and his interaction with the other powerful figures of his time. Harold L. Ickes's three-volume *Secret Diary* (New York, 1954) is often petty and always biased but it is entertaining throughout and presents one of the few uncomplimentary pictures of Harrison. Other critics include Rexford G. Tugwell, *The Democratic Roosevelt: A Biography of Franklin D. Roosevelt* (Garden City, 1957), and William O. Douglas, *Go East Young Man: The Early Years* (New York, 1974). Friendly to Harrison are Raymond Moley, *After Seven Years* (New York, 1939) and *The First New Deal* (New York, 1966); James F. Byrnes, *All in One Lifetime* (New York, 1958); James A. Farley, *Behind the Ballots: The Personal History of a Politician* (New York, 1938) and *Jim Farley's Story* (New York, 1948); George E. Allen, *Presidents Who Have Known Me* (New York, 1950); Frances Perkins, *The Roosevelt I Knew* (New York, 1946); and Charles Michelson, *The Ghost Talks* (New York, 1944). First-rate for its portrayal of and anecdotes involving Harrison is Turner Catledge, *My Life and The Times* (New York, 1971).

Among the more useful monographs are John A. Brennan, *Silver and the First New Deal* (Reno, 1969); David B. Burner, *The Politics of Provincialism: The Democratic Party in Transition, 1918–1932* (New York, 1968); Searle F. Charles, *Minister of Relief: Harry Hopkins and the Depression* (Syracuse, 1963); Paul Conkin, *The New Deal* (New York, 1967); Robert A. Divine, *The Illusion of Neutrality (Chicago, 1962);* Frank Freidel, *FDR and the South* (Baton Rouge, 1965); Warren F. Kimball, *The Most Unsordid Act: Lend-Lease, 1939–1941* (Baltimore, 1969); Gordon K. Lewis, *The Virgin Islands: A Caribbean Lilliput* (Evanston, 1972); Frank J. Munger and Richard

F. Fenno, *National Politics and Federal Aid to Education* (Syracuse, 1962); Jordan A. Schwarz, *The Interregnum of Despair: Hoover, Congress, and the Great Depression* (Urbana, 1970); and Robert Sobel, *The Origins of Interventionism: The United States and the Russo-Finnish War* (New York, 1960). The only intimate revelation of Harrison's views on racial matters is found in Ralph J. Bunche, *The Political Status of the Negro in the Age of FDR*, edited by Dewey W. Grantham (Chicago, 1973).

Two valuable collections of correspondence are Max Freedman, *Roosevelt and Frankfurter: Their Correspondence, 1928–1945* (Boston, 1967), and Elliot Roosevelt, *FDR: His Personal Letters, 1928–1945* (2 vols., New York, 1950).

Footnotes cite the many other books that provided useful facts and interpretations.

ARTICLES AND ASSAYS

Citations point to the several excellent articles on New Deal senators that appeared in the *Saturday Evening Post* written by Turner Catledge, Joseph Alsop, Robert Kintner, and Jack Alexander. Raymond Gram Swing, Robert Allen, and Max Lerner wrote illuminating essays for the *Nation* as did Raymond Clapper for *Reveiw of Reviews*. Footnotes indicate the dozens of other useful magazine articles.

Harrison's own writings are limited to "A Streamlined Tax Program" in *Nation's Business* (June, 1938); "Federal Aid to Public Education" in *State Government* (January, 1939) and *Elementary School Journal* (April, 1939); and "The Wages of Dixie" in *Collier's* (January 22, 1938).

Two lively vignettes on Harrison are the *Time* cover story, "Taxmaster" (June 1, 1936), and "The Portrait of a Politician from Jokes to Taxes" in *Newsweek* (December 13, 1936). The lengthy *Fortune* story, "The United States Senate" (February, 1935), is delightful. Of special interest is the *Life* poll of Washington correspondents on the ablest congressmen (March 20, 1939). Louis Cochran's "The Gadfly in the Senate" in *Outlook* (August 5, 1931) is representative of the lighthearted descriptions of the early Harrison. Albert D. Kirwan's sketch of Harrison in the *Dictionary of American Biography*, Supplement Three: *1941–1945* (New York, 1973) is good even though it contains minor errors. Topical articles of great interest are Thomas H. Eliot, "The Social Security Bill: 25 Years After" in *Atlantic Monthly* (August, 1960); Stanley High, "Whose Party Is It?" in *Saturday Evening Post* (February 6, 1937); and Louis Jiggitts, "Al's Chances in Dixie" in *Independent* (October 15, 1927).

There has been very little written in scholarly journals exclusively on Harrison or the New Deal in Mississippi. Extremely helpful are the essays on the senator by William S. Coker in the *Journal of Mississippi History*, "The Formative Years" (October, 1963) and "Strategy for Victory" (November, 1966). Useful also are Robert J. Bailey, "Theodore G. Bilbo and the Senatorial Election of 1934" (*Southern Quarterly*, October, 1971); Robert W. Dubay, "Mississippi and the Proposed Anti-Lynching Bills of 1937–1938" (*Southern Quarterly*, October, 1968); Wayne Flynt, "A Vignette on Southern Labor Politics—The 1936 Mississippi Senatorial Primary" (*Mississippi Quarterly*, Winter, 1972–1973); Philip A. Grant, Jr., "Editorial Reaction to the Harrison-Barkley Senate Leadership Contest" (*Journal of Mississippi History*, May, 1974); Tom S. Hines, Jr., "Mississippi and the Repeal of Prohibition" (*Journal of Mississippi History*, January, 1962); David Porter, "Senator Pat Harrison and the Reciprocal Trade Act of 1940" (*Journal of Mississippi History*, November, 1974); and Ben G. Edmonson, "Pat Harrison and Mississippi in the Presidential Elections of

1924 and 1928" (*Journal of Mississippi History*, November, 1971). On the Mississippi of the 1930s J. Oliver Emmerich has an apt account, "Collapse and Recovery," in Richard A. McLemore (ed.), *Mississippi: A History*, Vol. II (Jackson, 1973).

I have written three articles on Harrison that are fuller accounts of certain aspects of this story than space would permit in a book. See Martha Swain, "The Lion and the Fox: The Relationship of President Franklin D. Roosevelt and Senator Pat Harrison" (*Journal of Mississippi History*, November, 1976); "Pat Harrison and the Social Security Act" (*Southern Quarterly*, October, 1976); and "The Harrison Education Bills" (*Mississippi Quarterly*, Winter, 1977–1978).

Among the many scholarly appraisals of particular topics that were of much merit were: Richard M. Abrams, "Woodrow Wilson and the Southern Congressmen, 1913–1916" in *Journal of Southern History* (November, 1956); Roy G. and Gladys C. Blakey, "Two Revenue Acts of 1940" in *American Economic Review* (December, 1960); E. Cary Brown, "Fiscal Policy in the 'Thirties': A Reappraisal" in *American Economic Review* (December, 1956); Dewey W. Grantham, "The Southern Senators and the League of Nations" in *North Carolina Historical Review* (April, 1949); Arthur S. Link, "The South and the 'New Freedom': An Interpretation" in *American Scholar* (Summer, 1951); Van L. Perkins, "The A.A.A. and the Politics of Agriculture" in *Agricultural History* (October, 1965); and Jordan A. Schwarz, "John Nance Garner and the Sales Tax Rebellion" in *Journal of Southern History* (May, 1964). Indispensable are the interpretive summaries of successive congressional sessions by E. Pendleton Herring and O. R. Altman in the *American Political Science Review*.

UNPUBLISHED STUDIES

Several M.A. theses have been written on aspects of Harrison's public career, but none of them relied upon manuscript material beyond the limited Harrison Papers. (The papers were not even open when I wrote "The Senate Career of Pat Harrison, 1919–1929," Vanderbilt, 1954.) See Ben G. Edmonson, "Pat Harrison: The Gadfly of the Senate, 1918–1932 (University of Mississippi, 1967); Chellis O'Neal Gregory, "Pat Harrison and the New Deal" (University of Mississippi, 1960); and William S. Coker, "Pat Harrison: The Formative Years, 1911–1919" (University of Southern Mississippi, 1962). My own dissertation, "Pat Harrison and the New Deal" (Vanderbilt, 1975), is long, detailed, and often tedious, but presents a fuller context than this version.

Other M.A. studies on Mississippi include: Richard C. Ethridge, "Mississippi and the 1928 Presidential Campaign" (Mississippi State University, 1961); Donald Brooks Kelley, "Of God, Liquor, and Politics: The Mississippi Press in the Presidential Election of 1928" (University of Mississippi, 1962); Arthur L. Rogers, Jr., "Mississippi Banking During Depression and Recovery" (George Washington University, 1938); and Larry F. Whatley, "The New Deal Public Works Program in Mississippi" (Mississippi State University, 1965). Roger Tate is presently writing a dissertation of promise on Mississippi during the Depression (University of Tennessee, Knoxville).

Unpublished studies of varying degrees of quality on Harrison's associates are Creed Black, "Parsonage to Publisher: The Life of Silliman Evans, 1894–1955" (in the possession of John Seigenthaler, Nashville); Polly Ann Davis, "Alben W. Barkley: Senate Majority Leader and Vice President" (Ph.D. thesis, University of Kentucky, 1969); Nevin E. Neal, "A Biography of Joseph T. Robinson" (Ph.D. dissertation, University of Oklahoma, 1958); and Jefferson Frazier, "The Southerner as

American: A Political Biography of James Francis Byrnes" (Harvard College honors thesis, 1964).

Topical studies of great utility are: Kenneth E. Harrell, "Southern Congressional Leaders and the Supreme Court Fight of 1937" (M.A. thesis, Louisiana State University, 1959); Walter K. Lambert's extremely germane "New Deal Revenue Acts: The Politics of Taxation" (Ph.D. dissertation, University of Texas, 1970); and Robert L. Zangrando, "The Efforts of the National Association for the Advancement of Colored People to Secure Passage of a Federal Anti-lynching Law, 1920–1940" (Ph.D. dissertation, University of Pennsylvania, 1963). Bernard Sternsher's 1963 Harvard seminar paper "The Undistributed Profits Tax of 1936" helps clarify a difficult subject.

Index